Elements of an Evolutionary Theory of Welfare

It has always been an important task of economics to assess individual and social welfare. The traditional approach has assumed that the measuring rod for welfare is the satisfaction of the individual's given and unchanging preferences, but recent work in behavioural economics has called this into question by pointing out the inconsistencies and context-dependencies of human behaviour. When preferences are no longer consistent, we have to ask whether a different measure for individual welfare can, and should, be found.

This book goes beyond the level of preference and instead considers whether a hedonistic view of welfare represents a viable alternative, and what its normative implications are. Offering a welfare theory with stronger behavioural and evolutionary foundations, Binder follows a naturalistic methodology to examine the foundations of welfare, connecting the concept with a dynamic theory of preference learning, and providing a more realistic account of human behaviour.

This book will be of interest to researchers and those working in the fields of welfare economics, behavioural and evolutionary economics.

Martin Binder is a Research Associate at the Max Planck Institute of Economics, Jena, Germany.

Routledge Advances in Social Economics
Edited by John B. Davis
Marquette University

This series presents new advances and developments in social economics thinking on a variety of subjects that concern the link between social values and economics. Need, justice and equity, gender, cooperation, work poverty, the environment, class, institutions, public policy and methodology are some of the most important themes. Among the orientations of the authors are social economist, institutionalist, humanist, solidarist, cooperatist, radical and Marxist, feminist, post-Keynesian, behaviouralist, and environmentalist. The series offers new contributions from today's foremost thinkers on the social character of the economy. Published in conjunction with the Association of Social Economics.

Previous books published in the series include:

1. Social Economics
Premises, findings and policies
Edited by Edward J. O'Boyle

2. The Environmental Consequences of Growth
Steady-state economics as an alternative to ecological decline
Douglas Booth

3. The Human Firm
A socio-economic analysis of its behaviour and potential in a new economic age
John Tomer

4. Economics for the Common Good
Two centuries of economic thought in the humanist tradition
Mark A. Lutz

5. Working Time
International trends, theory and policy perspectives
Edited by Lonnie Golden and Deborah M. Figart

6. The Social Economics of Health Care
John Davis

7. Reclaiming Evolution
A marxist institutionalist dialogue on social change
William M. Dugger and Howard J. Sherman

8. The Theory of the Individual in Economics
Identity and value
John Davis

Elements of an Evolutionary Theory of Welfare

Assessing welfare when preferences change

Martin Binder

 Routledge
Taylor & Francis Group

LONDON AND NEW YORK

First published 2010
by Routledge
2 Park Square, Milton Park, Abingdon, Oxon OX14 4RN

Simultaneously published in the USA and Canada
by Routledge
270 Madison Avenue, New York, NY 10016

*Routledge is an imprint of the Taylor & Francis Group,
an informa business*

Typeset in Times by
RefineCatch Limited, Bungay, Suffolk
Printed and bound in Great Britain by
CPI Antony Rowe, Chippenham, Wiltshire

British Library Cataloguing in Publication Data
A catalogue record for this book is available
from the British Library

Library of Congress Cataloging-in-Publication Data
Binder, Martin, 1978–
    Elements of an evolutionary theory of welfare : assessing welfare
    when preferences change / Martin Binder.
      p. cm.—(Routledge advances in social economics ; 16)
    Includes bibliographical references and index.
    1. Welfare economics.   I. Title.
    HB99.3.B54 2010
    330.15′56–dc22   2009050704

ISBN 13: 978-0-415-56298-0 (hbk)
ISBN 13: 978-0-203-84955-2 (ebk)

Contents

Figures

Tables

Acknowledgements

Research fields can be likened to pastures or meadows on which the researcher works in the hope of reaping some flowers from his hard toil. Some of these pastures are more popular than others, and many a person plucks the flowers growing there, turning them into barren land and making it difficult to find more pretty flowers. Other pastures are less popular and thus avoided so that a lush vegetation may grow unfettered, creating a jungle abundant with many flowers yet unheard of.

Writing this monograph on the topic of an evolutionary theory of welfare has seemed at times like roaming such a jungle, full of the unknown, beautiful and dangerous, and with few other persons around. Having found his way out of the jungle, the author of these lines can only hope that some of the flowers he brought back with him will turn out to be interesting to his co-workers and prompt them to roam these grounds as well.

To bring such an expedition to its tentative conclusion, beginning with a doctoral thesis and ending with this book, could only have happened in the extremely stimulating research atmosphere characteristic of the Evolutionary Economics Group at the Max Planck Institute of Economics in Jena.

I therefore want to thank my advisor Ulrich Witt for giving me the opportunity of working in this group and for his continual support during the various phases of writing and revising this work. Equally important has been the detailed advice of my mentor Christian Schubert, who has not only helped me sharpen my arguments with constructive remarks but has generally provided much invaluable guidance. I also thank Andreas Freytag for supervision and advice.

But without the encouragement and critical support of all my other colleagues, such a project would certainly have been a hopeless task. To all of them goes my heartfelt gratitude for helping to improve this work in various ways. In revising my thesis for publication, and with thanks to the generous funding of the Max Planck Society, I was lucky in meeting Adelheid Baker, who proofread the manuscript and – beyond considerably increasing readability – also offered many insights into where some of my arguments might possibly be misunderstood. I have benefited greatly from all this advice and support; needless to say that any remaining errors are mine.

A special thanks goes to Tom Broekel, fellow soul travelling on those pastures, whose role is only incompletely described as having contributed to the above analogy long ago . . .

And last, but not least, I thank my parents for all their support during these years and for their inspiration and encouragement along the way.

1 Introduction

1.1 Motivation

It has always been an important task of economics to assess individual well-being and social welfare. The question of which economic states, or situations, should be considered 'good' and which developments could lead to better states has been of central concern to economists (Cooter and Rappoport 1984; Sen 1987). In theoretical welfare economics, the measuring rod for welfare is the satisfaction of the given and fixed preferences of the individual. Based on some additional assumptions regarding the preference structures (completeness, transitivity), an ordinal utility function $u(\cdot)$ can be constructed for which holds that $\forall \mathbf{x}, \mathbf{y} : \mathbf{x} \geqslant \mathbf{y} \Leftrightarrow u(\mathbf{x}) \geq u(\mathbf{y})$ (where $\mathbf{x}, \mathbf{y}$ are commodity vectors and $\geqslant$ denotes a preference relation). This ordinal utility concept is usually assumed to be interpersonally non-comparable. It is then examined how changes in income or prices affect utility with given preferences. That is, from t_0 to t_1, the preference structure has not changed, but some prices and/or an individual's income have. Based on these changes, different solutions to the utility maximization problem exist, and one can calculate whether $u_{t_1}(\mathbf{x})$ is larger or smaller than $u_{t_0}(\mathbf{x})$.

These considerations are straightforward with stable preferences. But behavioural economics has brought to light a fundamental problem of this view by pointing to inconsistencies and context dependencies of the preferences revealed in human behaviour (Conlisk 1996). If these revealed preferences cannot be considered consistent and if they are dependent on the situation or its framing, or more generally, if they can change from t_0 to t_1, the question emerges whether they can still fulfil their role as a measuring rod for welfare (Sugden 2006a): if an individual (weakly) prefers $\mathbf{x}$ over $\mathbf{y}$ in t_0 and $\mathbf{y} \geqslant \mathbf{x}$ in t_1, we can say that $u_{t_1}(\mathbf{y}) \geq u_{t_1}(\mathbf{x})$ and $u_{t_0}(\mathbf{x}) \geq u_{t_0}(\mathbf{y})$, but the utilities at the different points in time are not comparable due to the informationally sparse assumptions that are placed on the utility notion. A consistent comparison based on preferences is not given, and it is *prima facie* not at all clear 'what kinds of normative economics would be possible if conventional assumptions about preferences had to be given up' (Sugden 2004: 1015).

The same problem obtains in social choice theory. Here the given measuring rod are preference orderings of the individual. If one preference ordering represents the individual at t_0 and another represents the individual at t_1, one needs a criterion of intertemporal consistency in order to evaluate whether one ordering represents an improvement over the other. This cannot be done without some other measuring rod. This consistency problem points to a more general difficulty regarding the underlying assumption of given and unchanging preferences, which is a stake here because

> [t]astes are intractable in ways well known to economists. When described in terms of utilities, they are neither intrapersonally comparable with respect to cardinality nor interpersonally comparable ordinally. Nor is there in economics or elsewhere anything remotely like a theory of how they are determined; more important, there is no theory of how they differ between agents and how they change over time. Neoclassical microeconoinic theory circumvents these problems by treating tastes as 'exogenous'.
>
> (Rosenberg 1992: 153)

The assumption of fixed preferences has been justified after Robbins (1935) and in the wake of subjectivist positivism as a sign of ethical neutrality (Gintis 1974: 415), and both content and formation of preferences have been delegated to other sciences such as psychology. Apart from the alleged ethical neutrality, such an exogeneity assumption also allows to dodge the difficulty of how to normatively deal with the non-existent basis for judging economic states when preferences change (George 2004: 6). Because of this fundamental difficulty, changing preferences can be seen as one of the most important problems of social relevance for economic theory (Weizsaecker 1971: 346). The 'intractability of tastes' proves detrimental to a substantive welfare economic analysis as it tightly confines welfare economics, limiting it, e.g. to the weak criterion of Pareto optimality (Rosenberg 1985; Sen 1987). Based on the sparse informational assumptions above, there is no judging of tastes, not even a discrimination between basic needs and 'mere' wants. In the same vein, a comparison of economic states involving interpersonal comparisons of utility would be impossible: for example, if just one individual suffered a minimal decrease in utility while everyone else were made much better off, this state would be non-comparable with the status quo.

Apart from this confinement, there is also the danger of wrong policy conclusions when basing economic models on empirically unrealistic assumptions such as that of static preferences.

> The most neglected part of the economist's research agenda has been attempting to understand the process of economic change. Economic theory is static; and in the world of dynamic change in which we live a

static body of theory consistently and persistently yields the wrong policy prescriptions.

(North 1999: 80)

Moreover, arguing that preferences cannot change blinds the welfare analyst to the possibility that policies have an influence on these very preferences. While such preference change may happen as an accidental side effect of a policy measure, it is also conceivable that policies are instituted with the deliberate aim of changing individual preferences, an eventuality that warrants closer scrutiny, if only for the strong paternalistic connotations associated with this very idea.

The considerations on well-known anomalies regarding human preferences and decision behaviour (e.g. Knetsch 1995) reinforce the view that economics should incorporate more realistic assumptions into its models (Altman 1999; Berg 2003). It is therefore no wonder that many authors have called for an enrichment of economic theory with more plausible empirical but also ethical assumptions (see e.g. Buchanan (1994: 1, 83), Sen (1987: 7, 29), and Hausman and McPherson (2006: 3–10)). But as a consequence of taking the findings of behavioural economics seriously, namely as a descriptively more accurate picture of human behaviour, in addition,

> there will be a central welfare economic problem that needs to be addressed – a problem that is absent from a static world but strikingly present when information is incomplete and in flux and when tastes and values are constantly being reformed.
>
> (Nelson and Winter 1982: 369)

This 'central welfare economic problem' of assessing welfare when preferences change will inevitably prompt a revision of some of the standard welfare economic ideas. It has to be noted that the malleability of preferences, i.e. inconsistencies and context dependencies, is only one facet of the phenomenon of preferential change. Preferential change is not necessarily inconsistent or solely triggered by framing effects. A systematic change in preferences can be triggered by innovations, either in the form of a new preference being created in the face of new consumption possibilities or as a change in an already existing preference. Such change in preferences is governed by 'transition laws': learning mechanisms explain under what conditions preferences change, they constrain preference change patterns and paths.[1] In this respect, the assumption of changing preferences does not necessarily imply their total arbitrariness or complete malleability (Buchanan 1994: 74–7).

When preferences are thus allowed to change and some of them are no longer consistent, one could think about different ways of solving the 'central welfare economic problem'. While Sugden (2004), for example, has promoted a notion of welfare based on opportunities and on a concept of an individual's responsibility as an autonomous agent, a different train of thought has been suggested by authors such as Kahneman et al. (1997) and Ng (2003). They propose to go back, in a Benthamite spirit, to the hedonic foundations of utility and thus to step beyond the level of preference to the 'deeper' level of objective utility (Kahneman) or happiness (Ng) as the actual factor motivating behaviour and the ultimate measuring rod for welfare. To contribute to the last-mentioned strain of literature, I take an evolutionary perspective. It is therefore necessary to explain some core tenets of such a perspective.

1.2 An evolutionary perspective

Evolutionary economics has been established as a distinct research field of economics, offering a different methodological and substantive approach towards economic theorizing (e.g. Nelson and Winter 1982; Witt 1987, 2003b). Evolutionary economics, as understood in this monograph, could be paraphrased as the idea that the only constant of human activity is change. Evolutionary economics is decidedly dynamic, but not only so: opposed to a dynamic perspective that concerns processes of change in closed systems (with fixed elements), evolutionary changes show historicity in the sense of being irreversible, while change is driven by the creation and dissemination of novelty (Witt 2003b). The socio-economic systems under consideration are thus open systems. This focus on change is prominent in evolutionary thinking, as can be seen in metaphors such as the 'perennial gale of creative destruction' (Schumpeter 1942: 84) or the 'restless nature of capitalism' (Metcalfe 2001: 561). Of course, in these continuously evolving systems, optimization is impossible, the notion of equilibrium cannot be sustained any longer, and the focus shifts to a process perspective (Metcalfe 2001):

> For if the economic world is continuing flux, as our positive theory suggests is the case, the normative properties associated with competitive equilibrium become meaningless, just as that equilibrium is meaningless as a description of behavior.
>
> (Nelson and Winter 1982: 356)

Note that in these open systems, social order is generated and adapted by processes of spontaneous self-organization (a very central Hayekian theme, see e.g. Hayek 1960). The emergence of novelty is a key feature of such a process. However, resulting from epistemic constraints, novelty cannot be fully anticipated (perhaps even only in small parts).[2] In such a system, individual behaviour cannot be characterized by the well-known optimization calculus anymore, but is seen as adaptation to new environments through learning processes such as reinforcement and imitational learning. It can also be ventured that institutions play a key role in reducing uncertainty. From an evolutionary perspective, the systemic openness and the emergence of novelty in the economic context is reflected in the innovativeness of economies (Witt 1996b). Through innovations; new opportunities come into existence. It is this essential feature of innovativeness that renders the idea of unchanging preferences implausible. From an evolutionary perspective, it thus seems no longer possible to maintain the assumption of exogenously given and static preferences (Witt 1991, 2001).

Another key feature of evolutionary economics, as it is conceived here, is its 'naturalistic methodology', as described in Witt (1987): the strategy adopted in the present monograph will be a *naturalization* of welfare economics, taking recourse to the findings of other behavioural sciences, for example by adopting a naturalized theory of preferences. Psychology offers insights into how preferences are formed, what their material content is, and how they change systematically over time. Moreover, subscribing to a naturalistic methodology is also understood to aim at a theory that is informed philosophically. This will have a bearing on the normative content to be developed. While I largely abstain from a meta-ethical discussion of how normative judgements can be critically, if not rationally, discussed and evaluated (more extensively, see e.g. Hausman and McPherson 2006; Schubert 2006b: 41–61), I reject the outdated positivist contention that all ethical discourse is necessarily unscientific and meaningless: normative economics cannot avoid making certain value judgements. These should be made in a transparent fashion and can be subjected to critical deliberation. Some justificatory arguments in favour of a value judgement might be better than others, and a naturalistic methodology suggests that one possibility is to discriminate between such arguments based on positive (descriptive) knowledge.[3] Scientific knowledge can thus render some normative claims more plausible than others.[4]

Nevertheless, there is a danger involved in adopting such an evolutionary perspective. If preferences can change and welfare economic policies and institutional setups can have an impact on them, this might also concern our moral preferences (preferences over different moral principles or welfare criteria). If these moral preferences do change, can we still say something meaningful about welfare? If moral preferences are malleable and subject to historical change, are our standards of human welfare perhaps nothing more than a contingent expression of our times? How can they be justified if this is the case? Opening up the black box of human preferences could confront us with the philosophical question of moral relativism, and is likely to prompt scepticism if some more stable basis for a suitable welfare measuring rod cannot be found. This challenge needs to be kept in mind in the discussion to come.

As a last feature, the evolutionary perspective with its emphasis on non-perfect knowledge and (probably often irreversible) dynamics also places an alleged focus of evolutionary theorizing on *processes* as opposed to *outcomes*. While standard economics is usually preoccupied with outcomes, evolutionary economics is concerned with processes in open systems and not so much with outcomes. It can be argued that to try to bring about desired outcomes would be contrary to the notion of competition as discovery procedure of an open process. Structuring some processes, on the other hand, would not interfere with evolutionary exploration (especially if it is not *a priori* clear what a desired outcome would be). This has led Vanberg to conjecture that utilitarian welfare economics is not compatible with an evolutionary perspective:

> The outcome oriented approach of utilitarian welfare economics cannot be reconciled with an evolutionary perspective. Its claim to decide in advance which among potential alternative courses of action is 'best' is in fundamental conflict with the essential attribute of evolutionary processes, namely their open-endedness. The ambition to control outcomes directly leaves no room for evolutionary exploration.
>
> (Vanberg 2006: 204–5)

Such focus on processes could be reflected in the shift in emphasis from satisfaction of preferences to opportunities as welfare criterion. In order to provide evolution with the necessary fodder to work on, a maximization of opportunities is (often only implicitly) advocated. Wegner (1991: 8 & 121–2) has called such an approach 'evolutionary market positivism' because – implicitly – the adequacy of the market mechanism is supposed to lead to unknown but desired outcomes, which will be the result of the selection process operating through markets. The general preoccupation with processes as opposed to outcomes will provide a guideline for the following chapters. As I intend to show, a focus on processes does not necessarily mean to completely abandon an outcome perspective in favour of an opportunity-centred calculus. It does, however, entail certain qualifications, for example a concern with conditions conducive to desired outcomes or an evaluation of 'patterns of outcomes' (Vanberg 2006: 204, emphasis omitted), taking into account more moderate informational requirements. These reflections inevitably involve normative aspects of evolutionary economics.

1.3 On the status of normative evolutionary economics

Although evolutionary economics has been established as a distinct research field, it still lacks a well-defined normative branch (for a programme and the beginnings of it, see Nelson and Winter 1982: Ch. 15). While there exists neither an explicit normative framework for evolutionary economics nor a systematic basis for evolutionary economic policy advice (see, however, Wegner 1991; Witt 2003a; Freytag and Renaud 2007), there are some suggestions regarding possible welfare criteria. Schumpeter, in his seminal work on capitalist development, linked social welfare to innovative activity when talking about the 'perennial gale of creative destruction' (Schumpeter 1942: 84), leading to an increase in the 'standard of living of the masses'. Thus a welfare improvement in a Schumpeterian sense would be the 'significant long run increase in per capita real income in all percentiles of the income distribution resulting from innovative activities in the economy' (Witt 1996b: 116).[5] Underlying this idea is the assumption that innovativeness results in increases in productivity and an extension of consumption possibilities. In this way, innovativeness is beneficial and welfare enhancing. Subscribing to the causal relationship between innovativeness and welfare, the question to be answered is about the kind of conditions for such improvements in welfare, notably, which institutional arrangements should be advocated to foster innovativeness.

But there are some difficulties related to such an idea (see Witt 1996b: 116): First, an increase in wealth is only an approximation for the stipulated increase in welfare. Wealth *per se* is only instrumental as it serves to satisfy an individual's preferences. The approximation of welfare by income or wealth generates some problems as the relationship between wealth and welfare is by no means simple and linear. This may result from informational constraints when wealth is used in a way that does not increase welfare because of lack of information. Equally, it may result from social dynamics such as, for example, positional concerns (Frank 1985). Or it may result from rising aspirations or other psychological mechanisms such as adaptation to the status quo (Easterlin 2003).[6] Second, this definition includes two qualifications, namely, on the one hand, that individuals do *on average* experience an increase in their standard of living, and, on the other hand, the increase occurs in the *long run*. The first qualification implies that only some individuals profit from innovations, while others do not and thus do not partake in any increase in wealth (or even experience a decrease). The second qualification means that even those who do profit in the long run, might face (probably even severe) decreases of wealth in the short or medium run. An important shortcoming for such a Schumpeterian welfare notion can thus be found in the distributional concerns, which are largely left unanswered. Third and last, such a notion of welfare improvement constitutes an *ex post facto* concept. Going by evidence from the last centuries, wealth increases have resulted from an increase in innovativeness. But the necessary and sufficient conditions for wealth increases in the future are not exactly clear. Therefore a substantial explanation is needed as to why innovativeness increases welfare, to what extent innovativeness translates into welfare gains, and what the distributional consequences of innovativeness are.

If we follow Boulding and define economic development as the 'discovery and application of better ways of doing things to satisfy our wants' (Boulding 1958: 23), the question that needs to be answered is why the satisfaction of wants increases welfare and whether this is always the case. A material explanation of what constitutes welfare implies a shift in perspective from a supply-side view (analysis of innovations, competition, market forms and different firm setups, as has, for example, been done in the tradition of Nelson and Winter 1982) towards a demand-side view of the consumers who satisfy their needs and wants via old and new consumption opportunities and derive utility from these acts of consumption. Of course, from an evolutionary perspective the 'discovery and application of better ways ... to satisfy our wants' cannot be limited to a set of given wants (Witt 1996b: 114): when consumers face hitherto unknown consumption possibilities that have come

into existence through innovations, this can lead to their acquiring a preference for something new or to a change of an old preference.[7] In a static world,
we can make sense of an innovation that leads to cheaper bicycles because
of a more efficient production process. It is, however, difficult to explain why
individuals should adopt the consumption of a totally new (and previously
unknown) product, if they had not acquired a preference for it upon learning
of its existence.

Other evolutionary thinkers have abandoned the assumption of stable
exogenous preferences and put forward differing conceptions regarding welfare economic criteria. I have already hinted at the idea that the historicity of
preference formation might prompt one to adopt a sceptical position regarding the historicity of our welfare criteria as well. An example of such a theory
of change in our normative principles has been brought forward by Sartorius
(2003), arousing in him a certain scepticism whether an acceptable theory of
welfare can be specified at all by taking an evolutionary perspective. In a
purely descriptive manner, Sartorius has sketched how different social norms
and values evolve over time and are selected for the fitness contribution they
make for a given society. The social norms most conducive to survival in the
struggle for scarce resources are then selected. However, since environments
change, there is no optimal set of values and no moral principle that could be
identified as the best one and could thus be accepted as a general moral norm.

> Since evidence for a generally accepted principle is lacking, it may be
> a good alternative approach to analyze how the existing normative
> principles evolve and whether, possibly, the mechanism of this evolution
> process may lead to the suggestion of a basic, widely accepted, normative
> principle.
>
> (Sartorius 2003: 198)

In the end, Sartorius posits that no living being would want its own death
and the extinction of the species. Taking this as a minimal, but generally
acceptable, normative premise based on the principles of evolution, the result
of this analysis is that, beyond furthering the general adaptivity of the systems in which normative principles evolve, not much can be said at all (see
Sartorius 2003: 205–11). But there are less pessimistic accounts: often implicit
in evolutionary thinking is the idea that novelty generated by the system in
the form of newly arising opportunities (that come into existence) is a fundamentally desirable goal. The idea is taken from the principles of evolutionary change, namely the variation, selection, and retention (VSR) scheme, and
it is argued that, given enough variety to act on, evolution will inevitably lead
to increases in fitness. If justified at all, this kind of reasoning then prompts
innovation policy recommendations that uncritically favour variety without
paying attention to distributional effects of innovations. In this category fall
criteria that, on the individual level, conceive of welfare improvements as
increases in individual opportunities and liberties. A similar idea was already

defended by Hayek (see Hayek 1960; North 1999). Hayek developed his welfare criterion starting from the view of an economy as an open system which is highly complex and evolving (for which Hayek coined the term 'catallactic'). Decentralized decisions of agents lead to macro results that are not predictable. No single agent could hold the knowledge contained in such a macro phenomenon (Hayek 1945). According to Hayek, the key feature of spontaneous market order is the capacity to process those amounts of new knowledge. This shifts the focus to knowledge, away from the welfare-maximizing allocation of resources. The 'Hayekian welfare criterion' (Schubert 2006a: 163) is the system's capacity to process decentralized knowledge. For such a criterion, individual liberties/opportunities are very important. Hayek develops individual rights and liberties as maxim and for welfare analysis, but he justifies them as instrumental to the knowledge processing capacity (Schubert 2006b: 221).

Similarly, North has defended a welfare criterion based on this line of reasoning (North 1999). In a static world, the goal of policy intervention is to ensure the efficiency of the market, and divergence from this goal is interpreted as market failure. But from an evolutionary perspective, what should be analyzed is 'how open social systems that are capable of endogenously generating novelty *develop* in a continuous way.' (Schubert 2006a: 156, emphasis in original) An open system, then, is *adaptive* in the sense of maintaining its capacity to develop endogenously and generate novelty. Such a notion has been called 'adaptive efficiency' (North 1999: 95). Of course, there is also a tension between this criterion of adaptive efficiency and concerns about unintended distributional results of innovative processes (Schubert 2006a: 156).

But there are other reasons why an uncritical maximization of opportunities cannot be defended as easily from a naturalistic perspective: empirical research has shown that, while indeed a certain amount of opportunities are positively valued by the individual, this relationship is not linear and monotonically increasing. There seem to be upper limits to the increase in well-being that individuals derive from increased opportunity sets (cf. e.g. Loewenstein 1999; Schwartz 2000): with an increasing number of choices, humans tend to develop increased regret aversion to the number of alternatives not chosen. This has been called the 'multi-option treadmill' (Binswanger 2006: 370–3) because, although we constantly face increasing options, well-being does not necessarily increase significantly. Binswanger identifies three different kinds of constraints as being responsible for this treadmill, viz., first, an information constraint (more options require more information for decision making and thus higher search and filter costs), second, a constraint on mental accounting (we are not able to properly account for pleasures and pains associated with all the options, making us prone to non-optimal decisions) and, third, a time constraint (although options increase, our time budget does not, and so we have to forgo many options, which we then regret). Thus, from a psychologically informed perspective, we can at least have doubts whether we should increase opportunities if an increase eventually turns out to be negatively correlated with well-being.

A last category of approaches are to be found on the more applied levels of evolutionary policy making. Here the policy maker is also understood to be facing the fundamental Hayekian knowledge problem (Hayek 1945): as no one is able to attain the knowledge (that is) embodied in spontaneously emerging market patterns, economic policy making is confronted with a fundamental epistemological difficulty. A policy maker cannot be certain about the effects of the intervention because there is an inevitable element of surprise in any intervention (Wegner 1997). Taking the role of imperfect information seriously seems to call for a reinterpretation of the role of the policy maker (Witt 2003a). What might be a replacement for first-best policies is the role of a 'learning' or 'piecemeal approach' to policy. In that sense the policy maker himself becomes an 'adaptive policy maker' (Metcalfe 1994), who should be a facilitator of the processes of self-organization in the open economic system, not only reacting to changes but actively learning in the policy (reform) process (Freytag and Renaud 2007).

1.4 Outline and contribution

I have presented some unconnected, and in some cases extreme, positions that come under the heading of 'evolutionary normative theorizing'. While the closest resemblance to the standard economic view might be seen in the Schumpeterian welfare criterion through the 'perennial gale of creative destruction', the others were more extreme suggestions. Based on these lessons, it is now possible to formulate some main questions which have to be addressed in this monograph and which, ideally, should be answered by any evolutionary theory of welfare.

(1) Is it possible to formulate a plausible theory of welfare, given that one accepts a relaxation of some standard assumptions of economics? Especially the change in preferences prompts the question to what extent a different – consistent – measuring rod for welfare assessments can be developed.

(2) A second challenge that presents itself is to define a suitable notion of welfare and relate it to its sources and indicators. The main emphasis is on *development* of welfare, i.e. an analysis how welfare changes systematically over time. In the course of this, I examine to what extent the evaluation of outcomes has to be relativized in favour of a process perspective.

(3) In formulating this theory, a naturalistic methodology will pose a constraint in so far as the empirical adequacy of the evolutionary theory of welfare depends on its congruence with findings of other behavioural sciences. In light of positive knowledge, some normative proposals will thus appear more plausible than others.

As Nelson and Winter state:

> An evolutionary approach to positive economics thus calls for a com-
> plementary rethinking of normative economics – a difficult task. A
> normative theory consistent with an evolutionary approach to positive
> theory almost certainly will be complex and messy.
>
> (Nelson and Winter 1982: 356)

While it can indeed be conjectured that the above-mentioned constraints will increase the complexity of an evolutionary theory of welfare, they should nevertheless be taken into account. With this book, I hope to provide some important elements of such a theory and pave the way for an evolutionary welfare economics. This work expressly focuses on what I have earlier called a demand-side perspective, centring thus not around organizational setups and assessments of firms and market forms, but on learning individuals and their wants and needs. Tackling the 'central welfare economic' problem of welfare assessments under a regime of changing preferences certainly has a high relevance for evolutionary economics, but is also of significance for a more traditional welfare economics. This work offers an alternative way of conceptualizing the individual in economic thought, shedding light on the individual's dynamic behaviour and the dynamics of welfare. It may enrich traditional welfare economics with well-founded hypotheses on human behaviour and well-being, allowing for a more substantive welfare analysis by discriminating between different dynamics of welfare.

This book is structured as follows. Having introduced my motivation for the present work, a sketch of an evolutionary methodology, and the outline in this section, the next chapter proceeds with an overview of orthodox welfare economics. No theory is built into an empty space, and novelty often draws on the existing. Although evolutionary economics still lacks a well-defined normative branch, economists have a clear understanding of what a normative branch of economics is generally supposed to consist of. The aim of Chapter 2 is thus to introduce and define relevant notions and technical terms for use in subsequent chapters, e.g. key notions such as 'utility' or 'welfare'. I continue by specifying what it means to build a 'theory of welfare', discussing formal and empirical requirements for any theory of welfare. Subsequently, I present the most prominent existing theories of welfare because these are the starting point for building an evolutionary theory of welfare. Merits and disadvantages of these theories are discussed to give the reader a measuring rod to assess their quality as well as the quality and novelty of the author's own proposal. Having established the terminological basis and conventions, a short introduction to, and exposition of, traditional welfare economics is given, assessing its main problems. This is important because it enables the reader to evaluate to what extent my own theory of welfare allows for different welfare economic answers to be given.

Some of the deficiencies pointed out by critics are related to the 'hollowness' of the concept of utility (Samuelson 1947: 91), and there are some methodological difficulties at the root of the inadequacies mentioned in Chapter 2. It is thus not surprising that there have been several attempts at relaxing some of these problematic assumptions in order to make progress in welfare analysis. It is the aim of Chapter 3 to exemplarily present and analyze some prominent examples from the literature and locate them in my framework to assess theories of welfare. The following three approaches have been selected: first of all, a relaxing of the assumption of stable preferences. Von Weizsaecker (2001) has suggested a model of 'adaptive preferences' (inspired by Elster 1982), where welfare analysis is still possible despite changing preferences. The model presented by the former is very close to traditional welfare economics because except for the preference stability assumption, the usual assumptions on utility and preferences are still accepted.

The second approach is more radical in its assumptions. Brought forward by Sen, the capability and functionings approach (e.g. Sen 1985a, b) has spawned a large array of theoretical and empirical contributions. At the heart of this approach is Sen's contention that the informational basis of utilitarianism is too narrow and has to be enlarged with empirical facts about human behaviour. This behaviour is in turn evaluated on the basis of further criteria based on explicitly ethical considerations. Sen's approach departs from the utility concept *in toto*, replacing it with a dual conception of 'functionings' and 'capabilities to function'. Functionings (which can be broadly understood as different aspects of life, what a person is and does) include *inter alia* material well-being as well as other aspects such as being well sheltered and in good health. Sen's notion of welfare is thus much broader and arguably less subjective than individual subjective utility. Moreover, in incorporating capability as the freedom to choose between different functionings, a second dimension is added to the analysis, where substantive freedoms (understood as opportunities) are considered as well.

The third approach is the most radical departure from the traditional concept of welfare economics because the whole idea of welfare as related to outcomes is given up completely in favour of a view that what matters normatively are solely opportunities. As was already alluded to, Sugden (2004) conceives of individuals as agents that take responsibility for their actions, no matter whether these are taken on the basis of coherent preferences or not. In his formal approach, Sugden is able to show that an economy can be modelled even with individuals that have incoherent and unstable preferences, and that this economy satisfies his 'opportunity criterion', which is an analogue to the first fundamental theorem of welfare economics in opportunity space. I conclude the chapter with a discussion of the implications and insights that can be gained from these three approaches.

The discussion of Chapters 2 and 3 serves to prepare the ground for my own contribution by establishing the terminology and showing the pitfalls that lie ahead. Before sketching my own welfare-theoretic contribution, one additional requirement has to be fulfilled. Any normative theorizing is built on positive (descriptive) knowledge and theory. Thus, before specifying an evolutionary theory of welfare, it is necessary to lay out the positive theory and framework upon which my theory of welfare builds. Chapter 4 is intended to fulfil this requirement. There I discuss Witt's 'learning theory of consumption' (LTC), a theory of consumer behaviour and learning (Witt 2000, 2001, 2005). This theory provides the positive groundwork for my own theory of welfare. The learning theory of consumption is a descriptive theory connecting hedonic experiences (utility) with pleasure and pain derived from the satisfaction of innate needs and acquired wants. It has three defining elements: first, utility is conceived to consist of the net total of pleasure over pain. In that respect, the theory can be understood to be a return to the sensory underpinnings of utility as was the case in the early utilitarians. Second, utility is derived from the satisfaction of genetically fixed needs and learned wants. According to the theory, wants can be learned either in an associative or cognitively mediated way: while innate needs are associated with a basic set of reinforcers, acquired wants emerge from an elementary learning mechanism by which individuals learn to associate originally neutral stimuli with concurrent pleasant ones. When individuals satisfy such a want, they feel a conditioned rewarding experience. These wants also mark a departure from the well-known (axiomatic) preference theory. Third, the learning of wants follows regularities that are also genetically fixed. These elements all are based on material conjectures about the psychological and biological bases of human behaviour. The dynamics of want acquisition and change are based on learning mechanisms that function as transition laws governing the change in wants. To understand how wants (or for that matter the preferences they are giving rise to) *systematically* change is an important requirement of a theory of welfare addressing such dynamic (better: evolutionary) features. These learning mechanisms are empirically extremely well founded and genetically fixed. The discussion of the learning theory of consumption is also compatible with the suggestion of a different model of human (economic) behaviour, viz. melioration learning and the matching law (Herrnstein 1997), which does not stipulate exceedingly high requirements on individual rationality.

The core of this monograph are Chapters 5 and 6, at which point I have assembled all the necessary components to develop the framework of an evolutionary theory of welfare. In that respect, the fifth chapter can be regarded as the beginning of my contribution towards an evolutionary welfare economics, where I will develop some important elements of such a (utilitarian) theory. Based on what has been fleshed out in the previous chapters, I develop a theory of welfare with the 'learning theory of consumption' as a positive basis and present an argument in favour of building a *hedonistic* theory of welfare. My hedonistic interpretation of the learning theory of consumption includes two notions of well-being, which form the core of Kahneman's 'experienced utility' construct (Kahneman et al. 1997). Next, I discuss the issue whether we can or should understand utility to be a multidimensional construct, beginning with some general remarks regarding the issue of multidimensional utility. I hope to clarify some of the aspects of the debate with recourse to findings from neurosciences. My argument here is that a neuro-economic perspective favours a utility notion that is one-dimensional (on its affective level). Additionally, I relate the hedonistic notions of well-being to the concept of 'wants' and highlight some interesting (normative) features of this concept, such as a (restricted) priority of innate needs, while also examining how to relate Witt's idea of 'wants' to the standard economic preferences. Having elaborated on my naturalistic notion of welfare, I justify the attractiveness of hedonism as the value basis of my theory of welfare and refute some common objections that could be levelled against it. Although hedonism is often considered to be an unattractive position, I make a case that such a contention would be premature.

After such comments on the empirical, methodological, and normative adequacy of the theory, I turn to the evolutionary aspects of the theory, to be tackled in Chapter 6. I show in what sense hedonism as theory of welfare better fits a dynamic setting than the standard welfare economic view. Moreover, I discuss to what extent we need a kind of 'normative standard of rationality' in order to be able to distinguish different wants (respective preferences) or enjoyments (pleasures) and consider possible distinctions. In the following, I develop three exemplary dynamic facets of my theory of welfare. The first facet concerns the description of a process view of 'enjoyment', where I intend to show how this process perspective alters the focus when making welfare judgements. Positive evidence is presented that individuals are rather poor judges of their future enjoyment. Based on a systematic inability to correctly forecast future enjoyment, one can argue for a shift from predicted enjoyment as a basis for welfare judgements to actual enjoyments.

The foundations laid out in the previous chapters can serve to understand some dynamics of hedonism, i.e. by going directly to the layer of enjoyment and suffering. Regarding this, the second facet of my framework, I focus on welfare dynamics that relate to changes in well-being directly such as, most prominently, hedonic adaptation effects. These dynamics can be normatively distinguished, for example discriminating between different sources of enjoyment and suffering. I also argue that hedonic treadmill objections can be relativized with respect to our positive knowledge on reduced adaptation dynamics regarding innate needs. While adaptation is a problem to be dealt with by any dynamically oriented, and not completely objective theory of welfare, it would be premature to judge the striving for satisfaction of preferences or for enjoyments to be self-defeating because of mechanisms of hedonic adaptation. Other dynamic aspects concern the link between enjoyment and want formation dynamics, where I rely on the aforementioned well-known learning mechanisms and their peculiarities to distinguish the different ways in which wants can be acquired (and unlearned) over time.

Turning from enjoyment to wants, I deal in detail with questions concerning the welfare dynamics that relate predominantly to changing wants (and the corresponding preferences), the third facet of my framework. Different types of change of wants are discussed, and, again, a scheme for their normative distinction is suggested. The first of two important phenomena discussed is a normative evaluation based on different satiation patterns that can be found in innate needs and acquired wants. This complements and extends the discussion regarding a possible normative priority of innate needs. The second aspect concerns a distinction that can be made also on the basis of different forms of learning mechanisms and regarding the way wants are formed through these. These mechanisms serve for coming to a differentiated understanding of the conditions under which a want is formed 'autonomously'. Such an autonomy requirement can play a role in taking into account possible distortions created by adaptive preference formation. Based on a distinction first put forward by Chai and Schubert (2007), I elaborate on how insightful learning can be a first discriminating test criterion of whether a want was acquired autonomously. Going beyond this, a second criterion serves to check whether the deprivation resulting in adaptive preference formation is indeed reflected in many classes of innate needs not being satisfied.

In Chapter 7, I conclude with a summary and short outlook on further research opportunities and open questions. These mainly concern the practical relevance of the theoretical discussion conducted here. The actual measurability of well-being and some questions of distributive justice are not explicitly addressed. Possible implications and relevance for economic policies might encompass several fields, from innovation policy to consumer protection and issues of sustainability. The most obvious implication may relate directly to the possibility of preferential change: in a framework where preferences are allowed to be variable, it has to be taken into account that economic policies can influence these preferences and shape their development, something that is neglected in a static framework. Such influences may either be deliberate, for example when a policy is instituted with the explicit goal of shaping, i.e. creating or altering, preferences, or they may be an unintentional consequence of a policy measure. Especially the latter possibility should be seen as an additional constraint facing the 'adaptive policy maker', who does not only have to consider the effects of any intervention as regards given preferences but also the likely effects of such a policy in terms of altering these preferences.

In summarizing my contribution to an evolutionary welfare economics, I present an overarching framework of an evolutionary theory of welfare. Based on insights from various behavioural sciences, a hedonistic concept of welfare is presented and evaluated as to its plausibility. Although the framework does not have the simple charm of the standard (but materially under-specified) notion of welfare, it serves to integrate the plausible parts of different theories of welfare. The advantages of such an empirically founded, hedonistic approach are threefold. First, solid ground is gained for the resulting welfare implications by basing the positive parts of this work on empirically well-established assumptions regarding the behavioural foundations. Second, the informational basis of my welfare concept is considerably broadened by using the (hedonistic) 'experienced utility' framework. A purely formal, subjectivistic stance is avoided. Third, the approach is decidedly evolutionary and may shed new light on the normative implications of different preference learning dynamics. In this framework, I am able to coherently integrate preference (want) and enjoyment dynamics, thus connecting strands of literature that have so far been discussed largely separately. I use a naturalistic methodology to give a more realistic account of human behaviour, to decide on the plausibility of some existing normative distinction schemes or normative requirements, and to provide new evaluation schemes and tests (such as in the case of adaptive preference formation or differential satiation patterns of wants).

2 Conceptual background and welfare terminology

Although evolutionary economics still lacks a well-defined normative branch, economists have a clear understanding of what a normative branch of economics in general is supposed to consist of. The aim of this chapter is to survey relevant notions and technical terms for use in later chapters. This concerns such key notions as 'utility' or 'welfare'. I start by introducing the relevant terminology (in section 2.1) to clarify how these terms are going to be used and continue by specifying what it means to build a 'theory of welfare' and discuss relevant requirements. Subsequent to this, I present the most prominent existing theories of welfare and their merits and disadvantages (in section 2.2) because these will be the starting point for building an evolutionary theory of welfare. This is followed by a short introduction to, and exposition of, traditional welfare economics (in section 2.3) and an assessment of the main problems of traditional welfare economics, with special emphasis on the preference stability assumption (section 2.4). The chapter ends with a summary of the lessons learned (section 2.5).

2.1 Conceptual background

This section deals with the clarification of key terms. I start with a tentative definition of well-being and welfare (in subsection 2.1.1). In economics, well-being is often equated with utility, a vague and fuzzy notion that has undergone considerable change in its usage (subsection 2.1.2). This highlights the need for careful and unambiguous definitions when it comes to discussing the specific details of a theory of welfare (subsection 2.1.3). Subsequently, (subsection 2.1.4), some requirements are presented that comprise our toolbox to assess the adequacy of the theories of welfare presented in the following section.

2.1.1 The notions of well-being and welfare

What do we mean by welfare, this 'everyday, vague, and depressingly elusive notion' (Griffin 1982: 332)? For a first approximation, we could consult a dictionary. The *Oxford Dictionary of Economics* defines welfare as 'enjoyment of the necessary resources for a worth-while life' (Black 2002: 502); but that seems a rather narrow focus on 'necessary resources'. Welfare is certainly a much broader and much more central notion. As such, it is used not only in economics but plays a vital role in philosophy and ethics as well, where there exist many competing theories of welfare. Since the concept is widely used, different meanings attach to the term. What is probably common to these usages is the idea that *an individual's welfare is concerned with what it means for that individual to lead a good life*. It deals with the quality of that individual's life. When a particular individual is enjoying a high level of welfare, that individual should be able to say that life is going well. This much can already be derived from the word's etymological roots ('faring well' means doing well). This aspect is also reflected in the notion of 'well-being': an individual's well-being is concerned with the question of whether that individual is well.

Thus welfare means doing well with respect to something. And it is this *something* that I will further look into during the course of this book. Many different ideas can be associated with the concept of welfare, such as 'a person's good, benefit, advantage, interest, prudential value, . . . happiness, flourishing, eudaimonia and utility' (Moore and Crisp 1996: 599, emphasis omitted). I address the question what it means to say that one's life is going well to consider the implications for ethics and political advice. But let us first agree to distinguish between individual (personal) well-being or welfare, on the one hand, and social welfare as the aggregate of individual welfare, on the other. This means that, while I use the term 'welfare' as an umbrella for both individual and/or social welfare, I reserve the term 'well-being' to explicitly denote an individual's welfare. The notion of well-being is also reserved for a purely descriptive context, for example when referring to the psychological literature on individual (subjective) well-being. How aggregate social welfare is calculated is debatable, but the most obvious way would be the aggregation of individual well-being by summing up or calculating the arithmetic mean. The issue of aggregating individual well-being to social welfare is no trivial exercise; it involves value judgements as to whether different individuals' well-being should be given different weights or not. A straightforward solution would be the welfare egalitarianism of the early utilitarians, where each individual counted the same.

In everyday life, our own welfare (but also that of our loved ones) is one of our primary concerns. Our well-being seems to be valuable in itself; to promote our well-being is such a natural thing for us to do that, if someone were to ask us why we do this, we might think the answer is obvious. Most ethical theories also assign importance to the well-being of the individual. While utilitarianism claims that welfare is the sole value that counts, other ethical theories might argue that it is only one of many. However, it is difficult to think of an ethical theory that denies the importance of welfare as a fundamental value. The same holds for politics, where the welfare of the citizens is a vital goal. The welfare state and its institutions are one prominent example for this, but politics to alleviate poverty also come to mind. It is clear that the notions of welfare and well-being are of central importance to assess the quality of human life. To come to grips with the notion of welfare, I start with the meaning it has been given traditionally in economics, namely its synonymous use with the notion of 'utility' (Black 2002: 489), a concept no less puzzling. In view of its centrality in economics, we have to understand what the economist means by referring to 'utility'.

2.1.2 A short overview of the development of the utility concept

Similar to the terms 'welfare' and 'well-being', the notion of 'utility' is a fuzzy concept, used with considerable ambiguity even in the economic discipline proper (Broome 1991a,b; Sen 1991a). It has undergone major transformations in its history, and a brief sketch of this development is given in this section.[8] In ordinary English, utility means 'usefulness', but this meaning is not what economists have in mind when using the term. In the economic context, the notion of utility has originally been defined by Bentham. For the classic utilitarians such as Bentham and Mill, the notion of utility had a substantive meaning that was clearly related to pleasures and pains (Sen 1991a: 279). Bentham employed the notions of utility and happiness synonymously. The hedonistic character of his theory is clearly reflected in the way he has operationalized the concept of utility as:

> that property in any object, whereby it tends to produce benefit, advantage, pleasure, good, or happiness, (all this in the present case comes to the same thing) or . . . to prevent the happening of mischief, pain, evil, or unhappiness to the party whose interest is considered
>
> (Bentham 1789: 2)[9]

and '[w]hat happiness consists of we have already seen: enjoyment of pleasures, security from pains.' (Bentham 1789: 70) Bentham carefully discussed a long list of different types of pleasures and pains (Bentham 1789: 33–42), which he also distinguished along the four dimensions of 'intensity', 'duration', 'certainty' (or uncertainty with which it will occur), and remoteness or 'propinquity' (i.e. temporal proximity). This suggests that these pleasures and pains were for him very heterogeneous sensory experiences, pointing to a multidimensional conception of utility (this has been argued by Warke 2000a,b).[10] Among many others, Bentham's catalogue of different pleasures and pains contained such diverse sensations as the pleasure of the senses, of benevolence, of wealth and of imagination. Bentham identified individual welfare as the net total of pleasure over pain of an individual. Using the felific calculus, his idea was to simply add up the net balance of pleasure over pain of the individuals of a society in order to arrive at a measure of social welfare. For example, when judging on the appropriateness of an institution (e.g. a law), such a balance should be calculated for all those affected, and if the balance was positive, one had the justification to establish the institution: one was morally right to act this way. Accordingly, the morally best solution would be the one that would maximize this felific balance (the 'principle of greatest happiness').

The picture changed drastically during the marginalist revolution. The formal analysis of marginal utility and constrained maximization required modifications in order to allow for the utility variable to be maximized. Thus Jevons' goal in his *Theory of Political Economy* (Jevons 1871) was to develop a mathematical description of the utilitarian position, aiming at something like 'the mechanics of utility and self-interest' (Jevons 1871: 21), where – similar to classical mechanics – laws are expressed as functional relationships, which, in turn, can be treated by the extreme value analysis of differential calculus. To accomplish this goal, Jevons had to change the utility concept. He aggregated Bentham's naturalistic catalogue of pleasures and pains into the single homogeneous variable 'utility'. By relegating utility to commodities instead of actions, he eliminated the time dimension of utility, enabling him to analyze it within a static framework (cf. Steedman 2001: Ch. 1). Moreover, while comparisons of utility along the four dimensions mentioned were a legitimate possibility for Bentham, Jevons treated utility as a representation of purely subjective feelings. Interpersonal comparisons along these dimensions were no longer possible (Jevons 1871: 14–16) and the 'greatest happiness principle' was dropped as well (Jevons 1871: 23–7).

These changes gave utility theory a radically different orientation, moving it away from its normative origins. Not only did Jevons reject the idea that pleasures and pains are sensory perceptions that could somehow be made 'objective', but he also denied the possibility of deriving moral judgements from comparing the feelings of different individuals. This subjectivist stance, which has now been widely adopted in economics, was intended to make economics independent of insights from psychology (and related disciplines), making it difficult at the same time to develop more material conjectures about the content and process of preference formation. These changes have separated the utility concept completely from any naturalistic connotations (cf. Lewin 1996; Witt 2005; Bruni and Sugden 2007).

In the wake of positivist subjectivism, the notion of utility became more removed from its original meaning. First, Robbins advocated the banning of interpersonal comparisons of utility from economics as ethical and hence unscientific (Robbins 1935, 1938), a vastly exaggerated claim (Blaug 1992: 119): while interpersonal comparisons of utility are certainly not easily analyzed and probably difficult to test empirically, they are definitively not value judgements. Second, any other remaining psychological insights into the utility concept were removed due to Samuelson's theory of 'revealed preference' (Samuelson 1938, 1947; Wong 1978). Here preferences were solely determined based on the choices in which they were revealed, and no reference to psychological motivations remained. The material hypotheses of utility theory (viz. a decreasing marginal rate of substitution, marginal utility decreasing with the amount of a commodity consumed) were relegated in the hypotheses about the shape of utility functions and indifference curves. To achieve this, axioms had to be introduced that a preference ordering had to satisfy. The crucial step, which resulted in utility theory abandoning such material conjectures, was the transition from cardinal utility to ordinal utility, reducing utility theory to a theory of subjective preference orderings. Much relevant information (in assessing welfare) has been discarded and replaced with a narrow focus on preference satisfaction (its technical meaning is discussed below). As Witt notes, '[t]he mathematical details of abstract calculus of utility were preferred over the complexities of empirical conjectures about human behaviour competing with psychological approaches.' (Witt 2005: 10)

As a consequence, the concept of utility is very far removed from its original meaning. What Samuelson (1947: 91) describes as the 'hollowness of utility' is the fact that utility has become an abstract magnitude, an index number, which is supposed to be only ordinally measurable when an observer sees a person choose between somehow arranged alternatives. In today's axiomatic (expected) utility theory, the notion of utility is thus only used as a placeholder for *'that which represents a person's preferences.'* (Broome 1991b: 3, italics in original) The concept that is fundamental and with which axiomatic utility theory starts are individual preferences. Based on these, one arrives at a utility function if they obey some standard textbook assumptions (Mas-Colell et al. 1995: Chs 1&3): preferences are defined over *commodity bundles* (given N commodities) in the consumption set $X \subset \mathbb{R}^N_+$. A consumer's preferences are captured by the preference relation '$\geqslant$', being an 'at least-as-good-as' relation defined on X. The following axioms are then defined:

$$\forall\, x, y \in X : x \geqslant y \vee y \geqslant x. \tag{2.1}$$

$$\forall\, x, y, z \in X : (x \geqslant y \wedge y \geqslant z) \rightarrow x \geqslant z. \tag{2.2}$$

If preferences satisfy the conditions of completeness (equation 2.1) and transitivity (equation 2.2), they are called 'rational'. This notion of rationality demands that an individual has a complete ranking of all commodities in X, which means that the individual's own preferences can be completely specified for even the most exotic bundles of commodities and that this ranking must additionally be consistent in the sense of the transitivity requirement.[11] If the preference relation is also assumed to be continuous on X, there exists a continuous utility function $u(x)$. This function assigns a numerical value to each element in X and ranks these according to the preferences. We say $u : X \rightarrow \mathbb{R}$ is a utility function that represents these preferences if the following holds:

$$\forall\, x, y \in X : x \geqslant y \leftrightarrow u(x) \geq u(y). \tag{2.3}$$

There are other assumptions regarding preferences and the utility function as well,[12] but if there is some hedonic experience that is actually measured, and what that would be like, is unclear. What motivates individuals and why their preference ordering is the way it is, is left unexplained in this framework. Moreover, some of these assumptions on individual rationality are very strong and far removed from actual human cognitive capabilities (Qizilbash 2006). Of course, if welfare is identified as utility, the material emptiness of the utility notion transfers directly to the notion of welfare. Can such a notion still capture what it means when a life goes well? It is obvious that a more systematic treatment of the concept of welfare is needed. Thus, in the next subsection, I discuss what a *theory* of welfare should consist of.

2.1.3 A theory of welfare

What is a theory of welfare? Any inquiry into the nature of welfare can focus on three different aspects (Sumner 2006: 17): First, a theory of welfare (in the narrow sense of the word) specifies the *nature* of welfare, giving a formal account of what constitutes individual well-being and social welfare. At this level, it is specified what makes a life go well and under what conditions this takes place. As was shown before, classical utilitarians such as Bentham conceived of welfare as happiness in the sense of a balance of pleasure over pain (see Bentham 1789), a use that has changed towards the preference satisfaction view, where welfare consists of the satisfaction of individual preferences (see Harsanyi 1982; Griffin 1986). The latter 'identification is so automatic and so ubiquitous that economists seldom realize how controversial it is.' (Hausman and McPherson 1997: 17) Second, there is the question of what are the *sources* of well-being. Note that this is distinct from the point made above since specifying a list of sources of well-being does not say what makes an item appear on this list. However, a theory of welfare (in the first sense) would specify a criterion of how to assemble a list of sources of well-being. Third, there is a layer that consists of *indicators* of welfare. While a theory of welfare clearly focuses on the most theoretical and conceptual layer, indicators of welfare are the most practice-oriented layer, where concrete measures for the sources of well-being are proposed. These might be very crude, depending on available data. Varying with the concrete exercise, different approaches stress different layers. A theory of welfare in a wider sense, however, should ideally comprise of all three layers, i.e. should specify the nature, sources and indicators of welfare. To give an example of this trinity of layers: standard economics is based on a theory of welfare that specifies preference satisfaction as identical with well-being on the most abstract level (however, as has been argued above, it is very unspecific on the nature of utility and preferences). On the middle layer, the consumption of commodities is argued to be the source of satisfaction. Income is thus often used as a (crude) indicator of well-being on the most practice-related layer (but other consumption- or expenditure-based measures are also used). This relationship is depicted in Table 2.1.

Table 2.1 Elements of a theory of welfare (based on Sumner 2006: 17)

Level	Role	Example
(1) Conceptual Level	specifies nature of well-being, gives criterion for what is part of (2)	preference satisfaction
(2) Sources	gives list of sources of well-being, is the basis for (3)	consumption of commodities
(3) Indicators	measures that represent (2), serve to empirically capture (1) and (2)	income or expenditure

In order to derive a usable taxonomy of different theories of welfare, there are two important criteria according to which all theories can be ranked. The first criterion is whether the notion of welfare makes use only of utility information, or whether it includes other information such as rights, liberties, etc. as well. To only use utility information in order to conceptualize well-being has been dubbed 'welfarism' (Sen 1979c: 468). While I defend welfarism in a separate subsection (see subsection 2.1.5), the second criterion is concerned with the subjectivity of the welfare notion itself and merits some discussion here.[13] On the one extreme of this dimension, there are theories that defend the view that individual well-being is completely subjective: in terms of the preference satisfaction view, this means that the individual is the most competent judge of his own desires, and no material specification of welfare is possible since one's own preferences might be widely divergent from the preferences of others (it is mind-dependent and as Sumner calls it: 'subject-relative'; Sumner 1996: 20–1). If individual i prefers commodity A over B, that individual's welfare increases when the latter can consume more of A (given non-satiation). For another individual j, this could be the opposite so that j's welfare would increase when consuming more of B instead of A. In terms of a hedonistic theory of welfare, welfare subjectivism means that pleasures and pains are the private, and subjective, qualities of an individual (in terms of what causes them and how they are experienced) and are thus not comparable or measurable. This subjectivity is appealing with respect to the sovereignty that an individual is endowed with when forming one's own tastes (Scanlon 1975: 656–7). Indeed, it has always been important for economists to adhere to the principle of normative individualism, namely that:

> individual preferences alone provide the measuring rod that is needed in order to formulate normative statements on economic states and processes in general and policy measures in particular. It is not allowed to evaluate these preferences from some 'external' perspective, i.e. in a paternalistic way.
>
> (Schubert 2005: 2)

Therefore economists readily embrace a subjectivist theory of welfare, as has already been stated above. On the other extreme of this dimension are objective theories of welfare, objective in the sense that welfare is independent of individuals' evaluations or preferences and their satisfaction. For example, basic needs theories postulate that humans all share a set of basic needs whose satisfaction increases individual welfare. A fully objective theory would probably defend the view that the amount of welfare resulting from a certain source would be the same for everyone, perhaps comparable to the nutritional content of a loaf of bread which is (putting aside certain parasitic diseases) also the same for everyone.

To avoid a common misunderstanding; a qualification seems in order: a theory of welfare *per se* has to assess the 'prudential value of a life' (Sumner 1996: 20). When assessing the value of the life of a person, we want to know whether this life is good *for the person*. We can call such a theory a 'theory of the good' (whereas a 'theory of the right' is concerned with ethical value). Confusion might result from the entanglement of the notions of prudential versus moral (ethical) value. They are closely related and thus often confounded (Feldman 2004: 10). It is important to keep this distinction in mind when considering (for example) sadist preferences. Conceptually speaking, a purely positive theory of well-being could imply that humans take pleasure in acts of cruelty, for example a sadist enjoying the suffering of others. Regarding prudential value, the life of a sadist goes well (all other things neglected), if that individual can make other individuals suffer. In this situation, the sadist's welfare would have to be assessed as being quite high because that sadist's life is going well *for him*. It goes without saying that this is morally highly suspect, and a theory of welfare is therefore usually supplied with an additional 'moral (or normative) filter' to account for sadistic preferences and the like. A moral filter can be understood to consist of external value judgements to supplement a theory of welfare in order to make it compatible with our moral intuitions and to account for otherwise implausible implications of such a theory. A theory of welfare should thus ideally consist of two parts, one specifying individual well-being and another, normative part specifying social welfare and endowing it with a 'moral filter' in order to incorporate some value judgements regarding the desirability of different types of prudential value such that the theory does not contradict the moral values of a society.

2.1.4 Requirements for a theory of welfare

To evaluate competing theories of welfare, Sumner has suggested two main criteria (Sumner 1996: 8–10): on the one hand, it has to be assessed whether the theory of welfare is 'descriptively adequate'. This means deciding whether the notion of welfare is in line with findings of what constitutes well-being and how individuals actually assess their welfare. The second criterion is 'normative adequacy', and it captures to what extent a theory of welfare is in accordance with moral criteria and intuition. Sumner has further subdivided his criterion of descriptive adequacy along four dimensions, namely 'fidelity', 'generality', 'formality' and 'neutrality'. By 'fidelity', Sumner refers to the degree with which the notion of welfare corresponds with our intuition of what constitutes welfare. 'Generality' denotes the dimension that assesses what kinds of welfare judgements would be comprised by a theory of welfare. The 'formality' dimension maintains that a descriptively adequate theory of welfare should not simply list the sources of welfare but give an account of its nature (Sumner 1996: 16). The last dimension for descriptive adequacy is 'neutrality', which means that a theory of welfare should not be biased in any way. This amounts to a very heterogenous category of descriptive adequacy, comprising such different dimensions as methodological considerations (formality, generality or neutrality) and empirical considerations (fidelity). I therefore submit that a different categorization along three main criteria is better suited to assess the adequacy of theories of welfare, which I will label 'empirical', 'methodological' and 'normative' adequacy. I will discuss these three dimensions in turn.

By 'empirical adequacy', I refer to the descriptive correspondence of the notion of welfare with empirical findings from the natural and behavioural sciences. When specifying a notion of individual well-being, this notion should – in accordance with the naturalistic methodology introduced in Chapter 1 – be informed by positive knowledge of human behaviour (or at the very least, not contradict it). Thus empirical adequacy is less concerned with (folk) intuition regarding welfare or the formal (methodological) requirements of being general or neutral.

The second category, 'methodological adequacy', would then refer to exactly these methodological requirements that do not deal with the theory's empirical content. Of course, in a wider sense, all three dimensions are methodological requirements, but this category encompasses *formal* criteria, while the other dimensions encompass *substantive* empirical, respectively ethical, requirements. A theory of welfare is methodologically adequate if it formally specifies the nature of welfare, is general and comprises all three layers of analysis (nature, sources and indicators of welfare). Obviously, a theory of welfare should be complete and not only deal with a subset of welfare judgements. For example, an account that considers only the satisfaction of a few basic needs as welfare enhancing would not be sufficiently general if, in reality, the satisfaction of other preferences increased welfare as well. I also submit that a requirement such as Sumner's 'formality' is insufficient and a material (substantive) specification of the nature of welfare is necessary for a theory of welfare (for a similar distinction see Hausman and McPherson 2006: 119). The methodological stance of naturalism taken in this book suggests that a complete theory of welfare has to materially specify the notion of welfare. But one could also require other criteria in this category. Stigler, for example, has demanded that a theory should also be 'manageable' (Stigler 1950b). This can be interpreted to be a formal criterion ensuring the 'mathematical tractability' of the theory (Warke 2000b).

The third category is called 'normative (or moral) adequacy' and assesses the extent to which a theory of welfare is in accordance with our moral values. (Here I go along with Sumner's suggestion.) As an important requirement to assess the normative adequacy of a theory of welfare, it should at least be clear what kinds of moral value judgements it is compatible with or runs counter to. Consider, for example, the critique that objective theories of welfare can support paternalism because the individual is not the judge of his own well-being (see, e.g. Sugden 2006b). For this reason, anyone defending such an objective theory should at least make clear to what extent the theory is leading to paternalist implications and is thus not compatible with the value of individual autonomy. One test for moral adequacy could be how well a theory fits with our moral intuitions. While the correspondence of a given argument with 'common intuitions' is a widespread criterion to assess normative arguments in economics, one has to be aware of the fact that intuition can be a fickle source of justification, especially when judging on the adequacy of thought experiments requiring us to imagine very exotic things (similar arguments have been advanced also by Haslett 1990; Sumner 1996). Nevertheless, especially in ethical debates, intuition seems to be accorded great weight in critically assessing various theories. Griffin (1998: Ch. 1) rightly notes that some doubts are in order with such a methodology: it is not clear why our intuitive faculty should be producing unbiased, well-informed judgements about different normative arguments (how cultural biases influence our intuitions has been shown succinctly by Hauser 2006). A more plausible view (defended here) would recognize the value of using a 'criterion of intuition' to see whether an argument is in accordance with intuitions or not. If it is not, I would argue that it needs otherwise strong support in its favour, or else one would need to explain why intuition might be amiss in such a case. While intuitions are not the sole source of normative justification, they can nevertheless offer valuable insights, and if some aspects of a theory of welfare are not in accordance with widely held moral intuitions, at least some other reasoned arguments have to be offered as to why this is the case.

Note, finally, that there may be trade-offs between the three dimensions. It is possible that a theory of welfare is empirically, though not normatively, adequate and *vice versa*. Consider the example of sadistic preferences. Although one could argue that, for example, the preference satisfaction view might be empirically adequate, one would certainly find it normatively inadequate without some 'moral filter' excluding such sadistic preferences. Similar trade-offs might exist between empirical adequacy and aspects of methodological adequacy, for example when an empirically rich theory is no longer mathematically tractable. Ideally, a theory of welfare will meet all three requirement categories. But if trade-offs become plain, one has to decide which of the dimensions is accorded more weight, i.e. one either has to focus on its explanatory adequateness or on its normative role or method-ological requirements. While Haslett (1990) argues that the primacy should lie in defining a welfare notion with its normative purposes kept in mind, the naturalistic perspective taken in this work prompts a focus on empirical adequacy. Remember that it is the declared aim of a naturalistic approach to construct a theory of welfare that takes into account the findings of other (behavioural) sciences such as psychology. However, this does not mean that this theory will necessarily be philosophically uninformed or morally naive. The question to be answered in the chapters below will be whether the naturalistic approach can help us shape also the normative aspects of our endeavour.

2.1.5 *In defence of welfarism*

In this section I specify a line of criticism that is centred more narrowly on welfare economics and a class of theories of welfare. It concerns utilitarian-ism as a moral principle and has been forcefully made by Sen (Sen 1979b,c). The utilitarian framework is discredited by the former on the grounds of his criticism of welfarism, the principle that '[t]he judgment of the relative good-ness of alternative states of affairs must be based exclusively on, and taken as an increasing function of, the respective collections of individual utilities in these states.' (Sen 1979c: 468)[14] The identification of individual utility (no matter how one defines it) as the *sole* intrinsic value for ethical consider-ation is an important decision and, according to Sen, entails neglecting other important values which, in this view, become purely instrumental. It is important to note that what is criticized about welfarism is not that the welfarist holds that individual welfare is an important normative maximand, but that it is the one and only normative maximand. This criticism has two aspects, viz. the supposition, first, that well-being (understood as utility) is the sole criterion of a person doing well (with other things such as liberties and rights only playing an instrumental role) and, second, that well-being is best seen as utility and not something else (e.g. happiness, freedom, etc.).

The first point of criticism can be illuminated succinctly by the following example (adapted from Sen 1979b: 547). Table 2.2 shows what critics of welfarism hold to be the most problematic aspect of this position. For the following example, let us assume cardinal utility, which is measurable and comparable across individuals. These are strongly favourable assumptions about the informational basis of welfarism. Consider individuals r and p in

Table 2.2 Welfarism – an example; adapted from Sen (1979b: 547)

	(X) 'Status Quo'	(Y) 'Redistribution'	(Z) 'Insurrection'
(R) 'Rich'	10	8	8
(P) 'Poor'	4	7	7

the three different social states x, y and z. In x, r has command over many resources and r's utility is 10. p is worse off and can only consume few items such that p's utility is 4, leading to an overall social utility of 14. Situation y has come about through redistributive policies, where some resources of r were given to p. (It is obvious that marginal utility is decreasing.) Redistribution has increased social utility to 15. The utilitarian would hold that y is socially preferable to x. Now consider z, which has come about through an insurrection of p. Let us assume that no commodities are replaced but p burns down the home of r and tortures r in the process. This leads to an increase in utility for p through the sheer pleasure p derives from burning down the home and torturing r. The social utility in z is equal to the social utility in y. y is preferred to x, and, in consequence, z should be preferred to x on a purely utilitarian basis. This example highlights an apparently appalling conclusion that utilitarianism (being based on welfarism) is infamous for: in the interest of the greater good, important individual rights (in this case the freedom from harm) and other values deemed important *per se* are neglected. Consider also the example of a club of sadists: even if a utilitarian assumes that the pleasure gained by a sadist from torturing someone is only 1/100 of the pain that sadist inflicts on the victim, it would be perfectly acceptable if 101 sadists were to torture someone (Sugden quoted from Ng 1981: 529).

The second criticism regarding welfarism concerns the interpretation of well-being in terms of utility (Sen 1987: 45): for Sen, the judgement of welfare exclusively in terms of happiness or preference satisfaction has limitations that seem to be particularly problematic in interpersonal comparisons of well-being, the reason being that a subjective metric is relative to one's own expectations and to the comparative standard of one's social situation. For example, a 'hopeless beggar' (in a situation of objective misery) might be more easily reconciled with small pleasures; but attaching a correspondingly small value to those small pleasures would be ethically undesirable. This criticism of welfarism has to be dealt with when trying to argue for a utilitarian approach to welfare economics. First of all, rejecting welfarism on grounds of measurability problems seems mistaken. The argument that welfare cannot be adequately measured, or is practically difficult to measure, does not constitute a case against it on a conceptual level (Ng 1981). While it is perfectly in order to be a welfarist at the conceptual level, one can use non-utility information on the level of the indicators to measure welfare if no other approximation is available.[15]

But the examples regarding torture and the hopeless beggar argument indeed point to a problem associated with welfarism, namely the somewhat narrow informational basis of the approach. (This was the case even under the most favourable assumptions regarding cardinality and interpersonal comparability of utility.) Can welfarism be defended against these objections? Let me make clear that the latter are aimed at welfarism at a specific level. Moore and Crisp (1996) have argued that welfarism can be criticized for three different claims it makes: first, it contains an *existence thesis* stating that a concept like individual well-being does exist (which could be denied, see e.g. Moore 1903: Ch. 3). Second, it contains a *significance thesis* (individual well-being is a significant notion) and, third, it contains the *exclusiveness thesis* (the sole moral maximand is welfare). The above-mentioned objections clearly belong to the third category.[16] What about the exclusiveness thesis? Are other intrinsic values needed to cope with the objections presented above? Can a welfarist accommodate for the problem of social conditioning that leads to a beggar accepting his lot and striving for any small pleasures that might be available? There seem to be three possible ways in which the problem of the hopeless beggar could be accommodated by a welfarist theory (Moore and Crisp 1996: 604–5): one could either stipulate that with informed desires, the hopeless beggar would not be content with his lot (this equals a correction of preferences towards some criteria of rationality). Another way would be to argue for different kinds of pleasures so that, although the beggar might experience some small pleasures, that beggar might be fairly deprived regarding the pleasures that could be derived from self-respect, a pleasure that cannot be derived in case of the beggar's contentment with a miserable lot (as has been argued, e.g. by Mill 1863). A third way would be an objective theory of welfare that is still welfarist. It is thus clear that the problem of the hopeless beggar can be addressed in less narrow welfarist accounts of well-being (I return to the hopeless beggar objection in more detail below, see section 6.5.2).

This leaves us with the torture objection, which points to the question of value monism versus value pluralism. Can we defend a welfarist account of welfare against the torture example mentioned above? Ng (1981, 1990) has argued that, while a situation like z might be conceivable, it would in reality be impossible that the utility configurations have this distribution because the indirect effects of torturing a person would further decrease social utility. Taking all direct and indirect effects into account, it would be practically impossible that z came about, and therefore the welfarist need not worry. Ng goes so far as to argue that in such an (impossible) situation, he would give up his idea in 'no torture' as being a less fundamental value judgement than his belief in 'welfarism'. Ng bases his argument on the distinction between 'basic' and 'non-basic' value judgements (Sen 1967). The former hold independently of any factual information under all possible circumstances and without qualification. The latter, non-basic, value judgements are subject to qualification and might not hold unconditionally (they might become revised in the light of new factual information). This distinction is then applied to the value judgement of welfarism, which Ng characterizes as comparatively more basic than the no-torture value judgement. Given this assumption, the no-torture value judgement would have to be given up when it conflicts with the basic welfarism value judgement. Ng argues that it is obvious that welfarism is the more basic value judgement for everyone because the value judgement that torture is bad would mostly be justified through the harm caused by torture (be it that the direct effect on the victim is always taken to be higher than the gain for the torturer, or be it that there are many indirect negative effects such as the increased aggressiveness that the acceptance of torture would inflict on society). Since such an argument justifies the no-torture value judgement in terms of its welfarist consequences, welfarism is more basic (see similarly Blackorby et al. 2002: 14). Ng holds that even if the positive effects for the torturer would in some cases exceed the negative total effects, one would argue against torture but could still adhere to a welfarist theory of welfare. Why is this the case? Ng holds that one can be welfarist but acknowledge the fact that one cannot really calculate the consequences of each action in all situations. Therefore rules (norms) have been established that tend to foster the welfarist goals in average situations (this would be a pro rule-utilitarianism argument). These norms might be so deeply internalized in our behaviour that we do not recognize their being derived from welfarism in the first place.

To conclude this section, let me remark that the arguments in defence of welfarism are not fully bullet-proof, but that a case in defence of welfarism can be made on the grounds mentioned and '[w]elfarism remains a powerful and attractive position in contemporary ethics' (Moore and Crisp 1996: 613). While the focus in this section has been on defending welfarism against some objections, another strategy could be fruitfully adopted in making a case that no other value judgement has so much support as an ultimate goal to follow in life (Ng 1990; Shaver 2004). This would largely amount to holding a position of 'weak welfarism' (Adler and Posner 2008), which can be conceived of as having the structure $W = \{W^*, F_1, \ldots, F_n\}$, where W^* denotes well-being, while the F_i denote other concerns or values such as liberties, and so on. On such an account, the focus would be on the analysis of welfare, without denying the importance of other fundamental concerns, which could then be used to qualify some aspects of the account. I will argue below that well-being is a very important value. The original parts of this monograph will therefore be mostly (weakly) welfarist and may be criticized for this allegiance.[17]

2.2 Theories of welfare

In this section, I exemplarily sketch the most prominent types of theories of welfare and discuss their merits and weaknesses according to the requirements set out in the previous section. This discussion introduces the main questions and problems to be answered by a theory of welfare. Table 2.3 locates the more prominent examples of conceivable theories of welfare along the two axes of the degree of subjectivity and the binary dimension of welfarism. The examples listed in the table are not exhaustive but should be seen as exemplary theories of welfare which I discuss in the following subsections.[18]

2.2.1 An objective theory – the basic needs account

To begin the discussion at the objective end of the spectrum for theories of welfare, one can consider the so-called 'basic needs' account as an example of

Table 2.3 A typology of theories of welfare (author's exposition)

	Welfarist	*Non-Welfarist*
Subjective		
	Hedonism	
	Desire Theories	
		Capabilities & Functionings
		Basic Needs
Objective		

an 'objective list account' (Parfit 1984). A different example would be Sen's 'capabilities and functionings' account. Since the latter offers such a rich framework, which has departed from many of the standard assumptions of traditional welfare economics, I discuss it in greater detail in the next chapter (see section 3.2). The basic needs account has been established especially for use in assessing poverty and for policy advice in development economics (Streeten and Burki 1978; Chichilnisky 1980; Streeten 1984; Thomson 1987). Usually, basic needs accounts equate welfare with the satisfaction of certain *basic* needs such as the need for nutrition, unpolluted air, shelter, etc. While there is often disagreement on the exact nature of the needs (if they are speci-fied completely at all, cf. Jackson and Marks 1999), these needs are mostly related to commodities as 'needs for commodities' (Sen 1993a: 40 fn 30).

These needs are argued to be independent of human desires, and they are supposedly *fundamental* with respect to guaranteeing normal human func-tioning (Thomson 1987: 8 and 36–8). There are several peculiarities attaching to such an account that require attention. At first glance, needs seem to be sufficiently objective as opposed to 'mere' preferences. In comparison, needs lack the 'intentionality' of preferences (Sumner 1996: 53). As intentionality is always a characteristic of the mental (and thus the subjective), a needs account lacks one feature that subjectivist accounts share. Sumner gives the following example: although I have a desire for water, it doesn't follow that I desire H_2O because I might be ignorant of the chemical composition of water. If one needs water however, one needs H_2O, independent of whether one realizes this fact or not. In this respect, a needs account seems to be objective. Since one does not choose to have a certain need and needs are not changeable (they are givens and thus 'inescapable', cf. Thomson 1987: Ch. 4), one cannot be held responsible for having them (Griffin 1982: 341 fn 2). The satisfaction of these needs thus constitutes a more *urgent* goal than the satisfaction of 'mere' preferences (Scanlon 1975). Moreover, since we all share these needs, making them constitutive of welfare would satisfy our egalitarian intuitions.

However, there remain some difficulties with such an account: first of all, most accounts of basic needs give a list of needs whose satisfaction increases welfare. As mentioned earlier, a list of objects is not enough to really specify a theory of welfare. There is a difference between a formal theory of welfare and a mere list of sources of welfare as provided by a basic needs account. Such an account would have to specify why the needs on the list are actually on it, that is, why their satisfaction increases well-being. Most basic needs accounts do not specify this 'nature of welfare' since their aim is very practice-oriented, for example at the level of poverty reduction (e.g. Streeten and Burki 1978; Streeten 1984). This makes the accounts vulnerable to objections of the sort that important needs are neglected or unimportant needs are on the list, both of which threaten the claim of objectivity that is advanced as a favourable characteristic of such an account. Moreover, a basic needs account obviously cannot include all sorts of needs. For example, the need for electricity to cook the evening meal is too instrumental to qualify as a valid need because it is derivative. Central, or in that sense 'fundamental', in this context would be the need for nutrition. By narrowing down the list of basic or fundamental needs, such a theory of welfare inevitably loses generality. It could well be argued that we are benefited not only by the satisfaction of basic needs but also by the satisfaction of preferences and mere whims.

Another aspect concerns the assembly of the list of basic needs. To maintain the claim for objectivity, this list would have to be constructed naturalistically. It would have to be established that nature has endowed all individuals *qua* genetic make-up with these needs. Being deprived of their satisfaction would seriously harm the bodily (and mental) functioning. As Sumner correctly points out, any valuational or consensual exercise of constructing such a list (which he terms 'constructivist approach') would be inimical to the claim of objectivity of this theory of welfare (Sumner 1996: 56).[19] A promising strategy for a basic needs account could be what Thomson has in mind when arguing that a need is fundamental if its deprivation causes harm to the individual (Thomson 1987: 36–8). Note, however, the presupposition of a theory of welfare that lies below the level of needs in this account since the concept of 'harm' now fundamentally specifies the nature of welfare. I propose a related decidedly hedonistic account below, where basic needs play an important role as well, without being vulnerable to the criticisms mentioned so far. At that point, I am able to argue that, while inadequate on the level of the nature of welfare, basic needs can play an important role in operationalizing the concept of welfare at the level of sources and indicators of well-being (Chs 5 and 6). Summing up the main problems of objective theories of welfare, we have to conclude that it seems dubious whether a completely objective theory of welfare could actually be specified (Scanlon 1993: 190–1). Indeed, we see that defending these theories against common objections tends to introduce subjective elements into them so that objectivity is no longer given. This, then, brings us to the subjectivist theories of welfare.

2.2.2 *Subjective theories of welfare*

Two different kinds of theories of welfare fall into the category of subjective theories, namely the preference satisfaction (or desire) theories and the different forms of hedonism. While the terms 'desire' and 'preference' can often be used interchangeably, they are not one and the same, strictly speaking. The notion of desire is somewhat more general and does not have the relational connotations of the technical term of preference. Opposed to a desire for *A*, a preference is always of the form that one prefers *A* over *B*. The term 'desire theories' thus denotes the category name, while 'preference satisfaction theories' are one specific subclass. Desire theories are also called state-of-the-world theories because they detail which states of the world fulfil certain desires. Hedonistic theories, by contrast, are state-of-the-mind theories because welfare is considered by them to consist of pleasure and pain, which are states of mind.[20] Both are discussed in this subsection.

The preference satisfaction view/desire theory

As already discussed, the preference satisfaction view is that theory of welfare that underlies standard welfare economics; it is thoroughly *subjective*. Whatever an individual's preferences, their satisfaction (e.g. via the consumption of goods) is that what counts normatively. This does not necessarily imply, however, that such individual assessments have to be uninformed, biased, or otherwise fallible. The most common view on preference satisfaction is certainly the one by Harsanyi (Harsanyi 1955, 1982). But Griffin has presented another type of desire theory (Griffin 1986: Chs 1&2). The preference satisfaction view attributes value to something because of its being desired by an agent. In other words, to value something means to prefer it over something else. Such an account is concerned about those states of the world that bring about the fulfilment of preferences. Note that in a completely subjectivist account, it does not matter what is valued; a case in point might be preferences for counting blades of grass (Rawls 1971).

There are some difficulties associated with this sort of theory of welfare. Although the account is formally completely specified as a theory of welfare (welfare comes from the satisfaction of whatever preference an agent has), it is materially empty since it does not say anything about what might be the cause of this welfare gain.[21] It is neither clear why, and in what way, satisfaction leads to an increase in welfare, nor is it specified whether there are commonalities of desires in humans. For example, it might be conjectured that humans are biologically endowed with some shared preferences.[22] As long as a preference satisfaction theory makes no material propositions on the content of preferences, it remains materially unspecified.

Besides, Broome (2008) has shown that a utilitarian preference satisfaction view fails due to its inability to coherently integrate intra- and interpersonal comparisons of utility levels solely in preferentist terms. In short, his argument is that a preferentist utilitarian account needs to make some assumptions on the strength or intensity of preferences, for otherwise, no sense can be made of ideas such as the maximization of social welfare in terms of the individual's preference satisfaction. If that intensity of preferences were constructed based on the (hedonic) effect or sensation of the related event, the whole view would turn into a hedonistic account of welfare. The solution is thus to construe intensity of preferences in this account by using expected utility theory (Broome 2008: 230–2). But can the preferentist compare degrees of preferences between individuals? Harsanyi has suggested using 'extended preferences', i.e. preferences about whole histories of human lives (this means one has a preference for a history where one lives the life of an economist over the history where one lives the life of a philosopher). In an extended preference set, all possible states of being are included. When additionally assuming that everyone has the same identical extended preferences, individuals' preferences (and the utility levels derived from them) are indeed made comparable interpersonally. Although Broome (1993) has shown that the formal argument for such a universal preference ordering fails, Binmore (1998, 2005) has recently offered another hypothesis on how a long-term convergence of extended preferences could come about based on processes of social evolution. Basically, Binmore argues that individuals adopt the extended preferences of their successful peers (Binmore 2006: 22). Several weak points have been attributed to this proposal: First, both expected utility theory and the convergence hypothesis are based on very strong and unrealistic assumptions of individual rationality (individuals are more likely subject to the well-known Kahneman–Tversky-style anomalies in decision making than to obeying strict economic rationality). Second, the model of social evolution as suggested by Binmore has been criticized as descriptively too simple (Sugden 2001; Cordes and Schubert 2007). And, third, from the point of view of moral adequacy: even if we accept the model's strong assumptions; there is no argument to be found why the outcome of social evolution would really be a desirable theory of welfare, i.e. why people *should* behave as preferentists (Broome 2008).

Another problem already detailed above are preferences that are undesirable from an external viewpoint. This is usually subsumed under the heading of irrational preferences and, besides antisocial preferences (such as sadism, envy, resentment, malice), also includes preferences that were formed either ignorantly or involuntarily. As discussed in section 2.1.3, a remedy regarding antisocial preferences would be the introduction of a 'moral filter'. This is done by Harsanyi in a more or less *ad hoc* fashion and by appealing to common sense and 'general goodwill and human sympathy' (Harsanyi 1982: 56). A normative filter, however, presupposes an underlying moral theory and is thus subject to debate. While the exclusion of sadistic preferences may be reasonably defensible, there might be disagreement over the exclusion of other sorts of preferences (e.g. aggressive preferences). To account for ignorance or problems of self-control, Harsanyi has further argued for taking into account only 'true preferences', namely those preferences a person '*would* have if he had all the relevant factual information, always reasoned with the greatest possible care, and were in a state of mind most conducive to rational choice' (Harsanyi 1982: 55, emphasis in original). This is done in a similar fashion in other 'informed desire' accounts (Griffin 1986). Indeed, it seems necessary to make that shift in emphasis: although the standard economic view of 'actual desire' fulfilment is highly influential because it makes the individual the judge of his own desires (see section 2.1.3), it is nevertheless inadequate since we often fail to recognize what is in our own interest so that preferences are often mistaken. Many desires we have can be fulfilled but do not increase our welfare. In consequence, '[t]he objection to the actual-desire account is overwhelming' (Griffin 1986: 10).[23]

If we reject the actual desire view in favour of an informed desire view, this shift in focus entails some other problems. Corrections have to be made because a preference satisfaction account is always directed towards the future: potential discrepancies between *ex ante* expectations and the *ex post* experience of the satisfaction of a preference can cause distortions that would have to be corrected (Sumner 1996: 128–30). But constructing this account in terms of somehow 'idealized preferences' makes the whole endeavour dependent on a systematic notion of the good (of what is valuable) that lies outside the individual. When talking about informed desires, one presupposes a commonly shared eudaemonia or commonly shared interests according to which one can only judge whether the desires are indeed the 'true preferences' and not distorted (see Qizilbash 1998: 61). Even if one makes no material assumptions about idealized preferences but remains on the level of specifying procedural constraints on the preference formation process, the whole endeavour is not that simple and unambiguous anymore: what is the necessary information that an individual should possess for acquiring 'informed preferences', when is deliberation 'rational', and under what circumstances is the mind in a state 'most conducive to rational choice'? All this can be subjected to debate, making the account vulnerable to objections (not to mention the limitations such a modified account would place on an individual's autonomy regarding that individual's preferences, i.e. such an account would lose its probably most attractive feature).

Moreover, depending on whether one wants to put this objection forward as a separate category (instead of understanding it as subset of what it would mean not to be in a state of having true preferences), there still remains an open question, namely how to deal with adaptive preference formation (the 'hopeless beggar'): an individual being born into a very unfavourable situation (e.g. extreme poverty, war, slavery) might very rationally decide that having high-minded desires will only lead to frustration and thus (even under rational and conscious deliberation) opt for very few and humble desires only. Such an individual might be content even in an objectively very miserable situation, and one would certainly hesitate to say that this individual's welfare was high. The questions how to incorporate 'windfall gains' (an action that the individual did not desire leads to an increase in well-being) or the satisfaction of 'disinterested desires' (desires whose satisfaction does not increase well-being) also remain unanswered. Rather than addressing them myself, I refer to Sumner (1996: 122–37) for a more extensive treatment.

The fundamental problem involved in any desire or preference satisfaction view is, however, that it mistakes one of the most prominent sources of individual welfare (namely the satisfaction of a desire) for the 'nature' of welfare. Desire accounts:

> attempt to build an account of the nature of welfare around one of its standard generic sources. The symptom of the mistake is also the same in each case: whatever the favored source may be, its possession is logically neither necessary nor sufficient for our well-being.
>
> (Sumner 1996: 137)

This problem has already appeared in various guises in the objection regarding actual versus informed preferences because there is often a divergence between preference and welfare that may result from many of the above-mentioned mechanisms: one can desire something but may not be better off in terms of welfare because of an uninformed desire, a non-perfect foresight, an irrational urge (perhaps from addiction), and so on. As long as wanting (desiring) and liking (welfare) coincide, the desire account seems to work. But for the large class of cases where this does not hold, the divergence between wanting and liking leads to a biased estimate of well-being (Ng 2003).[24]

And, one may add from an evolutionary perspective: when one takes individual preferences as the measuring rod for welfare, it is not clear how to make sense of this in the context of changing preferences. When individual i prefers A over B at time point t_0, but i's preferences change such that B is preferred over A at time point $t_1 > t_0$, what can then be said about i's welfare? This objection points to the overall theme of this monograph, namely that some other measuring rod for welfare has to be found when one makes the assumption that human preferences may change. If no other welfare criterion is applied, it becomes problematic to weigh changing desires or to find a maximization calculus under a regime of changing preferences (for this diagnosis, see also Griffin 1982: 337). This makes hedonism seem a *prima facie* more attractive theory of welfare because there, no matter whether preferences change, the measuring rod for welfare are the pleasant sensory episodes.

Hedonism

Taking up these remarks, I will briefly discuss the features of a generic hedonistic account of welfare. Welfare is understood here as consisting of pleasure and the absence of pain (usually as the net total of pleasure over pain). Besides the main proponent (Bentham 1789), it has been put forward in modified fashion by Kahneman et al. (1997) or Feldman (2004). Since pleasure and pain are understood to be sensations and are thus states of the mind, this account is usually independent of states of the world. In this respect, hedonistic accounts of welfare are even more subjective than desire theories.

We should view with caution three different interpretations of hedonism

(Sumner 1996: Ch. 4). First of all, 'psychological hedonism' can be interpreted as a causal theory of motivation. It is an empirical question for psychology whether humans are solely motivated to act in terms of rewarding pleasant sensations (and pain avoidance, respectively). This interpretation is purely descriptive. While some economists (e.g. Harsanyi 1982) reject the idea that all is done just for the pleasure (or the avoidance of pain), one has to admit that pleasure and pain constitute two powerful motivating forces in human (and animal) life (cf. Cabanac 1979, 1992). I discuss the psychological evidence regarding psychological hedonism in more detail below (section 5.1). A second interpretation is 'ethical hedonism', where ultimately all moral value is attributed to pleasure (and evil is equated with pain). Thus judging the *rightness* of a state is done solely in terms of the pleasure and pain in that state. As a theory of the right, ethical hedonism is normative. Psychological hedonism can be regarded as a good justification for also accepting ethical hedonism. But of course, no strict logical implication to accept ethical hedonism follows from the fact that humans act according to psychological hedonism (similar to the case of preferentism: from the fact that individuals tend to satisfy their desires, it does not automatically follow that they should satisfy their desires). The third interpretation is hedonism as a theory of welfare. Here *prudential value* is assigned only to pleasure and pain. Recall from the above that a theory of welfare does not *per se* say something about ethical value. 'Welfare hedonism' as a theory of welfare would thus also require a moral filter to deal with the pleasures of a sadist. This objection concerns the normative adequacy of hedonism as a theory of welfare; it should be treated separately from the question whether hedonism could be an empirically accurate theory of welfare (and value). Note the similarity to the arguments for welfarism (section 2.1.5) that can be mustered to defend hedonism as a theory of welfare (e.g. no one would want to deny that pleasure is a very important value in human life).

But this is not the only distinction that is important. Hedonism (as a theory of welfare) can come in an 'internalist' or an 'externalist' version. The internalist model of hedonism claims that pleasure is a sensation that has a homogeneous feeling tone. This means that all pleasures are qualitatively the same, whether it is the pleasure one derives from reading a book or from strolling through the park, or whether it is carnal pleasure. One of the most common criticisms levelled against hedonism concerns exactly this homogeneity of sensation. Are, the critics ask, the pleasures we derive from the above-mentioned activities really of the same quality (Sen 1981)? The externalist version avoids this critique by arguing that pleasures are heterogeneous. What is the same, however, is the reaction to these pleasures, for example in the form of having a favourable attitude towards them (Sumner 1996: 90). While the externalist model seems more convincing regarding a potential incommensurability of pleasures, this comes at a certain cost: when having only one quality of pleasure, intra- and interpersonal comparisons of well-being are straightforward. This is no longer the case with a model of multidimensional pleasures (and well-being) and may even turn out to be impossible (Sen 1981: 200). While this objection can also be understood as a 'measurement objection', we should be careful to reject hedonism as there are promising attempts at measuring pleasure and pain (see Ch. 5).

Due to its peculiar nature, there are several other criticisms which have branded hedonism as a supposedly unattractive candidate as far as a theory of welfare is concerned. I examine these criticisms in order to assess whether the version of hedonism defended below stands up against the former. One important objection concerning both versions of hedonism is that one risks a solipsistic theory of welfare since well-being is only a mental state and not connected with the world: Nozick's famous experience machine thought experiment nicely illustrates this (Nozick 1974: 42–5): suppose there exists a machine that constantly stimulates your brain. While your body is resting in a vat you live in an illusionary world full of pleasant experiences. Would you tap in? Nozick and others say no and take this as an objection against hedonism because, obviously, there must be something else besides pleasure that is important, so they argue. The main point of this argument is that there seems to be a difference between having a pleasurable state of mind and really doing something pleasurable or being a certain kind of person. A hedonist would be committed to the position that the illusion of pleasure would be similarly valuable to a person as the equivalent 'real' pleasure. Another objection concerns the assumption that the value of a good life should consist only of pleasure. Proponents of this objection always describe simple hedonism as a 'depraved' view that only propagates mere sensualism, i.e. individuals are reduced to mindlessly seeking low pleasures – supposedly their sole goal in life. It seems other important values such as friendship, sympathy, achievement are neglected by this view. While this objection might be a problem for an (internalist) sensory hedonism with a narrow view of pleasure, it would not necessarily be a problem for a broader view of pleasure that also incorporates the pleasures gained from achievement or from having friendships and the like.

Lastly, there are two objections that carry more weight. One concerns 'non-existent pleasures', the other adaptation phenomena. I discuss them in turn. Imagine Stanley the Stoic who decides to live a life in reclusion, forswearing all sensual pleasures and living a life of quiet contemplation. At the end of his life, Stanley will surely have led a life valuable to him. The non-existent pleasures, however, would, in standard accounts of hedonism, lead to an account of low well-being for Stanley. How can the hedonist account for this? One way out is the externalist version of hedonism because Stanley would have reacted favourably to his life without pleasures. But the internalist hedonist, too, when subscribing to a broader view of pleasures, could claim that Stanley might have ranked low on the common sensual pleasures but might possibly have compensated for that by ranking high on the achievement component of pleasure for his leading the life he wants to live. What remains is the problem of adaptation, indeed constituting a difficulty for hedonism. The hopeless beggar might have been so miserable that his aspiration levels for pleasure had gone down considerably so that this individual would have been very content even with small pleasures. This is certainly a problem for the externalist version of hedonism, where a favourable reaction is derived even from small amounts of sensory pleasures. It is not entirely clear whether this is as problematic for the internalist version. Of course, a person might become used to living on few calories a day, but it seems to be the case that adaptation does not set in here as strongly, concerning the pleasure derived. This person will be constantly hungry, and while assessing the state of deprivation as not so bad due to lowered aspiration levels, the levels of pleasure might be quite low (not the assessment or favourable reaction to them; I address this in more detail in Chs 5 and 6).

Summing up, we have seen that both desire theories and hedonistic theories are subjected to severe criticism concerning their empirical, methodological and normative adequacy. What should have become clear is that all theories of welfare considered so far are heavily influenced by the ethical outlook one subscribes to. All theories of welfare thus have to be modified with a moral filter that depends on value judgements one is willing to defend. Moreover, we see that, on the one hand, purely objective theories of welfare are not easily conceivable, while, on the other hand, purely subjective theories need some kind of an objective link to the external world. One can thus agree with Sumner that in trying to build a plausible version of a theory of welfare, the objectivist has to introduce subjective elements while the subjectivist has to introduce some objective elements (Sumner 2006: 15). It can be conjectured that a defensible view of welfare will be halfway in between the dichotomy, and the question whether such a theory should be subjective or objective is therefore somewhat misplaced. Lastly, it can be conjectured that in accommodating all the objections to the standard views, our notion of well-being will no longer be a neat theoretical concept or a single index number. It is shown below how findings from psychology and the neurosciences impact on the plausibility of some of the objections discussed above. There is no reason to stick to these objections in economics once it has been established that the objections lack (empirical) validity.

2.3 Welfare economics

Let us now turn to a less abstract level and explore how a theory of welfare is used in welfare economics. To begin with, what is the concern of welfare economics? Basically, it is concerned with comparisons of social welfare in different economic states. As Ng defines:

> Welfare economics is the branch of study which endeavors to formulate propositions by which we can say that the social welfare in one economic situation is higher or lower than in another.

> (Ng 1979: 2)

As such,

> welfare economics is concerned with the critical scrutiny of the perform-
> ance of actual and/or imaginary economic systems, as well as with the
> critique, design and implementation of alternative economic policies.
>
> (Suzumura 2002: 1)

It is often argued that this general definition can be interpreted in two ways,
viz. either positively or normatively. One interpretation implies that social
welfare is a descriptive account of the aggregated well-being of the individuals in an economy. It is argued that welfare economics is a solely positive
endeavour, entailing no normative judgements on what is supposed to be a
better or worse economic state in terms of social welfare (such reasoning is
offered by Friedman 1967). Another interpretation implies that with 'higher
social welfare' a state is judged better (normatively) than other economic
states. The discussion of the most prominent theories of welfare has shown
that no concept of welfare is specified on a completely positive level. Normative considerations play a role, even when it comes to selecting a concept
of welfare. It is therefore misleading to think that welfare economics can
be done without resorting to normative claims.[25] For the sake of clarity, I
will adhere to the following terminological distinction, which is based on the
economic trichotomy (positive economics, normative economics and the 'art'
of economic policy) by J. N. Keynes (Keynes 1955: Ch. 2, §1). The following
three elements are part of welfare economics:

(1) *Positive Economic Theory*, being the positive side of the subject matter,
     where economists deal with the question of 'what is' and with 'establishing
     uniformities' ('economic laws').[26]
(2) *Welfare Economics* (in a narrow sense), being the normative part of
     economics, which deals with the 'determination of ideals' and thus invol-
     ves explicit ethical value judgements as to the desirability of different
     economic states or processes.
(3) *Practical Welfare Economics*, dealing with economic policy making, the
     'formulation of precepts'.

Welfare economics (in a wider sense) consists of all three parts. Doing welfare
economics proper (2) in this classification presupposes a positive economic
theory, describing the status quo of the economy and economic mechanisms
and their interrelationship. Assumptions on how individuals behave (and
which are likely to be part of an informed theory of welfare) belong to this
domain as well. Having such a mainly positive theory of welfare is a precondi-
tion for deriving normative statements in welfare economics. Other precondi-
tions are normative assumptions, value judgements of what one considers to
be better or worse. Only after having established the normative side of welfare
economics, can one derive policy implications in practical welfare economics.

Adopting one of the above-mentioned theories of welfare allows us to conduct welfare analysis on a more practical level. While traditional welfare economics is based on the preference satisfaction view, the material voidness of the concepts of preference and utility leads *applied* welfare economics settling for a notion of 'welfare [that] is broadly defined as the money needed to maintain a constant level of utility.' (Slesnick 1998: 2,110) The main focus, then, lies on the applied level of measuring welfare by its indicator 'income', which is ordinally equivalent to utility under certain conditions (see section 2.3.2). What are the consequences of adopting this view for welfare analysis? After the harsh ordinalist criticism (Robbins 1938, 1935: Ch. 6). banning the cardinal notion of utility and interpersonal comparisons of utility as unscientific, an ethically informed welfare analysis became increasingly difficult (the last proponents of such an analysis were Pigou and other members of what has been called the 'material welfare school', cf. Cooter and Rappoport 1984: 512).

It is possible to distinguish two influential schools of thought that have shaped what has now come to be known as the 'new welfare economics' (for a historical overview, see Suzumura 2002, 1999: 204–5): the first school centres around the Pareto criterion and other compensation principles. It is supposed to be based on very weak ethical assumptions to which anyone would readily agree. In the following subsection, I briefly present this welfare criterion and its successors. Although the Pareto criterion commands wide assent in economics, its practical scope is very limited because it is based on such a weak ethical value judgement. Confined to the Pareto criterion, welfare analysis is practically meaningless and runs the risk of being empirically irrelevant (Atkinson 2001). To gain more practical relevance, stronger assumptions and value judgements are needed. For example, the ordinality assumption of utility could be dropped for a cardinal utility notion, or interpersonal comparisons of utility could be reintroduced into the theory. This route has been chosen by the 'Bergson–Samuelson' school of thought, which has utilized the concept of the social welfare function (Bergson 1938; Samuelson 1947: Ch. 8). An example of such a welfare calculus is introduced in the subsection below. However, the assumptions of that school are no longer as innocent as those needed for the Pareto criterion. It is also clear that, in the tradition of this school, we have to interpret the famous Arrovian Impossibility Theorem (Arrow 1963), which will be at issue in the last subsection.

2.3.1 Pareto efficiency as welfare criterion

Perhaps the most important criterion of welfare economics is the criterion of Pareto optimality: a given allocation is Pareto optimal (or Pareto efficient) if no one could be made better off without making someone else worse off (see e.g. Ng 1979: Ch. 2).

This can be expressed formally as follows: assume a set of social states Y (which could be defined as a distribution of the commodity bundles for all individuals in the society) and any n-tuple of utility functions $u = (u_1, \ldots, u_n)$

representing a population of N individuals. Assuming welfarism, the set of Pareto optimal states $P(Y, u)$ is defined as:

$$P(Y, u) = \{x \in Y \mid \nexists \, y \in Y \text{ such that } \forall i \in N : u_i(y) \geq u_i(x)$$
$$\wedge \, u_j(y) > u_j(x) \text{ for some } j \in N \}. \tag{2.4}$$

The Pareto criterion has been welcomed by economists as being the smallest common denominator regarding ethical value judgements in welfare economics. As a normative principle, it is so weak that it supposedly commands uniform assent. It is this very parsimony that makes it vulnerable to criticism (Calabresi 1991; Buchanan 1954, 1959, 1977).

The Pareto criterion as such does not deal with distributive issues as it is a criterion of allocative (economic) efficiency. This means that, for example, the wealth of an economy could be in the hands of one person, while everyone else is poor; and such a state would still be Pareto efficient. Initial endowments are thus taken as given and excluded, and ethical considerations about distributive issues play no role. But taking initial endowments as given implies an ahistoricity that seems especially problematic from an evolutionary perspective: consider some processes that have led to a situation, where A has accrued almost the whole cake of the endowments and B only very little of it. A new state where A obtains even more and B's situation is left unchanged would also constitute a Pareto improvement. The distributive blindness is only one particular problem of the Pareto criterion when it comes to judgements about differing economic situations. For policy advice, its scope is even weaker since virtually all policy measures are such that there are winners and losers (Suzumura 2002: 7), situations (that are) not covered by the criterion. Note as well that the criterion of Pareto optimality is based on the assumption of given and unchanging preferences. This further limits the scope of meaningful normative propositions. While proponents of this approach acclaim the positive nature of such an endeavour, there have been several attacks on their assertion that Paretian welfare economics is really an entirely positive theory (cf. Blaug 1992: 124–6).

What is left to say for welfare economics under the conditions spelt out above? The most important results are the 'two fundamental theorems of welfare economics' (Koopmans 1957; Boadway and Bruce 1984: Ch. 3):

(*)   Theorem 1: given price-taking behaviour, utility-maximizing households and profit-maximizing firms, local non-satiation and no externalities, the resulting state (allocation of goods and factors) from a competitive general equilibrium is Pareto optimal.

(**) Theorem 2: given the assumptions of theorem 1 and assuming convexity of preferences and production sets, every Pareto optimal state (allocation of goods and factors) can be realized as the outcome of a competitive market equilibrium for some lump-sum redistribution of factors or goods.

Theorem 1 (the direct theorem) is descriptive in the sense that it establishes that the states produced by a competitive market equilibrium are Pareto optimal (formalizing Adam Smith's 'invisible hand'). It should be noted, however, that the assumptions under which the theorem holds are demanding (Boadway and Bruce 1984: 82–4 and Ch. 4). It is not clear whether an ideal market with self-interested utility-maximizing consumers, profit-maximizing firms, price-taking behaviour and the absence of any interdependencies (i.e. no externalities) can ever be attained in reality (the assumptions rule out envy or empathy in individual behaviour and technological externalities in production). But even if these idealized conditions were to hold, the state attained would be one Pareto optimum out of an entire set, and the full criticism regarding the Pareto criterion would still have force.

The second theorem is normative in the sense that it implies that a socially desired state (fulfilling the Pareto criterion) can be attained with the market mechanism satisfying certain conditions. Through this theorem, the role of government is constrained to the redistribution of factors and incomes. But there is no justification for allocative intervention except in blatant cases of market failure. Of course, this argument rests on the assumption of ideal markets, the possibility of costless lump-sum transfers of factors and commodities (an idealized condition because redistribution causes social costs by distorting incentives) and a further convexity assumption: the assumption of the convexity of production sets rules out economies of scale, which would be obtained, for example, in decreasing-cost industries. (The convexity assumption of consumer preferences has already been mentioned in section 2.1.2.)

The Pareto criterion and the two fundamental welfare theorems, besides being elegant results of welfare economics, yield important insights into the working of the price mechanism (given self-interest). Their ethical content is, however, rather small, as we have seen. While theoretically, the second theorem is more appealing because one can infer from it that the very best social state must at least be Pareto optimal, its practical relevance for policy is severely limited because the redistribution (to the social optimum) might involve radical transfer payments, which generally are not possible, so that other mechanisms are required which are not covered by the theorem.

An extension of Paretian welfare economics was attempted by the introduction of the Kaldor–Hicks criterion of potential Pareto improvements (cf. Kaldor 1939; Hicks 1939). The criterion judges an economic state superior to another (i.e. total welfare increases) when the gains of potential winners are higher than the losses of potential losers such that the losers could be compensated by the winners. Actual compensation is not necessary for such a situation to constitute a *potential* Pareto improvement. A number of objections have been raised to this criterion as well: if compensation is fictitious, it is doubtful why the mere possibility of compensation should count as a social improvement. On the other hand, if compensation is actually paid, the compensation principle is not needed anymore since the resulting state after redistribution would be Pareto efficient. Besides, there are internal (logical) inconsistencies that weaken the appeal of the Kaldor–Hicks criterion (e.g. Scitovsky 1941; Samuelson 1950; Gorman 1955). Scitovsky (1941) pointed to the fact that moving from a given state *A* to another state *B* could be a Kaldor–Hicks improvement, but that moving back from *B* to the original state *A* could be an improvement as well. Samuelson (1950) demonstrated that it does not necessarily have to be the case that a group *A* is better off than a group *B* even if the former has more of everything than the latter. This line of criticism has been extended more recently (Boadway 1974; Chipman and Moore 1978; Suzumura 1999): critics argue that it is not possible to arrive at definitive statements about welfare changes associated with different welfare policies in a general equilibrium framework. Estimates of income-compensated welfare gains at constant prices are partial equilibrium measures that coincide with general equilibrium measures only under very restrictive conditions (viz. when preferences are identical and homothetic, cf. Chipman and Moore 1976). In an extended framework, with changes in relative prices induced by the redistribution of income, potential Pareto improvements provide incorrect estimates of welfare changes: it is possible that those policy measures which lead to the largest monetary net increases are not necessarily the best anymore. Meaningful welfare analysis does not seem to be an easy endeavour without cardinal utility measures and without making distributional value judgements in the form of interpersonal comparisons of utility (Suzumura 1999: 219).

2.3.2 Welfare analysis

Besides the welfare analysis of compensation criteria, another straightforward way of welfare analysis is also centred on the individual consumer, maximizing that consumer's utility through the consumption of a bundle of goods constrained by available income. The standard textbook formalism can be represented as follows (e.g. Slesnick 1998, 2001). Assuming well-being w_i of individual i to be identical with individual utility u_i, we have:

$$w_i(\mathbf{x}) = u_i(\mathbf{x}) = u_i(x_1, \ldots, x_n), \tag{2.5}$$

where utility depends on the consumption of a bundle of n goods $\mathbf{x} = (x_1, \ldots, x_n)$. It is usually further assumed that individual utility is increasing in the different goods (marginal utility is positive), viz. $\frac{\partial u}{\partial x_i} > 0$ (assumption of local non-satiation). The utility function is assumed to be continuous and differentiable. Additionally, the individual has a given income I_i and faces a given vector of prices for the goods $\mathbf{p} = (p_1, \ldots, p_n)$. This amounts to the following utility maximization problem for the individual:

$$\max u_i = u(\mathbf{x}) \text{ subject to } \mathbf{p} * \mathbf{x} = I_i. \tag{2.6}$$

The solution to this maximization problem gives the Marshallian (or uncompensated) demand functions $x_i = x_i(\mathbf{p}, I_i)$ for the individual. They describe the demand of good x_i at given prices and income (and given preferences of the consumer). These can, in turn, be substituted into the utility function to arrive at the individual's indirect utility function. This corresponding indirect utility function V_i is then expressed in terms of the price vector and an individual's income, and is written as:

$$v_i = v(\mathbf{p}, I_i) = u_i(x_1(\mathbf{p}, I_i), \ldots, x_n(\mathbf{p}, I_i)). \tag{2.7}$$

The indirect utility function represents the maximal level of utility the individual can attain with a given set of prices and fixed income. Its inverse is the expenditure function e, which is the minimum total expenditure required to obtain a given level of utility at fixed prices:

$$e_i = e(\mathbf{p}, v_i). \tag{2.8}$$

Via the expenditure function, it is possible to translate utility levels into monetary equivalents. A money metric utility function π is defined as:

$$\pi = \pi(\mathbf{p_0}, v_i(\mathbf{p}, I_i)), \tag{2.9}$$

with $\mathbf{p_0} = (p_{01}, \ldots, p_{0n})$ being a vector of reference prices. The money metric utility function is ordinally equivalent to the indirect utility function and is a monetary measure of individual well-being. While the formalism does not change, the empirical measurement of individual well-being measured monetarily is often done at the household level, mostly because other data is not available. But it creates methodological problems and seems to require normative judgements in the form of interpersonal comparisons of utility (Slesnick 1998: 2,144–5).[27]

In this framework, social welfare is understood to be a function of individual welfare that somehow aggregates the well-being for all $i = 1, \ldots, N$ individuals of a society. These individuals are represented by the set of their utility functions $\mathbf{u_i} = (u_1, \ldots, u_N)$, given that individual well-being is represented by individual utility. We can denote this formally:

$$W = W(\mathbf{u_i}). \tag{2.10}$$

Such a social welfare function $W(y)$ in the Bergson–Samuelson sense assigns a numerical value to each social state $y \in Y$, where the social states in the example above are defined in terms of the given utilities $\mathbf{u_i}$ (see equation 2.10). In principle, other information can also be used to describe different social states. The aim of the policy maker employing such a social welfare function (SWF), then, is to maximize social welfare subject to given constraints. It is important to note that this aggregation exercise requires normative judgements regarding the form of the social welfare function. One route taken here to avoid this is to assume a representative consumer whose preferences are revealed by aggregate demand patterns. The techniques of individual welfare measurement detailed above are then used to measure the welfare change of the representative consumer. But market demands have been shown to be not necessarily consistent with the assumption of a representative consumer (preferences would have to be assumed to be identical and homothetic; see Gorman 1953). Other economists (such as Bergson) have argued that it is acceptable that the ethical judgements could be made by the economist, or outside of economics by a policy maker or by society in general. Then the economist would use the SWF and report on the properties of the resulting welfare measure (Suzumura 1999: 205). As Slesnick notes:

> Any effort to develop an index of group welfare must inevitably make normative judgements in which the gains to some are weighed against the losses to others . . . Due largely to economists' reticence to confront such normative questions, measures of group welfare used by practitioners have been developed in an ad hoc manner with little or no welfare economic justification. Rather than avoid the issue, a more appealing strategy is to confront it head on and make explicit the subjective judgements that are required to aggregate household welfare measures consistently into measures of social welfare.
>
> (Slesnick 1998: 2,137)

Let us follow this route here and briefly discuss an example of a social welfare function. There are different possibilities to aggregate individual well-being into a social welfare function W, the easiest example being simple unweighted aggregation:

$$W(u) = \sum_{i=1}^{N} u_i. \tag{2.11}$$

This is the special utilitarian case of a social welfare function that assigns weights a_i to the utilities u_i:

$$W(u) = \sum_{i=1}^{N} a_i * u_i. \tag{2.12}$$

Having established money metric utility functions as an exact representation of ordinal individual well-being, it would be straightforward to base the SWF on the aggregation of these functions. However, Blackorby and Donaldson (1985, 1988) have shown that this results in a flawed measure of social welfare.

Therefore the indirect utility function $v_i = (v_1, \ldots, v_N)$ is used to represent individual well-being in the aggregation procedure:

$$W = W(v_i). \tag{2.13}$$

One simple application in welfare economics could be to measure the (differentially small) welfare change resulting from a change in income:

$$dW = \sum_{i=1}^{N} \frac{\delta W}{\delta v_i} \frac{\delta v_i}{\delta I_i} dI_i. \tag{2.14}$$

The weights for the change in income can be denoted by $\beta_i(I_i)$. In this β, assumptions of the economist's distributive ethics are reflected (Slesnick 1998: 2,153) since β represents the marginal social utility of income:

$$\beta_i(I_i) = \frac{\delta W}{\delta v_i} \frac{\delta v_i}{\delta I_i}. \tag{2.15}$$

If social marginal utility of income is assumed to be constant and equal over individuals, it can be normalized to unity, and if we additionally choose the simple aggregative social welfare function, we again arrive at the utilitarian calculus:

$$dW = \sum_{i=1}^{N} dI_i. \tag{2.16}$$

A social welfare measure satisfying these conditions is the *per capita* income measure (it assumes cardinal measurability of welfare which is fully comparable across households). Note that this measure has been criticized for various reasons (Easterlin 1974; Scitovsky 1976; Sen 1985a). Qualifications also concern the rising standards of inequality accompanying rising incomes. It has been demonstrated in inequality research that often growth (as captured by rising national income) heavily benefits the rich, while the poor are left out (Peach 1987; Forbes 2000; Scully 2002). Whether a measure of social welfare such as *per capita* income is empirically adequate in representing social welfare is only one question that has been hotly debated. The other qualification concerns the question of how to arrive at an adequate social welfare function. It is this question that has been answered by Arrow (1963) by stating his famous 'general (im)possibility result'.

2.3.3 The Arrovian impossibility result

Arrow's findings deserve a place in this exposition because they directly deal with the questions that have been raised in the previous subsection. They are often interpreted as having caused severe negative consequences for doing welfare analysis based on social welfare functions. But this has to be relativized somewhat. I begin by stating the conditions and the General Possibility Theorem Arrow has proved (for proofs of the theorem, refer to Arrow 1963; Gaertner 2006):[28] an Arrovian welfare function is a functional relation f specifying a social ordering R for any n-tuple of individual orderings (called a 'profile') $\mathbf{R_i} = (R_1, \ldots, R_n)$ defined over the set of social states Y (an individual ordering is a ranking of all possible social states):

$$R = f(\mathbf{R_i}). \tag{2.17}$$

A numerical representation of the Arrovian welfare function R corresponds to the Bergson–Samuelson welfare function W; in other words, the *value* of the Arrovian SWF is a Bergson–Samuelson SWF. Preference profiles of individuals are supposed to obey rationality assumptions of reflexivity, completeness and transitivity (see section 2.1.2). In the Arrovian framework, utility is ordinal and interpersonally non-comparable. The following conditions, then, are imposed on the Arrovian welfare function for a society of $N = 1, \ldots, n$ individuals:

(U)   Unrestricted domain: the domain of f includes all logically possible n-tuples of individual orderings over Y.

(P)   Weak Pareto Principle: for all ordered pairs $x, y \in Y : (\forall i \in N, x >_i y)$ $\rightarrow x > y$ (if all individuals strictly prefer x over y, then society prefers x over y).

(D)   Non-dictatorship: there is no individual i in the society such that for all preference n-tuples in the domain of f and for all ordered pairs of $x, y \in Y$, $x >_i y \rightarrow x > y$ (there is no person such that whenever this person strictly prefers x over y, then society prefers x over y).

(I)   Independence of Irrelevant Alternatives: $\forall x, y \in Y$, $\forall n$-tuples $\mathbf{R_i}$ and $\mathbf{R'_i}$: $(\forall i \in N, xR_i y \leftrightarrow xR'_i y) \rightarrow (xRy \leftrightarrow xR'y)$ with $R = f(\mathbf{R_i})$ and $R' = f(\mathbf{R'_i})$ (if for two profiles of individual orderings $\mathbf{R_i} = (R_1, \ldots, R_n)$ and $\mathbf{R'_i} = R'_1$, $\ldots, R'_n)$, every individual in society has the same preference regarding any x and y, then society should have the same preference regarding x and y for the two profiles).

For a finite number of at least two individuals and at least three distinct states, Arrow has proved the:

(*)   General Possibility Theorem: there is no SWF f satisfying (U), (P), (D) and (I).

Or, in other words, given the assumptions (U), (P), (I), Arrow has shown that the only possible SWF is dictatorial. The importance of Arrow's results cannot be overestimated. They have established the field of 'social choice theory', spawning a huge research strand on how to relax the above assumptions so as to obtain other consistent SWFs.

But how does the result relate to welfare economics? The theorem does not deny the existence of a Bergson–Samuelson SWF, nor does it invalidate the field of welfare economics, as some may think (Samuelson 1967: 42). What it does deny, however, is the existence of a rational (in the sense specified above) decision process that associates a Bergson–Samuelson social welfare ordering with each conceivable profile of individual preference orderings (Suzumura 2002: 12 fn 20). Indeed, Arrow has shown that there are certain logical tensions in the kind of analysis introduced in the new welfare economics, which is based on assumptions of ordinal and interpersonally non-comparable utility (Bossert and Weymark 2006: 6). These two assumptions are seemingly too sparse to provide an informational basis to arrive at a consistent social welfare ordering (Sen 1974). With these assumptions, the classical utilitarian calculus would be excluded as a social decision rule. Sen (1979a, 1982) has discussed different informational assumptions and introduced the concept of a social welfare *functional* that constitutes a more general SWF, which collapses into the Arrovian SWF under the conditions of ordinal utility and non-comparability but can incorporate different informational assumptions as well. Sen has shown that with the possibility of different types of interpersonal comparisons of utility, one can get around the Arrovian impossibility result. Moreover, the assumption of an unrestricted domain has been criticized as being too strong for an economic context. As Bossert and Weymark observe:

> Arrow's Theorem is not directly applicable to economic problems. In economic problems, both the social alternatives and the individual preferences exhibit considerable structure and, therefore, a social welfare function only needs to be defined on a restricted domain of preference profiles.
>
> (Bossert and Weymark 2006: 2)

Thus more realistic assumptions on preferences or alternatives (in terms of the underlying individual motivations and other information) might turn the impossibility result into one of 'restricted possibility'.[29]

2.4 On the stability of preferences

In this section, I argue that the problems discussed above and those that were brought forward by critics of welfare economics stem from deeper methodological flaws inherent in the basic assumptions of the economic models discussed so far. While this also pertains to the rationality assumptions imbued in the utility functions of *homo oeconomicus* (cf. e.g. Scitovsky 1976; Simon 1979; Elster 1983; Schelling 1984), this section focuses on the unrealistic and psychologically uninformed assumptions found in preference theory. Of course, there have been attempts to justify the neoclassical assumptions, the most prominent of which being 'De gustibus non est disputandum' (Stigler and Becker 1977), where the authors state that:

> tastes neither change capriciously nor differ importantly between people. On this interpretation one does not argue over tastes for the same reason that one does not argue over the Rocky Mountains – both are there, will be there next year, too, and are the same to all men. . . . The establishment of the proposition that one may usefully treat tastes as stable over time and similar among people is the central task of this essay.
>
> (Stigler and Becker 1977: 76)[30]

This approach is the strictest version of adopting exogenous preferences since in the above Stigler/Becker version preferences are not only exogenous but also identical over time and individuals. This seems to be the most radical attempt to define away the problem of changing tastes. Although most economists would not subscribe to such an approach, assumptions on given preferences are often made in an aprioristic and *ad hoc* manner (cf. Rosenberg 1979; Witt 1991: 560–3). In such a manner, everything can be made plausible (Lewin 1996).[31]

All in all, the axioms of orthodox preference theory are not easily acceptable in terms of intuitive plausibility (Witt 1991, 2000). Some of them express material hypotheses containing quite strong claims, which can be empirically disputed (e.g. continuity/insatiability, excluding the possibility of lexicographic preferences). Some assumptions are of limited validity; the completeness axiom, for example, would hold only in an economy with very limited and unchanging consumption alternatives, or the transitivity axiom might hold for a certain share, but not for all observed choices. Reflexivity and convexity are assumptions which can best be characterized as idealizations (Witt 1991). Behavioural economics has produced a large body of evidence on how human preferences deviate from the standard assumptions discussed above (excellent surveys are provided by Lewin 1996; Conlisk 1996; Kahneman 2003). 'Anomalies' of the Kahneman–Tversky style (Tversky and Kahneman 1986; Kahneman and Thaler 2006), framing effects (Kahneman et al. 1982), the endowment effect and the non-reversibility of indifference curves (Knetsch 1992), the violation of the continuity assumption in the case of lexicographic preferences (making Kaldor–Hicks criteria inoperable and cost-benefit analysis meaningless, cf. Spash and Hanley 1995), hyperbolic discounting (Laibson 1997; O'Donoghue and Rabin 2000), the violation of the transitivity assumption and preference reversals (Loomes and Taylor 1992; Tversky 1969), and shaping effects (Loomes et al. 2003) are just a few examples of preferences that do not obey the rational choice assumptions in the textbooks.

Whether the standard assumptions have any empirical meaning can thus be contested, despite the elaboration of the theory of revealed preference (cf. Samuelson 1938, 1948). Moreover, this theory, in its positivist interpretation, is not as logically conclusive as was first claimed (Georgescu-Roegen 1954a; Wong 1978; Hausman 2000) since, for example, the assumption of consistent behaviour (formally: the transitivity assumption) would require independent testing data. From a dynamic point of view, it has to be stated that preference revelation is a time-intensive process since an indifference curve is constructed from the observed choices of a person. In empirical test cases, different choices have to be administered to experimental subjects, and the possibility that this repetition affects behaviour cannot easily be excluded (cf. e.g. MacCrimmon and Toda 1969). Of course, one might introduce a stationarity assumption, but then there would be a confounding of hypotheses since two hypotheses would have to be tested simultaneously in a preference revelation experiment. Moreover, to assume stationarity would be empirically very counterintuitive since there is enough evidence which points to a systematic change in preferences. Thus the empirical status of the theory is still unresolved. As tests of the theory have generally led to rather inconclusive results (Koo 1963; MacCrimmon and Toda 1969; Koo and Hasenkamp 1972), one is justified in stating that the high expectations economists initially placed in this approach have not been fulfilled by the theory (Georgescu-Roegen 1954a: 129). To conclude:

> In view of the little content that is left today in the theory of preferences and choices and of its unclear empirical status one may well feel inclined to try a reprise of those 'objectionable' utilitarian, physiological and psychological hedonistic conjectures that have dropped out of the theory in its process of being narrowed down to a few dry axioms.
>
> (Witt 2000: 10)

It seems that in order to escape the 'tyranny of a priorism' (Jones 1994), a naturalized theory of welfare will have to be grounded in findings of other natural and behavioural sciences such as psychology and biology.

2.5 Some lessons learned

What can we learn from the preceding discussion? Several points can be summed up, which should be kept in mind as guideposts for the following chapters. These are:

(1) The concepts of preference, welfare and utility are used in various meanings throughout economics. What is needed is a clear definition of these concepts (Griffin 1982: 366). A naturalistic methodology could, in turn, materially enrich these notions and imbue them with empirical content.

(2) A theory of welfare that makes use of these concepts should also account

for empirical, methodological and normative requirements. It is desirable that a theory of welfare should address the nature of welfare, its sources and its indicators.

(3) Existing theories of welfare have strengths and weaknesses. The question remains whether their strong elements might be integrated into one coherent theory of welfare. Especially the features of an objective needs account constitute a *normatively* interesting fact: 'such an extensive uniformity in our basic desires ... is an interesting *empirical fact* about human nature, which seems to be of some importance for ethics' (Harsanyi 1997: 139, emphasis in original).

(4) Armouring a theory of welfare against common objections leads to a compromise theory that cannot plausibly be an extreme position in the dimensions of our taxonomy (Sumner 2006: 15). Such a theory might lose its features of being simple and neat. This might also concern its mathematical tractability (consider e.g. multidimensional utility concepts and/or dynamic preferences).

(5) Welfarism is an attractive and defensible position; however, its status seems to rise and fall with the way it deals with the question of adaptation phenomena (the 'hopeless beggar' argument).

(6) The problems of applied welfare analysis can be traced to some methodological decisions. On a more concrete level, one could question whether assumptions such as the ordinality of utility, the assumption of the impossibility of interpersonal comparisons of utility and the abstaining from value judgements are still tenable.

(7) From an evolutionary perspective, the stability of preferences, in particular, can be considered as the fourth methodological assumption which is not easily defensible. Using additional information seems to be the key to restricting the domain of admissible preferences and preference change paths (cf. Sen 1977a). Dropping the idea of fixed preferences does not mean that they have to be totally malleable (Buchanan 1994: 74–7).

Summarizing, I have argued that welfare economics has been limited in its theoretical and practical relevance due to methodological decisions reflected in the lack of realism in its assumptions as well as in a deliberate confinement to ethically minimal value judgements. This has led to the Arrovian impossibility result and the political irrelevance of its most important welfare criteria. Enriching the welfare-theoretic foundations with a naturalistic perspective, especially regarding the content, formation and change in preferences, and the neurological and psychological substrates of well-being and utility, seems a promising route to take.

3 Other approaches to welfare economics

In the previous chapter, I have laid down conceptual and terminological foundations and have described a framework in which to assess different theories of welfare. Using this framework, it was possible to analyze traditional welfare economics and its notions of utility and welfare. It has become clear that there are some deficiencies associated with the 'hollowness' of the utility concept. It is thus not surprising to note that there have been several attempts at relaxing some of these problematic assumptions. My aim in this chapter is to exemplarily examine some prominent examples from the literature. While this will not be an overview of all competing approaches to welfare analysis, it nevertheless allows us to see to what extent changes in the fundamental assumptions lead to widely diverging concepts of welfare.

The following three approaches have been selected. First, von Weizsaecker (2001) has suggested a model of 'adaptive preferences' (inspired by Elster 1982), where the assumption of stable preferences is relaxed (see section 3.1). The model presented is very close to traditional welfare economics, as most of the traditional assumptions on utility and preferences are still accepted. The second approach is more radical in its assumptions (section 3.2). Brought forward by Sen, the 'capability and functionings approach' (e.g. Sen 1985a,b) has spawned a large array of theoretical and empirical contributions. At the heart of this approach is Sen's contention that the informational basis of utilitarianism is too narrow and has to be enlarged. The approach departs from the utility concept *in toto* and replaces it with a conception of 'functionings'. Moreover, by additionally incorporating the 'capability to function' as the freedom to choose between different sets of functionings, a second dimension is added to the analysis, where substantive freedoms (understood as opportunities) are considered. The third approach constitutes the most radical departure from the traditional concept of welfare economics because the whole idea of welfare as related to outcomes is abandoned in favour of a view that what matters normatively are solely opportunities (in section 3.3). In this way, Sugden (2004) conceives of individuals as agents who take responsibility for their actions, no matter whether they are taken on the basis of coherent preferences or not. Sugden is able to show that an economy can be modelled even with individuals that have incoherent and unstable preferences.

Such an economy satisfies the 'opportunity criterion', which is an analogue to the first fundamental theorem of welfare economics in opportunity space. I conclude the chapter with a discussion of the implications and insights that can be gained from these three approaches (section 3.4), which will be taken into account in the next chapters when developing an alternative, evolutionary theory of welfare.

3.1 Von Weizsaecker's adaptive preferences

Von Weizsaecker's approach starts explicitly with the guiding question of the present monograph, namely whether it is possible to use changing preferences as a measuring rod for welfare. Are two states under this assumption still comparable? He rightly acknowledges that exogenous preferences are a methodological simplification but an unsuitable approach for evolutionary theorizing (Weizsaecker 2005a: 44–5). His account deals with adaptive preferences and their welfare implications. To make (intertemporal) intrapersonal comparisons of welfare, von Weizsaecker develops a model, where preferences adapt to past consumption vectors (Weizsaecker 1971, 2001; 2005a,b), but he retains most assumptions regarding individual rationality and maximization of utility. In our taxonomy of section 2.2, his theory can be classified as belonging to the standard preference satisfaction view and is thus subjective (see Table 3.1). Before describing the model, it is worth discussing how von Weizsaecker conceives of preferential change.

3.1.1 *Sour grapes: adaptive preference formation*

The mechanism of adaptive, or reference-dependent, preferences has been introduced by Elster (1982). Von Weizsaecker uses this concept in the following way: preferences of an individual are dependent on the states the individual has been in in the past. For example, $(A; B) > (C; B)$ means that an individual prefers state A to C, given that the individual's past state has been B. The axiom of adaptive preferences can now be formulated as: *Let* $(B; A) > (A; A)$, *then* $(B; B) > (A; B)$. If adaptive preferences are defined in such a way, it is not

Table 3.1 A typology of theories of welfare revisited: von Weizsaecker

	Welfarist	*Non-Welfarist*
Subjective		
	Hedonism	
	Desire Theories: von Weizsaecker's Model	
		Capabilities & Functionings
		Basic Needs
Objective		

possible to have a situation, where an individual prefers *A* when adapted to *B*, and prefers *B* when adapted to *A* ('non-circularity').

Von Weizsaecker's definition is similar but not identical to the original meaning that adaptive preferences have been given by Elster. Adaptive preferences in the Elsterian sense can be neatly illustrated by Aesop's fable of the fox who wants the grapes but cannot reach them and then exclaims in defiance: 'They're sour anyway!' Adaptive preferences in this interpretation follow a certain pattern: an individual wants something but cannot attain it for external reasons and consequently adapts his preferences to the new situation. They are a reaction to a decreased opportunity set, resulting in a vexing problem for welfare assessments: 'For the utilitarian, there would be no welfare loss if the fox were excluded from consumption of the grapes, since he thought them sour anyway.' (Elster 1982: 219)

At the heart of adaptive preference formation lies an endogeneity problem: preferences are the basis for social choice, but social choice, in turn, feeds back to the preferences. While von Weizsaecker uses the concept of adaptive preferences as the sole force of preferential change, Elster has carefully distinguished adaptive preferences from other cases of how preferences can be formed and changed:

(1) While adaptive preference change can be reversed, this is not the case when a preference change results from learning or experience (in the latter case a reversal might happen if new facts are learned but, in general, the effect of learning cannot be reversed).

(2) Precommitment as a deliberate restriction of the feasible set differs from adaptive preference formation in the sense that the latter happens involuntarily. Precommitment is a *cause* for a restricted set of options, while adaptive preferences are a *result* of a restricted set of options.

(3) The deliberate manipulation of preferences by others differs from adaptive preference formation in that the latter is endogenous.

(4) Adaptive preference formation can be distinguished further from deliberative character planning (understood as the intentional shaping of one's desires) through the process of preference formation. It is also distinct in the end result because character planning upgrades accessible options, whereas adaptive preference formation downgrades the inaccessible ones. Moreover, it tends to 'overshoot' (Elster 1982: 224).

(5) As a last distinction, Elster mentions wishful thinking or rationalization processes which shape the *perception* of options, while adaptive preference formation shapes the *evaluation* of options.

Note that adaptive preference formation as conceived by Elster is psychologically explained in terms of reduction of cognitive dissonance (Festinger 1957). It is a process of resignation or habituation to a situation, which is distinct from the large class of other cases of how preferences can be formed and changed (as detailed above). Moreover, Elster argues that adaptive preferences are problematic in terms of the individual's autonomy. The Elsterian argument states that the welfare assessment of a preference should depend on whether it was formed by a process of adaptive preference formation. This is mostly a critique relating to the autonomy involved in the process of preference formation (see also section 6.5.2).

Von Weizsaecker's idea of adaptive preferences is different in that all preferences of an individual always adapt to each new commodity vector over time. In comparison with other possible consumption vectors, the one that is attained receives a more favourable evaluation. Indeed, it is only in this respect that von Weizseacker's concept is similar to Elster's version of adaptive preferences: the individual values less (and thus discounts) what this individual cannot obtain. But it has to be noted that most of the content of Elster's concept is gone when von Weizsaecker conceives of *all* preference changes as adaptive ones, a point I take up below. Even more, one could argue that a more appropriate psychological basis for von Weizsaecker's type of preference would not be the reduction of cognitive dissonance but the 'mere exposure' effect (Zajonc 2001), which describes how an initially neutral stimulus is evaluated more positively with increasing habituation. Von Weizsaecker further assumes a stable meta-preference of the kind that an individual prefers more income to less. This is important for his definition of improvement over time, since he argues that no matter what change in preferences occurs, on a meta-level the individual always prefers a situation where real income has increased (rising nominal income with prices staying the same). Moreover, von Weizsaecker argues that changes in preferences with a constant budget should also be seen as improvements (Weizsaecker 2005a: 4). Finally, the assumption of non-circularity of preference paths which excludes the 'Lucky Hans' phenomenon[32] plays an important role as a criterion of global consistency of preference change. Von Weizsaecker argues that it is hard to conceive of 'economic progress' in a situation where, after a series of changes, a person is back at the starting point but feels better off nevertheless than when he started from there. Von Weizsaecker here conjectures that this does not satisfy any notion of intertemporal consistency and rationality (Weizsaecker 2005a: 4 & 26). 'Anti-adaptive preferences', where the present attained status is discounted in favour of other commodity bundles ('forbidden fruit is sweet') or the valuation of change *per se*, are thus excluded from the model.

3.1.2 A model of preference change

Let us now look how von Weizsaecker can integrate his notion of adaptive preferences into the standard microeconomic theory of the consumer. As in the standard view (see section 2.3), we begin with the utility-maximizing individual (this section draws heavily on the exposition given in Weizsaecker (2005a)). Von Weizsaecker assumes a single-person economy with one consumer of a commodity bundle **x** in the positive orthant of n-dimensional

Euclidean space ($\mathbb{R}^n_+$). The model is continuous in time t and regarding the quantities of commodities. The individual follows standard assumptions in maximizing an instantaneous utility function $U(\mathbf{x})$ subject to a budget constraint. What is new in von Weizsaecker's model is that $U(\mathbf{x})$ is dependent on past consumption. This is captured by making utility dependent on an N-dimensional vector $\mathbf{q}$ (past consumption). Von Weizsaecker holds that it is not necessary that $n = N$ so that relatively large N (compared to n) can be interpreted as a long history of consumption experiences. The utility function is then written as:

$$U = U(\mathbf{x}; \mathbf{q}), \tag{3.1}$$

where U is continuously differentiable with respect to $\mathbf{x}$ and $\mathbf{q}$. Note that utilities with different $\mathbf{q}$ cannot be compared because different $\mathbf{q}$ represent different preferences of the individual.

The dependence of present consumption on past consumption is modelled by von Weizsaecker as follows:

$$\frac{d\mathbf{q}}{dt} \equiv \dot{\mathbf{q}} = \mathbf{Q}\mathbf{x} - a\mathbf{q}, \tag{3.2}$$

where $\mathbf{Q}$ is an $N * n$-matrix and a is either a positive number or a positive definite $N * N$-matrix (an example for the latter case would be a matrix with zeros outside the main diagonal and positive values on the main diagonal). The dependency condition 3.2 has the feature that with constant consumption $\bar{\mathbf{x}}$, the value $\mathbf{q}$ converges to

$$\frac{1}{a}\mathbf{Q}\bar{\mathbf{x}} \tag{3.3}$$

(if a is a matrix, $\frac{1}{a}$ denotes the inverse of the matrix).

The core of von Weizsaecker's model is the concept of the 'improvement path', a path through time in which the standard of living of a person never decreases, but increases at least at some points (this improvement path is a subset of the paths $\mathbf{x}(t)$ that consumption takes through time). The formalism of an improvement path needs some definitions: assume paths $\mathbf{x}(t)$ are piecewise continuous. Consider a path of the consumption vector $\mathbf{x}$ through time with $\mathbf{x}(0) = \mathbf{x}^0$ being the starting point and $\mathbf{x}(T) = \mathbf{x}^T$ being the end point. Let $\mathbf{I}_T$ be the interval of real numbers $[0, T]$ (it is possible that $T = 0$). Now let $\mathbf{J}$ be a set of 'jump points' $\mathbf{J} = \{t_1, \ldots, t_N\}$, a set with a finite number of moments in time (it can be empty) such that $0 \le t_1 \le \ldots \le t_N \le T$. Von Weizsaecker now considers paths $\mathbf{x}(t)$ such that $\mathbf{x}(t)$ is continuous in $\mathbf{I}_T - \mathbf{J}$.

If $\mathbf{q}(0) = \mathbf{q}^0$ is given, then $\mathbf{q}(t)$ is well defined for such paths by the differential equation 3.2 that defines the relation between present and past consumption vectors. The unique solution for that equation is:

$$q(t) = e^{-at}\left[q^0 + \int_0^t e^{az}Qx(z)dz\right].$$

(3.4)

The integral is well defined if $x(z)$ is piecewise continuous. The following expression $\hat{U}$ is defined for all points where $\dot{x}$ exists:

$$\hat{U} \equiv \sum_{i=1}^{n} \frac{\partial U}{\partial x_i} \dot{x}_i.$$

(3.5)

$\hat{U}$ can be given the following economic interpretation: a positive $\hat{U}$ means that real income increases (in our case: the budget rises or the price index falls). Therefore $\hat{U} > 0$ constitutes an improvement.

In order not to be restricted to differentiable paths $x(t)$, von Weizsaecker defines for a given path $x(t)$ a time point $\bar{t}$ which is called an 'improvement point' if there exists a non-empty interval $K(\bar{t}) = [\hat{t}, \bar{t}]$ such that for:

$$t \in K(\bar{t}) : U(x(t); q(\bar{t})) \le U(x(\bar{t}); q(\bar{t})).$$

(3.6)

At $\bar{t}$, utility evaluated at preferences for this point is equal to or greater than utility for smaller t. If $x(t)$ is differentiable at $\bar{t}$ and if $\bar{t}$ is an improvement point, then $\hat{U} \ge 0$. Given this definition of an improvement point, von Weizsaecker can now define the notion of an 'improvement path' and a 'weakly improving path'. For a piecewise continuous path $x(t)$, he defines $\{x(t); q^0; T\}$ as path of the piecewise continuous consumption vector $x(t)$ in the time interval $[0, T]$ with the initial value q^0 and preferences determined by

$$q(t) = e^{-at}\left[q^0 + \int_0^t e^{az}Qx(z)dz\right] \text{ (i.e. eqn. 3.4).}$$

Let $\{x(t); q^0; T\}$ be a piecewise continuous path of $x(t)$ with H jump points $J = \{0 \le t_1 < t_2 < \ldots < t_H \le T\}$ on the time interval I_T. $\{x(t); q^0; T\}$ is called a weak improvement path if:

(1) $\bar{t}$ is an improving point for any $\bar{t} \in I_T - 0$ and
(2) there exists $\varepsilon > 0$ such that for $0 < t < \varepsilon : U(x(t); q(t)) \ge U(x(0); q(t))$.

A constant utility path is also a weakly improving utility path. $t = 0$ does not need to be an improvement point so that the definition of a weakly improving path is independent of the path $x(t)$ outside the interval. The second condition excludes a negative utility jump point at $t = 0$.

Finally, an 'improvement path' $\{x(t); q^0; T\}$ is a piecewise continuous path of the consumption vector $x(t)$ with H jump points $J = \{0 \le t_1 < t_2 < \ldots < t_H = T\}$ on I_T if:

(1) the path is a weak improvement path and
(2) for $t_{II} = T \in \mathbf{J}$: $\lim_{t \overset{\leq}{\to} t_H} U(\mathbf{x}(t); \mathbf{q}(t_H)) < U(\mathbf{x}(T); \mathbf{q}(t_H))$.

On an improvement path, real income never falls, and it rises at some points: when there are jump points in $\mathbf{x}(t)$, the jump is not downward (in terms of the preferences at that point) and at the end is definitively one jump point with an upward jump (condition 2).

Armed with these definitions, von Weizsaecker postulates the following *axiom of progress*: a person prefers an improvement path on which that person's real income increases over a path where it stagnates or decreases. This criterion is a measure of economic progress, in so far as only movements in time that satisfy the improvement axiom are considered welfare-increasing. Formally, the axiom is written as follows:

(*) Improvement Axiom: let $\{\mathbf{x}^*(t); \mathbf{q}^{0*}; T\}$ be an improvement path. Let $\{\mathbf{x}(t); \mathbf{q}^0; T\}$ be a path where consumption remains constant, i.e. $\mathbf{x}(t) = \mathbf{x}(0)$ for $0 \leq t \leq T$. If $\mathbf{x}^*(0) = \mathbf{x}(0)$ and $\mathbf{q}^{0*} = \mathbf{q}^0 = \frac{1}{a}\mathbf{Q}\mathbf{x}(0)$ then the individual prefers $\{\mathbf{x}^*(t); \mathbf{q}^{0*}; T\}$ over $\{\mathbf{x}(t); \mathbf{q}^0; T\}$.

To compare consumption paths with different preferences, a sort of a meta-preference is needed (Weizsaecker 2005a: 49).[33] Von Weizsaecker assumes that the individual compares improvement paths and chooses the best of all locally possible paths to follow according to the meta-preference (basically a value judgement about different preferences, Weizsaecker 2005b: 11). Ultimately, it is this meta-ranking which is considered normatively relevant for the notion of welfare under a regime of changing preferences. The core idea of this axiom is that the consumer prefers these consumption paths (starting with the same preferences adapted to the initial consumption basket) which constitute an improvement over these paths where consumption remains constant, always conscious of the fact that the consumer's future preferences will adapt to the new consumption baskets. The consumer is not aware of anything else except that preferences will adapt to new consumption, but will not know what preferences look like in the future.

Given the previous discussion, von Weizsaecker now makes the following five assumptions in order to prove the central theorem of his model. $\mathbf{x}^* >_q \mathbf{x}$ means that $\mathbf{x}^*$ is preferred to $\mathbf{x}$ given preferences corresponding to the past consumption vector $\mathbf{q}$. This is equivalent to $U(\mathbf{x}^*; \mathbf{q}) > U(\mathbf{x}; \mathbf{q})$.

(1) Existence of a Demand Function. Preferences allow for the existence of the direct demand function $\mathbf{x} = f(\mathbf{p}, \mathbf{q})$. It is always assumed that budget $\mathbf{x} * \mathbf{p} = 1$. $\mathbf{R}(\mathbf{q})$ is defined as the set of consumption vectors $\mathbf{x}$ for which there exists a price vector $\mathbf{p}$ such that $\mathbf{x} = f(\mathbf{p}, \mathbf{q})$ or $\mathbf{x} = \mathbf{0}$. ($\mathbf{R}(\mathbf{q}) = \{\mathbf{x} \mid \exists \mathbf{p} \in \mathbb{R}^n$, subject to $\mathbf{x} = f(\mathbf{p}, \mathbf{q}) \vee \mathbf{x} = \mathbf{0}\}$). Then $\mathbf{R}(\mathbf{q}) = \mathbf{R}^*$ is independent of $\mathbf{q}$ and $\mathbf{R}^*$ is convex.
(2) Non-Saturation. $\forall i : x_i^* > x_i \to \forall \mathbf{q} : \mathbf{x}^* >_q \mathbf{x}$.

For assumption 3, the definition of a 'constant budget path' is needed. Consider a path without a finite end $\{x(t); q^0; T = \infty\}$. This path $x(t)$ is generated by the maximization of $U(x; q(t))$ subject to starting preferences q^0 and a constant budget constraint $x * p = 1$ with constant price vector p. A 'constant budget path' $[x(t); q^0; p]$ is then defined if for $t \geq 0 : x(t) = f(p; q(t))$ and $q(0) = q^0$. If $x(t)$ converges to $\bar{x}$, then $\bar{x}$ is called 'long-run demand' with respect to p and q^0.

(3) Existence of Long-Run Demand: there is a unique convergence point $\bar{x} = F(p)$ of a constant budget constraint path for each budget constraint $p > 0$. This means the convergence point is independent of the initial value q^0.

(4) Continuity: for each triple of vectors $\{x^*; x; q\}$ such that $x^* >_q x$ there exist neighbourhoods $M(x^*)$, $M(x)$, $\hat{M}(q)$ such that $z^* >_r z$ for $z^* \in M(x^*), z \in M(x), r \in \hat{M}(q)$.

(5) Adaptive Preferences: let $\{x(t); q^0; T\}$ be an improvement path and let $q^0 = \frac{1}{a}Qx(0)$. Then $x(T) \neq x(0)$.

The idea behind these assumptions is the following: assuming a unique demand vector (assumption 1) imposes a convexity requirement on preferences. This is needed because improvement paths only lead to local optimization because global optimization cannot be expected in the case of non-convex preferences. The same is true for assumption 3 because the independence of the asymptotic behaviour from initial preferences can only be expected if preferences do not show non-convexities. Assumption 4 extends the continuity requirement from fixed to changing preferences. As von Weizsaecker (2005a: 13) states, this assumption is essential for the proof of the theorem that would not work with Non-Euclidean commodity spaces. Assumption 5 reflects the adaptive preference formation process discussed in the previous section.

Von Weizsaecker furthermore defines the set $A(x^0)$ as the set of vectors (from $\mathbf{R}^*$) that can be reached with an improvement path starting from x^0 with preferences adapted to x^0: formally, for any given x^0 let $A(x^0)$ be the set of vectors $\bar{x} \in \mathbf{R}^*$ such that there is an improvement path $\{x(t); q^0; T\}$ with $q^0 = \frac{1}{a}Qx^0 \wedge x(0) = x^0 \wedge x(T) = \bar{x}$.

With these five assumptions, von Weizsaecker is able to prove the following theorem (for the proof, see Weizsaecker 2005a: 14–21):

(*)   Theorem 1, part A: the long-run demand function $F(p)$ satisfies the strong axiom of revealed preference.

(**) Theorem 1, part B: there exists a utility function $V(x)$ that generates the demand function $F(p)$. Let $B(x^0)$ be the set of vectors such that $V(c) > V(x^0)$. Then $B(x^0) = A(x^0)$.

This model results in an ordering of the commodity space that allows to maintain a notion of welfare based on changing preferences. A discussion of the features and peculiarities of the approach is now in order.

3.1.3 Implications and discussion

Von Weizsaecker's model is an important step towards a more realistic welfare economics. He has challenged a main assumption of standard economics, showing how a certain type of changing preference can be incorporated into a model of the utility maximizing consumer. In an extension, he has also shown how this model can be considered as the basis of a Bergson social welfare function for an economy with multiple consumers (Weizsaecker 2005a: 21–4). However, in this case the inter-individual influences of consumption are restricted such that everyone prefers a situation where one is on an improvement path, no matter how small one's improvement actually is and without taking into account the improvements of others. Thus a person feels no envy if that person's situation improves a little, but everyone else's situation improves much more. This assumption is quite strong and not in accordance with empirical findings on positional concerns (Easterlin 1974; Hirsch 1995; Frank 1988).

Von Weizsaecker's concept constitutes a dynamic version of Pareto optimality and a very minimal standard of welfare judgement. He acknowledges that his concept of adaptive preferences models preferential change as conservative and resistant to change (Weizsaecker 2005b: 5). It can be criticized along several different paths: first, improvement paths are, as the Pareto criterion, very restrictive and conservative in policy analysis. There might well be welfare improvement paths that lead to an initial decrease in the standard of living but to a very high standard of living later on. It is not clear why individuals would not want to follow such a path if they knew (or anticipated) the rewards their sacrifice would bring. The resistance to change comes from the way adaptation is modelled: a very favourable position C that (wrongly) looks inferior to preferences adapted to state A may look better once preferences have adapted to situation B, but there is no way that this preference change towards B could happen because preferences have adapted to A. This can lead to certain lock-ins at a given position and thus result in a 'status quo' bias. Second, von Weizsaecker does not part with orthodox methodology (though he claims otherwise) in several respects: for example, he equates welfare with material well-being, viz. income. His model uses orthodox assumptions of (full) rationality, and although he claims that it could be expanded to incorporate bounded rationality (Weizsaecker 2001: 440–1), he does not elaborate any further. Third, there is the assumption of 'non-circularity' of improvement paths which is the central assumption of adaptive preferences. This assumption rules out the 'Lucky Hans' phenomenon, where preferences would change such that at some point in time, they again become the original preferences from where change started: a situation where $(A; B) > (B; B)$ *and* $(B; A) > (A; A)$ is excluded *a priori*. This seems to be an important assumption for the model to work, but it is by no means an innocent assumption: von Weizsaecker does acknowledge that this belittles the value inherent in change, something which strikes as odd for a *dynamic* theory of preference change (Weizsaecker 2005b: 4–6). Fourth, von Weizsaecker does not say anything about content and formation of preferences, except that preferences are influenced by past consumption. This, however, is not substantiated but simply assumed so that we are left with a formal model that is appealing but lacking material enrichment. While adaptive preference formation is indeed one way in which preferences can change, not all preferences are adaptive, and it seems that preferential change through learning (as will be discussed below) is a more ubiquitous form of preference change that could account for many more cases of changed preferences. Preferential change through learning might also lead to very different results compared to adaptive preference formation. Note as well that the assumption of adaptive preferences prohibits some welfare comparisons: if two states A and B in the commodity space are separated by non-convexities (i.e. consumption vectors in A and B are in different subsets of the commodity space, and while preferences in these subsets are convex, they are separated by a non-convexity), then von Weizsaecker's model cannot compare them because there is no improvement path from A to B or *vice versa* (Weizsaecker 2005a: 55–6).

The following, and last, objection is normative and possibly the most relevant one in the case of a model of adaptive preferences. This criticism has been succinctly formulated by Sen in his example of the 'hopeless beggar':

> The most blatant forms of inequalities and exploitations survive in the world through making allies out of the deprived and the exploited. The underdog learns to bear the burden so well that he or she overlooks the burden itself. Discontent is replaced by acceptance, hopeless rebellion by conformist quiet, and – most relevantly in the present context – suffering and anger by cheerful endurance. As people learn to survive to adjust to the existing horrors by the sheer necessity of uneventful survival, the horrors look less terrible in the metric of utilities.
>
> (Sen 1984: 308–9)

Individuals adapt their preferences to their situation through social conditioning (cf. Elster 1982; Sen 1987: 45–6), and this malleability of human preferences in unfavourable circumstances poses a problem for any subjective welfare concept (as was already discussed in section 2.2.2). With his model, von Weizsaecker is especially vulnerable to the Elster-Sen critique that human preferences adapt even to very unfortunate conditions: the hopeless beggar's consumption bundle may be very small but the beggar's preferences adapt to it. The fact that the situation of the beggar is still dreadful remains neglected. In this respect, there is a difference to the Elster-Sen idea of adaptive preference formation because the authors criticize this kind of preference formation as one that distorts the welfare calculus. Thus there should be a modification of the welfare assessment of a person whose preferences have adapted to misery (Elster 1982: 228–34). Contrarily, in von Weizsaecker's model, adaptive preferences are taken at face value as the autonomous preferences of an individual. While the mechanism of this type of preferential change is the same for both Elster/Sen and von Weizsaecker, the normative connotations are very different in both approaches.

3.2 Sen's capabilities and functionings account

To deal with the criticism of the malleability of human preferences, and especially with the hopeless beggar problem discussed above, Sen has put forward a different welfare framework called the 'capabilities and functionings' approach (Sen 1984, 1985a,b, 1992, 1999). Owing to its features, it has the potential to incorporate different behavioural insights and a 'richness of ethical considerations' into economic theory (Sen 1987: 70). Sen's theory of welfare is located at the non-welfarist side in my taxonomy (see Table 3.2). but while Sen claims his framework is objective, it is shown below that this claim has to be qualified.

Table 3.2 A typology of theories of welfare revisited: Sen

	Welfarist	*Non-Welfarist*
Subjective		
	Hedonism	
	Desire Theories	
		Capabilities & Functionings:
		Sen's Approach
		Basic Needs
Objective		

3.2.1 The evaluative framework

The capability account is an evaluative framework to assess individual welfare. In this account, living is seen as consisting of a *set of functionings* which could be described as different aspects of life. Functionings thus describe the achievements of an individual. They provide information about what a person is and does. For an assessment of a person's well-being, Sen proposes not only 'being happy' (as in the utilitarian tradition) but other intrinsic values as well: other functionings are, for example, 'being nourished', 'avoiding premature mortality' (Sen 1992: 39) or 'being in good health', 'being well-sheltered', 'being educated' or 'moving about freely' (Kuklys 2005: 10). This approach is *multidimensional* as a person's state of being (and her individual activities) is a vector of functionings. This idea has been formalized by Sen (1985b).[34] In set-theoretic notation, a vector of functionings can be described as:

$$\mathbf{b} = f_i(c(\mathbf{x})|\mathbf{z}_i, \mathbf{z}_e, \mathbf{z}_s),$$ (3.7)

where **b**, the vector of functionings, is defined by the following elements: $\mathbf{x} \in X$ is a vector of commodities out of the set of all possible commodities X. This includes *expressis verbis* non-market goods and services as well. **x** is mapped into the space of characteristics (Lancaster 1966; Gorman 1980) via the conversion function $c(\bullet)$ so that $\mathbf{c} = c(\mathbf{x})$ would be a characteristics vector of a given commodity vector **x**. The characteristics of a commodity do not vary across individuals, i.e. they are the same for everyone. What does vary, however, is the way individuals can benefit from them. Think of a person who possesses a loaf of bread. Someone suffering from a parasitic disease would benefit less from the characteristic 'caloric content' than someone who is well-fed (Sen 1985a: 9). This is reflected by the conversion function of an individual $f_i \in F_i$ that maps a vector of characteristics into the space of functionings (F is the set of all possible conversion functions). This conversion is influenced by the conversion factors z_k, where we can distinguish individual (z_i), social (z_s) and environmental (z_e) influences (Kuklys 2005: 11). Individual factors could be sex, intelligence, physical (dis)abilities, etc. Social influences are legal regulations, population density, etc. Examples for environmental factors include, *inter alia*, climate and environmental pollution. These conversion factors can be seen as non-monetary constraints on an individual: functioning achievement thus depends on commodities (**x**) and non-monetary constraints (z_k).

When choosing which way of life to live, individuals, depending on their idiosyncratic preferences, choose from different functioning vectors. The individual's set of all feasible functioning vectors is that individual's *capability set* Q_i. It is a derived notion and represents an individual's opportunities to achieve well-being, reflecting the various functionings that are potentially achievable (given constraints X_i, z_k). This set can now be defined as:

$$Q_i(X_i) = \{\mathbf{b_i} | \mathbf{b_i} = f_i(c(\mathbf{x_i}) | z_i, z_e, z_s) \text{ for some } f_i \in F_i \wedge \text{ for some}$$

$$\mathbf{x_i} \in X_i\}. \tag{3.8}$$

Supporters of the capability approach usually centre *conceptually* on capabilities as the more important reflection of human well-being. Their disenchantment with traditional, outcome-centred utilitarian welfare economics has led to their renunciation of using achieved functionings as a primary basis for welfare measurement (although, interestingly, the measurement of achieved functionings is often used as approximation for capabilities, cf. Lelkes 2006: 288).

How could one evaluate the capability set $Q_i(X_i)$, i.e. the set of feasible functioning achievement vectors for given constraints? One could postulate a valuation function $v = v(\bullet)$ that assigns a numerical value to each vector of functioning achievement. A straightforward rule would be to evaluate a vector according to the best element. Note that it is left unspecified how the index number problem should be solved regarding the multidimensionality of a functionings vector. This difficulty set aside, Sen calls such a rule 'elementary evaluation' (eqn. 3.9), giving as reason that a wider choice set is only valued because there is a higher chance of choosing a better element (Sen 1985a: 61). The value of the set is thus the value of the best element of the set:

$$EV(Q_i(X_i)) = \max_{\mathbf{b} \in Q_i(X_i)} v(\mathbf{b}). \tag{3.9}$$

One could alternatively evaluate the set according to its number of elements. The basic supposition here is that the larger a set, the more freedom an individual enjoys (this is measured via the cardinality of the set: $|A|$ denotes the number of elements in the set A):

$$CV(Q_i(X_i)) = |Q_i(X_i)|. \tag{3.10}$$

The elementary valuation of equation 3.9, for example, would require a complete ordering of sets. The following rules (equations 3.11 and 3.12) yield the same result as equation 3.9 in the case of partial orderings. They are thus the more general evaluation rule (Sen 1985a: 62): let Q_1, Q_2 be capability sets, let $\mathfrak{R}$ be an 'at-least-as-good' relation for comparing vectors $\mathbf{b}_i$. Then we define:

$$\mathfrak{R}^* \; : Q_1 \; \mathfrak{R}^* \; Q_2 \; \Leftrightarrow \exists \mathbf{b}_1 \in Q_1, \forall \mathbf{b}_2 \in Q_2 : \mathbf{b}_1 \; \mathfrak{R} \; \mathbf{b}_2. \tag{3.11}$$

$$\mathfrak{R}^{**} : Q_1 \; \mathfrak{R}^{**} \; Q_2 \Leftrightarrow Q_1 \; \mathfrak{R}^* \; Q_2 \wedge \neg(Q_2 \; \mathfrak{R}^* \; Q_1). \tag{3.12}$$

Equation 3.11 ($\mathfrak{R}^*$) is the set-comparison relation 'at least as good' and equation 3.12 ($\mathfrak{R}^{**}$) is the set-comparison relation 'better set'.

It has already been shown in the introduction (see section 1.3) that a 'cardinality valuation' procedure is not in accordance with the empirical fact that individuals can experience large choice sets as actually welfare decreasing (Loewenstein 1999; Schwartz 2000; Binswanger 2006). It thus neglects procedural aspects related to the number of choices. Similarly, one could develop a valuation rule that depends on the number of options in a capability set as well as the best element in it (Sen 1985a: 68). Such kinds of valuation rules would have to be specified in more detail. According to our naturalistic methodology, one requirement for such a specification would be that it is not *ad hoc* but inspired by findings about how humans cope with different sizes of choice sets. It would, for example, be more plausible to distinguish between opportunities that increase the value of the opportunity set and opportunities that are neutral or decrease the value of the set (Sen 1993a: 34–5): compare, for example, an opportunity set O_1 = {bad choice, very bad choice, incredibly bad choice} with the set O_2 = {good choice, great choice, incredibly wonderful choice}. In terms of the 'cardinality valuation' rule (see eqn. 3.10), both sets, O_1 and O_2, would have to be ranked equally, a fact that strikes as odd. Or consider the opportunity set O_2 and the further addition of the choices O_3 = {being tortured, blink twice, have one's hand cut off} to the set.

Regarding the simple logic of the cardinality rule, the addition of O_3 to one's opportunity set would definitively be a good thing (without any qualification). But while some opportunities might be trivial ('blink twice'), others are outright negative ('being tortured'), and it is not clear why their addition to the choice set would improve it. One could thus argue that some sort of calculus is needed to evaluate the opportunities in the set. This calculus would then probably have to include an evaluation of the outcomes related to the opportunities (Sen 1991b).

3.2.2 Features and discussion

Let me now highlight some key features of the capability and functionings approach. The following features are essential in evaluating the approach. Table 3.3 gives an overview, comparing the relevant aspects of the capability approach with standard welfare economics. I discuss these in turn, beginning with some philosophical (or conceptual) differences. In contrast to welfare economic *theory*, the capability approach has been designed by Sen to be a *conceptual framework* to assess human welfare (Alkire 2005; Sen 1993b: 46–9). It is under-specified and in certain respects deliberately vague and opaque (Sen 1992: 46–9) so as to invite concretization. It can be used on different levels, ranging from quantitative empirical analyses to philosophical theorizing (Robeyns 2005b: 193–4). The foundation of central concepts differs significantly between both approaches: much ink has been spilt on the lack of sufficient foundations of much of (welfare) economic theorizing (recall the discussion in Ch. 2). A different stance is reflected in the capability literature by basing the underlying value judgements on our commonly shared human *eudaemonia* (this pertains to the objective capability literature part). Note, however, that this foundation is explicitly not embraced by Sen, who leaves his approach open (Sen 1993b: 46–9).

Both the standard welfare view and the capability approach are essentially static. Although the latter is no longer centred on preferences, the capability literature often seems to implicitly assume that capabilities and functionings, once properly identified, either form an eternally valid list or otherwise

Table 3.3 Traditional welfare economics vs. the capability approach

Feature	Welfare Economics	Capability Approach
Theoretical Status	theory	framework
Time Dimension	static	static
Centred on	outcomes	opportunity
Welfare (conceptual)	utility	capabilities & functionings
Dimensions	one-dimensional	multidimensional
Empirical Measure	income	several indicators
Foundation	a priori, ad hoc	common eudaemonia (?)
Theory of Welfare	subjective	objective (?)

should be identified fitted to the occasion.[35] For the latter interpretation, there exists no specification how the approach could handle the varying importance of different valuable functionings. Consider especially Sen's claim that his approach is open for different purposes on different aggregate levels of detail (Sen 1993b: 48–9). We can interpret this claim as essentially stating that at different points in time different functioning and capability sets may be relevant, even for the same individuals. Sen does not elaborate on the process of selection of relevant sets so that it is not clear how we can systematically account for changing capability sets. Why they might change, or why they change if they do, is not clear. Therefore it would be necessary to complement the capability approach with a dynamic perspective from which it would be possible to clarify how relevant functionings and capabilities change over time.

The capability approach's focus on opportunities also makes it radically different from traditional welfare economics, where human well-being is usually represented as a homogeneous utility measure (see Ch. 2). The capability literature emphasizes the capability to achieve a wide variety of functionings which are all considered as based on intrinsic values. Thus they are not reducible to others, making the approach in essence multidimensional. The list of values (including the utilitarian happiness, the liberal values of freedom, etc.) is often seen as open-ended and supposed to contain 'the plurality of our concerns' (Sen 1992: 70). One would imagine that it must be very problematic to accept this notion since it seems to imply that the weights attached to each functioning in the set must be the same for everyone. Sen argues, however, that his notion does not need to say much about those weights since he sees well-being as a 'broad and partly opaque concept' (Sen 1992: 46–9), which is often best represented by partial orderings.

There are also differences as to how well-being is measured by both approaches. Contrary to income or expenditure measures in the standard approach (see section 2.3.2), there is much less consensus regarding many important measurement issues in the capability literature (Kuklys 2005: 25–8). While it has been shown that measuring functioning achievement can lead to significantly different results than employing income-based welfare measurements, some scepticism remains as to how one can meaningfully operationalize the capability framework:

> It is difficult to imagine how this approach might be implemented empirically to provide a comprehensive welfare measure. Individuals' capabilities are not always the result of revealed preference so we have little prospect for measuring individuals' valuations of these capabilities. For example, it might be important to know how they trade off material well-being for, say, life expectancy. This can only be answered in an arbitrary way since data provide little information on this issue. Most empirical applications examine each capability separately but make no attempt to aggregate the joint effects into an overall measure of welfare.

Nevertheless, it is difficult to deny the importance of these issues in the assessment of social welfare.

(Slesnick 1998: 2148–9)

These doubts notwithstanding, there has emerged an extensive literature on the empirical measurement of valuable functionings (see Sen 1985a; Kuklys 2005: 25–8). But the indeterminacy of the approach has resulted in an empirical measurement literature that often measures welfare over an *ad hoc* range of different functionings. Indeed, Slesnick is right in asserting that, so far, the question of how to aggregate different functionings into one aggregate measure of social welfare has not been satisfactorily answered. A further difficulty lies in measuring the actual *capability* to function (for an attempt to do this, see Anand et al. 2005; Anand and Hees 2006). But the empirical examination of conversion factors and functions has also received comparatively less attention in the literature (but see Binder and Broekel 2008; Chiappero-Martinetti and Salardi 2007; Deutsch et al. 2003).

The questions of a theoretical foundation, that is, how to select a list of relevant functionings and how these might change over time point to a deeper problem of the capability approach, namely the question whether to conceive of it as objective or not. Recall from section 2.1.3 that in traditional welfare economics, individual well-being is a subjective matter. Contrary to that position, the nature of welfare in Sen's theory is *purportedly* objective as he stresses that welfare is constituted by the capabilities for fulfilment of a certain set of objective functionings that is independent of the individual's evaluation (Sen 1985b: 196).[36] However, taking a closer look at the objectivity of Sen's account, we are left with the following puzzle: living is seen as a set of functionings such as being educated, well-sheltered, etc. These functionings are supposedly objective features of individuals' lives. But, then, how can we arrive at a complete list of human functionings, and is this listing really objective? Even if, as Sen stresses, it is a question of the concrete purpose of the examination of which functionings should or should not be included (cf. Robeyns 2005a; Sen 1993b: 31–2 & 46–9), the question remains who decides about the (normatively) relevant functionings? This critique has been voiced by several scholars (e.g. Sugden 1993; Nussbaum 2003). It can be raised either in a strong or weak form (Robeyns 2005b: 195): a strong critique holds that one concrete list of functionings would have to be specified (as argues e.g. Nussbaum 2000, 2003). A weak critique holds that at least a consistent method for selecting capabilities and functionings needs to be spelt out (Robeyns 2005b).

If Sen's account were really objective, there would have to be a definitive list of functionings, regardless of the purpose of the examination. Nussbaum holds that such a list has to be specified and argued for (Nussbaum 2003: 41–2). To maintain the objectivity of the account, the list of functionings would have to be derived from a set of objective (moral) values. Nussbaum derives her list from an argument concerning our commonly shared eudaemonia (i.e. our concept of 'human flourishing', what it means to live a valuable human life, a concept derived from Aristotle's ethics). Critics have pointed out that such an objective list always implies the risk of paternalism, if it cannot be made plausible that the list is indeed one that is necessarily valued by everyone (Sugden 2006b: 50). Otherwise, there is the danger that an individual's evaluations are overruled by social decisions taken on the grounds of an allegedly objective criterion. For many critics, then, it seems implausible, that a list of relevant functionings that we identify today would have been universally valid in the past and will not have to be changed or amended in the future. On the other hand, if one cannot produce an argument along such lines, Sen's account is no longer objective because the normatively relevant functionings are ultimately a subjective matter. If the selection of individual functionings depends on the individuals' own valuations (Sen 1993b, 1985a: 48 & 57), we are left with striking similarities to a standard subjective theory of welfare: for instance, when debating on a list of valuable functionings, an individual A could prefer functioning set $F = \{$being sheltered, being nourished, being educated$\}$, whereas individual B could hold that set $G = \{$being sheltered, being barely nourished$\}$ should be adopted as being normatively relevant. On this account, the problem of adaptive preference formation can no longer be evaded since social conditioning could have led B to adapt preferences so as to accept set G. In the subjective interpretation of Sen's account, the malleability of human preferences is transferred directly to the question of the selection of relevant functionings. This so far unresolved tension in the approach has led Sumner to speak of 'Sen's subjective turn' (Sumner 2006: 9).

3.3 Sugden's opportunity criterion

The third alternative to an orthodox welfare economics is a recent contribution by Sugden (2004), who has reformulated the principle of consumer sovereignty in such a way that it can be retained even in the face of incoherent or unstable individual preferences. By abandoning the focus on preferences as the measuring rod for individual well-being and by putting normative significance solely on the opportunity set an individual is endowed with, his approach can be characterized as the most radical departure from standard welfare economics. It turns out that Sugden's 'opportunity criterion' makes demanding assumptions on individuals' responsibility by holding them responsible for whatever (irrational) preferences are revealed in their market transactions. In terms of the welfare typology used here (see Table 3.4), Sugden's approach can be characterized as being non-welfarist and objective in the sense that an increase in opportunities is considered an increase in welfare, regardless of an individual's evaluation of the opportunities. I proceed by discussing the intuition of the model and the formalism of the opportunity criterion in the next subsection, before turning to a discussion of its implications in the subsection following that.

Table 3.4 A typology of theories of welfare revisited:
Sugden

	Welfarist	*Non-Welfarist*
Subjective		
	Hedonism	
	Desire Theories	
		Capabilities & Functionings
		Basic Needs
		Sugden's Approach
Objective		

3.3.1 A model focused on opportunity

Sugden's core intuition is to derive a notion of consumer sovereignty for a
model of an exchange economy without the assumption of coherent individual preferences (Sugden 2004: 1017). With this model he elaborates on 'an
apparently simple normative intuition: it is good that each person is free to
get what she wants' (Sugden 2004: 1016), i.e. the normative idea that individual opportunities and responsibility are fundamental values (partly similar
to Sen's approach discussed in the previous section). Sugden's point of
departure is twofold. First, he takes into account the findings of behavioural
economics that preferences are subject to non-rational processes that distort
'true preferences' into actual preferences (recall the examples from section
2.4). Sugden's argument also addresses the main research question of this
monograph: context-dependent preferences cast doubt on the role they play
as measuring rod for individual welfare. If it is not possible to somehow
recover an individual's true preferences (which he doubts), it is not clear why
actual preferences should be given normative weight. This argument serves
Sugden as a justification to abandon preference satisfaction as the basis for
welfare assessments in favour of opportunities. His intuition is that the size
and richness of an individual's opportunity set are better objects of inquiry
than a distorted notion of preference satisfaction. But since, in economics,
the individual is always conceived of as a bundle of preferences, Sugden
also has to provide a different notion of a coherent self, if it is no longer
provided by the individual's preference structure. Therefore he postulates the
'responsible agent', a person who is a coherent locus of responsibility.
Responsibility for one's choices is thus the key defining characteristic of an
individual. From this perspective, any increase in the lifetime opportunities of
an individual is intrinsically good (without any assessment of the opportunity that is added).

Now let us consider the 'opportunity criterion' for a single individual i.
Assume that there exist $m > 1$ goods in the economy and the individual
holds a bundle of goods $\mathbf{x}_i = \{x_{i1}, \ldots, x_{im}\}$ as commodity bundle. Let $\mathbf{z}_i$

be the initial endowment of i. By opportunity, Sugden denotes i's opportunity to change i's initial endowment into another bundle of commodities through trade. The opportunity criterion now centres on the notion of the opportunity set O_i of i, defined as $O_i \in \mathbb{R}_+^m$ such that $z_i \in O_i$ and for each $x_i \in O_i$ there is a series of trades such that i can expect to come from z_i to x_i. Furthermore, i is assumed to know her opportunity set. From the point of view of the social planner, Sugden argues, there exists a non-empty set of feasible commodity bundles X_i. It specifies the initial endowments in terms of resources that the planner is able to give to i. The elements in the set of different commodity bundles reflect exogenous limitations on resource allocations the planner faces. The individual cannot choose a bundle outside X_i due to restrictions that are not specified, but i can choose any x_i in X_i as initial endowment. So in this case, in accordance with the principle of consumer sovereignty, the opportunity set of i should ideally contain the set of all feasible bundles: $X_i \subseteq O_i$. The opportunity criterion is now defined *ex post*: assume that after being given an initial endowment z_i, i gets to $x_i^* \in O_i$ through trade. The 'Opportunity Criterion' is satisfied if for any other bundle $x_i \neq x_i^*$ either:

(1) x_i is not feasible: $x_i \notin X_i$ or
(2) x_i belongs to the opportunity set: $x_i \in O_i$.

An example should clarify this: assume i is given an initial endowment z_i and gets to a bundle x_i^* through trade. Now think of the individual complaining to the planner why she is not given bundle $x_i' \neq x_i^*$. If x_i' does not belong to the feasible set (1), it is outside the planner's possibilities to make the bundle available to i. If, on the other hand (2), x_i' is in the feasible set and in the opportunity set of i, then it was the responsibility of i that has led her to have x_i^* and not x_i'. i cannot blame anyone else for not having attained x_i'. This is the formal version of Sugden's notion of responsibility.

So far, we have only considered the one-person case. How can the opportunity criterion be generalized to an n-person economy? Here a modification is necessary (Sugden 2004: 1020): again we start with an 'allocation' $x = \{x_1, \ldots, x_n\}$, being a profile of commodity vectors for all individuals. Similarly, the 'initial allocation' $z = \{z_1, \ldots, z_n\}$ denotes initial endowments. Each consumer has an opportunity set O_i, and the set of all feasible allocations is a set such that $z \in X$. Free disposal is assumed as well as the absence of transaction costs. Under these assumptions, X contains all these bundles x that satisfy the inequality $\sum_{i=1}^{n}(x_{ij} - z_{ij}) \leq 0$ for $j = 1, \ldots, n$. The generalization of the opportunity criterion now is as follows: given a profile of opportunity sets $O = \{O_1, \ldots, O_n\}$ that results in a feasible allocation x^*, the criterion is satisfied, if for every allocation $x \neq x^*$, either:

(1) $x \notin X$ or
(2) there is some individual j such that $x_j \neq x_j^*$ and $x_j \in O$.

The *n*-person form requires for the criterion to be satisfied that for each other alternative **x** to the actual outcome, the alternative is either not feasible (1) or is feasible, but some individual *j* would have to be assigned a bundle that she has not actually chosen (2). This second condition makes the opportunity criterion an analogue to the criterion of Pareto optimality because if the criterion is satisfied, all alternative feasible allocations would coerce at least one individual into a choice that this individual would not have made otherwise (Sugden 2004: 1020).

Having defined the opportunity criterion for the *n*-person case, Sugden has characterized an exchange economy and examined under what conditions the criterion would be satisfied. Such an exercise serves to prove that a suitably defined market economy would indeed satisfy the opportunity criterion in equilibrium. I will not recapitulate the details here but refer the reader to the original article. In order to derive the formal model of a market economy that would induce market clearing prices, Sugden has to introduce rational arbitrageurs who exploit profit opportunities of the individual (non-rational) consumers, resulting in a market clearing price mechanism. By this mechanism, it can then be shown that the resulting equilibrium in the economy satisfies the opportunity criterion (Sugden 2004: 1021–30).

3.3.2 Implications and discussion

Sugden's model can be considered an addition to the first fundamental theorem of welfare economics. But while this theorem, as the underlying theory of welfare, presupposes a preference satisfaction perspective and consistent preferences in the sense detailed in Chapter 2, these assumptions are not made in the Sugden model. In that sense, Sugden's model does incorporate insights of behavioural economics into the way preferences are formed depending on the situation. However, it seems that Sugden throws out the baby with the bathwater in using these findings to abandon completely the idea that welfare depends on the fulfilment of preferences. In this form, Sugden's theory of welfare is, of course, compatible with all mechanisms of preference change that are imaginable (and would be even with conflicting theories of preference change).

On the level of technical assumptions, two peculiarities can be found in the model: while consumers are modelled, on the one hand, as being able to have all kinds of possible preferences and no utility-maximizing behaviour is assumed, they are nevertheless required to trade always at the most beneficial prices, on the other. While they may thus exhibit all kinds of strange behaviour, they possess high skills in determining where to get the most favourable price in the whole economy. This seems to be a strange rationality assumption, given the otherwise lenient assumptions on individual behaviour. A similar assumption is made about the arbitrageurs, who have perfect information of profit opportunities. Of course, both assumptions are needed on the technical level in order to make the specific model work. However, in terms of realism, they can be disputed as being a step backward from the realistic modelling of human behaviour.

The opportunity criterion neatly captures the essence of normative individualism, namely that individuals should be free to act according to what they think is in their self-interest (Schubert 2005: 15–6). But as Schubert points out, this forces Sugden to include a complete ban on any external constraints (e.g. precommitment) on an individual's future choices:

> A person who identifies with her future actions will not want to impose external constraints on her future choices as a way of forcing those choices to match her current conception of what is good for her
>
> (Sugden 2004: 1018)

Finally, as was already noted in the beginning (section 1.3), the exclusive reliance on opportunities as a basis for welfare judgements seems to be a popular (although mostly implicitly held) view of evolutionary economists who value variation *per se*. But it can be disputed that variety is always good and that opportunities should be the sole normative maximand. While there is no denying that freedom of choice is valuable, the idea that opportunity should be the only value that matters, even if an increase in opportunities brings a decrease in utility, is not easily compatible with many normative intuitions. (The arguments presented section 3.2.1 against simple cardinality valuation rules apply here as well.) It is, of course, very attractive to invoke a welfare criterion that allows for an individual's autonomy and is non-paternalistic. But ultimately, one could make the criticism that, according to Sugden's theory of welfare, all choices an individual makes are rationalized through the opportunity criterion, no matter how irrationally they were arrived at. This amounts to a Panglossian sanctioning of the status quo. If all choices are rationalized as being in accordance with the opportunity criterion, there is no need for change, and all is well. The *prima facie* appealing recourse to an individual's freedom and opportunities thus turns out to have very strong normative implications.

3.4 Insights and implications

What have we learned from the models discussed in this chapter? It is time to recapitulate the most important findings.

(1) To assess welfare in terms of the satisfaction of preferences, it is necessary to identify the 'laws of motion' that govern preference change. These should be informed by empirical insights of the behavioural sciences in order to avoid the pitfall of assuming non-existent or rare mechanisms of preference change. *Learning* seems to constitute a ubiquitous law of motion for preference change. Identifying such laws, then, expressly

introduces an evolutionary perspective into the analysis. History matters in the development of preferences.

(2) By enriching the notion of welfare and turning it into a multidimensional concept, there is a clear trade-off between mathematical tractability and the strength of the resulting concept. This is especially problematic for an empirical assessment when non-arbitrary aggregation weights have to be found (a still unresolved issue in Sen's multidimensional approach).

(3) The same holds true for the general incorporation of ethical or psychological insights into a theory of welfare. The price to be paid for developing a naturalistically informed notion of welfare might be that it cannot be easily translated into a neat formal model. Or one might have to settle for comparing partial orderings.

(4) When arguing for an objective account of welfare, one has to specify the origin of objectivity. Our biological heritage might be more promising than the recourse to a commonly shared eudaemonia. But such an objective account might be vulnerable to objections of paternalism (there is a potential trade-off between welfare and autonomy).

(5) It is obvious that a deliberate openness of the welfare framework is needed (at the cost of rigour) to accommodate for the possibility of a changing moral filter should moral values indeed change over time.

(6) Abandoning an outcome-centred notion of welfare in favour of one of freedom or opportunity poses difficulties how to rank these opportunities. From an evolutionary perspective, it seems promising not to neglect the issue of opportunities, but completely abandoning a focus on outcomes might throw out the baby with the bathwater.

The insights gained from the discussion of the approaches by von Weizsaecker, Sen and Sugden illustrate that worthwhile concepts of welfare can be developed even when deviating from standard welfare economic assumptions. These findings are used in the following chapters to develop an evolutionary theory of welfare that draws on a broad array of positive insights into human behaviour. This theory will occupy middle ground between the extreme poles of these positions discussed in this chapter. To lay the groundwork for such a normative framework, I start with the positive parts of my theory of welfare in the next chapter.

4 A positive basis

The learning theory
of consumption

I have so far identified the standard contributions to welfare economics in Chapter 2 as well as promising alternative views on the topic in Chapter 3. This discussion has been necessary to establish the terminology and to point out some pitfalls that lie ahead. Before sketching my own welfare-theoretic contribution, one additional prerequisite has yet to be fulfilled. Any normative theorizing is built on positive (descriptive) knowledge. Before thus specifying an evolutionary theory of welfare, it is necessary to lay out the positive theory upon which my theory of welfare builds. The present chapter is intended to fulfil this requirement. I discuss the 'learning theory of consumption' (LTC), a theory of consumer behaviour and learning, developed by Witt (2000, 2001, 2005). It describes how individuals act in order to satisfy their wants.

In section 4.1, I outline the motivation for Witt's contribution, which aims at revoking some of the methodological assumptions discussed in the previous chapters. Following the naturalistic methodology of Witt (1987), this theory is informed by findings from the behavioural sciences. It has three defining elements, which will be discussed at length: first, utility can be understood to consist of the net total of pleasure over pain, a position found already in Bentham's sensory utilitarianism (section 4.2). Second, utility is derived from the satisfaction of wants, some of which are genetically fixed, while others are learned. These wants also mark a departure from the well-known (axiomatic) preference theory. In section 4.3, I spend some time on the exposition of key features associated with a theory of wants, drawing on the theory of wants by Menger, as both theories stand in the same venerable tradition. Third, the learning of wants follows regularities that are also genetically fixed. Based on LTC and on insights into how preferences (wants) change, long-term dynamics of consumption behaviour can be explained (section 4.4). The discussion of LTC, finally, leads to a suggestion of a different model of human (economic) behaviour that does not stipulate exceedingly high requirements on individual rationality, viz. the matching law (Herrnstein 1997), which I deal with in section 4.5. I conclude with some implications and insights to be drawn from this chapter (section 4.6).

4.1 Learning to consume

In section 2.1.2, we have seen the change that the notion of utility has undergone over time. From its sensory underpinnings in Benthamite utilitarianism, it has been a long way to the well-known axioms of (expected) utility theory. The purging of any vestigial traces of psychology from economic theory made it possible to formulate a more rigorous calculus of choice under constraints. But this came at the cost of eliminating helpful information that would have been needed for a theory of consumer behaviour and the assessment of consumer welfare (Lewin 1996; Bruni and Sugden 2007). As one of the most prominent critics of utilitarianism remarks, revoking this move might prove to be fruitful:

> The utilitarian conception . . . is narrow and inadequate, and it has been further impoverished in modern welfare economics by the imposition of some additional limitations . . . That additional impoverishment can be countered by returning to a more full-blooded utilitarian conception.
>
> (Sen 1987: 58)

In his recent work, Witt (2000, 2001, 2005) argues for a rehabilitation of a somewhat less subjective version of (sensory) utilitarianism. We have traced the 'hollowness of utility' (Samuelson 1947: 91) to the way the concept has changed from Bentham until today (see section 2.1.2), originating with Jevons (1871), who aimed at a mathematical description of utility theory in the spirit of 19th-century physics (i.e. 'energetics', cf. Mirowski 1991, 1988: Ch.1).[37] While Jevons paid lip service to Bentham's 'calculus of pleasure and pain', he had a different direction in mind when describing the 'mechanics of utility and self-interest' (Jevons 1871: 21): Warke (2000b) has shown that Jevons introduced three major critical changes to utility theory to increase its 'mathematical fitness' (cf. also Witt 2005: 5, who has modified Warke's list):

(1) Utility is no longer derived from actions. Instead, it is attributed to commodities (Jevons 1871: 37–44).
(2) Jevons merges all sources of pleasure and pain into the single category of 'feeling'; the multidimensional nature of different pleasures and pains is lost (Jevons 1871: 7–14).
(3) Jevons treats utility as a representation of purely subjective feelings. Interpersonal comparisons along the four dimensions mentioned by Bentham are no longer possible (Jevons 1871: 14–16).

For the purpose of normative judgements, Jevons goes so far as to divide these feelings into two categories: the 'lower calculus of utility' is separated from a 'higher calculus of moral right and wrong', leaving the latter aside in the investigation. These modifications have been taken up by the discipline and stretched to the utmost limits emptying preference and utility of any psychological content in the theory of revealed preference (Wong 1978). The three changes above are the modifications Witt wants to revoke with his learning theory of consumption in order to *partly* rehabilitate a somewhat more 'objective' (naturalized) notion of utility and preference (cf. as well Sugden 2001: F221–2). It is with such a richer theory that we might be able to also arrive at a richer theory of welfare. Let us now turn to the three elements that have been named as characteristic of the learning theory of consumption, namely utility as pleasures and pains, a theory of wants as a replacement for preference theory and the innate learning mechanisms that govern the change of wants (preferences). I focus on each of them in the next three sections.

4.2 Utility as pleasure and pain

The main characteristic of the learning theory of consumption is that it can be understood as an updated version of 'sensory utilitarianism', a return to the hedonic qualities of utility. This reinstates features of Bentham's utilitarianism which had been abandoned earlier. As I have alluded to earlier (see section 2.1.2), Bentham understood utility (or synonymously 'happiness') to consist of enjoyment of pleasures and security from pains (Bentham 1789: 70). He distinguishes four dimensions that are inherent in any pleasure and pain and determine its value for a person (Bentham 1789: 29–31). These are the 'intensity' of a pleasure (or a pain, respectively), its 'duration', the 'certainty' (or uncertainty) with which it will occur as well as the remoteness or 'propinquity', i.e. the temporal proximity of the pleasure or pain. When considering the pleasure or pain that is involved in an act, two additional dimensions can be added (but Bentham is careful to associate these dimensions with the act, not with pleasure or pain itself), namely the 'fecundity' and 'purity' of the pleasure that is caused by an act. By fecundity, Bentham refers to the chance that the act is followed by pleasure, while conversely, the purity is related to the chance that a pleasure is not followed by a pain or vice versa. A seventh dimension is then added with reference to a group of individuals and the value a pleasure has for them. This dimension is the 'extent', i.e. the number of individuals to which the pleasure extends.

But these are only what could be called the generic features of all pleasures and pains. In an extensive exposition, Bentham lists all conceivable types of pleasures and pains (Bentham 1789: 33–42). As was argued by Warke (2000a,b), this suggests that for Bentham pleasure and pain (as sensory perceptions) are not one single homogeneous feeling. Rather, they are a multitude of very heterogeneous 'interesting perceptions' (Bentham 1789: 33), some of which are simple, others complex (being composed of more than one simple pleasure or pain). On the side of pleasures, Bentham distinguishes *inter alia* between the pleasure of the senses, of wealth, of skill, of amity, of a good name, of relief, of power, of piety, of benevolence, of malevolence, of memory, of imagination, of expectation and pleasures dependent on association. Some of these kinds of pleasures are even further subdivided such as the pleasures of the sense, where Bentham identifies nine different pleasures such as the pleasure of the palate, of touch, of smell, of intoxication, of the ear, of the eye, of the sexual sense, of health and of novelty (the list goes on, of course, with many more subcategories of pleasures and a similar array of different pains). But that is not all. According to Bentham, apart from the existence of these different kinds of pleasures and pains, an individual's sensibility to these pleasures and pains also depends on various circumstances. Bentham understands pleasures and pains to be perceptions of the mind, which each individual might experience differently. To make them comparable, Bentham carefully compiles a large array of over thirty factors that influence an individual's sensibility, including, for example, one's health, strength, age, education, rank, religious profession, insanity and moral sensibility (Bentham 1789: 44–64).

Just as intriguing such a felific calculus seems at first glance, so problematic it becomes in its details. If Bentham's account of utility is understood as an irreducibly multidimensional one (Warke 2000a,c,d), one runs into a number of difficulties when taking it as a guide to welfare policy and institutional design. Bentham himself wanted his calculus put to use not only by the government but also by judges when deciding on the punishment of criminals. In the latter case, only the utility of a single individual is concerned. It seems *comparatively* easy to estimate the pleasures and pains for one individual, taking into account the different types of pleasures and pains and the applicable circumstances. But consider enlarging the set of individuals affected to include larger subgroups of the population or the complete population. How should one operationalize the calculus in this case? For each individual, different circumstances influence the sensibility to pleasures and pains. The intensity of pleasure an act (e.g. a law or a policy measure) entails differs according to these circumstances (of which Bentham has listed over thirty!). Moreover, one can conjecture that different acts are composed of different types of pleasures, which also cannot be readily compared by an individual. So how could one even remotely think of arriving at a definite index number that denotes the net amount of happiness resulting from an act of legislation? In dealing with the multidimensionality of pleasures, Bentham often seemed to stipulate that the pleasures and pains are to some extent homogeneous enough to be compared with each other (Bentham 1789: 45 fn 1).

As a last qualifying point, note that for Bentham pleasures and pains were the psychological basis of all human behaviour. That means, Bentham subscribed to a theory of psychological hedonism, advocating that human behaviour can be explained with reference to the pleasures and pains involved. As such, it is a motivational thesis. But additionally, Bentham also subscribed to ethical hedonism, the view that all human behaviour should aim at maximizing the net balance of pleasures over pains. In this section, the focus is on the former idea, namely that one can understand human behaviour in terms of pleasure and pain. When considering Bentham's original felific calculus, it has to be pointed out that what Bentham has defined in these categories of pleasures and pains encompasses a wide variety of sensations:

> From today's point of view, the different sorts of categories given by Bentham refer to quite a mixed bag of sensory perceptions, innate as well as learnt responses, and complex contingencies. However, the basic idea is a very modern one: the utility derived from an action . . . originates from a multitude of possible sources of pleasures (and of pains avoided).
>
> (Witt 2000: 4)

Witt rightly notes that Bentham's extensive catalogue is based on the right intuition, but has to be supported by scientific foundations, for example regarding the distinction of pleasures and pains. Psychology has moved forward in researching these phenomena. Psychological hedonism is an empirical theory that commands reasonable support nowadays (see e.g. Cabanac 1979; Kahneman et al. 1999; Feldman 2004). When considering a notion of utility that is based on the hedonic qualities of an action, a naturalistic approach, such as the one used here, might help us in exploring the viability of the endeavour. The 'experienced utility' approach suggested by Kahneman et al. (1997) offers a 'modernized' account of the hedonic qualities associated with actions. In their account, Kahneman et al. (1997) have developed a notion of utility, where two of Jevons' modifications are partly revoked: Kahneman et al. return to an account, where the hedonic experience is connected with the outcome of actions – modification (1) – showing how utility can be connected to temporally distinct episodes. This is not unimportant, since pleasurable experiences are not necessarily connected with commodities *per se*. Often, individuals derive 'procedural utility' (Frey et al. 2004) from mere participation in activities (where no commodities are involved). In this way, the basis of the theory is considerably broadened and more in line with empirical findings. With respect to modification (3), Kahneman et al. claim that hedonic experiences are sensory perceptions and can be *observed* and *measured* despite their subjective nature (they even describe the possibility of making interpersonal comparisons of utility, cf. Kahneman et al. 1997: 379–80 and 383). However, the authors retain modification (2), postulating a compound, homogeneous utility measure. Below, I am going to address the question to what extent the multidimensionality of utility is defensible in light of present evidence from psychology and neuroscience (see section 5.3).

4.3 A theory of wants

Probably the most distinctive feature of the learning theory of consumption is, however, the naturalization of preference theory. As a replacement for preference theory and by adopting insights from psychology, Witt suggests a theory of wants, where the satisfaction of different wants entails pleasure (cf. Witt 2000, 2005): a rehabilitation of the old utilitarian approach would come from focusing on these 'wants' or 'needs'. Witt defines these as 'behavioral dispositions . . . which arise from a state of deprivation of an organism' (Witt 2001: 26). Deprivation is the cause of unpleasant sensory perceptions. Satisfying a want, on the other hand, causes a pleasant sensory perception and is thus positively reinforced. I use the term 'wants' as a general umbrella term for the theory and concept of wants and reserve 'needs' for a special subclass of genetically fixed wants (see below).[38]

The idea of a theory of wants has been put forward in and out of economics before. For instance, a similar theory was adopted by one of the protagonists of the marginalist revolution, namely Menger, in his *Principles of Economics* (Menger 1871). Here we can already find the notion of needs as motivators for consumption, i.e. individuals have needs and have learned that their needs can be satisfied by the consumption of goods (Menger 1871: Ch. 1):

> Needs arise from our drives and the drives are embedded in our nature . . . [T]o satisfy our needs is to live and prosper. Thus the attempt to provide for the satisfaction of our needs is synonymous with the attempt to provide for our lives and well-being.
>
> (Menger 1871: 77)

I focus here on Menger's exposition of needs. He does not only present a list of needs, such as 'food, drink, clothing, shelter, etc.' (Menger 1871: 81), but also orders them hierarchically (Menger 1871: 125–7). This has been termed the *Principle of the Subordination of Wants* (Georgescu-Roegen 1954b: 514), referring to the intuition that only after the satisfaction of lower, more fundamental needs do higher, less important needs emerge. Menger even comes close to the concepts we know from Bentham, in classifying needs in the order of the pleasure they bring (along the dimensions of duration and intensity):

> As concerns the differences in the importance that different satisfactions have for us, it is above all a fact of the most common experience that the satisfactions of greatest importance to men are usually those on which the maintenance of life depends, and that other satisfactions are graduated in magnitude of importance according to the degree (duration and intensity) of pleasure dependent upon them.
>
> (Menger 1871: 122–3)

Similarly, individuals prefer satisfactions yielding a higher well-being (i.e. having either equal duration and higher intensity or equal intensity and longer duration).

Menger's theory of needs also incorporates what Georgescu-Roegen

(1954b) has called a *Principle of the Growth of Wants* (see Menger 1871: 82–3), meaning that although a single need can be satiated, all needs will (perhaps) never be satiated, since after the satisfaction of one need another new and unsatisfied need will soon emerge. Finally, Menger explains that for most goods and services, needs cannot be substituted and that complex goods can serve more than one need (Menger 1871: 129), an example of which would be the number of ways in which the need for food might be satiated and the different purposes for which one consumes food (Menger 1871: 124). This has been called *Principle of the Irreducibility of Wants* (Georgescu-Roegen 1954b: 515). Menger has referred to his exposition of a hierarchy of needs as a 'demonstration of a difficult and previously unexplored field of psychology' (Menger 1871: 128). While there have been other attempts to ground (not only) consumption theory with a concept of needs or wants (cf. e.g. Abbott 1953; Duesenberry 1949: 22), this idea is not intrinsic to economics. Psychology has amply dealt with needs and their interrelation. The perhaps most prominent example is Maslow's hierarchy of needs (Maslow 1954). Other psychologists have argued for interrelated sets of needs that do not form an ordered hierarchy (Reiss 2000). While theoretically appealing, it is indeed an altogether different matter whether *hierarchies* of needs are empirically sustainable, which can be seriously doubted (cf. Maslow 1954: 8–9, Wahba and Bridwell 2002: 61–4 and Franke and Kuehlmann 1990: 256–8). Maslow himself acknowledges the problem in a later edition:

> It is fair to say that this theory has been quite successful in a clinical, social and personological way, but not in a laboratory and experimental way … It seems for most people to have direct, personal, subjective plausibility. And yet it still lacks experimental verification and support. I have not yet been able to think of a good way to put it to the test in the laboratory.
>
> (Maslow 1987: xix)

Witt therefore argues for a further elaboration of the concepts of 'wants', since one of its key weaknesses is the *ad hoc* fashion in which wants or hierarchies thereof are established. What is needed would be a naturalistic theory of wants, along the lines of Witt's proposal made in his learning theory of consumption (Witt 2001), where wants are characterized as sensory experiences related to physical states of the organism: Witt, on the one hand, classifies wants as *innate* (or *basic*), for which the term 'need' will be reserved, and, on the other hand, as *learned*. He claims that there exists a finite (and possibly very small) set of innate needs, based on findings of behavioural psychology (Millenson 1967: 368). These are physiologically determined and include the needs for air, aqueous solutions, sleep, food, maintaining body heat, physical activity, achievement, arousal, internal consistency, social (status) recognition, sex, care, and affection as well as relief of pain or fear (Witt 2006: 11). This is captured by his first hypothesis:

[Hypothesis 1] Basic wants are part of the human genetic endowment. They can be satisfied temporarily either singularly or in more or less complex combinations by consuming appropriate items in suitable quantities, and the desire to satisfy the wants motivates the corresponding activity.

(Witt 2001: 26)

Being in a state of deprivation concerning these wants causes an individual to have an unpleasant sensory experience, whereas the satisfaction of them means pleasant sensory experiences for the individual. Via this hypothesis, Witt links the concept of wants to the (hedonistic) utilitarian framework discussed above. A key feature of some of those wants is that through consumption of certain goods (where these goods are consumed in the sense of literally being eaten up in the process) wants can be satiated for a certain period of time, during which excessive consumption could even lead to unpleasant sensory experiences (a prominent example is food, where, after having eaten a certain amount, hunger is satiated). Satiation in those cases is, however, temporary so that after a period of time, deprivation recurs. The other category of learned or acquired wants is possibly the more important one for economic and behavioural analysis, since Witt's conjecture is that those wants are not few. The argument in this case is based on innate learning dispositions that are common to all humans. The basis of these elementary learning processes are sensory perceptions with the capacity of innate or *primary* reinforcers (i.e. the innate needs). *Secondary* (acquired) reinforcers complement the picture sketched earlier by Skinner (1953: Chs 5&6). Secondary reinforcers are acquired via learning mechanisms. At least the mostly unconscious of those so-called behavioural programmes have a genetic basis (Lumsden and Wilson 1981: Chs 2&3). The most interesting ones are learning programmes such as classical and operant conditioning and elementary learning processes, which are similar in all humans and in other species (they are discussed in more detail in the next section). Additionally, there is a genetically programmed classification (a neural process) of those responses that feed back in a positively reinforcing way as pleasant stimuli (and vice versa, in a negatively reinforcing way, as unpleasant stimuli: cf. Pulliam and Dunford 1980: Chs 2&3).

These two mechanisms allow for a wide variety of learned behaviour that goes far beyond the simple learning mechanisms and the few innate reinforcers. With these mechanisms of learning, Witt provides a material basis to argue for the 'Principle of Growth of Wants', since a plethora of combinations of learned wants can emerge from the set of basic needs. 'Given the powerful associative capacity of the human brain it is easy to imagine that an elaborate structure of conditioned reinforcement can emerge in this way over an individual's life time from the few innate reinforcers' (Witt 2006: 11). This hypothesis is, however, not innocent, since the associations are contingent on the differences in personal learning histories: 'a huge inter-personal variety of idiosyncratic acquired wants is likely to result' (Witt 2005: 16). A question arising in this context is whether cultural and biological heritage would then be sufficient to account for systematic commonalities regarding those acquired wants (e.g. is it possible to argue that US American citizens share a common subset of acquired wants due to their common upbringing in the same country, or in the same cultural sphere?). Georgescu-Roegen (1954b: 517) argues that this is the case for members of similar cultural origins: hierarchies of wants are identical to a certain degree and even more so for cultural subgroups. This would, however, have to be substantiated beyond mere intuition and *prima facie* plausibility.

Our human cognitive capacity enables us to anticipate and predict future (un)pleasant stimuli and to plan and act accordingly. This cognitive capacity is very important in another respect as well, since some wants cannot be satiated via direct consumption but via indirect consumption, viz. the use of tools and services. Beliefs and expectations regarding these tools and services are thus motivating factors in consumption as well. In this case, it is not the satisfaction of the underlying want any more that motivates consumption, even though innate needs are concerned. The same is true for acquired wants, which are conditioned on underlying innate (basic) needs. For consumption theory this means that, given enough income, consumption might be extended until each and every single want is satisfied and/or the cognitive motivation to acquire a good is exhausted as well. Since acquired wants are often conditioned on more than one innate need, and these are rarely satisfied all together at the same time, one can expect the intensity of acquired wants to constantly be relatively high over time. Even more, some innate needs, such as the need for social status, might be difficult to satiate at all (see section 6.5.1). It can be concluded that the kind of utilitarianism Witt proposes in his theory, is partly objective (on the grounds of shared innate needs and learning mechanisms) but leaves much room for subjective diversity due to genetic variance and individual learning histories. Introducing shared innate learning mechanisms results in the endogenization of preferences (through the wants that give rise to them) within the theory.

4.4 Learning what we like – consumption dynamics

Having elaborated on the sensory underpinnings of utility and their connection to Witt's theory of wants, we can now examine the mechanisms affecting the formation and change of wants.[39] As highlighted in the previous section, innate behavioural learning mechanisms can be identified as the necessary transition laws to account for the systematic change of wants (Witt 1996a: 712). Learning mechanisms are part of the human genetic inheritance, and while the objects of learning may vary, the processes of learning are quite stable. 'Learning' refers to the procedures and mechanisms through which animals and human beings acquire, retain and modify modes of behaviour. These mechanisms mostly elude direct observation and are thus hypothetical entities explaining observed phenomena. We can broadly distinguish between two kinds of learning, viz. cognitive (social) learning and non- (or sub-) cognitive reinforcement learning. We will see, however, that this distinction is only a conceptual aid, as for humans reinforcement learning is also partly cognitively mediated (Bandura 1977: 38). In conjunction with primary reinforcers, which are genetically programmed and species-specific and thus serve as a 'guide to learning' (Pulliam and Dunford 1980: 25), learning mechanisms allow for a wide variety of behaviours to emerge (and become associated with these reinforcers). Especially in humans, cognitive abilities seem to allow for a wide range of learned behaviours (which, in the case of social learning, can be transmitted even across generations).

4.4.1 Classical and operant conditioning

Classical and operant conditioning are both important and well-researched forms of sub-cognitive learning (Domjan 2005; Staddon and Cerutti 2003).[40] Both forms have been intensively studied in animals and (to a certain degree) humans. Classical conditioning was discovered and studied by Ivan Pavlov in his famous experiments with dogs (Hilgard and Bower 1966: 48). Generally speaking, classical conditioning refers to involuntary behaviour that occurs whenever a certain stimulus induces a predetermined unconditioned response or reflex (UR). When such an unconditioned stimulus (US) is coupled with another stimulus sufficiently often (i.e. another stimulus precedes or coincides with the US), the new stimulus becomes a conditioned stimulus (CS), eliciting the same response as the US. This response is called a conditioned reflex (CR). This form of conditioning works largely sub-cognitively and allows for previously neutral stimuli to become conditioned either as appetitive (positive relation, e.g. when a certain stimulus is associated with a rewarding experience) or aversive (negative relation, e.g. when a certain stimulus is associated with punishment). This mechanism only works when US and CS are temporally related (principle of contiguity, cf. Anderson 1995: 56–8). The association of CS with US depends on the intensity of the stimuli and the number of repetitions in which CS and US are paired. If CS and US are decoupled after a while, 'extinction' (or 'unlearning') begins, and the CR does not occur anymore.

Some characteristics of classical conditioning limit its scope: unconditioned responses are part of our innate behaviour and not subject to change. Consider, for example, the increased pulse rate in case of pain or the reflex that closes the eyelids when something comes near our eyes. Such reactions are usually not subject to our control and occur automatically (Franke and Kuehlmann 1990: 122). Moreover, in classical conditioning no new modes of behaviour are learned since innate responses are (merely) associated with different stimuli. Thus classical conditioning cannot explain how humans acquire complex forms of behaviour. Although it is possible to associate chains of conditioned stimuli with an unconditioned stimulus, this works only partially with very intensive unconditioned responses such as the avoid-ance of pain. Classical conditioning has nonetheless been shown to be useful in advertising, where stimuli elicited, for example, by eroticism or recreation are associated with the products advertised (a classical example would be a girl in a bikini praising a brand of beer at the beach, see e.g. Corn 1982; Stuart et al. 1987; Shimp et al. 1991).

Similar to classical conditioning is operant conditioning (operant rein-forcement), which is closely related to the work of Skinner (1953). Contrary to classical conditioning, which starts with stimulus-linked behaviour, oper-ant conditioning starts with a behavioural response. When such behaviour is followed by a rewarding experience (a stimulus), an individual learns to adjust behaviour such that the shown response is more likely to occur in the future. The valuation of a sensory experience thus determines the probability of a repetition of that response. The difference between classical conditioning (which is called 'respondent behaviour' in Skinner's terminology) and oper-ant conditioning is that the former is a type of passive reaction, while the latter is behaviour for which no conditioned or unconditioned stimulus is observable beforehand. Operant conditioning allows us to learn behaviour, leading to certain behavioural consequences. This is why it is also called 'instrumental conditioning'. As for classical conditioning, operant learning requires a temporal vicinity of behaviour and its consequences ('contin-gency'). Events that follow operant behaviour and increase the probability of its future repetition are called reinforcers (Skinner 1953: 72–5).

There is a difference between 'positive reinforcers' such as food, whose presence increases future operant behaviour, and 'negative reinforcers' (or punishments) such as electric shocks, which increase future operant behaviour when removed. As has been mentioned previously, it is important to dis-tinguish two classes of reinforcers, namely primary and secondary rein-forcers. Primary reinforcers, such as food, are generally reinforcing (this is often species-specific). Their reinforcing character need not be learned, it is genetically programmed. Secondary (conditioned) reinforcers acquire their reinforcing power via their association with another primary or other strong secondary reinforcer (e.g. money, grades). Note that in classical and operant conditioning, no assumptions about inner cognitive processes are made (these are 'black box models').

While Skinner does not do so, reinforcers can be related to human needs: it can be argued that only those things are (positively) reinforcing that tend to satisfy human needs (cf. e.g. Hull 1943; Witt 2001). Since there is sufficient genetic variance in the weights individuals attach to the satisfaction of differ-ent needs (this is does not apply to the more physiological needs such as the need for air, warmth, etc.), this accounts for the differences that are experi-enced in experiments about what is reinforcing for a person (e.g. for some, grades or status are more reinforcing than money, for others not). Reinforce-ment learning has been shown to be effective in wide-ranging contexts, e.g. in improving punctuality and other aspects of work in companies (for a survey cf. Hamner and Hamner 1976). However, due to the complexity of the business environment, it clearly has its limits. Another instance of operant conditioning would be the business practice of trial subscriptions, where customers ideally learn to like the product due to its reinforcing characteristics (cf. Franke and Kuehlmann 1990: 140). Some reinforcing processes are clearly not conscious to the individual, but often operant conditioning does depend on cognitive processes as well, e.g. in attention processes: what we tend to notice can be experienced as reinforcing. The same is true when learning depends on the individual's knowledge of means–ends relationships. Thus classifying operant conditioning as a form of sub-(non-) cognitive learning is a simplification, which should be seen as a conceptual aid inasmuch as it highlights the relative unimportance of (highly) cognitive activities in this form of learning compared to social learning.

4.4.2 Cognitive (social) learning

It has become clear that new and complex ways of behaviour cannot be explained with the forms of learning discussed so far. For example, children do not learn language via continuous reinforcement by their parents. The same holds true for learning to behave correctly while driving a car. Trial-and-error reinforcement processes would soon reach their limits in such cases (Zimbardo and Gerrig 1996: 337). Psychologists have thus identified another important learning process. This process has been called social learning (synonymous with imitational learning, vicarious learning, observational learning) and is closely associated with important contributions by Bandura (1977; 1986).

Bandura conjectures that most learning (especially in humans) is accomplished by imitation. Social learning means that a person learns behaviour by observing (and later by imitating) someone else's behaviour, which is (more or less obviously) reinforced by its consequences. To understand the processes of observational learning, some assumptions about the underlying cognitive processes have to be made. This highlights an important difference to classical and operant conditioning, where the learner is seen as a black box and learning is solely interpreted in terms of overt behaviour. With imitational learning, (cognitive) psychology has opened this black box and begun to hypothesize about inner processes. In social learning models, two broad phases of learning are distinguished, namely the acquisition phase, where behaviour is observed and learned, and the performance phase, where this behaviour is exhibited after learning. Imitational learning can thus take place without the learner actually performing the learned behaviour, since learning takes place in the acquisition phase (Bandura 1965). While, initially, learning does not depend on actual reinforcement, performing learned behaviour does. In experiments with children, it was shown that they learned aggressive behaviour by observing it, but only performed this behaviour when being reinforced for doing so (Dubanoski and Parton 1971; Madsen 1968).

The consequences of behaviour thus only play a role in the second phase of learning. 'Vicarious reinforcement/punishment' (i.e. the reinforcement/punishment of the observed role model) influences the probability of displaying imitative behaviour later (Bandura 1986: 301–3). The more similar the observer is to the role model, the more readily such vicarious learning takes place (Paulus and Seta 1975).

Bandura has identified four sub-processes governing observational learning (Bandura 1986: 52). In sequential order, these are 'attentional processes', 'retention processes', 'production processes' and 'motivational processes'. Attentional processes govern the individual's attention towards a modelled event. That means, whether a situation is perceived at all by an observer and whether learning actually takes place depends on the salience of the event, its complexity, the prevalence, the affective valence (what kinds of emotions are attached to it) and the (known or inferred) functional value of the situation (Bandura 1986: 51–5). It is not solely the situation that determines attention, but also some 'observer attributes', i.e. the observer's perceptual and cognitive capabilities, the arousal level (partly depending on the situation) and existing acquired preferences. In the present context, wants and their learning histories influence attentional processes: wants guide attention towards means to their satisfaction. In the subsequent retention processes, cognitive skills and rehearsal govern the preservation of learned behaviours. On the production level, behaviour depends on the physical capabilities of the observer to reproduce the observed behaviour and on feedback information. The motivational processes governing imitational behaviour (not the acquisition phase) depend on several sets of incentives as well as some observer attributes. Learning often takes place without incentives, but learned behaviour rarely occurs without them. Incentives can either be external (direct) or vicarious (observed), or they can be personal standards. Some relevant observer attributes are internal standards or social comparative biases. For our purposes, attentional and motivational sub-processes are clearly the most important of the four categories, since they are closely related to the learning of wants.

Observational learning has been criticized for some of its assumptions: though it has proved fruitful in experimental research, the focus on internal (unobservable) processes is somewhat problematic. The same holds true for a sharp distinction of exactly what processes are involved in a certain learning situation, since many different characteristics of the modelled events and the observer can potentially play a role. As a final point, the sequential character of Bandura's model is also empirically contestable (Franke and Kuehlmann 1990: 146). Nonetheless, imitational learning is an important form of human learning and has been fruitfully employed in 'mental training', business life or marketing (think of the typical role models shown in commercials, cf. Kroeber-Riel 1992: 645–60). In the following section, I outline how Witt argues that learning plays a crucial role in the formation and change of wants.

4.4.3 *How learning affects wants and their satisfaction*

From the previous sections we can conclude that wants are shaped in a two-fold way: some wants are genetically determined, others are learned. Let us now examine how different wants are satisfied and how learning fits into the picture. In the case of physical needs (e.g. the need to eat or drink), these needs can be satisfied for a certain time period through the consumption of what Witt calls 'direct inputs' (Witt 2001: 26). These are, for example, the loaf of bread or the water that are consumed. This consumption satisfies the respective need for a certain period of time, but after a certain time span, bodily functions have used up the direct inputs, and the organism again enters a state of deprivation. But there are needs that are not satisfied in this way. Innate needs, such as maintaining a certain body temperature, require the 'service of tools' for their satisfaction (Witt 2001: 26). In this case, satisfaction depends on the tools that are available to the consumer, for example sets of clothing that can regulate body temperature. Note that for both kinds of needs there are satiation levels (per time period), but in the latter case (where tools are involved) the number and quality of tools are not subject to satiation. Witt believes that the consumption of the tools is not necessarily determined by the degree of relative deprivation of one of the underlying needs. In this context, other independently (cognitively) conditioned motives, relating to the instrumental relationship between tools and need satisfaction, influence the number of tools purchased. In these consumption processes, different kinds of learning dynamics play a role. First, as regards the more or less invariant set of innate needs, learning can occur in the form of associative learning, connecting previously neutral activities with already existing wants and needs. It happens frequently through the above-mentioned conditioning learning mechanisms and may often take place on a subconscious level. This gives rise to Witt's second hypothesis about the enlargement of the set of wants:

> [Hypothesis 2] By associative learning, acquired or learned wants emerge. Their satisfaction, which is obtained by carrying out the originally neutral activities in the association, is a conditioned rewarding experience. The strength of an acquired want fades if the association on which it is based is not at least occasionally corroborated.
>
> (Witt 2001: 29)

By way of associative learning, a subjective set of highly idiosyncratic wants is likely to emerge in different individuals. Furthermore, Witt asserts that, while the intensity of innate needs varies systematically with their level of deprivation, this relationship does not hold for acquired wants: these carry with them the special property that their deprivation is no longer specific, i.e. it does not matter whether the acquired wants have been satisfied recently. What counts in the case of acquired wants is the relative degree of deprivation of the underlying innate needs. As acquired wants are often conditioned on several innate needs, Witt conjectures that satiation with regard to acquired wants will be seldom reached (Witt 2001: 29). But learning also affects the way a consumer satisfies an existing want. Through learning, consumers can acquire the knowledge to satisfy a want in a novel way. This is a form of learning that is mostly cognitively mediated. The consumer learns that some direct input or a tool has the potential to satisfy an existing want more efficiently or in a different way. This is basically related, *inter alia*, to the instrumental relationship existing between wants and the means to their satisfaction (be they direct inputs or the service of tools). For this, Witt has coined the term 'consumption knowledge', which encompasses our knowledge stock of these instrumental relationships (Witt 2001: 26). This knowledge stock depends on an individual's cognitive capacity:

> [Hypothesis 3] People reflect and learn about how to instrumentalize direct inputs and the services of tools for the satisfaction of their wants, i.e. build up consumption knowledge, by personal experience and inventiveness. Knowledge implicit in socially practiced consumption technologies is also acquired by communicating with, and observing and imitating, other consumers.
>
> (Witt 2001: 28)

But these cognitive learning processes concerning the instrumental relationships between inputs or tools and wants do not describe the complete picture of cognitive learning processes in Witt's learning theory of consumption. Such processes can also interfere with the non-cognitive associative learning processes described above. According to Witt, the crucial insight here concerns the bounded cognitive capacities of the human mind (Witt 2001: 29–30). Information is not processed costlessly, instantaneously and effortlessly. Rather, information has to be filtered and is processed selectively. This selection of relevant information follows rules that are well known in psychology. One very important class, structuring the information processing, are attention processes (Anderson 1990a: Chs 3&5). Attention processes thus influence which elements of consumption knowledge we learn or which new wants we acquire. Of course, these attention processes also depend on our existing set of wants and current level of deprivation. Here cognitive mechanisms are intimately tied to non-cognitive learning mechanisms. But attention processes are also connected to collective behaviour because they are linked to communication with other individuals (Bandura 1986: Ch. 2). Consider, for example, the well-known 'agenda-setting effect' and the influence that role models have on the consumption activities of others. In this domain, we find other influences on the non-cognitive level because what is 'on the agenda' affects future consumption activities, for example by way of shaping which new wants are acquired. Through these mechanisms, we can expect subgroups of individuals to develop similar consumption patterns. These may shift when attention is drawn to other consumption possibilities, for example through role models or advertisements or in the ever-changing fashion cycles. The refocusing of attention to other ways of consumption could be labelled 'shift effect' (Chai 2007: 23). Witt has captured these relationships in his fourth key hypothesis of the learning theory of consumption:

> [Hypothesis 4] Because of selective attention processes, both cognitive and non-cognitive associative learning causes wants and consumption knowledge to selectively become more detailed and to induce specialization in consumption. To the extent to which selective attention processes are influenced by an agenda-setting effect which emerges within intensely communicating groups, specialization in consumption may become a collective 'sub-cultural' phenomenon specific to the respective groups.
>
> (Witt 2001: 30–1)

This has been called 'refinement effect' (Witt 2001: 31) because the dynamics described above lead to a refinement of consumer wants and their respective consumption knowledge over time. This refinement, then, entails a specialization of the consumer towards ever more refined consumption activities. Both 'shift effect' and 'refinement effect' thus relate to some basic consumption dynamics that have been identified in Witt's learning theory of consumption. Both effects together could serve as a basis to explain the unceasing growth of demand that has been observed so far. Assuming the necessary condition of an increasing real per capita income is met, this means that increases in per capita consumption expenditures imply that some wants are not satisfied. In the terminology of the learning theory of consumption, this indicates that either more direct inputs are being purchased or more tools, or either of them in more expensive variants. Considering direct inputs first, Witt conjectures that the satiation level for direct inputs would function as an upper bound for their consumption (Witt 2001: 32). However, in empirical terms, household expenditures on food (or other inferior goods) are still rising in absolute numbers (Lebergott 1993). While this might be explained by the fact that the lower classes have not reached their satiation levels, Witt argues in favour of the following explanation: first, kind and quality of direct inputs change with rising income (e.g. more exotic diets are consumed). Second, products are introduced where the (physical) satiation level is not reached so easily (e.g. artificial sweeteners, see Ruprecht 2005). Third, there are product innovations, which combine direct inputs and/or tools (and their services). These are supposed to appeal to several wants at once, preventing the consumer from ever reaching satiation.

However, the consumption of services of tools seems more important in accounting for the sustained growth of consumption expenditures (Witt 2001: 33). First, consumption of tools does not solely depend on the level of deprivation regarding the underlying want. It is conditioned on cognitive factors. But again, the bigger part of the growth in consumption of tools comes also from product innovations, which simultaneously satisfy multiple wants (on the cognitive level, producers try to provide new justifications to buy new tools). These effects have resulted in the growing consumption knowledge of the consumer (which has been historically supported by the improvement of the general public's education). The advertisement industry is a good example for the enhancement of consumption knowledge as well. The most dramatic effect, however, relates to the two learning processes described above. They contribute significantly to the possibilities of new product innovations, since by way of those processes consumers acquire a plethora of new wants, which need to be satisfied. As Witt argues, this has led historically to highly specialized consumerism. But can this explain why we have experienced a sustained growth of demand? Specialized consumerism differentiates consumers and allows for an increased overall variety of products. Under this specialization (and therefore small scales of specialized production) and rising wages (during the past century), growing consumption expenditures are possible because production costs (i.e. prices) are higher than those of non-differentiated products (which could have been produced on a much lager scale). We can see that a naturalistic approach to consumption yields interesting long-term explanations for the growth of demand. To conclude, it has to be pointed out that the learning theory of consumption does not explicitly address questions of (short-term) consumer choice. It is no theory of choice in the narrow sense, but aims at explaining behavioural regularities and their dynamics and the resultant long-term consumption patterns. Nevertheless, I will address a compatible model of consumer choice in the next section.

4.5 The matching law – a behavioural model

The entire approach discussed so far prompts a revision of the idea of individual optimization behaviour. If consumers have limits to their cognitive capabilities, on the one hand, while consumption possibilities increase due to ever new variants, on the other, it is open to question how an individual could form a complete and transitive preference ordering over these. If consumers are constantly learning and their consumption patterns are determined by shifting attention and idiosyncratic refinement of wants, a different model of actual human behaviour seems to be necessary, as opposed to the behaviour of the well-known omniscient consumer. This is even more so the case when taking an evolutionary perspective and acknowledging the innovative nature of an economy: innovations cannot be plausibly addressed from a static, orthodox perspective (Nelson and Winter 1982). Taking seriously the idea of innovations and the inherent novelty they represent, the epistemic constraints associated with novelty forbid that consumers can anticipate tomorrow's consumption possibilities and thus their future choice set. In this sense, truly unanticipated consumption possibilities emerge through innovations, and consumers have to learn if and how they can satisfy their needs and wants.

These considerations discredit the assumptions of 'homo oeconomicus' as an appropriate model of human behaviour. As has become clear in Chapter 2, a more realistic model of human behaviour might provide the necessary stepping stone for a substantive welfare economics. But how would one conceive of 'homo discens', the learning consumer?

It can be argued that the learning theory of consumption is compatible with Herrnstein's theory of choice of the 'matching law' and melioration learning (Herrnstein 1970, 1997; Herrnstein and Prelec 1991).[41] Matching behaviour could serve as a more realistic replacement for the conventional economic rationality postulate (see also Vanberg 2004: 10).[42] According to the theory of the matching law, an individual does not maximize the total satisfaction of wants over a time interval but, based on reinforcement learning, will *ceteris paribus* choose more reinforced behaviour more often than less reinforced behaviour. The dynamic process which subsequently yields this kind of matching behaviour in equilibrium is called melioration learning. Being a reformulation of the principle of reinforcement (Herrnstein 1990a: 219), melioration learning will in the long run lead to matching behaviour, where:

> an individual's behavior is distributed over alternatives in the choice set so as to equalize the reinforcement returns per unit of behavior invested, measured in time, effort, or any other dimension of behavior constrained to a finite total.
>
> (Herrnstein 1990a: 218)

Mathematically, the (strict) matching law can be formulated as:

$$\frac{A_1}{A_1 + A_2} = \frac{u(A_1)}{u(A_1) + u(A_2)}, \tag{4.1}$$

or equivalently:

$$\frac{A_1}{A_2} = \frac{u(A_1)}{u(A_2)}, \tag{4.2}$$

where the ratio of the frequencies of two actions (A_1, A_2) matches the obtained rewards (conceptualized here by their respective utilities $u(A_1)$, $u(A_2)$). The basic model of matching behaviour, as put forward, for instance, in Herrnstein and Prelec (1991: 141), has two components according to which an individual acts: the first one is called 'value accounting' and comprises the tracking of the average satisfaction received per unit invested for each alternative. The second one is 'melioration', the shift of behaviour to the alternative that provides the higher per unit return. In this simple formulation, matching behaviour is depicted with reference to two alternatives (but the model can be extended to n alternatives; see e.g. Brenner 2006: 43–5). In the case of the basic formulation, the resulting equilibrium of matching behaviour is then either the stable choosing of one alternative or a stable distribution of both alternatives and an equalized average return per unit.

Herrnstein has characterized the matching law as a 'particular sort of limited optimization' (Herrnstein 1990a: 218). To understand this remark, it may prove helpful to briefly compare it to the standard utility maximization calculus mentioned in section 2.3.2. In consequence, it turns out that the theory of matching behaviour is more general than the theory of utility maximization. While at times predicting behaviour that is at odds with utility maximization, these predictions are empirically better corroborated than those of the rival rational choice theory (Williams 1988; Davison and McCarthy 1988). The theory of matching collapses into the standard utility calculus for certain environments (see below). Both approaches have in common the idea that in a static environment, behaviour will tend to approach equilibrium. They diverge to the extent that the matching equilibrium is often different from the equilibrium (that) rational choice theory (understood as maximization of utility) would predict (Herrnstein 1990a: 218). As Herrnstein states, matching behaviour is 'generically suboptimal, though still orderly, and . . . optimality is the exception rather than the rule' (Herrnstein 1990a: 218). There are two important differences between both theories. An important criterion for the decision between the two alternatives according to rational choice theory is the comparison of their marginal utility. *Ceteris paribus*, the alternative chosen is that which yields the higher marginal utility. In Herrnstein's theory, the decision maker considers *average utility* as the relevant criterion and chooses the alternative that yields the higher average utility (i.e. the alternative with the higher reinforcement per unit return). The second difference lies in the requirements on mental accounting. For rational choice theory, reinforcement (utility) over the complete set of choices needs to be taken into account in order to calculate the optimum. The mental bookkeeping for matching behaviour is less demanding because only the correct attribution of (average previous) reinforcement to the particular alternatives is necessary (Herrnstein 1990a: 219). Thus requirements on rationality are considerably lower for individuals to exhibit matching behaviour.

Matching behaviour and utility maximizing behaviour converge in environments, where the reinforcement rates are independent of the sampling rates of the alternatives. This applies to repeated choices but also to the limiting case of only one decision to make. Consider the simple example of choosing between alternative A_1: 'getting 5 Euros' or alternative A_2: 'getting 10 euros' (assume $u(A_2) > u(A_1)$). Rational choice theory as well as the theory of matching predict (along with common sense) the superiority of alternative A_2. This is a trivial instance of the timeless choice assumption inherent in most of rational choice theory. But the hopes of rational choice theorists to smoothly extend this framework in a dynamic context seem to have been wrong

(Herrnstein 1990b: 363). Let us consider an example of choice, where a decision has to be made repeatedly and in which the payoff (in terms of reinforcement) depends on how often that choice has been made before (cf. also Vaughan Jr. and Herrnstein 1987; Herrnstein and Prelec 1991; Brenner and Witt 2003): consider having to choose between eating either a serving of hamburger or caviar over a period of several days, where the utility of eating caviar is initially higher than the utility of eating hamburger but diminishes as a function of having eaten caviar in the past. In this setting, the individual's taste for hamburger is less sensitive than that for caviar. Thus past consumption of hamburgers does not decrease the utility of eating more hamburgers. The maximizing equilibrium would yield an allocation between caviar and hamburgers, where the current utility received from caviar would be higher than that of hamburgers to offset the negative effects that future caviar consumption would entail. The maximizing individual would thus engage in a process of self-rationing of caviar to maximize overall utility. An individual obeying matching behaviour, however, would distribute choices between caviar and hamburger so that current average utilities are equal, thus overeating on caviar and diminishing the utility of caviar up to the point, where a further unit of caviar results (only) in the same utility as eating another hamburger. This behaviour results in a loss of total utility (Herrnstein et al. 1993).

This example is an instance of 'distributed choice' (Herrnstein 1990b: 363), which means that there is not a single decision made by the individual that holds once and for all time. In situations of distributed choice, several decisions (repeated choices) are made over a certain time period. It is obvious that this kind of choice is pervasive in many decision situations (as opposed to the timeless orthodox calculus): what to have for lunch is a repeated decision; whether to watch television in the evening, etc. are choices that are not made in a static context but routinely at more or less regular time intervals. Furthermore, in such contexts the reward values of the different alternatives often change over time as a result of previous choices. Economies of scale, changes in motivational states (e.g. deprivation), depletion of the rewarding resource or other time-dependent changes in the environment can all be reasons for such change in reward value (see section 6.4.1, cf. also Herrnstein and Prelec 1991: 144). In cases of distributed choice, the focus on average returns as opposed to marginal returns per unit of behaviour leads to total returns that are lower than optimal. The foregone optimum that matching behaviour entails in these environments has been labelled an 'internality' of the decision maker because the individual neglects the effect of a change in choice rate on the values (the reinforcement) of the sampled alternatives (Herrnstein and Prelec 1991: 147).

I end this section with some limiting remarks. The demanding rationality requirements necessary for utility maximization prompt a more suitable replacement theory. The theory of matching behaviour might be able to provide such a theory of actual decision behaviour. Matching behaviour has been shown to apply to a wide range of situations, and empirical evidence is abundant on animal experiments. As for human matching behaviour, evidence also exists but is not as impressive (see for surveys Williams 1988; Davison and McCarthy 1988). Based on empirical research, Baum (1974) has introduced the 'generalized matching law' (the modern version of the theory), where matching behaviour is represented by a power function of the form:

$$\frac{A_1}{A_2} = b * \left(\frac{u(A_1)}{u(A_2)}\right)^s. \tag{4.3}$$

Here parameters b and s denote bias and sensitivity, respectively. Both parameters are empirically determined. Sensitivity $s \neq 1$ captures a preference that is more or less extreme than the matching relation would predict. A value of s smaller than one has been termed 'undermatching', i.e. the alternatives are chosen less frequently than predicted, while a value of $s > 1$ represents 'overmatching', which means that the alternatives are more preferred than predicted by the matching relation. Bias b is a parameter used for an unaccounted preference for one alternative. It measures the preference for one alternative when the matching law would predict indifference between alternatives. A value of $b \neq 1$ indicates an unknown but invariant asymmetry between alternatives. If bias and and sensitivity equal 1, the generalized matching law collapses into the strict matching law. Usually, it is argued that this formalization of the matching law better fits empirical data (Baum 1974; McDowell 2005). Of course, the general twist of strict matching behaviour is still retained in this more complex version of the theory.

Note that matching behaviour is best at representing cases of routine behaviour without too strong a cognitive involvement of an individual. It fits less well in describing strongly involved problem-solving activities, where an individual has a complex and unfamiliar task at hand. Related to the notion of wants, melioration learning implies that when deprivation is higher for some wants than for others, processes of homeostasis make the elimination of this deprivation more rewarding, and the individual is likely to choose behaviours that address the most deprived wants. Of course, in any one decision, an individual is free to consciously refrain from exhibiting matching behaviour when deliberating on the options, for example after having read this section.

4.6 Implications

I conclude this chapter by summing up the most important insights to be gained from the outline of the learning theory of consumption provided in this chapter.

(1) The learning theory of consumption (LTC) is a theory that aims at a

more realistic description of *consumption* behaviour. Its three characteristic features are, first, the turn back to a notion of utility based on the
hedonic qualities of actions, i.e. pleasure and pain (making LTC a variant of sensory utilitarianism). Second, it is based on a theory of wants
and their dynamics, which is a replacement for orthodox preference theory. Third, it is evolutionary to the extent that it examines the dynamics
of these wants, mainly on the basis of their often irreversible development through learning.

(2) By introducing the theory of wants, which replaces or supplements the
orthodox notion of preferences, the idea of *materially* specifying an individual's preferences leads to a different layer between goods (or actions)
and utility. Actions or commodity bundles are multidimensional with
respect to the different wants they satisfy.

(3) LTC has connected a hedonistic utility concept to consumption activities
or to actions in general. This is a significant departure from orthodox
theory, where utility is directly connected to goods, thus ignoring the
time dimension (see also Steedman 2001). Connecting utility to actions
opens up the possibility to accommodate phenomena such as 'procedural
utility' (Frey et al. 2004). For LTC to become the basis of an evolutionary theory of welfare, it has to be complemented by a carefully specified
notion of well-being (see the next chapter). This has not been done in
LTC so far.

(4) The dynamics of want acquisition and change are based on empirically
extremely well founded and genetically fixed learning mechanisms, which
function as transition laws governing the change in wants. On account
of the dynamics of this theory of the learning consumer, a much less
pronounced role is attributed to an individual's rationality. *Homo discens*
is perhaps a more plausible version of man than *homo oeconomicus*.

(5) It is also important to keep in mind that LTC is a theory that seeks to
explain long-term behavioural regularities. It is not primarily concerned
with a decision-theoretic perspective of individual decision making. Also,
since most behaviours described here often take place subconsciously, it
is important to note that the theory only offers hypotheses and conjectures about *regularities*. Individuals are capable of reflecting on their
wishes and expectations and can therefore change their wants via more
reflective cognitive mechanisms. Moreover, they can decide not to satisfy
their wants in some instances. Individuals can refrain from impulse pur-
chases, and they ponder whom to vote for in elections, etc. Every single
action may be overridden by conscious interference of the individual.
While, for example, matching behaviour is well established in rats, one
would not be surprised to find that humans can deliberately avoid some
matching behaviours. In contrast to the huge class of everyday or routine
behaviour, it can be conjectured that important conscious decision tasks
individuals have to perform might be better represented by some sort of
optimality calculus.

(6) In that respect, different dynamics of LTC also have different 'stabilities' with regard to their effects. All behaviours that are non-cognitively based can be conjectured to be more stable than cognitively mediated behaviours. Thus the acquisition of a new want through reinforcement learning is more stable than behaviour that depends on a change in consumption knowledge.

Overall, LTC offers a more realistic account of human behaviour. But this comes at the cost of lacking the charm of simplicity. It is 'messy', as Nelson and Winter (1982: 356) have put it.[43] What can be gained from such a theory? Can we illuminate aspects of economic behaviour that cannot be adequately dealt with by orthodox theory using the more realistic premises of LTC detailed above? In consumption theory, LTC has given rise to different questions centred around consumption dynamics and has answered at least some of them. The material specification of the underlying bases of preferences and their change by drawing on insights from psychology has been fruitfully applied to explore the different dynamics of preferential change and consumption (e.g. Ruprecht 2005; Chai 2007; Buenstorf and Cordes 2008) and preferential change and institutional dynamics (Binder and Niederle 2008). In the next chapter, I explore how the theory presented in this chapter can serve as a basis for an evolutionary theory of welfare.

5 An evolutionary theory of welfare

At this point, all the necessary components have been assembled for a framework of an evolutionary theory of welfare. Based on what has been discussed in the previous chapter, I can build a *hedonistic* theory of welfare, with the 'learning theory of consumption' (LTC) as the positive basis. While I do not specify well-being either in terms of the satisfaction of desires (or revealed preferences) or in terms of an objective list of needs, both these aspects play an important role for the theory. My aim is to make a convincing argument so that the position developed here has the potential to incorporate the important aspects of these different kinds of theories of welfare into one integrative framework. In that sense, this chapter can be understood as arguing that there is a grain of truth in all the standard theories of welfare thus far presented.

Two goals are pursued in this chapter. The first goal is to give an account of well-being that is empirically adequate and useful to deal with the challenges presented in Chapter 1. This concerns the introduction of a time dimension into the theory and a possible shift in perspective from outcomes to processes. As has been shown in the previous chapter, LTC has shifted the emphasis from goods to (consumptive) activities in general, which means that utility is associated with actions that happen at a point in time and over time. My hedonistic interpretation of the learning theory of consumption will include two notions of well-being that will be at the heart of the envisaged theory of welfare (sections 5.1 and 5.2). Based on the learning theory of consumption and the different wants and needs posited there, the question arises whether to conceive of the utility that results from the satisfaction of these diverse wants and needs as multidimensional. I discuss this issue, beginning with some general remarks (section 5.3), before I clarify some of the aspects of the debate with recourse to findings from neurosciences (section 5.4). My argument here is that a neuro-economic perspective favours a utility notion that is one-dimensional. I also relate my version of hedonism to the concept of wants and needs dealt with earlier and highlight some appealing (normative) features (section 5.5). The gap between a thoroughly subjective notion of welfare and a less subjective one can be bridged by linking it to basic needs. This is also the appropriate moment to examine how to relate Witt's idea of wants to standard economic preferences.

The second goal consists in arguing that the concepts introduced here are also normatively adequate. I justify the attractiveness of hedonism as the value basis of my theory of welfare (section 5.6) and refute some common objections that could be levelled against it (section 5.7). This is not to say that my framework is completely immune to objections, but there are some good arguments in favour of it. Moreover, it can also be defended against some common methodological and normative objections. Although hedonism is often considered to be an unattractive position, I make a case that such a contention is premature. After these comments on the empirical, methodological and normative adequacy of the theory, I sum up this chapter in section 5.8 before turning to the dynamic aspects of the theory in the following chapter.

5.1 Well-being

Opening up the black box regarding the notion of well-being necessitates introducing concepts from the brain sciences and psychology. Research on the functioning of the brain has brought stimulating new insights into the neural correlates of utility. In order to present the physiological basis of human well-being, the following distinction will be useful. As shown in Table 5.1, brain processes can be categorized along the following two axes (Camerer et al. 2005: 15–9): along the first dimension, brain processes are divided into automatic and controlled ones (see e.g. Schneider and Shiffrin 1977). Automatic brain processes are the default mode of the brain (Camerer et al. 2005: 18): it is characteristic of automatic brain processes that they happen as parallel processes in the brain, are perceived as effortless (involving no subjective feeling of effort) and are not accessible by consciousness. An example is face recognition, which happens without conscious control, involves no discernible effort and is not open to consciousness because we cannot detail the steps involved in recognizing a face.

The opposite of automatic processes are controlled processes, which are processed serially. These are evoked deliberatively and are open to introspective access. Controlled processes are also experienced as involving some effort. As an example of a controlled process, consider solving a chess problem or setting up a mathematical task. Usually, controlled processes occur as the overriding modes of brain processes that (can) overrule automatic processes

Table 5.1 Types of Brain Processes (from Camerer et al. 2005: 15–9)

	Cognitive	*Affective*
Controlled	I	II
Automatic	III	IV

(Camerer et al. 2005: 18). This mostly happens when new problems are encountered or unexpected events call for a reaction. It is possible that over time formerly controlled processes can become automated (through learning) if they are repeated sufficiently often (e.g. many of the calculations of a chess genius become automated processes of pattern recognition through training). While it is sometimes possible to override automatic processes with controlled ones, more often this is not possible (Camerer et al. 2005: 21).

The second dimension distinguishes brain processes as either affective or cognitive (Zajonc 1980, 1984). The primary criterion for affective brain states is the role they play in motivating an individual. With all affects, a 'valence' of either positive or negative is associated. Most affects are associated with a distinct feeling state only if they reach a certain intensity. It is, however, conjectured that affect operates most often at a level below conscious aware-ness (LeDoux 1996; Carter 1999). Besides a valence, affects are often accom-panied by 'action tendencies', i.e. they motivate either approach or avoidance behaviour. Affects thus include drives such as hunger (see also Buck 1999).[44] By contrast, cognitive processes do not show these action tendencies. It is argued that cognition can only motivate behaviour in combination with affect (Camerer et al. 2005: 18); in that sense, a cognitive process could be described as addressing true/false questions.

While much of economic behaviour is *prima facie* seen as belonging to the cognitive and controlled sphere (brain process type 'I' in the table), the following discussion shows that this is not the case. In many areas, human behaviour is similar to the behaviour of our close animal relatives with whom we share the same brain systems (neural mechanisms).

> Many of the processes that occur in these systems are affective rather than cognitive; they are directly concerned with motivation. This might not matter for economics were it not for the fact that the principles that guide the affective system – the way it operates – is so much at variance with the standard economic account of behavior.
>
> (Camerer et al. 2005: 25–6)

Indeed, many of the enjoyment processes associated with what we experience as pleasure are of an automatic affective nature ('IV'), and their occurrence is therefore often even below our level of conscious awareness. Of course, the distinction drawn here is as clear-cut as above only in conceptual terms. Both dimensions are best represented as a continuum, where some processes are more controlled than others and some automatic processes can be overruled more easily than others. The same holds for the affective/cognitive dimension, where the boundaries are also blurred. In general, psychologists emphasize the primacy of the affect side of brain processes so that when cognitive and affective processes conflict, it is most likely that the affective processes will succeed, especially at high levels of affect (Zajonc 1980, 1984; Camerer et al. 2005: 29–31).

Having presented a framework of brain processes in general terms, I proceed to describe the neural substrates of utility by examining how reward is processed in the brain. The systems of reward processing determine what could be termed our 'liking' of something, i.e. the evaluation according to an action's hedonic qualities. In the following, I draw *inter alia* on the findings of Berridge (1996), Kahneman et al. (1997) and Shizgal (1999) on how to understand utility (and thus also well-being). Reward processing is a complex matter involving many different brain areas. Consider the example of an animal approaching food (food being a so-called 'goal object' or reinforcer). While *perceptory processing* identifies the object, its location and physical properties, *reward processing* simultaneously determines the worth of the goal, and a *timing system* tries to identify when and how often the object will be available (Shizgal 1999: 501–2). Based on the timing and reward system the payoff of the goal object is calculated internally. All three processes work together, and often all of them occur without the animal's awareness (be it rat or human; of course, in humans such processing can be cognitively mediated when some factors overriding the automatism hold such as a certain novelty of the 'goal object', etc.). Studies have been conducted with natural reinforcers such as food. Neuroscience, however, has advanced to a point, where in experiments (in rats) electric stimulation is applied directly to the reward areas ('brain stimulation reward', BSR), i.e. without the presence of a goal object. Reactions are similar to those reported in studies with natural reinforcers, but the absence of a reinforcer as trigger for the perceptory processes can lead to diverging reactions regarding learning processes induced by electrical stimulation (see Shizgal 1999).[45]

The *continuous* evaluation of the rewarding sensory experiences (relating to an action or object) has been termed 'instant utility' (Kahneman et al. 1997). Together with 'remembered utility' (see below), it is a special case of 'experienced utility' (referring to the experiential character of utility). Instant utility refers to the affective (hedonic) experience of an individual at a certain point in time. It has two main aspects: the hedonic aspect, which refers to its either positive or negative valence, and another aspect, which relates to an action tendency, biasing the individual towards a certain behaviour (approach) or impelling the individual (avoidance) when the valence is negative. Instant-(aneous) utility is associated with every moment, and the evaluation of sensory experiences is an automatic process, happening effortlessly and mostly without conscious interference. Instant utility better reflects the time dimension than the standard economic utility calculus, which associates a utility value with a goods vector. The automatic hedonic evaluation of the organism's state I call the 'enjoyment' that accompanies different actions. Of course, this term only makes sense when instant utility is positive. For negative instant utility, I refer to the 'suffering' that accompanies an action (or a time interval). Although I often use the terms interchangeably, I prefer the terms 'enjoyment' to 'pleasure' and 'suffering' to 'pain' for the following reasons: being opposed to the notions of 'pleasure' and 'pain', the time dimension is nicely reflected in the word 'suffering', which I use synonymously with negative instant utility (or pain). But the notion of 'enjoyment' also refers to the verb 'to enjoy' (pointing to an activity in time) and is hereafter used synonymously with positive instant utility (or pleasure). A second reason for my preferring enjoyment/suffering to pleasure/pain is that, when referring to pleasure and pain, this is often reduced to the pleasures of 'wine, women, and song', not taking into account other social and creative pleasures as well (compare also Crisp 2006a).[46]

The organism's internal evaluation of a goal object is dependent on internal and external factors, meaning that the strength of the rewarding sensory experience depends on the qualities of the goal object and the organism's internal state. One very important factor in these experiences is the state of deprivation of the organism. Let us briefly look at the factors that influence our hedonic experiences. Being biological products, humans have evolved not to be happy, but to survive and reproduce (Camerer et al. 2005: 27). This is achieved by 'homeostasis', a process that seeks to regulate bodily functions in reaction to changes in external and internal conditions (Damasio 2003: 30–5). The function of this process is to compensate for changes in environmental conditions. The regulation of body temperature, the regular intake of air, water and food are examples of homeostatic processes. These consist of two sub-processes. First, the organism detects a deviation from 'set points' as regards the parameters necessary to allow its continued functioning. For instance, when hot summer weather has increased body temperature, or the hunting for food has dehydrated the organism, certain mechanisms restore the balance conditions in these monitored parameters (set points comprise mostly of parameter ranges, not sharp levels). The organism produces sweat to reduce body temperature or develops thirst to replace lost fluids. These processes mostly work without any deliberate intervention. The negative hedonic feeling associated with the deviation from set points, i.e. the deprivation of innate needs discussed above, is nature's way of motivating action on the part of the organism to restore the homeostatic balance. In that sense, sensory pleasure is a sign of the presence of a useful stimulus (Cabanac 1979). Closely related, and complicating the account a little, is the concept of 'alliesthesia' (greek for: 'changed sensation'; cf. Cabanac 1979), meaning that a stimulus can be perceived to be pleasant or unpleasant, depending on the inner state of the organism. While deprivation is the negative motivator for action, alliesthesia is the positive one, making stimuli more rewarding when an organism is deprived of them. Indeed, pleasure and pain are 'sovereign masters' (Bentham), motivating human action (see also Cabanac 1992).

This discussion has the following implications: understood as (hedonic) experience, utility varies depending on external states of the environment and internal states of the organism. There are numerous studies providing evidence of how, for example, the hedonic evaluation of food depends on the organism's internal state (see Cabanac 1979; Berridge 1996). In these experiments, an individual derives differing pleasurable experiences from the same consumption item in different situations. Such differing evaluations have also been labelled 'valuation effect' (this can also include a 'devaluation effect' that decreases the attractiveness of other items, cf. Brendl et al. 2003). For example, the hedonic evaluation of the consumption of similar food items varies with the number of items already consumed (Small et al. 2001): eating pieces of chocolate one after the other clearly illustrates the law of diminishing marginal utility. It is important to examine the different circumstances and both internal and external factors that play a role in the hedonic evaluation of actions (most of the dynamic interactions will be discussed in the next chapter). In a static calculus, this can be largely assumed away by the condition of (local) non-satiation. But such an examination becomes considerably more urgent when utility is conceived of in a dynamic fashion.[47]

Overall, a good case can be made to base a notion of 'sensory well-being' on the temporal profile of instant utility: understood as the continuous (automatic and often not fully conscious) evaluation of an organism's state in terms of hedonic experience, sensory well-being ('enjoyment') is a concept of well-being that is very close to what individuals experience as rewarding. Since this continuous evaluation of reward is something that is linked to biological functioning and happens automatically and even without conscious attention, such a notion would be quite stable and not easily influenced by changing ethical norms. As such, the concept would be a (relatively) stable indicator of value *for an individual*. A further advantage consists in the fact that it is well researched in terms of the underlying brain processes, providing it with a strong empirical basis (see also section 5.4) and, in turn, putting a hedonistic theory of welfare on more solid ground as regards the nature of pleasure.

Kahneman et al. (1997) have introduced additional utility notions. These are situated at other levels in our overall classification of brain processes because cognitive and controlled functions are involved there. When trying to assess the utility of a certain temporal interval (a 'temporal episode') in retrospect, individuals assess their 'remembered utility'. Remembered utility aggregates a potentially very complex profile of instant utility into a total measure. As argued by the authors, this is done via certain heuristics. While such heuristics allow for a reduction of the complex task of calculating the overall utility of an episode, they do not conform to what might be expected from a normative point of view: it is empirically shown that the remembered utility calculated by an individual is not equal to the integral under the profile of instant utilities. Therefore remembered utility reflects the instant utility of a temporal episode in a distorted way. While it is not clear how exactly this calculation is done, it is clear that a consistent summation of the total past instantaneous utility cannot be given unless the individual can recall every pleasant and unpleasant moment encountered during the relevant temporal episode. Indeed, the longer the time span, or the more diversified the experience during such a time span, the more remembered utility will depend on simplifications (via heuristics), which might occur consciously as well as subconsciously (often depending on attention processes). Kahneman et al. (1997)

have found that a temporal profile is aggregated into remembered utility obeying a 'peak-end rule', where remembered utility turns out to be the average of the peak and end sensory experience (resulting in duration neglect and violation of temporal monotonicity).

Based on the concept of remembered utility, I now introduce the second relevant notion of well-being, which I term 'evaluative well-being'. Following the findings of Kahneman et al. (1997), I conceive of the evaluative well-being of an action or episode as the subjectively aggregated sensory well-being over the time interval of that action or episode. Evaluative well-being is basically an individual's more conscious *ex post* evaluation of a temporal interval. This is an appealing concept of well-being in so far as it accords normative weight to the individual's evaluation of what it means for that individual to lead a good life, one that is going well. As a result, the notion of evaluative well-being is much more cognitively mediated than sensory well-being and thus subject to certain biases and distortions. Evaluative well-being, as introduced here, is not strictly identical with 'remembered utility' because, as Schreiber and Kahneman (2000) state, this only concerns *small* temporal episodes. In my use of the concept, an extension to longer episodes is possible, but this would probably increase the distortions in reports of past remembered utility: while it might be relatively easy to consistently remember and evaluate the well-being experienced in the past minute in terms of hedonic tone, this might be less straightforward for the last year or even longer episodes. Nevertheless, there are studies on how these past episodes are evaluated, and one of the main findings is that remembered utility is calculated on the basis of cognitive operations (retrieval of hedonic values of points in time and their assignment to an overall measure). Schreiber and Kahneman (2000) put forward the hypothesis that the calculation is done via a 'judgement by prototype' heuristic: how do you imagine the sum total of the utility of your last day? Since the total instant utility of an episode has no realistic representation a heuristic processes and forms an evaluation on the basis of some salient subset of the original set of instant utilities that would have to be evaluated. It is likely that the most salient or some of the most extreme emotions (or instant utilities) will form the basis of this heuristic operation (Frey and Stutzer 2004: 5–6), which is in accordance with the main effect found in calculating remembered utility (namely, the neglect of duration and a violation of temporal monotonicity).[48]

The notions of sensory and evaluative well-being have to be distinguished from other, forward-looking concepts of decision making: besides the concept of experienced utility, Kahneman et al. (1997) have also introduced utility concepts such as 'decision utility' and 'predicted utility'. Predicted utility (i.e. utility of a future episode) is estimated based on the calculation of remembered utility. These notions of utility are not necessarily the same as the standard notion of utility used in economics. According to standard economics, an individual assesses the outcomes of some alternatives in question and then chooses the one with the highest expected utility (this would be 'decision utility'). But if predicted utility is internally calculated on the basis of remembered utility, it diverges from the standard view. This calculates utility as the temporal profile of the utilities properly discounted. Therefore individuals empirically assess their utility differently from the economic calculus. This distinction in terminology is vital. Using the notion of utility in the previous chapters involved a certain ambiguity as to its dual role as motivator of choice and measuring rod for welfare. This dual function is often confounded (Sen 1973: 253). It is therefore worthwhile to elaborate on this distinction. When facing a decision, a choice is made on the basis of certain preferences, and a forward-looking calculation (or estimation) of expected utility is made. That is, individuals decide on a course of action on the basis of their desires, which are directed to the future. This has also been called 'wanting' (Berridge 1996, 1999). In biology, the notion of wanting relates to appetite or incentive motivation. Having made the decision, individuals take an action and face the outcome of their decisions (e.g. the consumption of a food item). Such an act of consumption or, more broadly speaking, the satisfaction of a desire is accompanied by a feeling of reward, a pleasurable experience. This pleasure aspect of utility or, in other words, the 'liking' aspect (the experiential/evaluative side, not the motivational side) is what interests me in the following discussion. It is this notion of utility as liking or enjoyment that plays a role in assessing individual well-being. The pleasure aspect is an *ex post* evaluation or can also be the instantaneous evaluation of the moment. Contrary to wanting (or expected utility), it refers to the hedonic qualities of reward (of course, the forward-looking motivational utility can be based on previous experiences of 'liking'). Berridge has shown that, while both wanting and liking often go hand in hand, they can also be dissociated. Preference (or choice) and welfare are thus not identical. As Knutson and Peterson (2005) have made clear, both processes have different neural correlates. Because it is crucial for welfare analysis, my immediate concern here is the biological and neurological representation of utility as enjoyment,[49] i.e. the liking aspect of utility.[50]

Before examining the relation between the two concepts of well-being presented here, a discussion on their interpersonal comparability is in order. There is empirical evidence that instant utility can be reliably measured,[51] converted into a cardinal scale (under some logical axioms) and even be made interpersonally comparable between individuals (Kahneman et al. 1997; Kahneman 1999, 2000).[52] As the banishment of interpersonal comparisons of well-being from welfare economics has been labelled responsible, *inter alia*, for the somewhat precarious state of welfare economics (see Ch. 1), it is worthwhile to examine how a proposal of interpersonal comparisons of utility based on Kahneman's experienced utility notion would have to proceed. This involves two steps: the first step goes from a single moment's instant utility towards the experienced utility of a temporal interval (establishing an 'intrapersonal comparability of moments'). Based on such a measure, the second step requires to justify why the experienced utility number for such a temporal interval should be comparable across persons (interpersonal comparability). The first step depends on the properties of instant utility. For Kahneman's proposal to work, it is necessary that an individual can consistently order moments by the intensity of affect (Kahneman 1999: 5–6). The first requirement is that instants of pain (resp. pleasure) can be ranked ordinally so that a pain level of, say, 7 would always rank higher than one of 6, and a pain level of 3 higher than one of 2. In this, it is not necessary that the difference between a pain level of 6 and 7 is psychologically equivalent, or represents a similar difference in pain, to the difference between, say, pain levels of 2 and 3. This amounts to an ordinal ranking of the deviations from a neutral reference point. The second requirement is the existence of a stable neutral reference point to anchor the scale along which instants are ordered. According to the evidence discussed extensively in Kahneman (1999), both are not unreasonable assumptions.

If these two conditions are fulfilled, i.e. if instants can be ordered by an individual ordinally and there exists a neutral reference level, it is possible to transform the ordinal rankings into an equivalence that accounts for duration. An observer would thus be able to use judgements on trade-offs between different profiles (e.g. one minute of pain level 7 is equivalent to two minutes of pain level 6) such that 'a consistent rescaling is possible, yielding a ratio scale for instant utility that is calibrated by its relation to duration' (Kahneman 1999: 6). A measure of 'total utility' can be constructed based on this transformation under some further assumptions.[53] This total utility measure makes it possible to consistently (intrapersonally) evaluate temporal intervals of different duration regarding their intensity of pleasure and pain. It thus provides an intrapersonally comparable representation of the integral of pleasure and pain along a certain time span.

The second step serves to establish that individuals rank moments and episodes of pleasure or pain similarly, namely that their rankings of a certain episode or experience are similar. In this way, an interpersonally comparable utility measure for different episodes can be established. In fact, there is (tentative) evidence of a convergence of these rankings. For example, a consistent relation exists between physical contractions during childbirth and women's self-reported pain levels (Algom and Lubel 1994). Similarly, an observer's rating of pain via grimacing and groaning during a colonoscopy correlated quite well with that individual's self-reported pain rating (Redelmeier and Kahneman 1996). It is not overly surprising that individuals engage in interpersonal comparisons of utility with a certain success and reliability in everyday life (e.g. Harsanyi 1982: 49). An explanation why these comparisons are not arbitrary might have to do with our innate ability to put ourselves in the shoes of another (i.e. showing empathy). The capacity to empathize with others is based on our ability to understand others to be intentional agents (Tomasello 1999a,b), something already found in children, who do this most readily with respect to others' emotions (Meltzoff 1990). Such empathetic capacity is best achieved if connected to one's own affect. It can be conjectured that humans share an 'affective core' enabling them to relate to other's feelings (Gierer 1998). Such an explanation was put forward by Cordes and Schubert (2007) in the context of shared fairness norms, but seems to be extendable to the case of making interpersonal comparisons of affective states.

While the findings on such interpersonal comparisons of well-being are relatively new and need more empirical confirmation, for example in different settings and maybe for different sources of enjoyment and suffering, they underline that interpersonal comparisons of utility are not completely arbitrary, meaningless expressions of taste but can be addressed in a scientific manner (see also Blaug 1992: 119). Although outside the scope of the present theoretical context, issues of practical measurability and comparability of well-being certainly deserve more consideration (especially before placing these findings into a practical welfare policy context).

5.2 On the relation between sensory and evaluative well-being

Having discussed the two concepts of sensory and evaluative well-being, the question arises as to what notion of well-being should serve as the normative maximand in a welfare calculus if conflicts arise between them. From the preceding discussion, it is obvious that the human mind works on two different albeit interrelated layers (viz. the affective and the cognitive level). I have identified these as giving rise to two distinct notions of well-being. Which of the concepts captures better an individual's well-being? In this section, I clarify their mutual relationship and how they relate to other similar concepts of well-being.

In the psychological literature, sensory and evaluative well-being are related to the notion of 'subjective well-being' (also called 'happiness'). But there are some important differences. While there are theoretical contributions that distinguish between affective and cognitive layers of well-being, most of the (empirical) literature seems to be centred on a cognitive interpretation of subjective well-being. This is reflected in the notion of subjective well-being (or happiness) understood as life satisfaction: the interest lies in the cognitive aspect, making well-being a cognitive judgement-cum-endorsement, i.e. an attitude which one holds towards one's life (see e.g. Frey and Stutzer 2002a). Very similar to this tradition is research using the 'satisfaction with life scale' (SWLS, Diener et al. 1985). Although the proponents of this scale argue that both cognitive and affective components together build the psychological construct 'well-being', the cognitive components seem to dominate their scale. Haybron (2007: 118–9) suggests that this scale captures an individual's 'perceived welfare', not satisfaction with life.[54] Kahneman (1999) has also called his notion of experienced utility 'objective happiness', though this is somewhat misleading: although the adjective 'objective' points to a difference vis-à-vis subjective well-being concepts, it has to be emphasized that experienced utility is centred on affect. Therefore it is misleading to label experienced utility 'objective happiness' on account of the connotations of the term 'happiness' in the literature on subjective well-being, where most concepts are based on a cognitive interpretation of subjective well-being. Well-being, as it is conceived in this monograph, is centred on the affective part of experiences, i.e. the hedonic or reward component. From this derives the evaluation of one's stream of instant utility. Here 'sensory well-being' is the primary concept as it refers to the experiential process that underlies any aggregation of instant utility in the form of remembered utility. Arguably, sensory well-being also partly underlies all of our cognitive judgements on how happy or how satisfied we are with our lives (but see the next paragraphs for qualifications). Moreover, 'sensory well-being' is an evolutionary primary whereas cognition is a recent feat of nature, available only to very few creatures (viz. only humans). Positive and negative affect, on the other hand, seem to guide most other creatures as well.

The stream of affective experience might be difficult to elicit or measure empirically. Two possibilities are suggested by Kahneman and Sugden (2005), a 'day reconstruction' or an 'experience sampling' methodology. Participants in 'experience sampling' studies carry palmtops and have to report their hedonic state at random intervals. The 'day reconstruction method' requires that participants decompose each day retrospectively into short episodes, which they subsequently have to rate in terms of affective value. Both methods seem to work reasonably well on the individual level; but they are cumbersome, and it is not easily conceivable how they could be used in a wider assessment of welfare for large groups (to see how similar measures can be used for 'national well-being accounts', cf. Kahneman et al. 2004). The cognitive judgements on life satisfaction, on the other hand, are easier to elicit. But the above critique that a cognitive scale measures 'perceived welfare' is pervasive and can be extended to many of the concepts of subjective well-being discussed in this section (O'Neill 2006): do these reports really capture 'subjective well-being', or are they subjective reports of some underlying concept of well-being? If we understand that 'evaluative well-being' comes close to being a cognitive judgement about one's underlying instant utility (i.e. affective experience), it can only be very loosely related to the subjective well-being concepts discussed above (such as life satisfaction). This is the case because satisfaction with life can be conjectured to depend on many different things, of which positive affect is only one. In an excellent article, Haybron (2007) discussed how social conventions, moral norms and different potential perspectives towards one's own life can influence one's own assessment of how well one is faring: the assessment of our life satisfaction requires a judgement of ourselves and this judgement is affected by social conventions. For example, one would perhaps not readily admit that one is dissatisfied because it is expected that one should be a happy citizen of a country with mostly happy citizens (effects where subjects modified their judgements to reflect such aspects of social desirability have been found by Schwarz and Strack 1991: 42). This assessment might also be influenced by moral values, for example when we draw a comparison between our life and that of a poor person in a poor country. Who of us would say that their own life goes horribly bad? While one could attempt to capture the effects of social and moral norms by analyzing the *changes* in life satisfaction, these effects are not the only problems that might distort cognitive judgements of well-being.

According to Haybron, the other factor is the 'arbitrariness of perspective'. Depending on the area of life chosen as a reference point, the assessment of one's own welfare may differ. The economist hoping for a tenure decision in the weeks ahead might discount his private life in his assessment of well-being because he is completely focused on his career at that particular moment. Similarly, various events might focus one's attention on domains of one's life that are temporarily more important. These may be important events or even small, transient ones such as a rainy day. While these problems are certainly pervasive in the practical elicitation of judgements of well-being (Schwarz and Strack 1991, 1999),[55] one could argue that they are measurement problems that cannot call into question the theoretical adequacy of the concept. Moreover, how one looks upon one's life generally depends on the standard of comparison used. Do we consistently compare ourselves to others? What is our reference group? Our peer group changes with our employment, education or income, just to name a few examples (see, e.g. Frank 1985). Another standard of comparison might be our aspirations in life. Looking into the future, we might envision ourselves reaching this and that goal. Not having reached these goals, we may well come to a very different assessment of our well-being than when comparing ourselves with a reference group. Or we could evaluate our well-being in relation to what we think we deserve (maybe an evaluation based on ethical or religious ideas of desert or on purely egoistic grounds). Alternatively, we may look back at the past, how our life went, taking this as a standard of evaluation. Another standard might be how much our life has improved. Our 'needs' might be another standard. Compared to what we need, how much did we get? All these comparisons can be used by different individuals, or concurrently by the same individual, or in a changing order.[56] Even if it were clear which of these standards should be employed, how could one be certain that individuals would consistently assess their well-being on this basis? All these possible standards are not necessarily chosen by us with full awareness of this fact. In this respect, they are arbitrary to a certain degree, and can, moreover, adapt over time in ways that would have to be taken into account (Veenhoven 1991).

Such a perspectival contingency is inherent in the cognitive nature of these well-being constructs (well-being understood as life satisfaction). This objection goes deeper than addressing measurement problems because even under ideal epistemic conditions, these reports are perspectival, and it can thus be doubted whether they would capture well-being in a *consistent* fashion. The effects mentioned in the previous paragraphs cannot really be considered exceptional cases that only happen in rare and dire circumstances. Taking different perspectives on one's life can happen all the time, our endorsement of our life change capriciously, and moral values or social conventions have an impact on these reports on an often unreflected level. It seems inevitable that the former bring a measure of arbitrariness to the self-reported assessment of our well-being (as life satisfaction). These considerations are not meant to discredit self-assessments of life satisfaction. But as O'Neill (2006) rightly quips, such objections cast doubt on what exactly individuals report when asked about their subjective well-being. One should be cautious about the information contained in these assessments. Based on such reasoning, one could easily dismiss reports of life satisfaction as 'inherently ill-suited to serve as a proxy for well-being' (Haybron 2007: 113). In fact, the arguments presented here reinforce the point of the contingency of (cognitive) judgements of well-being. At least these doubts stress the desirability to go one level deeper, making enjoyment and suffering the bases for assessments of individual well-being. This aspect is also strengthened by the conjecture that individuals use their current affect (pleasure levels) as a proxy for judgements of life satisfaction (Schwarz and Strack 1991).

One has to be aware of the existence of feedback effects between affective and cognitive aspects of well-being. Positive affect or pleasant sensory experiences tend to positively influence judgements of well-being. For example, reaching one's aspirations may result in pleasure. Here a cognitive judgement could tend to positively influence the affective reaction. Similarly, one might experience some pleasures but, since they are deemed morally unacceptable, at the same time feel guilty for experiencing them. The relationship between the two notions of well-being is thus a very complicated one that does not need to be consistent. It has to be noted that evaluative well-being was introduced as the individual's cognitively mediated aggregation of a stream of affective experience. Conceptually, it is thus quite distinct from life satisfaction, which is used most prominently in the happiness literature. However, one could understand life satisfaction to be an indicator, or empirical proxy, for evaluative well-being. To the extent that life satisfaction is considered an empirical proxy for evaluative well-being, it is clear that the arbitrariness discussed above would probably make this indicator highly unreliable. A better representation (empirical proxy) would focus on reports of the underlying affect during the reported time intervals. Nevertheless, since even such a narrow notion of evaluative well-being is strongly cognitively meditated, it can be conjectured that many of the problems mentioned in this section regarding the perspectival character and instability of cognitive well-being constructs would carry over to such an assessment. We have seen, then, that the assessment of one's own well-being may be subject to many distorting effects such as judgement biases, attention processes, temporary satiation effects, and so on. All these effects can lead to biased reports of (evaluative) well-being. As the notion of sensory well-being is based more directly on the satisfaction of needs and wants, it seems to be more stable and consistent than the notion of evaluative well-being (which can be conjectured to be subject to a multitude of cognitive influences), and biasing influences are not as pervasive.

Table 5.2 systematizes the distinctive features of both notions of well-being. Both capture something different. The notion of sensory well-being shows a higher reliability in terms of consistently capturing what I take to be at the core of an individual's well-being (see also Kahneman et al. 2004). In a certain sense, individuals experience pleasure in the present, not in the future or the past, and this aspect is best captured by instant utility. At the heart of well-being lie moments in which our life goes, or does not go, well. Based on this assessment, I prefer this to the overly malleable notion of evaluative well-being. Of course, this is despite the fact that for practical reasons, one might be stuck with focusing on the other notion. But one should still not be blind to the fact that the nature of well-being is distinct from what one chooses as a practical indicator of it. Moreover, it is important to understand the interplay of both notions and their temporal relationship.

5.3 The multidimensionality of utility

Based on the learning theory of consumption and the different needs and wants posited there, the question arises whether to conceive of utility resulting from the satisfaction of these needs and wants as multidimensional. So far I have conceived of utility (and hence well-being) as one-dimensional. This treatment opportunely coincides with the way utility is usually treated in economics. But is it tenable? Doubts about the comparability of utility resulting from different activities have been succinctly raised by Sen:

> How do we sum up, on the basis of some objective measures of intensities, the respective desires for an ice-cream, freedom from a headache, writing the most beautiful sonnet ever written, going to bed with one's favorite film star, and being morally impeccable?
>
> (Sen 1981: 200)

Table 5.2 Two notions of well-being (author's exposition)

	Sensory Well-Being ('enjoyment')	*Evaluative Well-Being*
Defining Feature	deeper level, linked to biology	perspectival character (depends on attention process), derived notion (via heuristics)
Brain Process	automatic, affective	controlled, cognitive
Stability	high	low (judgement that changes easily), depends on norms and ethical values
Adaptability	limited adaptability when related to needs	high (to aspirations, comparisons with others, previous life, expectations, desert, . . .)
Elicitation	difficult	easier, e.g. via questionnaires

Do we have empirical evidence that supports a multidimensional utility notion?[57] Before presenting empirical evidence, especially from neuropsychology, in the following section, I discuss the possible difficulties associated with a multidimensional utility notion.

In the economics of today, utility is conceptualized as a one-dimensional variable derived from the consumption of different goods (see section 2.1.2): drinking water, enjoying one's fame or reading a stimulating novel all result in a comparable utility that can be evaluated on the same scale. The one-dimensionality of the utility notion is something that the classical utilitarians did arguably not subscribe to. As Warke (2000a,b,c) has persuasively shown, Bentham's utility notion is irreducibly multidimensional, i.e. utility is a vector of qualitatively different pleasures and pains (a distinction between higher and lower pleasures can also be found in Mill 1863). This multidimensionality poses a severe problem, which Bentham himself had already identified. When using the concept for the greatest happiness principle, one encounters the index number problem, which refers to the impossibility of arriving at a ranking of some states that differ with respect to more than one independent quality: given n persons and m qualitatively different pleasures, one needs a matrix of $m * n$ intra- and interpersonal aggregation weights in order to arrive at a numerical representation of social welfare. Without these weights, it would be impossible to use Bentham's felific calculus except in trivial situations (such as those where differences in pleasures and pains only relate to one type of pleasure) because in such an account, there is no common natural denominator, no generic pleasure according to which acts can be ranked. To address the question of intrapersonal weights, Bentham has put much effort into classifying the different kinds of pleasure (see section 4.2). He seemed to be aware that weights for intrapersonal comparisons might depend too much on introspection and could differ from observer to observer; he admitted that precise measurement might not be easily possible (Bentham himself seemed to rely on these concepts more for *qualitative* investigations; cf. Warke 2000b: 9). While the same problem of determining weights also holds for interpersonal comparisons of utility, Bentham could, in this respect, avoid the measurement problems by introducing a strong ethical value judgement, namely that of '[e]verybody to count for one, nobody for more than one' (cited from Warke 2000b: 9–10), effectively equalizing all weights. It should be noted that making such a value judgement was not considered to be problematic by the early utilitarians since they explicitly wanted to offer a normative approach.

But let us put normative considerations aside and examine the positive side of an irreducibly multidimensional utility notion. When contemplating which action to choose, a severe problem arises as to the specification of determinate choice. To exemplify, consider a person's motivation to act in a multidimensional utility framework. Facing two possible actions, A and B, and the question whether to choose A or B, that person would be guided by the utility associated with these actions, viz. $u(A)$ or $u(B)$. Let us assume equal duration and exclude questions of uncertainty. The intensity of the pleasure associated with actions *A* or *B* still seems to be subject to considerable subjectivity. In order to make a decision whether to choose action *A* or *B*, a person has to be able to trade off different pleasures against each other and, subsequently, different pleasures against different pains. Suppose, for example, the simplest case of only one type of pleasure and one type of pain being related to both actions. Assuming cardinality, if *A* results in a pleasure of 5 units and a pain of −3 units, and *B* in pleasure of 7 and pain of −6, what action should be chosen? The person in question would have to be able to specify how many units of pain are traded off against one unit of pleasure (assume the ratio is one to one, then one could calculate $u(A) = 2$ and $u(B) = 1$, and the person would prefer *A* to *B*. If such a trade-off cannot be specified, it is unclear how to order $u(A) = \{5, -3\}$ and $u(B) = \{7, -6\}$). In case there are even more than two pleasure dimensions, one would have to have more weights to internally compare the components and thus calculate a utility index. Such an index number problem can then be transferred directly to the theory of consumer behaviour, where commodities are bundles of qualitatively different pleasures and pains (Warke 2000a: 375).

   In a more systematic fashion, there are three different strategies for the economist to deal with the index number problem (Warke 2000a). The first strategy is to argue that in each different type of pleasurable episode a feeling of enjoyment or satisfaction occurs that is homogeneous across the types of pleasures and pains. If such a feeling of enjoyment occurs and can be argued to be sufficiently homogeneous, the index number problem would not arise, and utility as an index number could be calculated by summing up the enjoyment of different activities. In consequence, determinate choice would favour the action that maximizes this feeling. The second strategy would be to assume a state of 'indifference equilibrium' in which the individual contemplates different actions. While the first strategy solves the problem of determinate consumer choice from the bottom up by asserting the homogeneity of pleasures and pains, the assumption of an indifference equilibrium does so top down (Warke 2000a: 382). The argument basically goes that the consumer chooses between bundles of goods in such a way that the pleasures resulting from a marginal increase of expenditure on any of the goods are equal, even if the pleasures are qualitatively different. With this kind of equilibrium as a starting point and the assumptions of reflexivity and continuity, a complete and transitive ordering over the set of alternatives can, again, be arrived at. However, it would be a strong assumption to visualize the consumer in such a state of indifference equilibrium all the time because such an assumption rules out the idea of out-of-equilibrium consumer behaviour and, as Warke succinctly puts it, it is at least questionable whether the chosen pepperoni/ham ratio on our pizza reflects our long-run indifference equilibrium regarding the pepperoni/ham ratio on a pizza (Warke 2000a: 383). The third strategy would be to impose *a priori* restrictions on an individual's preference set. These restrictions are rationality assumptions chosen to imply that a determinate choice will be possible. This is done in axiomatic utility theory, which starts with an individual's preferences. From these, one arrives at a utility function if the preferences obey the previously discussed standard textbook assumptions such as completeness and transitivity. As discussed above, with this strategy all connotations with sensory experiences or psychological qualities are lost in the technical meaning of the term utility (see section 2.1.2). Is it possible to decide which of the strategies should be chosen? Is utility best conceived of as one- or multidimensional? From a naturalistic point of view, such a question should not be decided in an *ad hoc* fashion or based on introspection but on sound empirical evidence. In order to decide the case, I review some evidence from psychology and the neurosciences in the following section.

5.4 A neuro-economic perspective on utility

Studies on reward processing have opened up the black box of the human brain and allow us to understand what happens when an individual encounters a rewarding object (e.g. McClure et al. 2004). While not going into the details of brain imaging (e.g. PET, fMRI, etc.), I will link the findings of brain sciences with established results from psychology. As shown above, there exist different notions of utility. Especially the distinction between 'experienced utility' and 'decision utility' or, for that matter, between 'liking' and 'wanting' plays a crucial role. Both processes have different neural correlates (Knutson and Peterson 2005). Here I address the biological and neurological representation of utility as pleasures, i.e. the liking aspect of utility, in accordance with my argument for an 'experienced utility' concept as the basis of a notion of welfare.

Seeking rewards is one essential feature serving the survival and reproduction of all animals. From a biological perspective, it is not the pursuit of pleasure and pain that is the ultimate goal, but reproductive success. Nevertheless, nature has endowed animals and humans alike with an elegant solution that tends to favour those actions that are generally beneficial for reproductive success. This is achieved by ensuring that these actions are rewarding for the organism. Rewards can be understood to be all those stimuli that positively reinforce behaviour. As a result, they increase the probability of a behaviour occurring (McClure et al. 2004: 260). It has also been shown that there are many primary reinforcers that are genetically hardwired to be reinforcing. As they are well established *fact* in psychology (Damasio 2003: 131–2), I take for granted the different innate reinforcers provided by Millenson (1967) and discussed in the previous chapter (see section 4.3). We have seen that via associative learning (see section 4.4) previously neutral stimuli can become reinforcing as well. For example, one can conjecture that the most prominent secondary reinforcer, money, is conditioned on other primary rewards. In principle, all learned reinforcers are conditioned on primary reinforcers (even if the chain of associations may sometimes be quite large and idiosyncratic: cf. Cabanac 1979; McClure et al. 2004). But how are these rewards mapped onto brain functions? It has been established that there are certain brain regions in which rewards are processed (these regions differ from the regions where 'wanting' or 'decision utility' is processed, see Knutson and Peterson 2005). As Camerer et al. (2005: 10, italics omitted) submit, 'the study of the brain and nervous system is beginning to allow direct measurement of thoughts and feelings'. Especially, the neurosciences have furthered our understanding of what happens when an individual encounters a natural or conditioned reinforcer, where and how reward is processed in the brain (i.e. the neural substrates of experienced utility) and how it relates to the satisfaction of human needs and wants. Based on empirical evidence, a case can be made that although there is diversity at the level of wants, the rewarding experience (i.e. the 'enjoyment') associated with the removal of deprivation is largely a unitary one.

Before enlarging on the hypothesis that reward is processed 'along a single final common pathway' (McClure et al. 2004: 261) and translated into one single 'common currency' (McFarland and Sibly 1975), I give a brief description of the brain areas involved in reward processing. While different tasks activate different brain regions, it is a well-established fact that rewarding stimuli consistently increase activity in the regions of the orbitofrontal cortex (OFC), the amygdala and the ventral striatum/nucleus accumbens (NAcc).[58] Note that 'activated' brain regions consume more oxygen. From the increased blood flow in these regions, an increased neural activity is therefore inferred. This is measured non-invasively through functional magnetic resonance imaging/tomography (fMRI). The measurements do not report absolute levels but relative increases in blood flow (Kenning and Plassmann 2005: 345). To establish the role of these regions in brain processing, a wide array of brain imaging experiments have been conducted with a host of different stimuli presented such as food, juice, water (e.g. Berns et al. 2001; O'Doherty et al. 2002), smells (e.g. Gottfried et al. 2002), sexual stimuli (e.g. Arnow et al. 2002), sexual behaviour (e.g. Komisaruk et al. 2004), conditioned rewards such as money and positive feedback (e.g. Delgado et al. 2000; O'Doherty et al. 2001a), but also abstract conditioned rewards such as light flashes (e.g. Pagnoni et al. 2002) and social rewards (e.g. Aharon et al. 2001; Rilling et al. 2002; Rolls et al. 2003). Although the functional mapping onto the OFC-Amygdala-NAcc complex is crude in terms of exact location, it seems fairly well established that reward processing (evaluation) in general takes place in this region.

While the OFC has been found to receive direct input from primary taste and olfactory cortices as well as from higher-order visual and somatosensory areas (Rolls 2000), being thus an ideal place for the storage of reward values of sensory stimuli (McClure et al. 2004: 260–1), the amygdala seems to be involved in processing the intensity of positive and negative stimuli (Anderson et al. 2003).[59] The ventral striatum also plays an important role for rewards because of its connection with the mesencephalic (midbrain) dopamine system: the release of dopamine from the ventral striatum onto the NAcc is experienced as highly rewarding (Johnston 1999: 116).

> Output from the limbic system, the pleasure pathway [i.e. the MFB, the medial forebrain bundle, the pathway from striatum to NAcc], appears to be the common neurophysiological correlate of hedonic tone, and this output establishes the important link between feelings and learning.
>
> (Johnston 1999: 116)

As such, this pathway plays an important role in assessing reward and pleasure:

> Incredibly, the release of dopamine onto the nucleus accumbens has now been established to underlie almost every form of pleasure that animals can experience. Blocking the action of dopamine at the nucleus accumbens will ... block the pleasurable effects of a host of natural rewards, such as food and water and sex. In addition, it has now been established that all addictive drugs ... either directly or indirectly activate the pleasure pathway and eventually release dopamine onto the nucleus accumbens. The release of dopamine onto the nucleus accumbens, then, appears to underly all of our reward feelings.
>
> (Johnston 1999: 116)

Shizgal (1999) discusses evidence from research on brain stimulation reward (BSR), where rats received direct electrical stimulation in the brain reward centres. This stimulation differs from a natural situation in that no deprivation of physiological resources is required (ibid., 501), but it generally simulates natural reward very well (see also Conover and Shizgal 1994a,b), namely by providing instant utility. However, direct stimulation of brain areas in rats[60] is subject to problems of precision. Is there any evidence of how reward is processed for natural reinforcers? The answer is yes, there is. While the neural activities remain partly mysterious to science, reinforcer-related behaviour is increasingly well researched. I will stick to the model of Shizgal (1999) (introduced above) of what happens when a so-called 'goal object' (a reinforcer) is encountered. Three different brain processes work in parallel: first, there is perceptual processing, which discerns the identity, location and physical properties of the object. Second, there is evaluative processing, which determines goal worth. Third, a stopwatch timer process computes when the goal object is available and how often this will be the case. The latter two processes then provide the basis for calculating the payoff of the object (i.e. the reward or utility). Regarding the two processes, there is a certain multidimensionality in the 'payoff record' of a reinforcer because reward depends on intensity, amount, time of occurrence, kind of reinforcer, etc. But this kind of multidimensionality differs from another kind that would assert that the pleasures resulting from different reinforcers differ with respect to their qualities. Reward processing itself has been found to take place in certain regions of the brain:

> A large body of evidence implicates specific regions in reward processing, including midbrain dopaminergic nuclei and target areas such as the striatum, as well as orbitofrontal cortex and amygdala (see Everitt et al. 1999; Rolls 2000; Schultz et al. 2000). Two distinct components to reward processing are an anticipatory component, often signalled by the presentation of a cue which reliably signals the subsequent delivery of reward, and a consummatory component relating to reward receipt (Berridge 1996).
>
> (O'Doherty et al. 2002: 815)

These areas are frequently cited for the computation of reward. But if stimuli differ regarding time, reward intensity, and so on, the question arises how the organism computes the reward and adjusts behaviour. The information contained in the multidimensional payoff record is condensed into a common internal unitary valuation by means of a 'currency function' expressing the value of the goal object on a common scale (Shizgal 1999: 509). The same is argued by Montague and Berns (2002: 279): 'Together, these results suggest that the OFS [orbitofrontal cortex and striatum] circuits act to generate a common internal currency (scale) for the valuation of payoffs, losses, and their proxies (predictors of payoffs and losses; . . .)'. Note that:

> [w]ithout internal currencies in the nervous system, a creature would be unable to assess the relative value of different events like drinking water, smelling food, scanning for predators, sitting quietly in the sun, and so forth. To decide on an appropriate behavior, the nervous system must estimate the value of each of these potential actions, convert it to a common scale, and use this scale to determine a course of action. This idea of a common scale can also be used to value both predictors and rewards.
>
> (ibid.: 276)

It can be argued that this internal condensation of a multidimensional profile of the payoff record results in the continuous calculation of 'instant utility' (Kahneman et al. 1997; Shizgal 1999). Summing up the evidence presented here, a case can be made for the following view: reward is processed in some fixed brain regions. The brain converts multidimensional payoff records into one common (neural) currency, which is the basis of our decisions but also of our evaluation of goal worth. Were this not the case, we would be the proverbial Buridan's ass, unable to decide between sonnet and food. The internal currency can be conjectured to be the feeling of reward that is associated with goal objects. There is no evidence that this reward (termed 'utility' in economics) is multidimensional as regards its neural correlates. This lends support to the hypothesis that reward is also best understood to be one-dimensional. Of course, while there is a difference in the feeling tone when one eats something to remove hunger or drinks something to remove thirst, the internal evaluation in terms of hedonic tone is of the same quality.[61]

5.5 On the status of wants and needs

I have argued above that the theory of welfare presented here introduces a middle level between utility and actions in the form of wants giving rise to materially specified preferences. Contrary to the standard notion of preferences, where these are formally specified and have to obey certain *a priori* rationality assumptions, a materially specified, or 'substantive', preference is one whose content goes beyond mere formal specification (Binder and Niederle 2008).

We can fill the concept of preference with life by referring to Witt's notion of wants. Recall that wants are 'behavioral dispositions' and part of the input into a materially specified preference. While preferences in the standard economic sense involve a relational comparison; i.e. an individual i prefers a over b (formally denoted as $a > b$), wants are, in this sense, absolute: an individual i has a want for a. Kahneman and Sugden (2005: 164) have suggested characterizing preferences as extensional, which would mean that preferences are comparisons between states of the world. From this, one could surmise that this is not true for wants, i.e. that wants are non-extensional (such as e.g. an 'attitude': it describes a state of the mind that is prompted by the world). However, this is not the case. Wants are also extensional and relate to states of the world (this is the link that anchors this hedonistic account in states of the world and not merely in states of the mind), but they involve no binary comparison of these states and are directed to one state of the world (mainly an individual's deprivation regarding that want and the relevant means of removing that deprivation). Furthermore, it seems plausible to argue that having a certain want might give rise to a more concrete preference (in the usual meaning of the term): suppose i has a want for cognitive arousal (or *vulgo*: entertainment). The individual learns that a certain television set a allows to satisfy this want better than another television set b. Therefore a preference for a over b is developed.

As has been outlined in Chapter 4, the learning theory of consumption offers the positive hypotheses of how human wants change over time. Besides these laws of motion for preference change, the theory proposes substantive hypotheses about the content of human preferences (albeit on the relatively low level of *innate needs*, including the needs for air, aqueous solutions, sleep, food, maintaining body heat, physical activity, achievement, arousal, internal consistency, social (status) recognition, sex, care and affection as well as relief of pain or fear, cf. Witt 2006: 11). Such needs give rise to *materially* specified preferences. Since acquired wants are always conditioned on existing wants or innate needs, we can (in principle) trace back every acquired want to its basis, namely one or more basic innate needs (McClure et al. 2004; Cabanac

1979: 17). Although individual learning histories might vary widely across cultures, all wants have the same basis in the set of innate needs. The approach discussed here shows similarities with the 'basic needs approach' (see section 2.2.1), which I have discussed as an example of a suitably objective theory of welfare. But as opposed to the basic needs approach known from developmental economics (e.g. Streeten and Burki 1978), this approach is broader since it takes into account basic needs such as those for entertainment, status or achievement, including not only needs for commodities but also for actions (e.g. the act of consuming goods, but not limited to this category). The claim of similarity has been made on the grounds that needs are objective in the sense that everyone has these needs and they constitute an important source of welfare for everyone: our individual biological make-up has endowed us with a capacity to experience pleasures from the satisfaction of innate needs. These innate needs (reinforcers) constitute an *empirical fact* of biology (Damasio 2003: 131–2). The existence of primary reinforcers is neither a matter of value judgement nor an *a priori* assumption; a list of innate needs can be assembled with scientific precision. With the same precision, one can ascertain in which range the deprivation of a need is tolerable and in which it causes severe harm.

A prominent example is the need for food, which is well researched (e.g. Cabanac 1979; Berridge 1996). On the basis of biological and psychological research, one can establish ranges of daily caloric intake necessary to ascertain the continued health and functioning of an individual. A similarly obvious case concerns the intake of liquids. Even more trivial is the need for air. These examples stem from the physiological character of these needs. Based on findings from the life sciences, a naturalistic approach regarding these needs could specify this aspect more fully. A similar case can be made regarding psychological needs such as cognitive arousal. *Prima facie*, there seems to be a systematic difference between physiological needs (if we are deprived of them, this will sooner or later result in death) and psychological needs (such as social recognition or cognitive arousal), where deprivation might not result in imminent physical shock and harm. It can, however, be conjectured that continuous deprivation of these psychological innate needs will also result in severe harm: take, for example, the need for cognitive arousal and novelty. Findings in psychology and neurobiology show that humans experience a certain level of cognitive stimulation as positive (Scitovsky 1981; Anderson 1990b; Wasserman et al. 2004). If novel stimuli are too high or too low, this is experienced as unpleasant. Serious harm occurs if an individual is completely deprived of all sensory inputs. The harm caused by sensory deprivation has been demonstrated by the effects of certain torture methods or solitary confinement (see, e.g. Spjut 1979; Grassian 1983).

These examples illuminate the fundamental character of basic needs for human flourishing and well-being. Basic (innate) needs are independent of human desires and preferences as well as *fundamental* with respect to guaranteeing normal human functioning (Thomson 1987: 8 & 36–8). That is, if an organism operates outside the bounds sketched above, well-being decreases as negative sensory experiences accumulate. If one or more needs are not satisfied to a sufficient degree, the individual suffers. If, on the contrary, deprivation is removed, pleasurable sensory experiences result, increasing individual welfare: the individual enjoys the action that removes deprivation. This fundamental connection exists by virtue of our human biological heritage. As has been noted, the empirical existence of these basic needs constitutes 'an interesting *empirical fact* about human nature, which seems to be of some importance for ethics.' (Harsanyi 1997: 139, emphasis in original) In this context, an important connection between pleasures and needs (and wants) could be identified. If we subscribe to the view that more pleasure is better than less pleasure and less pain better than more pain, basic needs constitute a very important category of *sources* of welfare. Their deprivation harms an individual, while their satisfaction brings pleasure. In this sense, one can argue that innate needs do have a normative significance. If deprivation reaches a critically high level, its removal is vital because otherwise the individual would die or suffer serious harm. But note that in terms of the three layers a theory of welfare should address, wants are on the layer of *sources* of welfare, while the theory presented here argues that the nature of welfare is fully specified by the enjoyment and suffering (that results from the satisfaction of wants). Note also that the fundamental character of innate needs refers to the fact that they are on a lower level than concrete preferences (see Thomson 1987). Innate needs are fundamental in the sense that they (do not yet) specify concrete goals or preferences. Needs can be satisfied by different means. While some needs can be satisfied only in a limited number of ways (we cannot eat iron bars, but chocolate bars will do), other needs can be satisfied in a myriad of ways. Consider, for example, the many ways in which we can satisfy our explorative motivations for cognitive arousal or the need for status seeking.

Consider now the relation of innate needs to preferences. It has always been a source of discontent among critics of economic preference theory that a distinction between such needs and mere preferences is difficult if not impossible because of the intractability of the preference concept (Rosenberg 1985). By using a naturalistic methodology to identify these needs, such a distinction becomes tractable. Compared to preferences, innate needs lack the 'intentionality' inherent in preferences (Sumner 1996: 53). As intentionality is always a characteristic of mental states (and is thus subjective), a needs account lacks one feature that subjectivist accounts share. Recall the example given in section 2.2.1: although one can have a desire for water, it does not follow that one desires H_2O because one might be ignorant of the chemical composition of water. If one *needs* water, however, one needs H_2O, independent of whether one realizes this fact or not. In this respect, such an account is suitably objective. This less subjective stance carries over to the hedonistic account I have sketched here. Usually, hedonism suffers from the standard objection of being too subjective. This would not hold for the position defended here. Moreover, the fundamental character of innate needs is intimately related to their 'givenness' aspect: one does not choose to have a certain (basic) need, and needs are not changeable. They are givens and thus 'inescapable' (Thomson 1987: Ch. 4). While the means of satisfaction of a given innate need is subject to moral considerations, it would be much more difficult to hold someone responsible for having a need. Therefore a plausible case can be made that one should not be responsible for having such an innate need (Griffin 1982: 341 fn 2). Furthermore, to satisfy these needs is a 'natural necessity' (Thomson 1987: 88), and as it has been shown how important pleasure and pain are in regulating individual behaviour, it is not surprising why these two 'sovereign masters' make it so difficult (if not outright impossible) to escape our needs (at least in the long run).

In the following, I want to highlight an argument stating that the subset of innate needs can be given normative priority due to the objectivity and biological significance these *innate* needs have for human functioning and well-being. Their satisfaction, then, constitutes a more *urgent* goal, as Scanlon has put it, than the satisfaction of mere preferences (Scanlon 1975). Note that here the 'urgency' of innate needs pertains to their status in moral deliberation. This urgency allows us to give more weight to some need-based preferences on the grounds that they reflect an objectively more important concern than other preferences. Consider a utilitarian framework that establishes the distributive criterion that everyone should be entitled to the same amount of utility. If a person has 'expensive tastes', for instance always preferring caviar to bread, that person would require much higher resources (to reach the same level of utility) than another person having the opposite preference. For a criterion of distributive justice that advocates equality of welfare (utility), expensive tastes are a challenge. Strength of preference cannot be a suitable criterion from a moral perspective in such a framework. Even if person *A* has a desire for caviar that is as strong as person *B*'s desire for good health, we would not readily concede that we should treat both desires equally. This problem is inherent in the subjectivity of well-being. But it seems that for a moral evaluation, it would not be the subjective importance an individual attaches to a specific interest that counts, but something less subjective, like the importance or urgency of a preference, as Scanlon argues. This importance of preference would have to be justified by giving reasons for having a certain preference (Scanlon 1975: 660).

From a purely formal preference satisfaction view, it is very difficult to give non-arbitrary reasons why some preferences should be urgent. In such accounts it is usually argued that all preferences are chosen by the individual and are thus consciously and willingly adopted. From this perspective, the analyst has no additional information on preferences to trade off one against the other in terms of importance. The dark side of the intractability of preferences is that there cannot be any disputing of tastes (see section 1.1). In section 3.3 it was shown that this argument can be carried to the extreme by suggesting, as Sugden (2004) has done, that individuals should be held responsible for all preferences they form, no matter how incoherent these might be. The importance of some preferences in moral deliberations results from their role in promoting some important interests deemed valuable by a society. Scanlon acknowledges that this is a 'relative urgency' for a society, one that might change over time or be different in different cultures (Scanlon 1975: 662). Just as ethical norms might differ, so we can imagine differing views of what it means to lead a 'good life', i.e. what promotes these urgent interests and what these interests are. (This is a conventionalist view of the concept of 'urgency'.) But a naturalistic view of the concept is possible as well. From a naturalistic perspective, the (relative) importance of some preferences is not a matter of societal consensus. Rather, the reasons for their urgency stem from the fundamental and objective character of basic needs (the view does not seem overly optimistic, namely that giving priority to the satisfaction of innate needs would command fairly high rates of consent, even across cultural borders). My point is that we have good reason to argue that the satisfaction of innate needs is urgent because of their fundamental, inevitable character. Not being able to satisfy these needs causes harm, and this provides a suitable link between needs and the obligation to moral consideration: we are better justified in arguing that it is our obligation to avoid harm to an individual. This is accomplished by creating the opportunities to satisfy these needs. Hence we have an obligation to give special, moral consideration to these needs.

Besides the theoretical appeal, the idea of giving priority to basic needs has received empirical support in an experiment, where the subjects decided on different rules of distributive justice, depending on whether preferences or needs were concerned. Yaari and Bar-Hillel (1984) found that the participants of the study would favour leximin rules of distributive justice (i.e. rules where the position of 'least well-off' was given priority) when needs were concerned, whereas a utilitarian rule of division was favoured when the satisfaction of preference was concerned. But subscribing to the view that basic needs should be accorded normative priority does not imply that any means to satisfy these needs is acceptable. This qualification is an important one as it shifts the burden of criticism regarding the moral filter of a theory of welfare to the means of satisfaction of innate needs. Thus what one can be held responsible for is the means of satisfying a need. Yet even in this category, the limited control individuals have over their basic needs has prompted regulations taking this into account: for example, in German legislation, there used to be a provision differentiating between ordinary theft and the theft of food for immediate consumption because of hunger (so-called 'Mundraub', or petty larceny of food), where the latter was punished more leniently than the former, acknowledging the existence of a fundamental need.

To prevent any misunderstanding regarding this distinction: I have already argued that in some cases there might be a difference between what individuals experience as valuable and what is morally acceptable (see sections 2.1.3 and 2.1.4). I have related this aspect to the moral filter of a theory of welfare. The primary descriptive aim of a theory of welfare is to empirically investigate what individuals value *themselves* (prudential value). However, some items individuals value for themselves are not acceptable from an ethical point of view. I have argued that any normatively appealing theory of welfare has to account for the fact that prudential value and ethical value might diverge. But for the sake of clarity, both kinds of value should be kept separate. Therefore I have maintained that the moral filter of a theory of welfare should reflect exactly these sources of prudential value that should be discounted.

Of course, the argument under review marks a relatively weak distinction. One might satisfy the basic need for food with caviar or bread. So even when distinguishing basic needs from acquired wants, a critique of the *means* of satisfaction of these needs is necessary. But at least a distinction can be made between *some* preferences. Leaving preferences completely unspecified (except for their formal properties) does not even allow for such a distinction. Furthermore, the distinction between innate needs and acquired wants should be understood only as a first step in terms of normative evaluation. As I discuss in the next chapter, a finer classification can be made even for innate needs in terms of their differential satiation patterns. For example, innate needs could be further subdivided, depending on how (in)satiable they are (see section 6.5.1).

From a dynamic perspective, these basic needs moreover exhibit a special feature, namely their resistance to adaptation phenomena. This point has been raised by Veenhoven (1991), and is clearly related to the biological function that the pleasure resulting from need satisfaction has for homeostasis. Since pleasure and pain work as signals of our bodily functioning, they have a built-in resistance to adaptation. That means the pains associated with deprivation and the pleasures from removing this deprivation tend to operate within fixed bounds. I have described the example of the pleasure that comes from eating one piece of chocolate after another. After hunger is satiated, an alliesthetic process starts and makes further pieces taste less pleasant up to a point where the next bite might be outright unpleasant. Satiation occurs with respect to all food (this is the upward direction of the phenomenon). These adversity reactions mark upward maximum levels of need satisfaction (per time interval). In the other direction, being hungry brings discomfort and pain. Being deprived of sensory stimuli or being lonely is also experienced as unpleasant and discomforting. It seems that adaptation or habituation to a state of continued deprivation is only possible up to a certain degree. One does not easily (if at all) adapt to eating only a piece of bread a day: such an existence is probably accompanied by constant discomfort if not outright suffering. A similar point should hold for the other innate needs as well. However, since this is an important dynamic aspect, I will defer its treatment to the next chapter, where I fully discuss the different satiation and adaptation patterns related to different wants (see chapter 6).

One last remark in this connection concerns the idea of a normative priority of needs. It has been argued by Rosenberg (1985) that a schedule of needs would solve the problem of different or changing tastes and the associated problems by *dissolving* it. This is indeed the case. Consider for one moment the idea that all humans share the same fixed set of innate needs. If no other wants existed except for these needs, the problems of preference theory would disappear. As Rosenberg elucidates, such an approach could be neatly integrated into Becker's theory of household production (see e.g. Michael and Becker 1973) and serve as an explanation why every individual shares the same set of preferences and therefore has the same utility function. Becker has stipulated that in his framework of household production theory, preferences are identical for everyone and stable over time (see especially Stigler and Becker 1977). While this assumption seems blatantly false when understanding preferences to reflect tastes, it gains in credibility when preferences are understood to reflect (or be identical to) a finite and fixed set of biologically innate needs. Indeed, if all individuals had the same needs, the utility calculus, as suggested by Becker in his theory of household production, would be quite straightforward. Given identical needs, a household k would derive utility from the consumption of n so-called 'household commodities' $\mathbf{z} = (z_1, \ldots, z_n)$:

$$U_k = U_k(\mathbf{z_k}). \tag{5.1}$$

These household commodities can be understood to cater to the finite set of needs which are identical for everyone. Household commodities are produced by the individual from the market goods $\mathbf{x} = (x_1, \ldots, x_n)$ that the household can buy. One could understand these household commodities to be, say, 'need satisfaction produced' by the household from market goods. The household's production function, which converts market goods $\mathbf{x}$ into household commodities $\mathbf{z_k}$, depends on the invested time t_i and an environmental variable E. For a household commodity i, this is formally described as

$$z_i = z_i(x_i, t_i, E). \tag{5.2}$$

Besides this constraint on household commodity production, a constraint on total income I of the household specifies that all income is spent on market goods (no savings):

$$I = \sum_{i=1}^{n} p_i * x_i. \tag{5.3}$$

A last constraint concerns total household time T that is spent on labour to earn the wage (t_w) and on the production of the household commodities (t_i):

$$T = t_w + \sum_{i=1}^{n} t_i. \tag{5.4}$$

The allegedly attractive side of this approach is that differences in household utility from the consumption of market goods can be relegated to differences in income or in household production technology, the latter being reflected in a difference in the environmental variable. In this calculus, optimization conditions (when utility is maximized) can be derived, for example that the ratio of two household goods must equal the ratio of their prices, etc.

Rosenberg rightly notes that such a reformulation of the standard utility calculus can only (dis)solve the problem of exogenous or changing tastes if the identical utility function of all households derives from a schedule of identical needs. The intractability of tastes would otherwise merely be deferred to the equally intractable question of how households choose a production function or how they determine preferences for household com-modities. In other words, Becker, in his original formulation of the theory, has not solved the problem of changing or divergent individual preferences because the role formerly played in the theory by the preferences is now also relegated (in parts) to the equally unobservable differences in production techniques. In this respect, Becker's theory has probably even magnified the problem of changes in tastes as intra- and interpersonal differences in utility can now derive from (unobservable) differences in tastes for household com-modities *and* household production techniques (E). Without Rosenberg's twist, Becker's theory of household production is as intractable as the stand-ard utility calculus (Rosenberg 1985: 55–7). Only if we can stipulate a fixed set of needs that is identical for everyone (and Becker seems to have alluded to such an idea, cf. Michael and Becker 1973: 145), could Becker's theory be put on a more solid footing. Such an assumption would have far-reaching *normative* implications since differences in household utility could then be attributed to less efficient household commodity production techniques. From this point of view, the welfare economist could suggest policies aimed at improving household production technology in order to decrease existing inefficiencies. This would be a very important and tempting route for the welfare economist. If, as in Becker's framework, differences in behaviour do not stem from differences in tastes but from differences in the efficiency of catering to identical needs through the production of 'need satisfaction' (through household commodities), the welfare economist could judge these differences in behaviour in relation to their productivity. Becker himself acknowledges the importance of this line of argument for welfare economics: for instance, if education alters tastes, it is not possible to evaluate the effect of education on an individual's utility. But if education simply altered the efficiency of household production functions, it could be unambiguously decided which situation would be more beneficial (viz. the one that has higher household commodity output).

I have discussed this assumption here to make two points. First of all to make clear that this cannot be argued from the point of view of the theory discussed in this and the preceding chapter. Rosenberg's idea to interpret Becker's theory of household production as catering to the satisfaction of fixed and identical needs (for everyone) is attractive on account of its dissolution of the problems of preference theory. But it critically neglects the fact that we are able to learn preferences (acquire wants), with the result that individual preference sets differ due to idiosyncratically divergent, individual learning histories. The existence of basic needs is only one (albeit integral) part of the theory presented here. Although humans share innate needs, the whole set of wants of an individual is likely to differ in important ways from the set of wants of other individuals. Therefore the approach of Becker, understood in the way suggested by Rosenberg, is inapplicable. But is it possible to restrict the analysis to the set of innate needs and argue that, regarding the latter, different efficiencies in satisfying them could be evaluated from a welfare-theoretic perspective? I think that this move would be just as problematic since different behaviour (and utility levels) can no longer be unambiguously associated with different efficiencies regarding the production of need satisfaction for the subset of innate needs. It could always be argued that these differences in observed behaviour result from the existence of different acquired wants. While these wants have a connection to innate needs (by being conditioned on them), this aspect does not suffice for the dissolution of the taste problem à la Becker/Rosenberg. Second, even if such an argument were possible, it would be subject to concerns on the applied policy level as it would favour large-scale paternalism, which, on a theoretical level, would strongly restrain an individual's autonomy. Based on the argument that everyone has the same preferences (in the form of needs) and some individuals are just not efficient in producing household commodities, the policy maker could claim that, since preferences are identical and known, the inefficiencies in household production require intervention. These concerns should not be taken lightly (cf. also Lawson 1997: 279–80). In a limited respect, they might also arise for a bounded set of innate needs, which could become the target of such intervention.

While it is thus not possible to use the idea of primary and secondary reinforcers specifying different sets of wants to arrive at a welfare calculus such as the one suggested by Becker/Rosenberg, a more promising route will probably lie in the analysis of wants and needs and how they evolve over time. Nevertheless, it could be shown that the material preference specification described in this section has promising normative implications. In the following sections, I will concentrate on the more philosophical and methodological foundations of my version of hedonism and a discussion of some important objections that could be made against it.

5.6 Foundations of hedonism

To explore some further normative implications, the first question to be answered is what exactly the ultimate source of value is according to our theory: what constitutes the *nature* of welfare? Let me therefore briefly refer to the *axiological* foundations of such a theory (see Table 5.3). In contemporary utilitarian accounts, the satisfaction of preference is what is considered to be inherently valuable. No content of preferences is specified whatsoever, but whatever the preference may be, its satisfaction is the ultimate source of value. The learning theory of consumption, the way it is interpreted here, and the associated theory of welfare shift the focus of that which ultimately constitutes welfare from preferences to pleasurable experiences (enjoyment and suffering). Although insights from psychology and evolutionary biology serve to relate the concept of wants (and the preferences these wants give rise to) to the concept of 'experienced utility', the source of intrinsic value are the 'pleasant sensory episodes' (in that respect, the absence of pain should always be understood similarly). This is a difference from contemporary utilitarian positions: for the evolutionary theory of welfare presented here, intrinsic value does not lie in the satisfaction of a preference *per se*. This has only instrumental value. Rather, intrinsic value lies in enjoyment (pleasure), but it is associated with the pleasant sensory episode enjoyed by the individual when a want is satisfied (a similar position has been defended by Ng 2003).

This shift in focus has an important consequence: while views based on preference satisfaction would hold that any instance of preference satisfaction is valuable in itself, the hedonist argues that this is only the case if preference satisfaction causes either a pleasant sensory episode or the removal or avoidance of pain. The axiological basis of the theory presented can be defined by the following three elements (compare Feldman 2004: 27):

1. Every temporal episode of enjoyment (pleasure) is intrinsically good; every temporal episode of suffering (pain) is intrinsically bad.
2a. The intrinsic value of an episode of enjoyment varies with the intensity

Table 5.3 Elements of a theory of welfare revisited

Level	Role	Example
(1) Conceptual Level	specifies and explains nature of well-being, gives criterion for what is part of (2)	sensory well-being (enjoyment)
(2) Sources	gives a list of sources of well-being, is the basis for (3)	satisfaction of innate needs and acquired wants
(3) Indicators	measures which represent (2), empirically captures (1) and (2)	not discussed here

of the pleasant sensory experience (and duration); the intrinsic value of an episode of pain does likewise.

2b. The pleasure results from the satisfaction of different innate needs and acquired wants, and enjoyment and suffering are in principle measurable.

3. The intrinsic value of a human life is (largely) determined by the intrinsic values of enjoyment and suffering (episodes of pleasure and pain) experienced in that life. Individual well-being is constituted by these episodes and is the net total of pleasant over painful episodes, captured by sensory well-being.[62]

This 'welfare hedonism' can be understood to be a modest form of hedonism because it does not necessarily assume that enjoyment is the only intrinsic value (see item (3) above). Nevertheless, I call it hedonism because I assume that enjoyment is the most important of these values.[63] In the course of this and the following chapter, it is shown that other values such as an individual's autonomy can be used to modify the well-being of an individual and to deal with some of the objections levelled against hedonism. Thus a plausible hedonistic account will likely have to acknowledge the importance of other values besides enjoyment. Also remember that the learning theory of consumption deals with 'behavioural regularities': we have to acknowledge that human individuals *tend* to strive for pleasure and pain. In the same vein, I would argue that welfare hedonism holds for all individuals with the usual genetic variance (cf. similarly, Veenhoven 1991: 31).

Although hedonism is often deemed unattractive, some authors have recently argued for a rehabilitation (Sumner 1996; Kahneman et al. 1997; Feldman 2004; Crisp 2006b). The *prima facie* appeal of a theory of welfare arguing that, for the individual, value lies on the level of pleasure and pain – this appeal is similar to that in the case of welfarism; and by and large, similar arguments can be made to defend both (recall the discussion in section 2.1.5). Especially when we deal with a modest form that would admit other intrinsic values besides enjoyment, it should not cause much controversy if it is argued that pleasure and pain are very relevant for the specification of the nature of welfare. It has to be pointed out that a subtle distinction can be made as to what should be dealt with in a theory of the good (Temkin 1993: 262–3): monist hedonism seems implausible when understood as a theory of the goodness of *outcomes*, because apparently there are other values that are important when judging the 'goodness of outcomes'. Monist hedonism seems more plausible, though, when understood as a theory of the 'good *for persons*', i.e. as a theory of what is in their best (self-)interest. It seems less problematic to hold that what is good for a person should be related to how it affects that person's mental states.

Modest hedonism as I discuss it here is thus best understood in such a restricted way. In a theory of welfare, we are interested in what is good *for persons*. To define this in terms of enjoyment does not seem totally implausible. While, in the following sections, I discuss to what extent hedonism could even be defended as the sole relevant value for a theory of welfare, it should be kept in mind that the weaker claim of a framework of pluralist values is less controversial.[64] Nevertheless, subscribing to a hedonistic axiology, some peculiarities of such an account need to be explained, and some objections have to be dealt with. This occupies the remainder of this chapter.

In the previous chapter, I have introduced the common distinction between motivational (psychological), ethical and welfare hedonism. Here I am concerned with 'welfare hedonism', i.e. the position that identifies welfare with enjoyment and suffering. There is a slight difference between welfare hedonism and ethical hedonism: welfare hedonism is about what is good for the individual (it is (a part of) a theory of the good). This might be different from what is considered ethically right (which is treated in a theory of the right). In typical utilitarian positions, these two aspects are usually lumped together, i.e. what is good for the individual is usually also assumed to be (ethically) right. Whether welfare hedonism should also be accompanied by ethical hedonism is debatable. Ethical considerations should not be confused with prudential considerations. In a later section, I therefore discuss to what extent welfare hedonism can also serve as the basis for ethical hedonism, which is a question that relates to the normative adequacy of the theory (see section 5.7.3). In the following, I focus mainly on hedonism as a theory of welfare.

Recall the distinction between an internalist and an externalist interpretation of hedonism. Both view pleasure and pain as distinct experiences. In the internalist version, enjoyable experiences are understood to share a common 'positive feeling tone: an intrinsic, unanalyzable quality of pleasantness which is present to a greater or lesser degree in all of them' (Sumner 1996: 88). On the grounds of simple introspection, this view is usually discarded as opposing the everyday fact that pleasurable activities such as sports, eating, reaching a goal or having sex share no common quality of enjoyment (as was discussed in section 5.3). This prompts critics to endorse an externalist version of hedonism, where:

> what all pleasures share is not a homogeneous feeling tone but the fact that they are experiences which we like, or enjoy, or seek, or wish to prolong for their own sake – in short, the fact that they are objects of some positive attitude on our part.
>
> (Sumner 1996: 90)

Such a view is held by (Sumner 1996) and Feldman (2004).[65] The unifying feature in externalist hedonism would be to adopt a favourable attitude towards the inhomogeneous experiential pleasures. In a recent paper, Crisp (2006a) has argued that the externalist view of pleasure is vulnerable to some objections regarding the pro-attitude accompanying the pleasurable experience. The question an externalist has to answer is what kind of pro-attitude that should be? As the quote shows, such an attitude could be, for example, to maintain that these pleasures are 'desirable' (such an account was proposed by Sidgwick 1874). But desirability is problematic. Characterizing a pleasure as desirable is an individual's cognitive act and too far removed from enjoyment: one could imagine that an individual characterizes a pleasure as desirable, but does not actually desire it. What is needed to connect enjoyment and desire is the act of desiring, not an abstract desirability. A different way to argue could be to say that one 'desires' these experiences to continue for their own sake (see e.g., Brandt 1966: 268–9). This pro-attitude of desiring different pleasures to continue (which could be called 'preference hedonism') seems thus more plausible. But such a move has unwanted consequences. I have argued above that wanting and liking may often diverge (see section 5.1). We desire things we do not like once they materialize. Or we enjoy things we have not desired. Merely desiring them cannot be counted as a sufficient specification because this would be based on an *ex ante* expectation that the continuation will still be pleasant. One can think of pleasures where the continuation might not improve the experience, such as giving birth or romantic moments (Sumner 1993: 111), or the 'subtle whiff of scent' of a perfume or the breaking of good news (Gosling 1969: 65).

By this reasoning, one comes back to the idea that an experience is enjoyed because it makes one 'feel good'. Crisp rightly argues that this turns the externalist account full circle, making it into an internalist account of pleasures. But then, what becomes of the different qualities of pleasure? Could one not conceive of a pluralist version of internalist hedonism? This would have to be a kind of hedonism, where enjoyableness is understood internally but with a plurality of feeling tones. I think Crisp is justified in his arguing for such a version (see Crisp 2006a: 623–30, for a more extensive account). Let us reconsider the heterogeneity argument. According to internalist *pluralist* hedonism, pleasures are intrinsically good because they 'feel good'. Their character of 'feeling good' is shared by all enjoyable experiences, and although they may differ on many other accounts, this is their unifying feature. As Crisp remarks:

> there *is* a way that enjoyable experiences feel: They feel enjoyable ... Enjoyment, then, is best understood using the determinable/determinate distinction, and the mistake in the heterogeneity argument is that it considers only determinates. Enjoyable experiences do differ from one another, and are often gratifying, welcomed by their subject, favoured, and indeed desired. But there is a certain common quality – feeling good – which any externalist account must ignore.
>
> (Crisp 2006a: 628, emphasis in original)[66]

Such an interpretation is plausible in so far as the common factor in the diverse enjoyable experiences cannot be understood as a sensation or feeling that occurs in a certain body part. While 'feeling good' is not a particular kind of determinate feeling, it is a determinable. Such an account of enjoyment is not far from our common use of the concept. One can ask whether an individual enjoyed a particular experience, be it strolling through the park, reading a novel or eating a piece of cake. Moreover, the individual can give an ordering after enjoying any of these experiences. (Of course, an individual's account of enjoyment can be somewhat different from the question whether that individual would prefer to have another experience of that sort.) The point about such an internalist interpretation of hedonism is that it is supported by my argument on the neural representation of utility in section 5.4. Relevant research has shown that there is a unitary brain representation of pleasure (reward), which is a correlate of enjoyment in the brain. This can be argued to be the correlate of the determinable quality of 'feeling good'. By way of this argument, we can preserve the appeal of the internalist account of hedonism (namely its link to pleasures 'feeling good') without it becoming vulnerable to objections regarding heterogeneous pleasures. Granting that this definition of enjoyment is accepted and we conceive of the hedonistic theory of welfare presented here as an internalist pluralist species of (modest) hedonism from now on, we are still left with the fact that hedonism is a mental state account of well-being (of course, this would also hold for any externalist version). Contrary to state of the world accounts, mental state accounts describe well-being as a mental state that bears no direct connection to the world. Solely the introspective sensation of 'feeling good' matters, making the account vulnerable to objections concerning delusions, which constitute one class of important objections to be discussed in the next section.

5.7 Discussion of objections

So far I have presented my account of welfare hedonism by giving arguments and evidence in its favour. The previous sections have demonstrated that such an account can be made plausible by means of the naturalistic methodology subscribed to in this monograph. What still needs to be shown is whether such a theory of welfare can also be defended against common objections. In this section, I discuss the most important objections critics could raise against such an account and present refutations. Based on a variety of allegations, hedonism has at times seemed a somewhat unattractive position to defend. These allegations encompass a wide spectrum of different concerns, some of which reflect conceptual criticism, while others have to do with moral implications or with practical problems, including the purportedly self-refuting nature of hedonism (subsection 5.7.1). A different category of objections are related to the idea of innate needs and their role in the theory (subsection 5.7.2). While these objections largely concern the conceptual level of the theory, I will briefly discuss the question of changing ethical norms and the moral filter of my theory of welfare (subsection 5.7.3). I aim to show that some common objections are misguided and hedonism is not easily to be dismissed.

5.7.1 Objections regarding hedonism

Mere sensualism / narrow view of the good

The first objection is that hedonism promotes 'mere sensualism' and sensation seeking, thus advocating shallow over deeper pleasures. While by virtue of its being based on a learning theory of *consumption*, pleasures of 'wine, women and song' are included in the formulation of hedonism presented here, consumption can be understood in a wider sense. Focusing on enjoyment has nothing to do with promoting a life of excessive drug abuse, overindulgence in vulgar and carnal pleasures at the expense of arts, culture and other things. Pleasures may as well result from social, cultural or creative activities. Moreover, the stipulation of hedonism promoting overindulgence in carnal or 'low' pleasures certainly neglects the aftereffects of such behaviour. Overindulgence of alcohol leads to the inevitable hangover or possibly to addiction and its aftereffects later on. Many other sensualist pleasures have similar drawbacks that would have to be considered in the long run. A balanced theory of welfare is concerned with the *lifetime well-being* of an individual rather than that individual's welfare within a short time frame. Whether the welfare of someone indulging excessively in 'wine, women and song' would really be greater than that of someone aspiring to other pleasures as well can be doubted due to the effects of excessive pleasure seeking (see Feldman 2004: 29–30).[67]

Moreover, the welfare hedonist does not necessarily have to be concerned about the objection that hedonism is a narrow view of what one should be morally obliged to promote because of the difference between 'welfare hedonism' and 'ethical hedonism': a hedonist about welfare does not need to be an ethical hedonist. Thus to argue that the good for an individual lies in pleasures is not tantamount to arguing that everyone is morally obliged to strive for pleasure. Related to this is the objection that assigning intrinsic value only to pleasures is a narrow view of the human good and neglects important dimensions of value. Indeed, there are many other things in human life that have an impact on our welfare. But are these really substantive goods that are intrinsically valuable in their own right, or are they valued because they tend to be prerequisites or conditions for achieving a more pleasurable life? It could be well argued that these other substantive goods have 'only' an instrumental character, namely in that they are important because they ultimately (tend to) bring about pleasure. Enjoyment as the ultimate goal in life does not deprive these other goods of their status. Why should we value having freedom, rights and opportunities? Would we really value these if they had no effect on our welfare (understood as enjoyment)? In the end, many things are probably valued just because they are enjoyed (see also Crisp 2006a: 637–8).[68] In any case, it is uncontroversial even for critics of hedonism that pleasures are at least one very important class of what constitutes human welfare.

A similar point can be made against the 'paradox of hedonism' objection (see also section 6.4.2), which holds that, regarding pleasures, those individuals who strive the most are the least likely to attain them. Noting that, in some cases, actively seeking enjoyment runs counter to finding it, does not invalidate the claim that the ultimate object of intrinsic worth lies in enjoyment. Similarly, the hedonist has no problem admitting that situations can be imagined where it is best to behave as if one was not seeking to attain pleasures in order to eventually attain them (Crisp 2006a: 638): focusing on some goal (instead of the pleasure that would accompany it directly) is not incompatible with making pleasure the ultimate goal and value. Moreover, critics seem to overestimate the importance of the paradox, as has been shown by Veenhoven (2003), who finds that hedonists (understood as individuals actively seeking pleasures) seem to be happier than non-hedonists. Although the statistical relationship is small in effect size, at least one can say that empirically we do not find strong negative relationships, as proponents of the paradox would allege. In light of these arguments, both the 'sensualism' and the 'narrow view of the good objection' (or 'incompleteness objection') lose much of their force.

Incommensurability of heterogeneous pleasures

Related to the incompleteness objection is the objection that a hedonistic account of one-dimensional pleasure lacks plausibility. This objection is also known as 'Brentano's cigar' (Feldman 2004). Brentano asks us to:

> [c]onsider how ridiculous it would be if someone said that the amount of pleasure he has in smoking a good cigar is such that, if it were multiplied by 127, or say by 1.077, it would be precisely equal to the amount of pleasure he has in listening to a symphony of Beethoven or in viewing one of Raphael's madonnas!
>
> (Brentano 1969: 31)

It is possible to interpret this remark in two different ways (Feldman 2004: 45–9). First, one can argue that pleasures are heterogeneous and lack a sufficiently homogeneous quality to make them comparable. In this form, the argument captures the essence of the externalist critique. As I have argued in the previous section, the internalist hedonist does not have to deny that the phenomenological qualities of diverse actions are different. Nevertheless, the unifying element of pleasures lies exactly in their being enjoyed. At the level of the nature of welfare, it is thus not necessary to conceive of pleasure as multidimensional. That does not preclude arguing that a multidimensional view of the *sources* of pleasures can also be a solution to the objection that it is unrealistic that the value of a good life should consist only in pleasure. While it was shown in section 5.4 that from an empirical point of view, it is fair to conclude that the evidence for a truly multidimensional utility concept is lacking, normative arguments might still be given in its favour.

According to the second interpretation, Brentano's cigar could also be understood as hinting at the practical incommensurability of pleasures, namely, that it is not possible to measure them (exactly) and thus compare the (exact) amounts of pleasure entailed by different actions. I call this interpretation the 'measurement objection' and discuss it separately below. Here I am interested in clarifying in what sense a *normative* argument for heterogeneous pleasures could be understood. From a normative point of view, one argument in favour of a multidimensional utility construct is that it would satisfy our introspective intuition. If we introspectively experience the utility of such diverse actions as being unrelated and qualitatively different, should this intuition not be taken into account? A view arguing that utility is one-dimensional runs the risk of paternalistically imposing a utility notion that runs counter to common (normative) intuitions. This is the standard objection that is raised against internalist accounts of pleasure (Griffin 1986; Sumner 1996: 92–8). Additionally, one could argue that some pleasures should also be accorded a higher prudential worth than others. The argument is exemplified in Mill's dictum, 'better to be Socrates dissatisfied than a fool satisfied' (Mill 1863: Ch. 2).

This argument has been refined in terms of a thought experiment (see also Crisp 2006b: 112–17, for an extensive treatment). If pleasure is ranked only according to intensity and duration, the hedonist is committed to swallowing the following bitter pill: suppose you could choose between living the life of the composer Joseph Haydn (having a duration of 77 years, with all the ups and downs of a creative artist's life) and living the life of an oyster, which is continuously subjected to very small amounts of pleasure. Imagine that the duration of the oyster's life is successively extended. At some point, the sum of pleasures of the oyster would outweigh the sum of pleasures of Haydn's life. Would the hedonist not be committed to the absurd conclusion of choosing the life of the oyster? By contrast, if one acknowledges the existence of higher pleasures, one could claim that there is some discontinuity between the pleasures of Haydn's life and those of the oyster's life. According to such a view, no matter how much oyster-type pleasure one could attain, it would always be worth less than the higher pleasures of Haydn's life. But in order to rank pleasures higher or lower, one would have to introduce other non-hedonistic values, thus rejecting pure hedonism.

There are different types of counter-arguments. First, there is the thought experiment, which is not exactly easy to fantasize about. How do we envision, say, 2,000 years of an oyster's life being continuously minimally pleasant. Would that amount to the mild pleasure of being tickled all these 2,000 years? Can we really imagine how it would be to experience that pleasure during a life of 2,000 years (keeping in mind that we do not adapt to the pleasure). Part of the experiment is the idea that this pleasure does not lose its appeal. It is as strong and pleasant in the beginning as in the end. If we enjoy the first second, we will similarly enjoy each of the remaining 63 billion seconds of the experience following that first second. Such an imagination taxes our faculty of correctly assessing the comparison. I have earlier presented findings of Schreiber and Kahneman (2000) that, when forming such aggregative judgements, we tend to use heuristics like the peak-end average resulting in duration neglect. These findings are usually not mentioned in the oyster example. When assessing the oyster's life according to such a heuristics, the resulting peak-end average will be pitifully low. I think this is a prime example of how a naturalistic approach can enrich normative theorizing: the thought experiment draws its force from a faulty aggregation humans employ in assessing periods of pleasure and pain. I submit that this explains why our intuition tells us that an oyster's life is unattractive.

Ryberg (2002) has given arguments that cast further doubt on the thought experiment. While our preference for Haydn's life may be clear, a restatement of the problem may challenge this idea. Consider a 'higher pleasure' such as listening to Bach's organ works, on the one hand, and a 'lower pleasure' like, say, eating an apple, on the other. Now imagine how many apples it would take to make that pleasure equivalent to the higher pleasure. Many would say no (finite) amount of apples would suffice. But what about some other higher pleasures, which are not ranked as high in enjoyment but are of a longer duration? It would certainly be easier to trade off half an hour of Bach's organ works against, say, one hour of Schubert's violin concertos, and these maybe against two hours of Shakespearean theatre, and this maybe against three hours of a delicious meal, and so on. Thinking of more examples, we would probably arrive at the least high of the higher pleasures and the highest of the lower pleasures. Would one be willing to sacrifice the higher pleasure for a much longer lower pleasure? Such a chain of trade-offs could show (against our *prima facie* intuition) that there is a continuum of pleasure between the highest and the lowest pleasure with no discontinuity involved.

What Ryberg has shown is that the test of whether we would prefer Haydn to the oyster may be an example where no trade-off seems possible, but that there are many other cases where a trade-off is indeed possible. This weakens the objection. Ryberg has refined the argument further by introducing probabilities, for example attaining the higher pleasure with only a very small probability (say, listening to Bach with $p = 0.00000001$) but the small pleasure with very high probability (eating an apple with $p = 0.99999999$). Here the preference might be reversed, and many of us would probably stick with the lower pleasure. One could even add pain to the example. Imagine a life filled with many lower pains and a small chance of achieving higher pleasures. On the other hand, imagine a life filled with many lower pleasures. According to the view that higher pleasures are discontinuously more valuable, one should choose the first alternative. But would our intuition still suggest that this is the case in the present example? Based on these counter-examples, I think it is fair to conclude that the Haydn–oyster objection is not as impeccable as it *prima facie* has seemed.

As a final note on this issue, the idea that some pleasures should be ranked higher (and thus be morally more relevant) than other pleasures may constitute a powerful argument in favour of a multidimensional view of utility as well, not only from a prudential but also from a moral point of view. Apparently a 'vector view of utility' can incorporate different classes of moralities, as Sen has argued, and this would enable the welfare economist to differentially weigh different pleasures according to moral worth (Sen 1981: 193). To do so, one would have to come up with a *normative* weight scale to trade off different utility components. Whether an argument can be made as to what this scale should look like (equal weighting or discounting of some pleasures and not of others, etc.) is not clear and has been doubted (see also Sen 1981). Of course, this weighing problem translates to any utilitarian prescriptive theory of the right, in which the rightness of actions is determined through a felific calculus that forms a net total of pleasures over pains. While the standard utilitarian calculus suffers from the high rationality and perfect foresight requirement on the individual or social planner who would have to calculate the future expected consequences of an action (in terms of utility), this problem would be even more pronounced if utility were irreducibly multidimensional. If one were to base a welfare measure on a multidimensional concept of utility (i.e. assuming multidimensional welfarism such as the position defended by Blackorby et al. 2005), it would also be crucial what informational requirements the underlying utility notion can meet. This has been formalized in a theoretic social choice setting. Similar to the impossibility result obtained by Arrow (1963) for a one-dimensional utility concept and a welfare aggregation based thereon, List (2004) has shown that in a multidimensional framework, one would have to meet certain informational requirements regarding 'interdimensional comparability' (List 2004: 120) in order to avoid an Arrovian impossibility result for that case: interdimensional non-comparability, in particular, leads to an Arrovian impossibility result in multidimensional utility space.

Thus, from a normative point of view, the stipulation of various dimensions of utility that are non-comparable cannot be considered attractive. Not being able to meet more demanding requirements on interdimensional comparability constitutes another normatively relevant objection (for the welfarist) against a multidimensional utility framework. In summing up this discussion, I doubt whether it is attractive to claim that utility should be conceived as multidimensional for normative reasons, especially since different pleasures can be represented in the framework above, where, although enjoyment is unitary, the different weighting could take place at the level of different wants.

Measurement objection

The argument of Brentano's cigar alludes to the impossibility of putting a concrete value to the pleasure of smoking a cigar or listening to a piece of classical music. Interpreted as 'measurement objection', the above argument is that pleasure and pain cannot be measured accurately and, therefore, hedonism is useless and should be abandoned. But this objection is beside the point because it attacks the validity of hedonism at the conceptual level by referring to problems that relate to the level of indicators and measurement. Understood as a general theory of welfare, hedonism is an axiological theory, and the concrete measurement problems that might exist would not invalidate its conceptual core. To argue that welfare lies on the levels of pleasure and pain does not require that pleasure and pain can be measured in all cases or even be traded off.[69] On the other hand, the level of indicators is always quite coarse for most theories of welfare. There are doubts concerning the elicitation of data on subjective well-being as happiness and related measurement objections. Are questions like 'How satisfied are you with your life overall?' really suitable to elicit happiness understood as subjective well-being? Or are they, as O'Neill (2006) suggests, more likely to elicit subjective assessments of (whatever) notions of underlying individual well-being? Similar measurement problems confront the capability approach and related approaches measuring freedom or opportunities: but expenditure or income-based measures of welfare (see section 2.3.2) are also beset by such problems. The objection that pleasure is not readily measurable does not refute the claim that the relevant welfare concept should theoretically aim at pleasure.

False pleasures and the experience machine

In section 2.2.2, I presented Nozick's thought experiment of the 'experience machine'. The gist of the argument suggests that *prima facie* there seems to be a difference between the illusion of a pleasure and the real pleasure. Even if the machine could provide us with an experience (or for that matter a pleasure) that is indistinguishable from the real experience, one is tempted to argue that there is a difference and one would prefer the real experience. In other words, not only does one's mental state matter, but also what one does and is. This objection can be qualified to a certain extent. First of all, such a thought experiment is relatively far removed from our everyday experiences so that intuition might no longer be helpful (Sumner 1996: 94).[70] Arguably, the objection's force seems to result largely from the possibility that potential 'dreamers' are aware that it is an illusion they are indulging in, or that a fear remains that some technical problem might occur during the stay in the pleasure machine. After accounting for these possibilities, there is no longer anything clearly objectionable to the thought experiment (see also Feldman 2004: 42–3 for such argument). Would you not want to live out your dream with full enjoyment on condition that you don't know it is an illusion (and will never find out) including the guarantee that nothing will go wrong with the pleasure machine? In taking care that these conditions are fulfilled, it is no longer clear whether this 'argument from false pleasures' is really an objection against hedonism any more.[71]

Let us consider a different version of the objection, as discussed by Nagel (1979: 1–11) and Kagan (1998: 35). Suppose Tim, the travelling salesman, lives a life he very much enjoys. For him it is full of pleasure, such as having a beautiful wife, nice children, nice colleagues and being in excellent health. Tim is certainly happy and content with his lot. But assume that Tim's apparently happy life is only pleasurable to him and he is seriously mistaken. Assume Tim's wife hates him, has an affair and only play-acts when Tim is around. His children, being on his wife's side, also hate their father but keep up appearances when he is present. Similarly, his colleagues make fun of Tim when he is absent. To top it all, the experiment adds a terminal illness afflicting Tim (which has gone unnoticed and has not caused any pain so far). Would you accord weight to Tim's false pleasures? Or would you even prefer a life full of misery (but knowing the truth) over a life full of false (unsubstantiated) pleasures? Critics of hedonism argue that the theory must remain blind to this distinction. A hedonist is not able to accommodate for the difference between real and illusory pleasures. Based on our intuition that we would not want to exchange lives with Tim, the critics say, hedonism is refuted.

There are two ways out of the predicament such that we can still remain hedonists. First, the case of Tim is incomplete. If we assume that Tim never finds out, we are presented with a similar (but less exotic) example of the experience machine. Tim unceasingly enjoys pleasures, but only by virtue of his being ignorant of the true state of things. In that respect, the enjoyment is real; Tim has a pleasurable state of mind but is mistaken about the source. In that case, the same logic applies as above, and there is nothing wrong with the hedonist arguing that Tim leads a life of pleasure (very valuable to him), enjoying substantial well-being. One could argue, of course, that Tim might want to know the truth. But then again, sometimes ignorance can be bliss! If Tim was told about the deception, he would certainly be very unhappy. But the enjoyment he had in the past would not be diminished through this revelation (Tim's retrospective evaluation of it would probably change, however). Moreover, from a perspective of modest hedonism, one could also acknowledge that there exist other values besides pleasure, and that this was a case where one would have to trade these values off against enjoyment. For someone who holds that knowing the truth has intrinsic value (as a dimension of welfare), there is no doubt that Tim might score considerably lower on welfare because, although he enjoys many false pleasures, he scores quite low in the truth dimension of welfare. It could also be that Tim's level of autonomy is low because he deluded himself as a result of 'objectively' adverse circumstances. Nevertheless, to conclude that Tim's false pleasures should not count towards his well-being introduces a somewhat patronizing element into a theory of welfare. While the subject-relativity of a hedonistic theory of welfare would accord a certain sovereignty to Tim as the sole judge of his well-being, a requirement that would discount enjoyment resulting from delusions calls for some external authority to decide what counts as a delusion. If Tim is not allowed to find solace or enjoyment in deluding himself, 'philosopher kings' (Plato) would be needed in order to decide on such cases. This does not seem overly attractive (see also Sumner 1996: 158–61).

A second way out of the predicament would be to recall that on a plausible hedonistic account, we are assessing the lifetime well-being for an individual. Our common intuition that Tim might prefer to know the bitter truth, to be devastated by the revelation that all his pleasures were false, might be considered an investment in future increased enjoyment because he can adjust his life, find a new, truly loving wife, a different job with nicer colleagues or change his behaviour such that his future pleasures will increase. The knowledge that his former pleasures were based on wrong beliefs might be painful for Tim in the present, but they do not extinguish past pleasures (although Tim might consciously evaluate them differently; there is no denying that he has enjoyed his previous period of life). Much of the intuition that we would consider Tim's life as going badly might also come from a possible failure to discard our privileged knowledge. Being spectators, we know that Tim lives a deceived life, and if some of his deceivers decided to tell him, he would be shattered. As Feldman argues, Tim's life is on the brink of a catastrophe, and that might explain why we would not want to be in Tim's shoes. But if one exchanged lives with Tim, one would lose that knowledge, thus leading a pleasurable life (Feldman 2004: 42–3).

It is worth pointing out that the proposed account of welfare opens up another possibility to rebut the argument from false pleasures. As this objection is based on the mental-state nature of hedonism, we could appeal to a sort of 'experiential requirement' linking pleasure and pain to real experiences, i.e. to states of the world. This could be done via the link between pleasurable experiences and needs and wants. The link to objective needs would then serve as a link between pleasurable mind states and states of the world. In this respect, a pleasure is always warranted by the fact that there is some state of the world that this pleasure is connected to. As long as pleasure is connected to the satisfaction of objective needs, pleasures are sufficiently grounded in experience to satisfy the experience requirement. In such an interpretation, we would only count pleasure as increasing well-being if and only if they satisfy the experience requirement. Cases like direct brain stimulation and the resulting pleasure would thus be not counted as they are not linked to the satisfaction of a need. Such a line of argument would then allow to reject the pleasures derived from the experience machine on the grounds of their not being linked to an objective state of the world (but this would not settle Tim's case, if his delusion satisfies a want, i.e. for cognitive consonance, care or affection).

Non-existent pleasures

Having discussed the argument from false pleasures, one might also reconsider whether someone leading a life devoid of pleasures can still enjoy a high level of well-being. Recall Stanley the Stoic (section 2.2.2), whose life is one of quiet asceticism with no pleasure in it whatsoever. If Stanley looked back on his life, would he not conclude that it went very well for him despite non-existent pleasures? According to the argument, no sensory pleasures are involved, but the hedonist could be saved if Stanley regarded his life with a positive, favourable attitude. Thus, from the point of view of the externalist (or attitudinal hedonist), Stanley's life, though devoid of pleasures, is full of attitudinal pleasure (favourable attitudes), and thus his welfare is high. The case of non-existent pleasures is indeed a challenge for any hedonistic account that is limited to sensory pleasures which are narrowly defined. But in the account presented above, I have followed Witt's suggestion to link pleasurable experiences to the satisfaction of innate needs and acquired wants. Psychology also suggests a possible way out of the dilemma. If achievement or consonance count as primary reinforcers, their satisfaction provides us with enjoyment. Although pleasure from achievement, in its phenomenological expression, might differ from the pleasure from drinking wine, it still qualifies as sensory (but not 'mere sensual') pleasure. I think, therefore, the argument of non-existent pleasures gains high plausibility from a narrow view of pleasures as 'mere sensualism'. A wider view of pleasurable experiences, resulting also from the removal of deprivation and stemming from the need for achievement or consonance, could shed new light on Stanley. According to this view, Stanley would have had pleasures, not of the 'mere sensualist' kind, but other pleasures derived from the sources mentioned above.

5.7.2 Objections regarding basic needs

Besides the objections relating to hedonism, some criticism can be levelled at the material preference specification via the link to innate needs. The approach presented here avoids the three objections to the basic needs account (see section 2.2.1). The first objection brought forward stated that an objective list account of welfare was under-specified in the sense that no theory of the *nature* of welfare was given but only an account of the *sources* of welfare. This criticism does not apply to the framework presented here because both layers are addressed by linking the satisfaction of wants to hedonic experiences. Moreover, since the ultimate measuring rod for welfare is (un)pleasant episodes, the fact that these result from the satisfaction of wants is additional knowledge that can be used in this framework.

The second objection concerned the criteria of selecting a list. Objective list accounts usually draw criticism for the *ad hoc* nature in which the objects that make it onto the list are assembled. This criticism has been levelled against the applied versions of the basic needs account known from development economics (e.g. Streeten and Burki 1978) but also against a similar objective list account, namely the capabilities and functionings account advocated by Sen (see section 3.2). While Sen has argued that the openness of his list account of valuable functionings constitutes a positive feature as it allows for deliberative decision (the 'constructivist' approach to list selection), the account presented here enables a different route. Any constructivist approach to the assembly of a list of valuable functionings or basic needs would lead to the criticism that such a list would then reflect an (inter-) subjective consensus of what constitutes welfare, which, at worst, would only reflect a certain culture's ethical values. From a dynamic perspective, this consensus could change arbitrarily over time as well. The naturalistic method has the advantage that the selection of the list can be done according to more permanent criteria. And the criteria for selecting which needs should be on the list are less arbitrary in the sense that it is an empirical matter what 'basic needs' are, not one of valuational (or ethical) discourse. Using a naturalistic approach to construct a list of basic needs offers the possibility to justify list selection with well established psychological and biological findings. In this respect, the list of valuable basic needs is better justified than comparable lists such as those in Sen's or Nussbaum's 'functionings approach', Rawls' 'primary goods' and Harsanyi's 'substantive goods' (Sen 1985a,b; Nussbaum 2000; Rawls 1971; Harsanyi 1997). While all these lists show a certain overlap and a high degree of plausibility (Qizilbash 2002), a list of basic needs as in the approach presented here can explain why so many of the items on comparable lists are similar. Moreover, this approach is less subjective because of the naturalistic justification (taking into account relevant empirical insights).

The focus on innate needs and their systematic selection (being primary reinforcers) also takes care of the third objection that only fundamental needs should be addressed, not instrumental ones. The fundamental character of innate needs lies exactly in their biological determination. Accordingly, a naturalistic list selection criterion would not suffer from the problem of admitting instrumental needs to the list. It has been noted by Sen that the standard basic needs approach is narrow in its 'commodity fetish' since it is centred only around needs for commodities (Sen 1993a: 40 fn 30). In other words, Sen has argued that typical basic need accounts have always revolved around basic needs for commodities. Although the idea of basic needs presented here is, in principle, very similar to the basic needs approach of developmental economics, the hedonistic framework, in conjunction with the idea of innate needs, is more broad-based, in view of its focus on actions, on the one hand, and a better founded, more general set of innate needs, on the other.

The fourth objection, which I have not discussed yet and which can be raised especially against a naturalistic theory that stipulates innate needs as primary sources of welfare, concerns biological determinism. One could argue that if needs were genetically determined and were the motivators of human behaviour, this would add up to a bleak picture of humanity, describing all human behaviour as completely biologically determined. Without going into a philosophical debate on free will. I think such an objection is misguided, for two reasons. First, needs are not sufficient for choices because there exists also the side of constraints. Second, as has been noted in the previous chapter. Witt's learning theory of consumption, and the theory of welfare based on it, are concerned with *behavioural regularities*. While wants and needs might play a role in determining behaviour especially on a sub-cognitive level, conscious intervention in such processes is often possible. In a concrete choice situation, one can always consciously refrain from satisfying a deprived want or need. Behaviour is thus not completely determined by these wants and needs. Only in the long run, one can argue, will behaviour follow these regularities, such as when individuals tend to satisfy their wants for reasons detailed in this and the previous chapter.

5.7.3 Changing ethical norms and the 'moral filter'

Some questions bearing on the normative adequacy of my theory of welfare remain to be discussed before concluding the chapter. They concern the distinction between a theory of the good and a theory of the right (see section 2.1.3). In standard utilitarianism, what is good and what is right are lumped together and thus easily conflated because utilitarianism is at the same time a theory of the good and of the right. In the utilitarian tradition, the right is often defined in terms of the good.[72] It is not implausible to claim that the basis of our morality lies in our prudential values (Griffin 1998). A theory of welfare can deal with both aspects.[73] But the fact that utilitarianism is usually understood as a theory both of the good and the right should not make us blind to this distinction. Arguing on the positive level that hedonism can be defended as a motivational hypothesis and a (positive) theory of well-being is different from defending ethical hedonism. Both can be combined, but the arguments in favour of the former may differ from the arguments in favour of the latter. However, I have argued that a theory of welfare should primarily be a theory of the good (for a person). Considerations about what is right should be addressed by the 'moral filter' of a theory of welfare. This distinction helps to keep apart the levels of prudential and moral values. Nevertheless, to assess a theory of welfare, one also needs to discuss the moral filter as to whether it is aligned with our moral values and intuitions. In other words, a theory of welfare would be normatively inadequate if it failed to take into account that some things, though good for a person, might be at odds with our moral values.

In discussing hedonism as a theory of welfare, I have primarily focused on its empirical adequacy, whether it captures what *empirically* constitutes well-being for an individual. I want to take up one aspect here which is commonly taken as a normative counter-argument against hedonism, viz. the 'argument from worthless or base pleasures' (Feldman 2004: 39–40). Consider a person who derives pleasurable sensory experiences from the most depraved activities such as torturing other persons, engaging in horrific sexual activities, killing people, and so forth. Imagine further that this person does not experience any other painful sensations in life. According to the theory of welfare developed here, this person would enjoy a rather high level of welfare, thus leading a good and valuable life. This interpretation is usually taken as a powerful rejection of hedonism, but the problem actually poses itself in all subjective theories of welfare, where individuals are the ultimate judges of their well-being. But is this so? The 'depraved person' leads a morally damnable life according to most moral systems ever adopted by humanity. Acts such as murder, rape or infanticide are (almost) universally considered as immoral. But although we can say that there seem to be some universally agreed moral principles, the question here lies on a different level. The 'depraved person' lives a life which that person enjoys. There is thus nothing wrong with conceding that this person's welfare is, by the person's own judgement, quite high. The ethical worth in this case is no doubt very low. But it would be wrong to state that this person's life has no prudential value for that person. The fact that 'base pleasures' pose a problem for subjective theories of welfare is to a certain degree offset by the fact that the latter accord high autonomy to individuals judging their own well-being. Quite obviously these are two sides of the same coin: if individuals are the ultimate judges of their own welfare, one has to put up with the possibility that there exist some individuals whose judgements of their own welfare are far removed from one's own judgement of what constitutes one's own welfare.

A similar case is the argument from 'worthless pleasures', where the pleasures involved are not necessarily harmful to someone else, but where intuition might tell us that they have no intrinsic worth. While Bentham held that pleasures from pushpin or poetry should be ranked only according to their intensity and duration, critics would argue that pleasures resulting from some activities are higher pleasures while others are lower or even worthless. Feldman has discussed this using the example of 'Porky', someone who takes pleasure in certain sexual activities involving swine in a barn (Feldman 2004: 40). Again, assuming there is no pain or harm involved for him or others (maybe including the swine), Porky would lead a life that is *valuable to him*. But most would find that conclusion repugnant. This argument is a variant on the depraved person, and a theory of welfare that leads to such a conclusion is deemed unsatisfactory by critics. But as with the 'depraved person', this argument is not as obvious a refutation of hedonism as might at first seem. Both examples concern episodes of low moral value. But in both, the individual involved enjoys them. In consequence, much of the criticism in the examples is motivated from a conflation of scales concerning prudential and ethical value. Disentanglement is hard, where morally repugnant cases are involved because our moral intuitions interfere with our assessment of prudential value. Especially in the case of 'worthless' pleasures, Arneson has rightly noted that criticizing preferences for counting blades of grass (or for the hedonist: the pleasures derived from counting blades of grass; the example is from Rawls 1971) is paramount to not taking seriously the subjectivism of the theory of welfare (see Arneson 2006: 17). As long as no harm is done, the subjectivist has to put up with the individual counting blades of grass, or for that matter, with what Porky is doing in the barn. Maybe it is a small price for the subjectivist to pay for the high degree of individual autonomy that can be retained in the theory.

Moreover, Feldman notes that many critics would perhaps also argue that they would never want to swap lives with Porky, even if his welfare was higher than the one they attributed to their own lives at that moment. Would you want to swap lives with Porky, if his lifetime welfare was twice as high as your lifetime welfare was going to be? Or ten times as high? Or would you never exchange lives anyway? Swapping lives with Porky does not only mean that we exchange our economics department for Porky's barn, something we would probably find repugnant, compared to our present situation. Swapping lives with Porky would mean that we would have his wants and enjoy his life circumstances. That is part and parcel of a subjective account of well-being. Taking this into account, would we not be forced to conclude that his (our?) life is going well? I think Feldman is justified in his argument that this is a problem of perspective we are facing when trying to evaluate such a situation. For us, with the specific preferences that we have, such a life is not attractive. But being in Porky's shoes, having his preferences, we would find it attractive. We would have his wants and, again, find this kind of life attractive. Is the argument of worthless pleasures perhaps based on a failure to grasp this perspective? At least, these considerations cast doubt on the alleged strength of the argument from base or worthless pleasures.[74]

Welfare hedonism holds that it is enjoyment in general that is the bearer of intrinsic value. The pleasure of the sadist or the 'worthless' pleasures of Porky are considered problematic because of their morally questionable source. They are considered base because the activity that initiated them might have violated someone's rights or our moral or social norms. But the point that some *ways* of achieving pleasure are morally repugnant does not constitute a refutation of the position that pleasure is what is intrinsically valuable. Therefore the distinction between the nature and sources of welfare makes clear that a moral filter should operate on the level of sources of welfare. A naturalistic methodology can further help us understand why some people find pleasure using questionable means. One could argue that to associate pleasure with a morally repugnant activity could indeed have a different moral status, depending on whether the association comes from genetic variance or has been learned. If someone has learned to act immorally, for example via associative learning, removing the association ('extinction' of learned behaviour) can have an effect, whereas this is not the case if genetic variance accounted for such behaviour.[75] The theory presented here thus offers a framework for assessing the moral worth of activities instead of pleasures *per se*, since our capacity for pleasure as well as the innate needs we all share are inborn. This opens the way towards differentiated justifications concerning the permissibility of actions to satisfy these innate needs. Moreover, as these can be separated from acquired wants, a second normative distinction can be made by arguing that acquired wants may be liable to criticism regarding their moral status. Having made the case that 'base pleasures' can still contribute to an individual's well-being, a normatively plausible theory of welfare would reject some sources of welfare or means of satisfaction of wants by virtue of the moral filter. However, I have no intention of gloss-ing over the fundamental difficulty inherent in this argument. If a moral filter does reflect our moral values, taking an evolutionary perspective might be problematic. As has been elaborated in the introduction, the norms that form the basis of the moral filter might change over time and thus make it impos-sible to arrive at some shared concept of welfare that could be the basis for economic policy making.

Clearly, the problem of changing preferences is two-faced. On the one hand, changing preferences can be a problem for the consistent assessment of individual well-being. On the other hand, they are significant for our moral preferences (i.e. our preferences for moral norms). Changing preferences can give rise to changing moral norms (Sartorius 2003). While I have shown that prudential value as reflected in sensory well-being is a relatively stable criterion of the good (we are biologically endowed with the capacity to enjoy the satisfaction of wants via primary reinforcers), the 'moral filter' of a the-ory of welfare probably cannot be assumed to be (very) stable. The problems of changing norms and the moral filter can perhaps best be illustrated by the concept of evaluative well-being. Judging how well my life is going is a matter that seems to be heavily influenced by many different considerations, includ-ing moral norms and biases (this has been discussed in section 5.2 on the perspectival character of judgements regarding how well our lives go accord-ing to our own view). This is an element of relativism in any theory of welfare that is subjective. Our own standards to assess welfare do change.[76] Can this problem be solved? The perspectival and unstable nature of the moral filter, in short: the relativism of the moral filter brought about by changing norms and moral values poses a challenge for every theory of welfare. It can only be solved to the extent that the philosophical problem of moral relativism is solved first. Here we enter the terrain of metaphysics. Do moral values exist? Are they objective or socially constructed? Are they eternal or ephemeral? I do not pretend to have an answer to these questions. Maybe Nussbaum and others are right in asserting that our moral values are shaped by a common *eudaemonia* that goes back to ancient Greece (Nussbaum 2000; Putnam 2002). This might give enough stability to the moral filter or even a measuring rod to talk of moral progress (Putnam 1990). From an evolutionary perspec-tive, the fundamental openness of the moral filter to revision (and perhaps: the possibility of moral progress through learning) should, at any rate, be considered as an attractive feature rather than a deficiency. Taking an opti-mistic position here, one could argue that human cognitive capacity has the potential to improve our moral norms, be it by blind experimentation or by insightful learning from an ever increasing store of non-moral and moral knowledge.

Before concluding this section, some remarks relating to stability of moral norms are in order. Hauser (2006) has made a convincing argument, namely that we have reason to think that humans are genetically endowed with what he calls a 'moral grammar'. Hauser has borrowed this analogy from

Chomsky's work on human language instinct (Chomsky 1986), in which the author has argued that humans are biologically endowed with a universal grammar allowing us to learn a language. The gist of the argument is that while, in an empirically contingent way, we learn the language of the region where we were born, we are already biologically equipped with certain universal principles of language learning that are independent of the concrete language we are actually learning. According to Hauser, the analogy to the case of moral norms is that we are genetically endowed with universal principles, i.e. a moral grammar that puts constraints on the concrete morality we can learn from our environment. Our judgements on what is morally permissible, forbidden or obligatory 'emerge from a universal moral grammar, replete with shared principles and culturally switchable parameters' (Hauser 2006: 43).

Such a 'moral faculty' (Hauser 2006: 36) allows us to make ethical judgements automatically and effortlessly. By virtue of being hard-wired processes, these are features of quadrant 'IV' in our scheme of different types of brain processes (see Table 5.1). Hauser has extensively researched his proposition and let a wide range of experimental subjects decide on moral dilemmas. One conclusion that he draws is that at first we (automatically and instantly) find actions permissible, obligatory or forbidden. Our moral faculty, argues Hauser, then triggers emotions such as guilt or disgust or empathy relating to the instinctive judgements. Only in a conscious and effort-involving stage of rational deliberation do we subsequently find reasons why we feel that these actions are permissible or forbidden. Such deliberate justifications only serve to rationalize our initial moral judgement (Hauser 2006: Ch. 1). According to Hauser's view on morality, our moral norms are thus partly genetically constrained and partly culturally mediated. While genetically fixed principles are the backbone of our moral systems, cultural variation sets the concrete parameters. This might be best illustrated by an example regarding universal concepts of fairness: Henrich et al. (2001) have extensively researched fairness norms in small-scale societies. While judgements of fairness seem to constitute an important universal feature of human morality, the exact parameters of what is considered to be fair vary. In terms of the ultimatum game played in Henrich's study, fairness norms varied from offers of 15 to 50 per cent. If Hauser's conjecture about a moral grammar is right, fairness norms outside the range of 15 to 50 per cent are impossible according to the innate structure of the human moral faculty (Hauser 2006: 83–5).

There are reasons to assume that five main principles might provide the structure of our moral grammar, and these concern harm/care, fairness/ reciprocity, community/loyalty, authority/respect and purity/sanctity (see, more extensively, Haidt and Joseph 2004; Haidt and Graham 2007). All five principles have clear evolutionary roots and can be related to our biology. But their order or the weights, so to speak, that are attached to them, and the trade-offs we make between them, might heavily depend on our cultural background. Based on the findings of a moral grammar, the naturalist has the means to argue that morality is something that can be researched empirically and is not totally arbitrary. Changes in the moral filter of a theory of welfare would be constrained by these principles and the possible parameter ranges. Whether such a 'skeleton of a morality' (Wong 1995: 389) would suffice to narrow down the possibilities for acceptable moral filters of a theory of welfare is open to debate. Proceeding along this way, one could outline a fitting structure for the moral filter of a theory of welfare (e.g. address all the areas mentioned above and include provisions regarding harm, fairness, community, etc). I am aware that more questions are raised in this section than have been answered. However, there are no easy answers to these questions, and they are certainly beyond the scope and focus of this work. My primary aim has been to provide a theory of welfare based on the learning theory of consumption, that is, a theory of the good. In my view, it can be convincingly argued that the notion of sensory well-being is a robust one that draws its stability from primary reinforcers. These tend to produce pleasure since humans are genetically hard-wired to experience them as pleasurable.[77]

5.8 An evolutionary theory of welfare: a summary

Summing up, it can be said that the theory of welfare presented here has established a connection between hedonic experiences and preferences by linking 'sensory well-being' to the satisfaction of the set of innate needs (or the much larger set of acquired wants based on innate needs). Within a naturalistic framework, I have specified the *nature* and *sources* of well-being. Adopting a hedonistic approach towards well-being in conjunction with a material preference specification has produced some promising normative implications. Moreover, the resulting theory is in accordance with findings from the behavioural sciences (and major findings from behavioural and neuro-economics). I have also argued that the particular theory of welfare presented here provides the tools to address the specific challenges that an evolutionary theory of welfare should, in fact, address.

While it does not have the simple charm of the standard (but materially under-specified) notion of welfare as utility (as discussed in section 2.1.2), the reasons have now been made clear why all the various theories of well-being have a grain of truth in them: hedonism captures the idea that humans experience situations or actions as either pleasant or unpleasant and that they seek to experience more pleasant situations (owing to research in the neurosciences we are increasingly better informed about what happens in these situations). The desire accounts 'understand' that a common source of these pleasant experiences is the satisfaction of desires. In the (less subjective) needs account, it is rightly argued that there are shared elements that shape our desires, and although there is some variance, a sizeable basis remains that is common to all humans. As I have claimed, my theoretical framework is predominantly hedonistic though not as subjective as standard varieties of hedonism (see Table 5.4, showing where the theory could be located on our

Table 5.4 A typology of theories of welfare revisited: evolutionary approach

	Welfarist	*Non-Welfarist*
Subjective		
	Hedonism	
	Desire Theories	
	Evolutionary Approach	Capabilities & Functionings
		Basic Needs
Objective		

conceptual map). By incorporating these insights into this new integrative framework and using the naturalistic method, my aim has been to make the connections between the essential elements of the various theories of welfare. By way of enumeration, I summarize the main features of the present theory and their relevance in a welfare-theoretic framework.

(1) In this theory the notion of welfare has been materially specified as opposed to the usual formal specification of the preference satisfaction perspective used in standard (welfare) economics. Opening up the black box of welfare, utility and preference are an important requirement for a naturalistic approach towards welfare. While the satisfaction of wants is an important source of welfare, the error that has been a cause for criticism concerning theories of preference satisfaction (namely mistaking the sources for the nature of welfare; cf. Sumner 1996) has been avoided. This relates also to the difference between this account and the basic needs account, or the capabilities and functionings account, because all these accounts merely stipulate lists of needs or functionings whose fulfilment purportedly increases welfare; but no systematic relationship exists between those sources of welfare and the nature of welfare. It should be noted that the account also has some advantages over the standard utilitarian accounts since it more precisely states the nature of welfare.

(2) The evolutionary theory of welfare qualifies as a connection between the subjective-objective poles of the spectrum of theories of welfare. It satisfies Sumner's conjecture that a defensible theory of welfare cannot lie at the extremes of these poles, as previous debates on theories of welfare have shown (Sumner 2006). The theory is subjective at the level of the (un)pleasant experiences and the adaptation phenomena occurring there as well as at the level of the idiosyncratic learning histories of acquired wants. It is objective at the level of innate needs and learning mechanisms, which are a feature shared by everyone.

(3) Two different notions of well-being have been suggested. It has been shown that sensory well-being is better able to deal with the scepticist objection that the notion of welfare is malleable and changes over time.

By contrast, the assessment of evaluative well-being is very prone to changing values and social norms. The reason is that a moral filter operates comparatively more strongly at the cognitive level of evaluative well-being.

(4) By separating the positive theory of welfare from the moral filter, both problems can be treated separately. The concept of sensory well-being is much more stable and thus constitutes a good basis for welfare assessments. Nevertheless, the moral filter is kept open for revisions in light of new 'moral knowledge', a feature that might even be attractive for an evolutionary theory of welfare. Our social norms and values do not change wholly capriciously, and by and large there is still a connection between the Aristotelian notion of a good life and the notion of a good life of our times (e.g. Sen 1987; Nussbaum 2000; Putnam 2002).

(5) The focus on the satisfaction of wants also addresses the objection regarding the 'commodity fetish' of the basic needs approach (made by Sen 1993a: 40 fn 30). Wants and needs are only indirectly related to commodities, and the theory's focus is much broader. In addition, it has been argued that innate needs should have a higher normative priority than acquired wants.

The focus on actions, or even more generally on distinct temporal intervals, has been brought in as a means to address the qualification (made in the introduction) that processes should matter as opposed to outcomes. Moreover, the theory is evolutionary in that it shifts attention to the dynamics of want and enjoyment changes, which merits an extensive treatment in the next chapter.

6   Evolutionary welfare economics

In the previous chapter, I have put forward my suggestion of a hedonistic theory of welfare based on the idea of understanding well-being in terms of enjoyment linked to the satisfaction of innate needs and learned wants (Witt 2001). One main aim has been to provide a better psychological and biological underpinning of the concept of well-being by turning to the findings of the other behavioural sciences. But the broader-based empirical foundation provided by these naturalistic insights can also be used to normatively discriminate between different sources of well-being and their respective dynamics. By taking an evolutionary perspective, this second important contribution of the present work is tackled in this chapter.

I show in what sense hedonism, rather than a preference satisfaction view, is more desirable in a dynamic setting (section 6.1). Moreover, I discuss to what extent we need a kind of 'normative standard of rationality' in order to be able to normatively distinguish different wants (and preferences) or enjoyments (section 6.2). Following this, I turn to a systematic discussion of possible distinctions of types of wants (and preferences) and enjoyments. Next, I discuss three important dynamic facets of my theory of welfare to elaborate more fully on such distinctions. First, I describe a process perspective of 'enjoyment' and show how this process view alters the focus on making welfare judgements (section 6.3). The foundations laid out in the previous chapters can also be used to understand some dynamics of hedonism, going directly to the layer of enjoyment and suffering: regarding the second facet, in section 6.4, I thus concentrate on welfare dynamics and their possible normative distinction, which relate directly to changes in well-being (e.g. hedonic adaptation effects). The third facet, in section 6.5, concerns welfare dynamics that relate to changing wants. Different types of want change are discussed and normatively distinguished. The two most important phenomena discussed here are a normative evaluation based on different satiation patterns that can be found in innate needs and acquired wants. This complements and extends the discussion of the normative priority of innate needs in the previous chapter. A second distinction is then made on the basis of different forms of learning mechanisms and regarding the way wants are formed through these. Here it is possible to come to a differentiated understanding under what conditions a want is formed 'autonomously'.

6.1 From preferences to enjoyment

In section 2.2.2, we have seen the different kinds of criticisms that were levelled at the preference satisfaction view. I complement these considerations with a discussion of how taking a dynamic perspective brings additional difficulties for a preference satisfaction view. To assess individual well-being in terms of pleasure and pain, one can (in principle) assess the enjoyment felt at each point in time and aggregate these instances for the period under consideration. For example, to assess the impact of an action *A* on enjoyment, one estimates, and adds up, enjoyment for each successive point in time. This could be depicted as in figure 6.1, where the upper line measures the well-being of an individual over time after policy measure or action A. The area between the upper line and the baseline shows the effect on well-being. (For expositional ease, I abstract from measurement, estimation, or knowledge problems.) In a similar fashion, individual well-being could be assessed in terms of preference satisfaction when preferences are assumed to be fixed (one would estimate the degree of preference satisfaction for each point in time and aggregate the estimates). For some policies and purposes, one can reasonably conjecture that preferences will be fixed, remain stable and are unaffected by the policy or action in general. This is probably more so for a shorter time frame. For a long time frame (e.g. an individual's lifetime), this assumption is inadequate. One might now argue that the typical time frame for welfare analysis is neither very short nor as long as an individual's lifetime. While there are areas where a comparatively long time frame is called for, such as in educational or health policies, the usual time frame lies somewhere between these extreme cases. But also for less extended time frames, a preference stability *hypothesis* would have to be justified and not be stipulated *ad hoc*, especially when it is acknowledged that the very policy that is to be assessed can lead to a change in preferences.

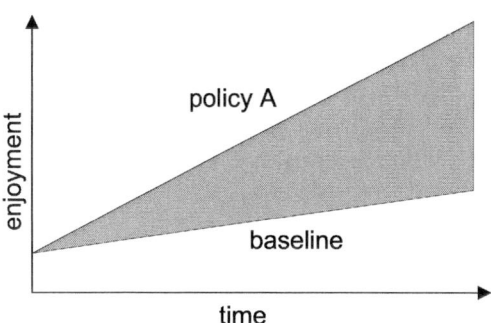

Figure 6.1 Impact of action *A* on enjoyment.

What happens if the stable preference assumption is dropped? In terms of the hedonistic view, nothing changes. It is still conceptually clear how to go about assessing the impact of an action on individual well-being by aggregating enjoyment. If one is to assess individual well-being in terms of preference satisfaction, however, some difficulties arise under a regime of changing preferences, making it conceptually problematic (if not 'unintelligible', cf. Brandt 1979: 251). This is a fundamental and puzzling problem of the preference satisfaction view (see e.g. Brandt 1992: 168–9; Griffin 1986: 16). Consider assessing the impact of action A on individual well-being understood in terms of satisfaction of preferences that change. Which preference set is to be taken as the measuring rod, the old or the new one?

Let us examine this problem in more detail. Imagine the welfare analyst is deliberating at t_0 whether to implement a policy A at t_1 that will last from t_1 to t_2, based on the effect on well-being (in terms of preference satisfaction) of individual i. Under the assumption that preferences may change, for example as a result of the policy's implementation, which preference set is used by the analyst to assess the impact of action A on i? Are individual i's preferences at t_0, at the time when the policy maker deliberates on the policy, taken to reflect i's well-being? Or would it not be more justified to assess A in terms of the preferences of i at t_1, i.e. the time when the policy takes effect? Now consider that action A affects i's preferences in the sense that the policy maker knows that at t_2, i's preferences will have been changed due to A. Would it then not be better to assess A in terms of the preference set of i at t_2, thereby taking into account the effect of A on the preferences?

These points in time have been chosen with reference to action A, but any other point in time could also be a candidate to assess the well-being of i. If we broaden our perspective towards a lifetime view of well-being, why should i's well-being not be measured in terms of the preferences at the end of i's life? Arguably, these preferences will be the most informed preferences that i will ever have, considering that experience accumulates in the course of a lifetime. So why not take this preference set? There seem to be good reasons to argue that i's preferences generally tend to get more informed with time. If it is not going to be the above set, then one might consult i's adult preference set. But which adult set? Brandt has argued similarly, that even i's end-of-life preferences might not be the best contender either to assess i's lifetime well-being. A simple example makes clear that it is not *prima facie* obvious whether these preferences should be privileged (Brandt 1979: 250): consider the elderly lifetime atheist who knows he will die within a week and asks for a priest to be called to his deathbed. So the atheist has changed his preferences. Some would perhaps object that it would seem odd to take the new preference set as the definitive measuring rod, considering that the new preference set has replaced one that had been fairly stable over a long life and changed only recently.

Similarly, it seems individuals rethink their life towards the end more in terms of what they could (or should) have achieved and what they actually leave as a legacy to the world, inducing them to acquire a new and unfulfilled preference for achieving B. If this preference for the achievement of B was not very important during i's entire life but gained in importance during the last few years, would it not be justified to measure lifetime well-being in terms of the preference set that gives high weight to a preference for the achievement of B (practically leading to a decrease in well-being since the preference was not fulfilled at all or only for a short time)? Or would that belittle the well-being the individual has derived earlier from the satisfaction of other, previous preferences? On the other hand, someone aware of the 'insidious social conditioning' effects on preferences might be more inclined to select a preference set during an early period of i's life to assess well-being because this might be less distorted by social conditioning. Since i had these preferences in the past, they could still be satisfied in the present or the future even if i no longer has them. These considerations are intended to show that under a regime of changing preferences, it is no longer *prima facie* clear which preferences should count in the assessment of individual welfare (Sugden 2006a; Griffin 1986: 16). Certainly, some of these suggestions are more easily discarded than others. It would probably be arbitrary to assess preference satisfaction in terms of i's youth or childhood preferences. Early preferences, in particular, might have resulted from a character not yet fully developed (consider evaluating i's life in terms of the preference for becoming a nurse, a fireman or astronaut at the age of six. Most of us would probably consider our lives a failure if assessing it according to such preference sets).

It has been discussed in the previous chapters that preferences can change, and important sets of preferences that change regularly are those related to processes of bodily functioning (see section 5.1). Just as an individual is observed expressing a preference for a food item when hungry (based on a need for nutrition), so the same individual expresses a complementary preference when that individual is satiated (see also section 6.5.1 below). It can be conjectured that many preferences are of a cyclical nature and tend to vary with deprivation levels. Depending on the concrete point in time, an individual's preference set might be substantially different from another set at another time. The most plausible way out of this evaluation question for the defender of preference satisfaction would be to argue that well-being in terms of preference satisfaction is assessed at every moment according to the momentary preference set. But what does that mean? If the welfare analyst aims at identifying the well-being of i in terms of the preference set of each moment, the whole view collapses into some sort of hedonism because the main idea of a particular well-defined preference set is lost. If preference sets are allowed to differ from each other from one moment to the next the reason for satisfying them seems to lie in the momentary enjoyment they bring the individual (Broome 2008). But in that case one could return directly to a hedonistic view. Preference sets that are undefined, ill-behaved and ephemeral could be justifiably abandoned for a conceptually more clear-cut view of well-being as enjoyment.

Another possibility to retain the preference satisfaction view in the face of changing preferences has been adopted in the form of the multiple selves view (e.g. Schelling 1984; Elster 1985; Thaler 1991) or in views that postulate stable meta-preferences (e.g. Frankfurt 1971; Sen 1979c; George 1998). Here preferences are allowed to be different at each point in time (or for any conceivable state), and the individual is assumed to be endowed with a set of meta-preferences that are preferences for preferences.[78] But such suggestions are not entirely convincing. Why should these second-order preferences be any more authoritative than first-order preferences (Anderson 1993: 163)? If we argue that an individual has a set of meta-preferences, we have to ask why these meta-preferences could not change as well. If, for example, one interprets meta-preferences as a sort of global preferences that rank important life choices or whole lives, one still could argue that these meta-preferences could also change, for example through learning about new opportunities or via critical reflection. Additionally, meta-preferences could be susceptible to processes of social conditioning (maybe they have come about by processes of social indoctrination, see Sumner 1996: 168–9, on the infinite regress being involved in such arguments). Thus it would be necessary to give an argument to what extent these meta-preferences are not variable and subject to social conditioning. Moreover, similar to the objection against an 'informed preference view', welfare in terms of meta-preferences is dependent on a substantive notion of the good to make sense of the concept, and removes welfare probably too much from the individuals and what is good for them.[79]

A similar point has to be made about the proposal of 'true preferences' (which are preferences formed with all relevant information, deliberated on with great care in a situation conducive to rational choice, cf. Harsanyi 1982: 55). Arguing that an individual's true preferences are stable over a lifetime and that only the set of actual preferences is distorted, maybe incoherent, and subject to change, seems to be a sleight of hand to avoid the issue. Considering that individuals learn throughout their lifetime, it is completely unclear why true preferences should be stable. A similar point holds for extended preferences for an entire life: it is equally unclear why such preferences should be stable. It has to be added that the informational requirements that are involved in these concepts seem too far removed from actual human cognitive capabilities. Given the cognitive limitations of the human intellect, the assumption of a complete set of extended preferences over all conceivable states is not tenable.

The questionable assumption of a higher stability of meta-preferences extends also to the *prima facie* similar multiple selves views. Here the individual is treated as consisting of multiple selves at different points in time, each self residing in the individual and having a different preference ranking. Opposed to the meta-preference view, where one individual has a ranking of multiple rankings of bundles of goods (i.e. the meta-preference set ranks different preference sets), here each self has a ranking of outcomes (not of preference rankings), and an individual has only one preference set at one point in time. This set can be different at different times, depending on which self is in control (George 2004: 32–3).[80] The multiple selves view interprets this metaphor differently depending on the respective authors: the interpretations are derived from considerations that have been put forward in analogy to interpersonal conflict situations (far-sighted vs. short-sighted selves), as an intrapersonal collective action problem or as a principal-agent problem, where planner and doer diverge in their preference sets (e.g. Schelling 1984; Elster 1985; Thaler 1991).[81] If multiple selves are hypothesized, the question is whether (and when) these are all present and have equal control, or whether there is a struggle for control. In the first case, if all multiple selves have equal control, the welfare economist does not gain much because welfare assessments will be fraught with the well-known problems from social choice theory (e.g. how to aggregate the selves' preferences into one ordering). A consistent aggregation would only be possible with strong assumptions similar to those on the interpersonal comparability of utility. If one allows for these, the whole multiple selves approach becomes obsolete because then one already has an appropriate welfare measuring rod (in the form of comparable utility such as discussed in the previous chapter). If one does not allow for these comparisons, one would be left with a view such as that put forward by Sugden, and the problems associated with it, where individual preferences can be incoherent and unstable (see sections 3.3.1 and 3.3.2).

On the other hand, if one self is favoured and its preferences provide the measuring rod for welfare, it remains to be explained which self is favoured and for what reasons. It is usually argued that the far-sighted ('rational') self is favoured over the short-sighted ('impulsive') self. This could be questioned in itself (Cowen 1991): should weight really be accorded to one's far-sighted preferences versus the short-sighted ones? What of the cases where a short-sighted self liberates itself from the self-constraint imposed by the far-sighted self (consider cases where the individual becomes frustrated and inhibited because the far-sighted self frustrates all impulsive behaviour, at least some expressions of which can be considered welfare-increasing; are the restraining, inhibiting and controlling preferences of the far-sighted self really a more appropriate measuring rod of an individual's welfare?) Moreover, the far-sighted self's preferences (since they are cognitively mediated) might be subject to biases and social conditioning. It is also questionable why, in these types of model, only the far-sighted selves collaborate (and are capable of strategic behaviour), while it is usually not the case that the near-sighted selves work together against the far-sighted ones (showing strategic behaviour). Moreover, and similar to meta-preferences, the far-sighted selves' preferences are often assumed to be more stable in order to be used as a measuring rod. Again, no matter how far-sighted a self is, it just does not seem to be the case that its preferences can easily be assumed to be unchanging. It might also be possible that, at a future point in time, the short-sighted self's preferences have improved through learning but are still constrained by the now less knowledgeable behaviour of a former far-sighted self (George 1998). These remarks show that a substantive theory of the good underlies these multiple selves views, which is often not explicitly acknowledged.

These considerations bring us back full circle to the conceptually clearer measuring rod of enjoyment because it can be argued that neither meta-preferences nor multiple selves views are sufficient to address the problems of preferential change (e.g. through learning); moreover, they come at the cost of an increase in complexity not present in the enjoyment view.[82] These conceptual considerations aside, we ought to be aware of the fact that enjoyment and satisfaction of a preference often coincide, as the satisfaction of a preference is one, if not the most important, source of enjoyment. This overall high correlation between preference satisfaction and enjoyment might also be more pronounced in a practical policy context. Therefore shifting focus from preference to enjoyment does not mean that preferences should be completely ignored or belittled. They can still play an important role in such a framework, not only as source of well-being, but also as something that may (intentionally or otherwise) change as a result of policy intervention. Nevertheless, it is important to note that the shift in focus from preference satisfaction to enjoyment offers the possibility to understand preference satisfaction also to be a means to an end, not as the end itself (Ng 2003).

6.2　Remarks on normative distinctions and a standard of rationality

6.2.1　*A standard of rationality*

Before discussing a typology of normative distinctions in more detail, a 'standard of rationality' is needed for making these distinctions. As this does not concern the descriptive view of how individuals act but the prescriptive side of how they should act, this standard is one of *normative rationality*. Based on such a standard, a theory of welfare specifies what is in the best interest of an individual viz. under what conditions an action can be understood to be in an individual's best interests (usually, and as in the present context, this is discussed with reference to an individual's *self-regarding* interests to avoid complications associated with other-regarding interests). A normative standard of rationality can be understood to instil a more precise meaning into a measuring rod of welfare in the sense that the standard suggests how to act in order to score high in terms of welfare. Such a standard can be used to consistently evaluate different wants or enjoyments regarding their contribution to welfare.

Different normative standards of rationality are possible. The traditional utilitarian calculus evaluates actions in terms of their consequences for utility. On this view, it is rational to choose that action which maximizes utility. In economics, this view has been gradually replaced in favour of a preference satisfaction view. Here it is rational for individuals to choose the action that maximizes the satisfaction of their preferences (without reference to any hedonic experience). But, as has been shown in the previous chapters (see especially section 2.4), other standards of rationality can be applied as well. In the revealed preference view, an action is termed rational when exhibiting internal 'consistency of choice'. Of course, still other standards of rationality are conceivable, for example where these actions count as rational when carried out under conditions of maximal freedom, or when maximizing freedom. These rationality standards are very demanding. To maximize utility or consistently satisfy preferences (obeying the transitivity axiom and having a complete set of preferences over all possible commodity bundles) imposes extreme requirements on the individual in terms of informational capacities and consistency of choice. Findings from behavioural economics have cast doubt on whether individuals come anywhere near such a standard, making it questionable whether such a normative principle is at all useful in guiding behaviour (Chapters 1 and 2): instead of labelling all human behaviour irrational if it consistently violates the above standards, it might be more appropriate to rethink the standard of rationality.

Doing so, one could depart from a standard of rationality that posits maximization and claim that a less demanding ideal could apply. Several possibilities exist: for instance, based on the positive knowledge of how humans behave, one could argue for a less strict normative standard of rationality that would classify an action as rational if it results in a certain amount of well-being, such as being above a certain 'aspiration level'. In that sense it would be normatively rational to 'satisfice' (Simon 1955). Similarly, one could take it to be normatively rational to show 'matching behaviour' (see section 4.5). But other standards are possible as well: Brandt (1979) has linked a standard of rationality for preferences to the idea of 'cognitive psychotherapy' (roughly: deliberating on a preference based on vivid information, in a suitable mindset), calling only those preferences rational that would survive such treatment. Vanberg (2004) argued that rational behaviour is that behaviour that obeys some agreed-on rules. Or a normative notion of rational behaviour could be different for different environments, thus basing the criterion of rationality on the idea of 'ecological rationality' (e.g. Smith 2003; Gigerenzer et al. 1999). These are all conceivable versions of a *normative* notion of rationality.

To be able to distinguish between different types of wants or enjoyments in a systematic fashion, a suitable standard of rationality is thus needed. Based on the insights gained so far, my argument rests on the following two points. First, the hypothesis of motivational hedonism was brought forward, i.e. it was argued that individuals tend – as a behavioural regularity – to strive for enjoyment and to avoid suffering (see Chapters 4 and 5). Second, if we agree further that an individual's well-being depends to a large part (or completely) on enjoyment and the absence of suffering (i.e. if we accept 'welfare hedonism'), it is 'rational' for the individual to attain enjoyment and avoid suffering. This suggestion of enjoyment, as being relevant for normative rationality, is not based on an *a priori* value judgement but on empirical insights as to what motivates individuals and why. On this view, a plausible normative standard of 'rationality' means it is rational for an individual to achieve a favourable net lifetime balance of enjoyment over suffering. Based on this criterion of rationality, one can evaluate preferences and even different kinds of enjoyments in terms of whether they are conducive to this goal. Especially on the basis of our positive knowledge about humans' cognitive capacities, it can be argued that a stricter notion of rationality, which requires an individual to *maximize* lifetime enjoyment, would be too demanding in terms of its informational requirements. Empirical evidence supports the conjecture that a less strict standard is more conducive to an individual's well-being than the attempt to maximize well-being: studies by Schwartz et al. (2002) and Schwartz (2005) have shown that 'maximizers' tend to be less happy than 'satisficers', probably because they engage more often in processes of social comparisons, show higher levels of regret and incur higher costs of information gathering, which are less easily compensated by the resulting enjoyment. These findings support the appeal of a favourable balance of enjoyment as a normative ideal. For the present purpose, we can thus take the rationality postulate of increased lifetime enjoyment as a normative guiding principle ('increased enjoyment principle').

Depending on the concrete evaluative purpose, such a standard of rationality can be constrained in terms of other values if one holds that welfare is only one part of a theory of the good among others (pluralist value view). Subscribing to a modest hedonism view, other important values such as autonomy,[83] freedom, or opportunity could be traded-off against welfare. If, on the other hand, one held a theory of the good that completely equated the good with an individual's welfare, one would have to conceive of these other values as merely instrumental to the good, and autonomous preferences, for example, would only be valued as promoting an individual's good if they increased that individual's well-being.[84]

6.2.2 *Normative distinctions*

Having specified a measuring rod for welfare as well as a criterion of normative rationality, we can turn to the objects of possible normative evaluation and discuss different types of preferences P_i (or wants) and enjoyments E_i.[85] Based on relevant psychological and behavioural knowledge, we are able to examine and normatively distinguish welfare-related phenomena, concerning P_i and E_i. These phenomena can be analyzed along two different dimensions: the first dimension deals with whether the analysis is performed purely formally or whether it is performed with regard to the content of preferences or enjoyments. The second dimension refers to whether the analysis takes into account static or dynamic aspects of P_i and E_i. An example of the former type of analysis would be the *formal* specification of the properties that make a preference addictive or of the formal criteria according to which a preference would count as uninformed. An example for a substantive specification of content has already been given regarding the content of innate needs. As for the latter type of analysis, considering static aspects, this is concerned with identifying structural features of a preference, which lead to a discrepancy between satisfying the preference and an increase in well-being. A prominent example are 'uninformed preferences'. These differ in their structure from other preferences in so far as they are based, for instance, on false beliefs: consequently, their satisfaction does not result in the expected increase in well-being. The analysis considering dynamic aspects, on the other hand, refers to dynamic or temporal characteristics of preferences or enjoyments which warrant a distinction. An example are hedonic adaptation phenomena (relating to enjoyments) or addictive preferences (which exhibit a characteristic intertemporal structure).

The different categories of normative analysis are depicted in Table 6.1. In the following, I discuss them in the order they appear in the table and focus on types of normative analysis that have so far been neglected or could be augmented by infusion of naturalistic insights. Since the last three types of phenomena constitute especially important classes for a subjective hedonistic theory of welfare, I discuss them in separate sections (see section 6.4.1 on hedonic adaptation, 6.5.1 on satiation and 6.5.2 on adaptive preference formation). Before discussing the above-mentioned phenomena, it should be noted that from the point of view of hedonism, the principle of normative individualism (see section 2.1.3) has to be understood not in terms of preferences but of enjoyments, i.e. individuals are understood to be the best judges of their *enjoyment*. This is a departure from the dearly held notion that preferences are taken as given and cannot (should not) be criticized. In a hedonistic welfare framework, preferences have a different status and can very well be seen as instrumental and subject to evaluation. As enjoyment is the basic measuring rod in the suggested framework, enjoyments can only be evaluated in relation to other enjoyments, or in relation to other values that are extrinsic to welfare. An example of the latter case would be to trade off enjoyments against values such as autonomy when arguing, for example, that enjoyments that are non-autonomous should count less towards an individual's welfare.

Table 6.1 Categories of normative analysis (author's exposition)

Phenomenon	Analysis	
	is of type	*is dynamic*
Informational Deficits	formal	
Habits	formal	x
Addictions	formal	x
Hedonic Adaptation	both	x
Satiation Dynamics	both	x
Adaptive Preferences	both	x

This would be a case, where the value of autonomy trumps well-being. Moreover, according to the standard of rationality specified above, a preference can be based on a false belief but still be rational if it leads to higher well-being. One could only justify labelling such a preference as problematic and discounting it in normative reasoning, if one accorded high normative weight to other values (such as truth). However, it can be conjectured that the satisfaction of such types of preferences will also tend to lower enjoyment.

Informational deficits

The first type of normative distinction is related to the information underlying enjoyments or wants (or the preferences they give rise to). These can be the result of mistaken beliefs or false, outdated or otherwise distorted information (e.g. faulty generalizations), or they can be context-dependent, or else biased by framing or similar effects (the behavioural economics literature is full of examples of how preferences are formed, based on simple heuristics and other related processes, see section 2.4 and the literature referenced there). These are the paradigm cases of an 'uninformed preference'. Even for central preferences in an individual's life, we can think of cases where these preferences are fulfilled, although the individual is not better off afterwards (Griffin 1986: 10–11). The structural characteristic of uninformed preferences lies exactly in the discrepancy that exists between their satisfaction and an increase in welfare: uninformed preferences are seen as problematic because their satisfaction does not contribute to welfare. Analogously, an acquired want may be based on a false belief. Consider Tim seeing Alice being praised for an action. But suppose that Tim wrongly infers that this action led to the praise (maybe it was only one of a series, and only performing all of the actions led to the praise). Via imitational learning, Tim might acquire a want for such an action. Tim would then have acquired this want via imitational learning based on false beliefs. Note, however, that Tim might lose the want in the future when he performs this action to satisfy his want and is not reinforced (no pleasurable experiences result). Another instance of a preference based on false beliefs would be the lack of knowledge of satiation patterns of wants. Tim could form a want that cannot be easily satisfied (or not satisfied at all). Had Tim known of the futility of his future endeavours to ever satisfy that want, he might not have developed it. Such a want is based on lack of information. (The picture is more complex if, despite this information, Tim chooses to acquire an insatiable want.)

Informational deficits are also problematic when they concern an individual not considering future wants or enjoyments. The difficulty of future preferences, and how to reflect them in a welfare calculus, has already been discussed, but this also extends to the enjoyment view: if individuals do not take into account changing preferences due to future changes in their enjoyments, they might also be tempted to choose an action in the present that does not increase their lifetime enjoyment. The question then is whether

it might be possible to make 'educated guesses' on potential future preferences and enjoyments and how they might affect an individual's actions.
To what extent is it possible for individuals to incorporate the positive
knowledge on such mispredictions into their deliberations? This is not a
trivial matter, and will be taken up later when I discuss evidence on how
individuals systematically mispredict their future enjoyments (see section 6.3).
It might be even more difficult to try and predict future preference changes
or associated satiation patterns. Critics rightly point out that the informational requirement of taking into account future desires poses a difficulty
for the preference satisfaction account because such a requirement would
demand truly Herculean capacities of an individual (Sobel 1994; Rosati 1995;
Qizilbash 2006).

   Arising from this is the question as to what should count as a reasonable
informational requirement. Obviously, one would need the right kind of
information to be able to assess one's interests. The most demanding criteria
require that preferences be based on true beliefs and complete information.
These are highly susceptible to the above-mentioned critique of requiring
Herculean cognitive capacities on the part of an individual. A less demanding criterion was suggested by Griffin, who proposed to call a preference
informed if it advances one's life plans, and further information would not
alter that preference (Griffin 1986: 13). This seems to link the informational
requirement to a person's interests as well as limit the amount of information
required to call it informed. One can conceive of this as a consistency test:
if new information does not change a given preference, it can count as
informed. However, the requirement is still a formal one: given sufficient
knowledge, some wants would be absent, while others would be acquired.
This leaves open how such a criterion would be operationalized or used.
Even as a hypothetical device, it is difficult to make sense of it (Sobel 1994;
Rosati 1995). Conditions relating to the state of mind of an individual who
is forming a preference, or that relate to the form in which information is
presented, are less demanding. One could thus argue that information should
be 'de-biased', delivered and assessed in a cool state of mind, in which no
emotions or 'visceral factors' distort deliberations (Loewenstein 1996). Of
course, even these fairly mild requirements entail the likely objection that
even the framing of options, or the 'de-biasing' of information, constitutes an
intervention in an individual's autonomy and thus a form of paternalism,
albeit a moderate one (although defenders of 'libertarian paternalism' would
hold that there is no decrease in autonomy involved in cases where information is framed or default options are specified in a certain way, see, e.g. Thaler
and Sunstein 2003). This is not debated here; but the objection is slightly
beside the point in the present context. In terms of *welfare*, such a procedure
would be beneficial to the individual. It is clear that there are trade-offs
between welfare and autonomy involved in this case, but they are neglected
here, as they should not be the primary concern in a discussion of how to
assess an individual's *welfare*.[86]

With respect to some preferences, one could also argue that their being rooted in experience can be taken as a criterion that they are suitably informed (Elster 1983). But does an informed preference always presuppose experience? This seems plausible for cases where, for example, one acquires a preference for good wines through educating oneself to taste the subtleties of such wines. Without such experiential learning, one would probably never acquire a taste for a good Château Lafite-Rothschild or an otherwise complex wine. As Griffin (1986: 10–12) points out, to be fully informed, one often needs not only the information itself but the history of previous informational states in order to be able to appreciate the information. An individual's informed preference in such a case might be for the Château Lafite-Rothschild instead of a cheap supermarket wine, but only if the individual has a learning history regarding wine preferences. Without such experiential learning, the individual would not be better off even if the 'informed preference' was satisfied. Such an individual would probably not be in a position to understand why this preference should count as 'informed'. But in what sense does this experiential requirement hold for all preferences? Would one, for example, regard a preference relating to drugs such as heroin as fully informed only if one had experienced their consumption (for example, preferring consumption of peanuts to that of heroin)? Whether such a requirement is tenable seems questionable, at least in such extreme cases. A different case concerns childhood preferences, which are largely acquired through associative learning (Zajonc and Markus 1982). Many preferences are acquired in this way, but having acquired them (via experience) does not imply that one has reflected on them or is even aware of their existence. To call such preferences 'informed' seems inappropriate. Similarly, preferences acquired via imitational learning can be considered informed only if an individual can adequately empathize with the role model's situation. This concerns large classes of preferences that are acquired based on 'second-hand information' (and implicitly on conjectures about the role model's situation). Overall, the human capacity for empathy probably limits the idealization one can project onto an informational criterion. If we were aware of our limited cognitive and empathic capacities, there would be – as with the considerations on a normative standard of rationality above – no point in demanding an idealized situation in which an individual can completely identify with whatever situation.

It is clear that one needs to define an informational requirement carefully, maybe even depending on the type of preference. Moreover, information can be useful, but does not necessarily have to be. In the last chapter, we 'met' Tim, the travelling salesman, who was deceived by his wife, friends and colleagues. In his case, is more information really leading to higher welfare (which was ultimately the idea of better informed preferences)? Probably not. Welfare and preference are dissociated, and more information is not a sufficient criterion for bringing the two together.[87] Based on a naturalistic understanding and the discussion so far, my proposal to differentiate between wants in terms of their degree of informedness is along the following lines: more promising than the above-mentioned formal requirements would be an informational requirement that specifies the conditions under which preference change can lead to comparatively more informed preferences. Regarding wants and their degrees of deprivation, one could consider a change of wants triggered in a state of high or of extremely low deprivation (i.e. satiation) as leading to potentially less informed wants because, in these states, the individual is prone to affectively misconstruing the future average level of deprivation regarding the underlying want (this is similar to a condition stating that preferences formed in 'hot' emotional states are potentially less informed than those resulting from reflections in a 'colder' state, cf. Loewenstein 1996). One could, moreover, demand that the individual be aware of forming a preference. Wants formed via 'associative learning' can be the result of an unconscious process, i.e. the individual is not aware of forming them. The learning mechanism involved in forming the preference can thus give a first hint whether the latter is informed or not: one could require that a want be acquired via 'insightful learning' (see section 6.5.2 and Hergenhahn and Olson 1997) so that an individual is at least aware of being in the process of acquiring it.

An informational requirement of this type puts a value on correct information leading to a want and thus seems more attractive than the overly strict requirements of full information or truthfulness. We could label the suggested situational requirement as a 'conducive condition', tending to promote the formation (or change) of a preference that is (by tendency) reasonably informed. Of course, in terms of a purely hedonistic value framework, a preference would count as informed when its satisfaction leads to the anticipated enjoyment. Nevertheless, in such a framework, the information problem extends to the question whether an enjoyment is sufficiently informed. This could encompass the delusional enjoyments of Tim, the misled salesman (whose pleasure results from his failure to grasp the true situation). While one could understand the connection of pleasures to the satisfaction of wants to be a further minimal experience requirement (noting, however, that Tim's delusional enjoyments could well satisfy some of his wants), this would not encompass cases where enjoyments adapt over time (see section 6.5.2), or where an enjoyment is sought out that leads to an insatiable preference (see section 6.5.1).

A moderate informational requirement for a normative distinction of enjoyments could similarly be conceived in terms of 'conducive conditions': given that an individual is aware of the generic adaptation and satiation effects of an enjoyment over time, and that the same individual has contemplated the enjoyment in a non-deprived and non-satiated (middle-range) state of his organism, then that individual's seeking the enjoyment should be considered informed. But even these attempts at normatively distinguishing between enjoyments in terms of their informational status can be prone to limit an individual's 'enjoyment sovereignty'. In particular, informational requirements that are stronger than the specification of 'conducive conditions' are unattractive because they tend to detract from an individual's sovereignty: for example, if one required that only wants based on true beliefs count normatively, one would adopt the point of view of an external observer with perfect knowledge. Who is to decide on the truth of the information? When criticizing preferences based on informedness, there is a clear trade-off between the degree to which one is judge of one's own well-being and the epistemological status involved in making that assessment. I submit therefore that informational requirements going beyond specifying conditions under which a preference should be formed would limit an individual's authority too much and diminish the *prima facie* appeal of a subjective account of welfare. On the other hand, purely formal requirements, such as the ones discussed above, are of limited use as they cannot be operationalized.

Habits

The second phenomenon to be discussed shifts our focus towards an intertemporal analysis: habitual preferences (as e.g. modelled by von Weizsaecker, see section 3.1.2) are preferences that depend on an individual's past consumption patterns (Pollak 1970; Naik and Moore 1996). Most often, habitual preferences are modelled similar to addictive preferences (e.g. Pollak 1976) and thus diverge from the common sense use of a habit, where an action is performed without much deliberation and probably often without bringing much enjoyment. Habitual preferences can also overlap with adaptive preferences if they were formed through socialization or cultural transmission processes (Brandt 1979). They can thus reflect a preference formation process that is either uninformed or non-autonomous. More in line with the common sense definition of a habit, habitual preferences can also be analyzed in terms of an informational deficit that hinders preference change because it might be conjectured that some habitual preferences would change if the habit was critically deliberated on. In this vein, they could be characterized as having been formed in the past without much deliberation and were kept over time, or were once formed deliberately but no longer thought about, their satisfaction becoming a ritual. In this case, the evaluation of habitual preferences in terms of enjoyment is not problematic. The preference for an activity that once brought a certain amount of enjoyment could serve as an example. If an activity brings no enjoyment but is still carried out to satisfy the preference for the purpose of enjoyment, an assessment is straightforward. If, over time, the enjoyment has decreased due to adaptation to stimulus repetition, the matter of a 'habitual preference' has to be assessed according to criteria pertaining to adaptive enjoyments: the problem lies not so much in the preference as in the underlying enjoyment structure.

The idea that habitual preferences should perhaps not serve as a basis for social welfare assessments if the habit is due to lack of imagination or reflection has already been expressed by von Weizsaecker (1971), who suggests an important role for the education of preferences in such cases. Nevertheless, if a social planner tried to fathom the long-run preferences (or the meta-preferences) of individuals, i.e. the preferences a process of habit formation would lead to, then the difficulties discussed above would ensue: one would have to outguess the process of preference change. It seems that in such cases, a preference satisfaction view reaches its limits, whereas it might turn out to be less complicated to estimate effects on enjoyment especially in terms of its most prominent sources such as the satisfaction of innate needs.

Addictions

'Addictive preferences' are another class of preferences that could be labelled as problematic. Similar to habitual preferences, the structure of addictive preferences is such that past consumption has an influence on present consumption, in the sense that an increase in past consumption leads to an increase in present consumption. Depending on the definition of an addictive preference (see e.g. Stigler and Becker 1977; Becker and Murphy 1988; Robinson and Berridge 1993; Bernheim and Rangel 2004; Gul and Pesendorfer 2007), such preferences can be characterized by the following features: a consumption that provides initially high levels of utility; a withdrawal that causes suffering; a tolerance to higher consumption doses. The dynamics of such preference formation is assumed such that, while the marginal utility of consuming the addictive good is increasing, a stock of harmful 'consumption capital' ('tolerance') is built up at the same time. This decreases the overall utility from consumption of more units of the addictive good (e.g. Becker and Murphy 1988). In their theory of *rational* addiction, Becker and Murphy (1988) go so far as to argue that one becomes addicted rationally: one decides on getting addicted as a result of a utility maximization calculus. Moreover, the authors argue that there exist some beneficial addictions such as classical music: one has to learn to appreciate classical music, and with increased consumption, one experiences an increased benefit from it (increasing marginal utility) so that, therefore, classical music is addictive (however, no tolerance is developed in this case). This idea of beneficial addiction has to be considered as part of Becker's larger programme of his theory of household production and idea of the production of consumption capital.

While the notion of rational addiction is popular in economics (see e.g. Andersson et al. 2006), insights from psychology and neurosciences prompt some scepticism (Robinson and Berridge 1993; Berridge 1999): findings of the behavioural sciences suggest that addictive processes work differently than stipulated in Becker's theory. Indeed, in the case of harmful addictions, it has been established that addicts do not experience increased utility from consumption doses, or at least the resulting well-being (liking) does not reflect the intensity of preference (wanting). In a framework where preferences are inferred from actions and are identified with welfare, this subtle dissociation must remain invisible (because intense craving is equated with intense well-being). But what largely happens in addiction is a 'sensitization' of wanting, not liking (the intensity of the preference increases without proportionately increasing well-being if that preference is satisfied).[88] That means, the craving for a drug is much stronger than the pleasure resulting from its consumption. It has been shown that even very small doses of a drug administered to experimental subjects without their knowledge motivated them to work to obtain higher doses (of the apparently neutral liquid), while their pleasure rating remained neutral (Berridge 1999: 542). These addicted individuals showed high levels of wanting which were disproportionately higher than one would have expected in terms of the resulting reward derived by the drug. Robinson and Berridge (1993) have provided evidence that the intensity of wanting in these circumstances is even higher than could be explained by the pleasure resulting from drug consumption or the removal of pain associated with withdrawal.[89] By contrast, in the so-called 'beneficial addictions', Becker and Murphy describe a sensitization of liking. Listening to classical music or deriving pleasure from high-quality wines are activities that result in increased marginal utility as one learns to appreciate the features of particular goods, learning to take pleasure in them. Such refinement of enjoyments is not problematic for the assessment of welfare, however. Welfare is represented correctly, and such cases can even be labelled as desirable. There is also a neurological difference between both phenomena, because in the case of harmful addictions, processes of sensitization modify the brain's dopamine system in ways that differ vastly from the acquisition of a normal preference for, say, classical music (Robinson and Berridge 2001).[90] It would therefore be misguided to conceive of addictive preferences in the way argued by Becker and Murphy (1988).

Addictive preferences could be given less normative weight for the following reasons: First, as opposed to other preferences, their withdrawal causes suffering. Second, as opposed to non-addictive preferences, and resulting from an increased discrepancy between wanting and liking, the resultant satisfaction does not stand in proportion to the craving as is the case with a standard preference (where welfare and intensity of preference coincide). Finally, as opposed to normal preferences, and due to increased sensitization, other activities are crowded out, which turns out to be welfare decreasing as well (Herrnstein 1990a: 365).[91] Having thus paved the way in terms of a general discussion how to normatively distinguish wants and enjoyments, I now embark on a closer analysis of three dynamic facets of my theory of welfare. The first is the description of a process view of well-being, where I show how this process perspective alters the focus when making welfare judgements.

6.3 A process view of well-being

6.3.1 Well-being as process of 'enjoyment'

Adding a time dimension to the welfare calculus opens up a different, process perspective on well-being: if enjoyment is a process that happens over time, and if different components work together in that process, it is important to understand their interrelationship. In a static calculus, well-being is associated with an outcome so that when an individual faces a decision task, the decision is made based on an estimate of the well-being associated with the future outcome of that decision. Introducing a time dimension, there is not one measure of well-being that is associated with an outcome; depending on the concrete stage of the individual's process of enjoyment, well-being is experienced differently. During the temporal episode, the individual experiences enjoyment as a continuous flow of instant utilities. Looking back at the episode, the individual remembers this flow in way that differs from the continuous evaluation (see sections 5.1 and 5.2). And looking ahead, an individual predicts the utility of an action or temporal episode based on the memory of previous similar episodes (using remembered utility as a basis for the estimate) or on some other cognitive steps, which are the focus of this section. This forward-looking utility estimate is important because preferences an individual might state or reveal in behaviour will be based on it, for example in the context of cost–benefit analyses for different policy measures. From a hedonistic perspective, the question arises whether individual estimates of future well-being (predicted utility) would be a welfare measure that reflects actual individual well-being more accurately than stated preferences.

In order to decide on this issue, it is helpful to develop a process view of enjoyment and discuss empirical evidence on individual estimates of future enjoyment. The three different concepts of well-being, corresponding to past, present and future well-being can be conceptually distinguished as three different stages of an overall process view of enjoyment.[92] During all three stages, different psychological processes occur (Mitchell et al. 1997: 426). I have already discussed the idea of 'enjoyment' as instant utility: it is the core of my concept of 'sensory well-being' and constitutes the 'present stage' of the process view, where behaviour is executed and the individual experiences the stream of utility associated with that behaviour. In the backward-looking 'past stage', an individual retrospectively assesses an episode or an action and evaluates it (in terms of remembered utility; see sections 5.1 and 5.2). The memory of enjoyment can be one basic ingredient of the future evaluation of actions by the individual. Besides these stages of the process of enjoyment, the forward-looking part, i.e. the 'future stage', concerns the individual planning a future action, making a decision, or forming a preference, influenced by previous experience with an action (or knowledge of similar actions as well as other relevant information). A relevant concept is an individual's predicted utility, which can be based *inter alia* on factors such as the remembered utility of previous similar episodes (Kahneman et al. 1997).

In the previous section, I have highlighted the possibility of informational deficits that may lead to a discrepancy between preference satisfaction and enjoyment. These pose a problem in the preference satisfaction view when the welfare analyst elicits individuals' preferences. Shifting emphasis from preference towards well-being, the question arises whether individuals are better at estimating their future well-being rather than their future preferences and preference satisfaction. If enjoyment is the measuring rod for welfare, and forecasts of future liking are distorted, problems may arise similar to those encountered with the preference satisfaction view. For example, if one's preference for buying an expensive, luxurious car is based on an affective forecast that overestimates the enjoyment one gets out of driving such a car (neglecting that one gets used to driving one very quickly), then the purchase of it will only partly satisfy the new preference. Many important life decisions, not only concerning expensive durable goods such as cars and houses, are based on individuals' forecasts of the resulting enjoyment. A systematic misprediction will thus have important consequences for individual well-being. In the next subsection, I therefore discuss empirical evidence relevant to such mispredictions. This discussion can be seen as an instance of how our positive knowledge of what we like can inform our understanding of why some preferences do not lead to increased well-being. But it can also provide a justification for not basing welfare judgements on predicted utility in concrete policy contexts.

Let us briefly look at some distortions occurring when an individual anticipates future affect, i.e. future utility. Under the label of 'affective forecasting', several phenomena have been shown to be influential in determining an individual's future affect (Wilson and Gilbert 2003). And this prediction is made in a biased way, misrepresenting the enjoyment that is subsequently experienced during an episode. More generally, affective forecasting can be biased in terms of its different components: the forecast can be misspecified in terms of the valence of a future episode (i.e. something positive is predicted to be of negative valence or vice versa), it can be misspecified in terms of wrongly attributed emotions (e.g. one expects to experience fear but experiences anger instead), or the prediction can be wrong regarding the intensity or duration of the affective experience. Such a biased specification of intensity and duration has been called 'impact bias' (Wilson and Gilbert 2003). The causes of impact bias and the resultant faulty affective forecasting are manifold and lie in the peculiar way in which the human cognitive apparatus works. They may contribute to individuals basing their actions or preferences on distorted information. The literature has identified the following causes as contributing to impact bias: the first and most straightforward cause is incorrect information, be it lack of information or distorted information due to framing effects or biases in information processing. If individuals base their affective forecast on a wrong construction of reality, the affective prediction can be inaccurate. Such misconstructions can occur because an individual has never experienced a relevant situation and bases the forecast on untypical examples or seemingly similar situations. One can easily think of how one forms expectations of events one has not yet experienced, based on information that is not accurate: consider events such as marriage, childbirth or becoming tenured (e.g. imagining childbirth and holding a child in one's arms after birth, but not thinking of the phase of being in labour, cf. Gilbert et al. 2002; Wilson and Gilbert 2003).

Such a wrong construction of reality can also result from relying on lay theories of enjoyment, when an individual predicts own future needs or future states of deprivation based on a lack of knowledge of adaptation or satiation processes (Kahneman and Snell 1992; Loewenstein and Schkade 1999). For example, individuals seem to overestimate the diversity of dishes they may want to consume (Read and Loewenstein 1995). Even if taking these factors into account, individuals might not correct their estimate accordingly, though (Kahneman and Snell 1992; Gilbert et al. 2002). Besides such misspecifications, individuals often tend to focus on just one, special aspect of an episode or action. So-called 'focalism' was found in a study, where individuals were asked about the impact of a tenure decision on their well-being. They neglected the importance of other events happening concomitantly and thus overestimated the impact of a possibly negative tenure decision on their well-being (Wilson et al. 2000). Similarly, neglecting other aspects of the same episode or action can also misinform the affective forecast. Attention processes play a strong role here, focusing the individual on the more salient or even random aspects of an episode, depending on a variety of external factors (including most prominently the effects of current weather on mood).

Expectation effects can also be misleading (Wilson and Gilbert 2003): if individuals already have a normative expectation about a future event, they would focus their attention on aspects related to the expectation. As a result, the forecast is biased in terms of the expectation. It has been found that individuals seem to have a 'rosy view' regarding life events that are generally seen as positive, such as holidays: these or similar occasions are more positively predicted and remembered than actually experienced (Mitchell et al. 1997). The authors speculate that the congruence between anticipation and memory be the result of a consistency effect: one wants to have congruence between what one anticipated and how one remembers an event. A distortedly high anticipation of these events might even lead to an actual experience that is negative, that is, when anticipation was so irrealistically high that no actual experience could live up to it. Similar to these misconstructions of reality, which constitute a failure to properly represent an episode cognitively, is the case of a wrong prediction of the affective component of a future episode, for example when an individual mispredicts that some event will be pleasurable but it turns out to be painful (Wilson and Gilbert 2003). Furthermore, at the moment of predicting future affective states, our own affective states seem to play an important role in influencing the forecast. If deprivation is high enough, 'visceral factors', such as being deprived in terms of needs satisfaction or emotional influences, seem to have overriding influences on decisions (Loewenstein 1996). In the extreme, this can lead to decisions that are not deliberate (sleep deprivation is an example: an individual does not 'decide' to fall asleep at the wheel). Visceral influences on our behaviour can result in decisions that do not contribute to an increase of our long-term enjoyment. A certain class of behavioural differences has been identified by Loewenstein as decisions that are made in a 'hot' visceral condition (being deprived, e.g. due to being hungry or sexually aroused) and fail to take into account that the subsequent condition of the individual will be 'cold'. This effect also works in the opposite direction, for example, when, in a 'cold' state, we fail to take into account that we will be in a 'hot' state later. These failures to properly account for future visceral states constitute an 'empathy gap': individuals fail to empathize with (or imagine) their future selves' needs and wants, leading to a discrepancy between predicted and experienced utility (see also Read and Leeuwen 1998).

While some of the mechanisms mentioned so far are the result of an individual's unconscious attempt at sense-making, there are other mechanisms for sense-making in the face of adverse events. When such events happen, individuals tend to rationalize them, using self-affirming biases or positive illusions, or reducing cognitive dissonance to cope with them. This happens largely unconsciously and operates, as Gilbert et al. (1998) suggest, analogously to our physical immune system (the authors call these processes 'immune neglect'). While these mechanisms are beneficial for well-being, they also influence affective forecasting and contribute to impact bias. This can happen when individuals have to assess the impact of an accident on their future well-being. Another relevant aspect of the way our psychological immune system works in this respect concerns the reversibility of decisions (Gilbert et al. 1998; Gilbert and Ebert 2002; Wilson and Gilbert 2005). One could argue that it is always better to be able to reverse a decision, for example to buy a car or an expensive laptop, as this option increases our opportunity set. But findings in connection with immune neglect suggest that an individual's well-being is often positively influenced if an important decision is non-reversible because, if the individual knows of the impossibility of reversing a decision, unconscious mechanisms set in, helping that individual to accept and cope with that decision. In terms of a biological explanation, this means the individual does not waste more energy on a situation that cannot be changed anyway (Gilbert et al. 1998). In the above example, the individual would thus look at the positive aspects and ignore the negative aspects of buying a car.

The causes of impact bias and the resultant faulty affective forecasting have been demonstrated experimentally in many different settings, going beyond the examples given here (see especially the literature in Wilson and Gilbert 2003). The mechanisms giving rise to discrepancies between prediction and actual experience are 'normal' in the sense that they are part and parcel of an individual's cognitive functioning. Apparently, individuals do not easily correct for their faulty forecasting through experiential learning. As Loewenstein and Schkade (1999: 99) argue, there are impeding factors that effectively forestall such learning, namely conformity bias (the tendency to focus attention only on information that confirms an individual's intuitive theories of how the world works), systematically distorted memories of pleasant experiences, and the need for repetition to learn from experience (many situations are repeated involving some dimensions that differ from the initial experience and are thus sufficiently different to make such learning more difficult). Knowledge about the process perspective of enjoyment and individual mispredictions of future affect can be accounted for in a normative context.

6.3.2 Normative aspects of a process view

A process view on well-being emphasizes the differences with which individuals assess their well-being at different points in time. This leads to the difficulty of deciding which of these welfare measures should be considered the best measuring rod for individual well-being, i.e. which of them best captures individual well-being, or whether all should play a role in assessing well-being. The latter has been suggested by Dolan and White (2006) and could be called a 'piecemeal approach': the authors argue that, depending on a concrete policy or welfare exercise, any of the above standards (i.e. expected utility, experienced utility, remembered utility) might be appropriate. This is (implicitly) justified by virtue of the different information included in the different stages and a postulated general impossibility to specify one general 'indicator' of well-being.

The piecemeal approach has two deficiencies, however. First, the authors treat the above standards as 'mere' indicators of well-being. That is, they assume that there is some unspecified concept of well-being that underlies these notions, but which they do not explore further. If one considers the above standards as *indicators* of well-being, it is left under-specified what well-being consists of at a deeper level. This is unsatisfying from a theoretical perspective (see also section 2.1.3). How these indicators would interact can only be explained with reference to the underlying structure. Stopping at the level of indicators leaves open a crucial question. A second objection is of greater concern for practical purposes. If all concepts are to be used as indicative of well-being, it is not at all clear in what cases each indicator would be appropriate. The authors advocate the use of the information of all stages for policy purposes. For elucidation, Dolan and White (2006) apply their reasoning to health economics (examining well-being related to loss of vision). In their example, they discuss relevant well-being information that corresponds to the different stages. But despite claiming that different weight can be given to different stages depending on the concrete policy context, the authors fail to show how this can be done in the concrete example at hand. For this or a similar policy measure, all of the indicators could deliver different and conflicting estimates of well-being. So which one should be chosen? The one yielding the highest welfare gain? Or the one which is most easily elicited? Or perhaps the one that suits the policy maker best? Arguing for the value of all these welfare measures neglects the issue where to put normative weight at all and makes the whole approach open to manipulation in an unnecessary way.

The positive knowledge discussed so far sheds some light on the issue between an 'ex ante' or 'ex post' approach to welfare economics. I have already argued that the relevant concept for assessing welfare has to lie on the level of 'liking', not on a forward-looking concept related to 'wanting' (see section 5.1). Apart from a few proponents (viz. Camerer et al. 2005; Ng 2003), such a view is quite controversial in welfare economics. The common view is that an individual's stated preference is what is normatively relevant in this context. That is, the actual forward-looking preference would be used as the basis to decide on policies. This view is known as the *ex ante* view because it takes into account the preference and information that an individual has before a policy is implemented (Harris and Olewiler 1979; Hammond 1983). In the context of a hedonistic notion of well-being, using forward-looking predicted utility as a relevant measure of welfare would suffer from similar problems as a preference-based approach, namely a divergence between the estimated well-being and the actual well-being. When ranking uncertain outcomes, according to standard *ex ante* welfare economics, it is the individual's subjective probabilities concerning the occurrence of an outcome that are to be taken into account. Hausman and McPherson (1994) give an example of implementing a plant location policy involving a chemical plant in a certain region, the waste of which may pollute a river and cause cancer in the occupants of the region downstream. An *ex ante* view could take housing prices from a region with a similar plant and compare them with the prices in a region where there is no such a plant. From these, one would infer individual preferences, taking into account only the information of the individual regarding possible welfare effects. Of course, the *ex ante* view could also be expressed in terms of predicted future enjoyment (affect) rather than in terms of predicted preference satisfaction. But if one assesses welfare in terms of enjoyment, our positive knowledge of individuals misconstruing their future liking suggests that the *ex ante* view is problematic.

The opposite view is an *ex post* view, arguing that a relevant calculus should take into account the *ex post* information of a policy measure (naturally, in the *ex post* view, too, this information is used *before* the policy is implemented). This view would advocate taking into account an individual's updated beliefs, i.e. the information that an individual would have after the policy was implemented. This has usually been discussed solely with regard to beliefs, for example in terms of the subjective probabilities that an individual would attach to different uncertain outcomes resulting from a policy.[93] For example, one could let experts ascertain the probability of contracting cancer and try to estimate the individual cost caused by cancer in order to evaluate the policy. In this example, the ignorance of individuals living near such a chemical plant could lead to a very different estimate between the *ex ante* and the *ex post* welfare impact of the plant location policy (the *ex ante* welfare impact could be estimated lower, due to ignorance, or higher if activist campaigns stir up irrational fears). It has already been pointed out by Hausman and McPherson (1994) that information and desire (belief and preference) cannot be neatly separated. For example, with updated information on the probability of outcomes, an individual's preference might be different from the *ex ante* preference (it could be based on a scientific estimate or, for instance on the activist campaign information). As the authors state, this entanglement puts doubt on whether an individual's predicted preference satisfaction or predicted enjoyment should be taken as the basis of a welfare calculus. In both cases, estimates of a future event by an individual are systematically distorted.[94]

According to the empirical evidence discussed so far, there is no reason to assume that predicted enjoyment is a good estimator of actual enjoyment. Therefore the welfare economist should be interested in an individual's actual welfare that is conceived as accurately as possible. This is also what the *ex post* school of welfare economics seems to have in mind when trying to infer individuals' preferences from more objective information regarding beliefs and probabilities (Hausman and McPherson 1994; Broome 1991b: Ch. 7). In terms of the above distinction, impact bias and faulty affective forecasting constitute a case where relevant information is lacking to the extent that it gives rise to a preference (want) that might not have been formed, had the individual known of the working of the bias and taken the distortion into account. But since in some cases, even the knowledge of this bias does nothing to offset the effect, faulty affective forecasting is more than a mere informational deficit (Wilson and Gilbert 2003: 393–6). The economic consequences of such mispredictions of future affect have been analyzed by Frey and Stutzer (2004) in the context of commuting decisions, where individuals' commuting decisions are based on wrong predictions of future utility and overstate the increased utility from higher income as opposed to more leisure time via less commuting. Positive insights into how future enjoyment is mispredicted could be used to inform individuals of these distortions such that they can take them into account when deliberating on policies. This information could be used as input in a public deliberation process (in the spirit of Habermas 1987; Rawls 1971) as relevant information for the individual to arrive at more accurate estimates of future enjoyment. These could then be used by the welfare analyst. 'De-biasing' individuals' affective forecasts can be conjectured to lead to individuals basing their decisions on estimates of their actual future enjoyment, not on their predicted utility. However, if Loewenstein and Schkade (1999: 99) are correct in hypothesizing that individuals cannot easily correct their faulty forecasting through experiential learning, there might be limits to the strategy of de-biasing estimates.

If the basis for an *ex post* approach to welfare is actual enjoyment, the welfare analyst (in a practical context) could also take the positive insights discussed above directly into account. But such an approach might draw criticism on the grounds of promoting paternalism. While I cannot go here into a full-fledged discussion of the issue of paternalism, some remarks are in order. Most importantly, there is a difference between being theoretically interested in an individual's 'true' well-being as opposed to distorted versions such as '(mis)predicted utility'. Questions of whether a social planner does in fact have better information on individuals' welfare or is interested in really promoting individual welfare require rigorous discussion in order to decide on whether actual policy should use this information (some authors seem a little quicker in advocating the 'laundering' of distorted preferences, cf. Adler and Posner 2006). However, informing the participants of a policy deliberation process about possible distortions constitutes a minimal implication that could be made without the risk of constraining an individual's 'enjoyment sovereignty'. Finally, being interested in enjoyment, not preference, does not mean a complete denial of the importance of an individual's preferences. This is even more so when subscribing to a view of welfare that conceives of (the satisfaction of) preferences as the single most important source of welfare (see also Broome 1991b: 162–3). What this section should clarify is the need to theoretically aim for an undistorted estimate of well-being. This aim can probably be achieved only when correcting future predicted enjoyment for all the above effects. The resulting welfare measure is the 'actual enjoyment'.[95] In this section, my argument has therefore been that, from a theoretical point of view, our positive knowledge of a process model of enjoyment prompts us to decide that the relevant measuring rod for welfare is an individual's actual enjoyment (sensory well-being), not an individual's remembered or predicted enjoyment.

6.4 Welfare dynamics relating to hedonism

The analysis of the dynamics of enjoyment, the second facet of my theory, constitutes an important contribution of any evolutionary theory of welfare. On account of the measuring rod of welfare, namely enjoyment, and a standard of normative 'rationality' positing that it is rational for an individual to strive for a more beneficial balance of lifetime enjoyments, we are now able to assess some dynamics of enjoyments and their impact on lifetime well-being. A highly relevant phenomenon I discuss in this section is the process of hedonic adaptation, which 'refers to any action, process, or mechanism that reduces the [hedonic] effects . . . of a constant or repeated stimulus' (Frederick and Loewenstein 1999: 302). Hedonic adaptation[96] plays a role in what I call 'partial welfare dynamics' as well as in 'general welfare dynamics' and can give rise to preference change. By 'partial welfare dynamics', I refer to welfare dynamics of hedonism connected with adaptation phenomena of a single class of enjoyments. These phenomena can, for example, be related to wants (section 6.4.1). 'General welfare dynamics' relate to the 'big picture' of overall enjoyment dynamics (section 6.4.2), which may, of course, consist of several 'partial welfare dynamics'. General welfare dynamics include the evaluation of different welfare development paths (e.g. paths where welfare is continually increasing as opposed to paths that start with a high, but subsequently decreasing, level of welfare) and an explicit introduction of a time dimension into the analysis. In this category belong the kind of dynamics that are often discussed as the 'paradoxes of hedonism'. The other category of enjoyment-induced preference change finally builds a bridge from the dynamics of enjoyment to an analysis of want or preference change in terms of the enjoyment associated with it (section 6.4.3).

The normative relevance of the dynamic features of enjoyment is apparent. If hedonic adaptation were to lead to continuous decreases in well-being, this could be taken as justification for arguing against making such a concept the basis of a welfare measure. Veenhoven has labelled this the problem of the 'relativity of well-being' (Veenhoven 1991: 7–9). Indeed, if either a large proportion of an individual's enjoyment were not significantly affected by external circumstances (for example because the baseline levels of enjoyment are largely genetically fixed, cf. Lykken and Tellegen 1996), or large parts of enjoyments were ephemeral over time because of large-scale adaptation phenomena, one could question to what extent an enjoyment-centred view of well-being reflects what it means for an individual's life to go well. If enjoyments were arbitrary and fleeting, would it make sense to make them the basis of a theory of the good or of a theory of the right? I provide a tentative answer to this question in the following subsections.[97]

6.4.1 Partial enjoyment dynamics: hedonic adaptation

A discussion of adaptation phenomena

As defined above, hedonic adaptation is the reduction of the affective effects of a constant or repeated stimulus. Besides *hedonic* adaptation, there are other forms of adaptation. These might often go hand in hand with hedonic adaptation or depend on similar processes in the organism. Hedonic adaptation can be related to adaptive preference formation (see section 6.5.2) in so far as cognitive processes that bring about adaptive preference formation can also play a role in hedonic adaptation. But adaptive preferences are usually understood to be the result of a decreased feasible set (i.e. reduced opportunities), while hedonic adaptation may result from an increased feasible set as well, which is the case when continued enjoyments become progressively duller due to hedonic adaptation. The interplay between all these processes can best be illustrated by an example (Frederick and Loewenstein 1999: 302). Consider Tim: after a tragic accident, Tim becomes a paraplegic. As he is now unable to walk, several processes can be observed such as his chest muscles becoming stronger by doing exercises in his wheelchair, making it easier to move around. This is a process of physiological adaptation. Or Tim starts setting new goals and developing new interests, and instead of running

a marathon discovers his love for playing chess. Such a process would probably be one of cognitive adaptation and can be labelled as adaptive preference
formation (Tim's feasible set has decreased due to the accident). Shifts of
attention to his possibilities and away from his disabilities would help to
attain and then maintain a higher level of well-being. Also, Tim has episodes
of pain that are gradually becoming duller. This process is probably the
closest to hedonic adaptation of enjoyments, where a repeated and painful
stimulus becomes hedonically less intense.[98] Tim's friend Alice, on the contrary, is successful in her job and has a salary allowing her to regularly
indulge in exquisite food. Dining in expensive restaurants on a regular basis,
she adapts to the enjoyments that certain foods bring her. After a while,
though, it is not as rewarding to eat in these restaurants as it used to be. Note
that Alice is a 'victim' of hedonic adaptation, but here it is a result of the
increased feasible set, not of adverse circumstances.

In its most narrow definition, hedonic adaptation decreases the intensity of
a repeated stimulus such as the enjoyment of eating a piece of chocolate or
the enjoyment that comes with a rise in income or from an aversive situation.
Although I will later discuss adaptive preference formation in more detail, I
restrict myself at this point largely to the most basic form of hedonic adaptation, namely that which is narrowly defined. Adaptation (in general) serves
two important functions. First of all, it is a protective mechanism (similar to
immune neglect, see section 6.3.1) that helps the organism to cope with the
impact of external stimuli. In that sense, shivering or sweating are adaptive
bodily processes that are a reaction to external circumstances. Such adaptive
processes are aimed at guaranteeing the continued functioning of our organism. Second, perception is enhanced through adaptation because the signal
value of changes in stimuli from the baseline levels is enhanced. This becomes
clearer in the case of some adaptive processes, for example adapting our
vision to changing lighting conditions. Our eyes adjust to the current baseline, enabling us to better discriminate visual stimuli in the new situation.
Frederick and Loewenstein (1999) conjecture that enhanced perception is
also relevant in hedonic adaptation because it would direct attention to those
needs that are unsatisfied. But as persistent strong hedonic states can have
physiologically negative consequences (high levels of stress or arousal are
detrimental to health, see Sapolsky 1999), hedonic adaptation reduces this
impact over time. Moreover, hedonic adaptation can make an individual
more sensitive to changes from the baseline when external circumstances
change. Stimuli that would barely be rewarding for a healthy individual can
have higher affective relevance after that individual has adapted to adverse
circumstances such as becoming a paraplegic.

From the examples discussed so far, it is clear that hedonic adaptation
can happen in two ways. First, the level at which a stimulus is experienced
as neutral can be shifted ('shift in adaptation levels'). Second, the subjective intensity of the stimulus is decreased ('desensitization'). Frederick and
Loewenstein (1999) exemplify both ways of adaptation within the framework

of a prospect theory value function, which captures utility (Kahneman and Tversky 1979): the zero points in the diagram (see Figure 6.2) represent the baseline levels at which a stimulus is experienced as neutral. The curve is concave for positive changes and convex for negative ones: one peculiar feature of such a value function is that it is kinked, i.e. a negative change of the same magnitude is experienced more strongly negative than a positive change of the same amount (the slope of the curve is steeper in the negative area). This has been termed 'loss aversion' (see Figure 6.2a). A shifting adaptation level means that the curve is shifted in position (Figure 6.2b), while desensitization alters the shape of the curve.[99] The consequence of a shifting adaptation level is that the sensitivity to stimulus changes is preserved or enhanced, while a desensitization reduces the sensitivity to stimulus changes. In the example of Tim, this can be exemplified as follows: from his healthy baseline level, being deprived of 80 per cent of his activities through disability (point 'A' in Figure 6.2b) is experienced as slightly better than being deprived of 90 per cent of his activities (point 'B'). Having adapted to his disability, i.e. being deprived of 90 per cent of his activities (the baseline point in Figure 6.2c); he is much more sensitive to an improvement in terms of only being deprived of 80 per cent of his activities (point 'A'). If Tim adapted to his disability in terms of a desensitization, reflected in a dampening of the curve, the sensitivity to change would be decreased. Tim would be 'hardened' or 'jaded' by the adaptation and less motivated to change his situation (Frederick and Loewenstein 1999: 305).

Apart from these general considerations, adaptive processes are not yet well understood, and firm empirical evidence on their functioning is lacking (Frederick and Loewenstein 1999: 311–20): few empirical studies, most of which are not experimental but rely on the subjects' memories, have targeted the phenomenon so far (the fact that most stimuli do not remain constant as well as the existence of context and demand effects complicate measurement). While there is *some* evidence, 'few general conclusions' (Frederick and Loewenstein 1999: 320) can be drawn on the prevalence of hedonic adaptation except for the fact that it seems to be highly domain-specific. It will therefore be illuminating to study some of these domains in order to learn

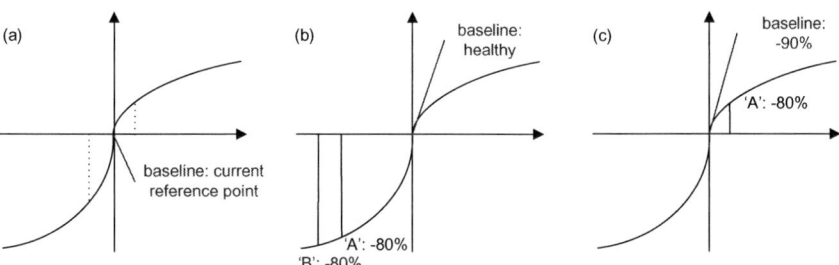

Figure 6.2 Mechanisms of adaptation, adapted from Frederick and Loewenstein (1999).

more about the cases where adaptation occurs. Perhaps the most prominent of these results are the well-known findings of happiness research showing that we adapt to increases in income (and material conditions) quite fast (Oswald 1997; Frey and Stutzer 2002a; Easterlin 2003). Evidence on adaptation to food is mixed: in some cases, there is adaptation, in others the opposite seems to be the case (consider the examples of getting used to coffee, chilli, etc.; see Rozin and Schiller 1980; Kahneman and Snell 1992). The time interval of consumption is significant as to whether one can speak of adaptation here. It seems more appropriate to refer to satiation in some cases. The question, which has so far not been answered sufficiently clearly, is whether in addition to satiation there exists long-term adaptation to food. Similarly mixed is the evidence on adaptation to sexually arousing stimuli: while adaptation is found in the studies by Meuwissen and Over (1990) and Koukounas and Over (1993), contradicting results are described in other studies (Smith and Over 1987; Laan and Everaerd 1995). Although some authors claim that there is no adaptation to friendship and other companionable pleasures (e.g. Frank 1999; Layard 2005; Kahneman and Sugden 2005), these arguments seem to rest mostly on armchair empiricism (but see Myers 1999). A different and large class of findings concerns marriage, showing (at least) quite slow rates of adaptation: while it had first been conjectured that one did not adapt to the pleasures of marriage at all (Frey and Stutzer 2002a; Easterlin 2003), later findings seem to suggest that adaptation does occur, albeit slowly (Lucas and Clark 2006; Stutzer and Frey 2006). A last class of positive stimuli that have been researched were cases of cosmetic surgery, where no adaptation effects to improved beauty were found (Wengle 1986; Young et al. 1994). However, it cannot be excluded that this is because of strong demand effects distorting the results. Frederick and Loewenstein (1999) argue that adaptation seems to work faster for positive stimuli in general.

Regarding negative stimuli, there is some evidence that one does not adapt to noise (Weinstein 1982; Schreiber and Kahneman 2000). As for pain, there is some adaptation, but it seems to be quite limited (Frederick and Loewenstein 1999; Kahneman and Sugden 2005). In the case of disability, the famous study by Brickman et al. (1978) seems to imply that paraplegics adjust quickly even to severe disability. However, adaptation is not complete (Veenhoven 1991; Oswald and Powdthavee 2008) and – despite the high prominence in the literature – some doubts have been voiced regarding the methodology used in that and similar studies (Veenhoven 1991: 13–16): for example, the disability victims were interviewed personally, a technique that tends to elicit higher well-being responses as compared to using telephone interviews, which were used for the control group. As opposed to disability, which allows for cognitive adaptation (such as adaptive preference formation) to happen, patients who suffer from chronic diseases and chronic pain do not seem to adapt easily to their conditions (Smith and Wallston 1992; Oswald and Powdthavee 2008). Studies in this field are complicated by the progressive nature of some of the diseases. Similar problems of adaptation pertain to cases of loss and bereavement. Adaptation in terms of regaining previous levels of well-being after the loss of a loved one can take a decade or, if measured by depression rates, even up to two decades. Here adaptation seems to work very slowly (Weiss 1988; Dyregrov 1990; Carnelley et al. 2006). One would also expect that incarceration is experienced quite negatively; however, adaptation seems to protect inmates from despair. What one does not seem to adapt to in prison is the loss of relationships (Flanagan 1980; Suedfeld et al. 1982). A last class of negative stimuli is the loss of job, where adaptation works less well for males who take longer to adapt and never seem to recover their previous levels of well-being (Clark and Oswald 1994; Frey and Stutzer 2002a; Lucas et al. 2004).

What is probably worth noting is that adaptation is less strong with respect to phenomena that are necessary for survival and reproduction or would compromise survival and reproduction (Frederick and Loewenstein 1999: 314). As Veenhoven notes:

> To a great extent happiness depends on the gratification of innate biopsychological needs which do not adjust to circumstances: needs mark in fact the limits of human adaptability. The better these needs are gratified the better we feel and the more satisfied we are with life. People cannot be happy in chronic hunger, danger and isolation: not even if they have never known better and if their neighbours are worse off.
>
> (Veenhoven 1991: 32)

Such a resilience in the adaptation to basic needs that are necessary for survival seems unsurprising because of its high functional role. Thus what we can summarily conclude is that hedonic adaptation is comparatively more limited in the case of innate needs than enjoyments resulting from acquired wants. In the short term, there seem to be upper and lower bounds regarding stimulus variation. Consider eating: within a certain time interval you can only eat so much before satiation sets in. But the levels after which satiation sets in can vary in the long term (malnutrition being a case in point for lowering the set points of a homeostatic process, and obesity another for the opposite). But what does this mean for the related hedonic experiences? A person might get used to living on very few calories a day; but apparently, adaptation does not occur here in terms of the pleasure derived (i.e. of the actual enjoyment experienced). The person will be constantly hungry, and while probably assessing the state (of constant deprivation) as relatively good due to lowered aspiration levels or adaptive preference formation, the profile of instant utilities would more accurately reflect the deprivation. This person will not have a high welfare in terms of these experiences. If sensory well-being were measured it might capture this adaptation phenomenon or at least, it might be comparatively less influenced by adaptation effects than the evaluative well-being concept, which is strongly cognitively mediated.

Normative evaluation of hedonic adaptation

A normative evaluation of adaptation phenomena related to enjoyments is largely absent in the literature for three reasons (but see Frank 1999; Layard 2005): first, the empirical findings on adaptation are still neither complete nor uncontroversial. There is still considerable controversy in such important fields as the enjoyment stemming from being married or adaptation to severe disability. Second, as adaptation is highly domain-specific, it is difficult to come up with a simple rule on how to assess adaptive processes in a welfare calculus. Third, since adaptation concerns enjoyment as well as suffering, the phenomenon can be a good or bad. In consequence, there is no simple classification scheme that would hold for all cases alike. Nevertheless, I will here put forward a tentative suggestion how to normatively deal with the phenomenon that takes into account the specificities highlighted above.

Let us first consider the 'bright side of adaptation', namely where adaptation increases well-being, for example when adverse circumstances are involved. While this is obviously a good function of adaptation for the individual, it has to be noted that it leads to a bias in an individual's own assessment of welfare as compared to (less subjective) outside appraisals of that individual's welfare. In the case of the severely deprived or handicapped, their levels of well-being would be distorted to a certain degree by adaptive processes. This is problematic with respect to interpersonal comparisons of well-being in the context of a theory of justice, for example when considering questions of distributive justice (Bruelde 2007: 30–1). While it can be considered fortunate that such adaptive processes help those afflicted with disability in coping with misery, this aspect should not lead to a neglect of their 'objective' situation in a welfare calculus (this line of reasoning is the basic thrust of Sen's or Nussbaum's arguments against utilitarianism, see section 3.2). Overstated enjoyment or understated pain in reaction to adverse circumstances could lead to a decrease in an individual's entitlements if this welfare measure is taken as basis for considerations of distributive justice.

Moreover, one can argue that the overly optimistic self-assessment in such circumstances is also problematic in the context of solely assessing individual well-being (not drawing on interpersonal comparisons of well-being between individuals). Similar to the argument in favour of discounting preferences that are not sufficiently informed, one can make a case that adaptive enjoyment should be properly discounted to reflect the distorting factor. This has also been suggested by authors of other accounts of well-being (e.g. Sumner 1996; Bruelde 2007). An argument can be given in favour of providing special provision in a welfare calculus regarding hedonic adaptation in the case of suffering (i.e. in all negative domains where adaptation occurs). Of course, in the case of suffering where adaptation is not possible, the welfare calculus correctly reflects an individual's well-being. While the evidence seems to support that there are pains and pleasures to which one does not adapt at all (e.g. chronic pain), it cannot be excluded that there is adaptation nonetheless, albeit a very slow one. But for sake of conceptual clarity, I will call these enjoyments and sufferings non-adaptive. In the case of non-adaptive suffering, I believe a clear case can be made to give it special emphasis by focusing on its abolishment. I here agree with Layard's conclusion that in the case of non-adaptive suffering, it seems uncontroversial to demand more efforts to decrease it (Layard 2005: 69). Such a demand is justified by directly appealing to the badness of pain in a hedonistic value framework. Giving priority to the abolishment of suffering can also be justified by the higher behavioural relevance of pain, which is reflected in humans who experience losses more strongly than equal gains (see e.g. the kink in the value function of prospect theory or the well-known endowment effect).

On the other hand, the 'dark side of adaptation to enjoyments' is that, over time, we lose (often permanently) the enjoyment of pleasurable things. Should one adopt a symmetric treatment here and correct any welfare assessment for these effects? I believe this is not as straightforward as in the case of the overstatement of actual well-being in adverse circumstances. While the counting is straightforward in cases without adaptation, it becomes more difficult where adaptation decreases the enjoyment resulting from a positive stimulus: consider two pleasurable activities, one adaptive and one non-adaptive. In order to derive the same amount of pleasure from both over a certain time horizon, an individual has to put comparatively more effort into the adaptive rather than the non-adaptive activity. One could say that this individual could derive the same amount of pleasure with less effort by sticking to the non-adaptive activity. In that sense, adaptive pleasures are comparatively inefficient or wasteful. By this line of reasoning, devoting more resources to non-adaptive activities is more efficient overall and should be encouraged or given higher normative weight.[100] Such a distinction could be realized, for example, in discounting adaptive enjoyments. Consider successful Alice who is adapting to eating in exquisite restaurants. Her initial enjoyments of such experiences will be quite high, but later on, she will experience them as lower by comparison because of her adaptation to these stimuli. While one could argue for an asymmetry property here and say that it does not really matter for a welfare calculus that Alice has adapted and reports lower well-being levels, I think such a suggestion would become problematic at the level of distributive justice (for a theory of the right), when making interpersonal comparisons of well-being. Here Alice's lower levels of enjoyments would introduce a distortion into the calculus when considering distributional issues. Based on the hedonistic value framework, in the case of both adaptive enjoyments and adaptive pains, these should be reflected in a welfare calculus as well as in the context of interpersonal comparisons of well-being.[101]

Going even beyond such a view, Layard (2005: 154–5) has suggested taxing adaptive enjoyments, justifying this with the similarity between adaptation to enjoyments and addiction: as soon as we adapt to the pleasures we derive from a set of activities in one period, we strive for more income to finance higher enjoyments in the next period. Based on such treadmill properties, Layard points out the addictive character of further income and advocates taxing it. This would imply that beyond the negative effects of adaptation on one's well-being, these are additionally penalized. As I have already argued, in addictive processes wanting is over-sensitized, and an individual is not able to assess correctly the well-being resulting from adaptive enjoyments. In adaptive processes, it is liking that is desensitized, which is something different. While in addictive processes, the individual is not able to correctly assess the over-sensitization of wanting based on pathological changes in brain chemistry, adaptive processes are different. It would therefore be misleading to characterize such processes as 'addictive'. While the analogy between addiction and adaptation is somewhat flawed, the reasoning underlying such a tax might be defended on the following grounds: corrective taxation can be used to internalize the costs of externalities. This argument is sound in the case of a positional treadmill, where the relative position of an individual is a source of enjoyment. When an individual does not take into account the external effects of a choice between leisure and work, a socially inefficient solution will come about. For example, assume that if an individual works one hour longer than everyone else, that individual's chances at promotion will increase. But if everyone works one hour longer, relative ranking remains the same. Individually rational behaviour leads to a situation in which everyone works more than in the social optimum. It was shown that lawyers would unanimously prefer that everyone worked a little less (Landers et al. 1996). Taxing overworking in this case could create the right incentives.

The reasoning supporting a tax to stop the hedonic treadmill is similar, although one would mainly rely on the tax to reduce an 'internality' (Herrnstein et al. 1993):[102] to the extent that individuals do not take into account the effects of today's consumption on their future consumption, such a tax could be corrective and be labelled desirable (in order to achieve internalization of the internality). However, such a corrective tax would strongly curtail the affected individuals' autonomy in making their own consumption decisions. Moreover, such a proposal is not easily defensible for practical reasons: it would have to encompass only adaptive enjoyments, not consumption in general (as would be the case with the progressive consumption tax suggested by Frank 1999). The domain of such a tax as well as its boundaries are thus subject to considerable imprecision. As long as processes of adaptation are as poorly understood, such a measure will not be practical.

One could go one step further, though in a different direction, and advocate an asymmetric treatment that ranks pains higher than enjoyments in a welfare calculus, thereby giving higher priority to the decrease of suffering than to the promotion of enjoyment. Such an 'asymmetry requirement' could be justified on the basis that adaptation generally works less well in the case of suffering, and that the sources of suffering are more uniform across individuals than the sources of enjoyment (Layard 2005). Moreover, a justification of such a treatment could be derived with a naturalistic methodology based on the following insight: the behavioural relevance of badness seems to be higher than the relevance of enjoyment if one considers that individuals experience suffering from losses more strongly than gains. The kink in an individual's value function in prospect theory is one example, another is the endowment effect (Knetsch 1992). Based on such a higher relevance of pain, it might be easier for an individual to empathize with the suffering of another individual, as opposed to empathizing equally strongly with another's enjoyment. Such a justification would basically use arguments similar to those used to defend forms of negative utilitarianism. While debatable on a normative level, it might be less controversial on a more applied policy level: to argue for policies that aim at increasing enjoyment might be more controversial than arguing for policies that aim at abolishing suffering, because of the more uniform distribution of sources of suffering.

6.4.2 General enjoyment dynamics: hedonic treadmills

Based on the insight that adaptive processes diminish our enjoyment of certain activities, critics have claimed that any striving for pleasure is doomed to failure as it will never be possible to attain lasting happiness. The classic 'paradox of happiness', which seems to justify the critics' claim, refers to the idea that, although incomes rise, individuals do not seem to become happier as they adapt to rising levels of income. A discussion of some general dynamics of hedonism would not be complete without addressing this objection. Following that, I turn briefly to a suggestion of how to evaluate different development paths of general enjoyment. Both topics are relevant because of the explicit introduction of a time dimension into my analysis.

Treadmill objections

In section 5.7.1, I have already defended hedonism against some common objections regarding its allegedly self-defeating character.[103] From a dynamic point of view, there is an important category of objections, which is centred on what has been called the 'paradox of happiness'. In particular the empirical literature on subjective well-being has found puzzling developments of subjective well-being over time. While I will not go into detail with respect to all these findings (but see e.g. Frey and Stutzer 2002a; Easterlin 2003; Layard 2005), there is strong evidence that well-being (as measured by the standard constructs of the happiness literature, such as self-reported life satisfaction) has not increased substantially in the last decades even though incomes have risen strongly. For example, in the US, real incomes have risen from 11,000 USD to 27,100 USD from 1946 to 1991, (measured in 1996 dollars, Frey and Stutzer 2002a: 76–7) while happiness levels have dropped from 2.4 to 2.2 (average happiness on a three-point scale). Similar findings were presented by Oswald (1997: 1818–20), who reports a slight increase in happiness with increasing income over time for the US and Europe. In a recent study, these findings have been qualified by Stevenson and Wolfers (2008), who have reappraised the data and were able to assess longer time horizons for the different countries. Based on a comprehensive data set, their main finding is that the paradox of happiness cannot be corroborated for European countries and Japan, while the US data confirm the previous analyses. These findings cast doubt on the strength of the empirical evidence for such intertemporal dynamics.[104]

So to what extent are we becoming richer without becoming happier? Can such a potential happiness treadmill be explained by adaptive processes and, if so, how should this be evaluated in normative terms? Two kinds of treadmills are important here: the 'hedonic treadmill', which is related to the adaptation of our enjoyment (Brickman and Campbell 1971), and the 'positional treadmill', which links our well-being to concerns of position and relative income (Frank 1985, 1999). Indeed, it is a characteristic of our biological endowment that we derive pleasure from comparing ourselves with others as long as the result is in our favour. As position is a relative matter and at most 50 per cent of a sample can be above average, positional concerns are also a self-defeating zero-sum game. When buying a positional good for the pleasure of its being unique (or rare), i.e. its status-signalling characteristics, rising incomes put us in a treadmill because as soon as others are also able to afford such an item, we have to go and buy the next better version of it. Frank (1999) has compellingly shown how this leads to upward spiralling circles of the purchase of 'better' items, ranging from luxury watches to cars and houses, and so forth. The positional treadmill cannot be discussed here for want of space (but I will discuss some aspects of it separately as an example of the insatiability of wants in section 6.5.1). The treadmill seems *prima facie* plausible and plays a certain role in a dynamic context. Here I concentrate on the classic hedonic treadmill, since it is related to the (above) discussion of hedonic adaptation. Although the findings of Stevenson and Wolfers (2008) partly contest the larger consensus regarding the existence of the phenomenon, theoretical explanations for stagnating well-being have been brought forward (see Veenhoven 2003; Layard 2005). Stagnating levels of well-being have been attributed to negative influences such as increasing crime rates, decreasing trust, or less emphasis on the community and related values (Layard 2005). It has been argued that individuals and society as a whole have decreasingly aimed for sources of lasting well-being and created sources of suffering through various developments in these fields. Hedonic adaptation can be credited with having influenced this development.

Based on such explanations, the paradox of happiness poses some problems for any hedonistic theory of welfare. Or does it not? To begin with, it has to be remarked that hedonic treadmills would pose a significant problem for *any* dynamic theory of welfare that is not fully objective. From a preference satisfaction perspective, this problem does not go away but is restated, i.e. whether preferences can ever be satisfied. In such a perspective, the question shifts to how to deal with the problem that, after one preference has been satisfied, other, new preferences come to the fore instead of the old one. The paradox can be qualified somewhat by saying that seeking enjoyments is, to a certain extent, not subject to hedonic adaptation. In this respect, it is also not self-defeating. What can be accomplished by this is to show that the para-doxes of hedonism are only half-truths, drawing appeal from illegitimate generalizations from salient but untypical examples (Martin 2008). In order to alleviate the effects of hedonic adaptation, normative priority should be shifted towards enjoyments where adaptation is slower or inexistent. Here the discussion from the previous subsection helps in distinguishing enjoyments as to their adaptability in order to avoid the effects of the hedonic treadmill. Based on our positive knowledge, we are able to relativize the claim of the self-defeating nature of seeking enjoyments at least to some extent. Pleasure and pain have been identified as playing a clear role in human biology in regulating homeostasis. They are a 'natural signal', crucial to securing our survival (Veenhoven 2003: 440). This also explains the relative resistance to adaptation in relation to our innate bodily needs. Here, as has been argued above, adaptation is less pronounced, and therefore the striving for such enjoyments will be a continuous factor in human life. To the extent that human striving for enjoyments is thus directed towards the reduction of pain, to which one cannot adapt, and to the attainment of enjoyments, to which one does not adapt easily, such striving is neither futile nor self-defeating over time. Of course, many of these everyday activities pursued by us are not direct quests for enjoyment; but many of them can be understood to be indirect attempts, such as performing a certain action with the knowledge that it may result in increased enjoyments.

Knowledge of the above mechanisms bears important consequences. While it seems premature to advocate the taxing of adaptive enjoyments, we should put emphasis on the prevention of pain to which one cannot adapt. Such a 'negative focus' is reinforced by findings that causes of suffering are much more homogeneous across humans than sources of enjoyment (Layard 2005). Similarly, one can normatively prioritize these enjoyments to which one does not adapt quickly (give them higher normative weight, in general, or subsid-ize related activities, on a more concrete level). Such a prioritization would presumably lead to a different policy focus that could include giving much more weight to these policy measures which promise lasting increases in well-being (examples could be health-related policies subsidizing pain relief or release from chronic depression, policies aiming at more self-determined working conditions and promoting long-term family relationships, policies improving commuting conditions and reducing commuting times and stress, etc.). My aim here is not to discuss any concrete policies; but these few examples show the different areas where long-lasting increases in non-adaptive enjoyments can be gained. The impact in such areas tends to be underestimated now because, by and large, the dynamic aspects of hedonic adaptation processes are being ignored.

Besides the justification of the above distinction regarding the badness of pain and suffering, further legitimacy can be provided on the grounds of an efficiency argument. Based on the reasoning in the previous subsection regarding the differences in efficiency between adaptive and non-adaptive enjoyments, we can label certain developments in general welfare as more desirable than others. While it is clear that shifts from pain to enjoyment are beneficial and desirable, we can also evaluate these shifts in a more differentiated fashion: thus any change in welfare that replaces an adaptive enjoyment with a non-adaptive one is 'welfare-progressive' as it tends to increase future welfare. As I have argued that hedonic adaptation in adverse situations should be normatively discounted, a shift from non-adaptive to adaptive pains cannot be said to be 'welfare-progressive'. I believe it is not very attractive to conceive of policies aiming at a shift from non-adaptive to adaptive suffering, instead of aiming at a reduction of suffering. Enjoyment paths that increase the proportion of adaptive enjoyments, on the other hand, are 'welfare-degenerating' because, although they might increase enjoyment in the beginning, the treadmill dynamics discussed above would lead to their decrease over time and necessitate inefficient amounts of resources just to maintain a level of well-being, once it has been reached. In this respect the development sketched above has been welfare-degenerating because the increase in personal income, which has been experienced from 1946 to 1991, has been largely used to maintain a constant level of enjoyment. Had this income been used on sources of non-adaptive enjoyments, higher levels of well-being could have been realized. The accumulated rise in income during this period thus shows the maximum efficiency gain that could have been reached if enjoyments had been completely non-adaptive. These rises in income could have been used to further reduce suffering or increase enjoyment lastingly, had they not been necessary merely to keep adaptive enjoyments on a constant level.

Before concluding this discussion, it is worth noting that the hedonic treadmill could also be explained differently, as a 'satisfaction treadmill' (Kahneman 2000). Thus, leaving hedonic adaptation aside, the alternative explanation would be that an increase in enjoyment also leads to a rise in individuals' aspiration levels. According to this explanation, an important source of well-being lies in reaching our aspirations. As a result, after a rise in aspirations more enjoyment is needed in order to increase reported satisfaction. In this account, the hedonic treadmill could result from the following development: even if enjoyments actually rose over time, the risen aspiration levels would lead to a constant level of *reported* satisfaction with these enjoyments. This clearly points to a certain deficit in the elicitation of evaluative well-being constructs such as reported life satisfaction or remembered utility. The satisfaction treadmill shows that it is necessary to measure enjoyment and suffering more directly rather than through reports of life satisfaction. If levels of enjoyment have in fact risen (while only the evaluation has remained constant), then, according to the welfare framework presented here, an increase in well-being has taken place. In order to arrive at such more direct welfare measures, one could try not to elicit the overall assessment of 'satisfaction with life' but the proportions of time in which individuals have experienced enjoyments or suffering. As has been suggested by Kahneman and Krueger (2006), such applied accounts of well-being would then lead to shifts in policy makers' attention towards increasing the proportion of time spent on enjoyable activities over painful ones. It is important to note that such concepts only come to the fore through the explicit acknowledgment of a time dimension in the welfare framework. Based on the framework provided here, we have a unified theory of how enjoyments relate to the satisfaction of important classes of innate needs (which could thus be the basis for systematic policies). One major disadvantage of the literature on subjective well-being is that research and policy advice are fragmented and focused on certain areas (e.g. the effects of marriage or unemployment), without giving systematic guidance as to which other factors might play a role. Based on the ideas expressed in the learning theory of consumption, these findings can be systematized and put on a sound footing, showing their importance (as sources) for well-being.

Enjoyment paths

Besides the enjoyment paths discussed above, a different evaluation is offered in this section, based on the structure of some dynamics of enjoyment in general. By taking a dynamic perspective on hedonism, can we label some general development paths of enjoyments as more desirable than others? There are cases in which this is possible. However, for reasons of space, I limit myself to one example of such enjoyment paths. Consider the three profiles of net enjoyment depicted in Figure 6.3. Let us consider the enjoyment from t_0 to t_6. Enjoyment in case (1) is the integral below the function $y_1 = f(x) = x$. Enjoyment in case (2) is the integral below the function $y_2 = g(x) = 6 - x$ and similarly in case (3), where enjoyment is the integral below the trivial function $y_3 = h(x) = 3$. Under the assumptions on instant utilities spelt out in the previous chapter (see section 5.1), all three provide an individual with the same amount of enjoyment over the time span ($U_1 = U_2 = U_3 = 18$). Could we. nevertheless; label one enjoyment path as more desirable than the others (in mostly welfarist terms)? Based on the positive insights gained so far, one

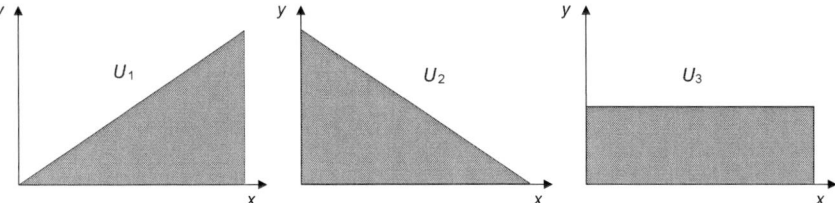

Figure 6.3 Different enjoyment paths (author's exposition).

could argue that path (1) is more desirable than the enjoyment development paths (2) and (3). We could label path (1) as 'bonum progressionis' as opposed to the 'malum regressus' path (2).[105] If we compare these three paths, path (1), when assessed retrospectively, will be evaluated by the individual according to a higher peak-end average than paths (2) and (3). While the individual would 'objectively' have enjoyed a similar amount of well-being in all three paths (in terms of sensory well-being), that individual would rank the first one more favourable (according to the peak-end heuristic) and the second and third one with the same value, since their peak-end averages are the same. Based on this reasoning, path (1) is the most favourable an individual can attain. The evaluation according to peak-end average might also explain the finding by Loewenstein and Sicherman (1991) that individuals prefer having rising incomes over constantly high incomes, even if the lifetime amount of both income paths might be the same.

Ranking path (1) higher than paths (2) and (3), as suggested above, amounts to normatively discriminating between enjoyment paths that are objectively equal (regarding the enjoyment contained in them) by giving higher weight to the former, which is additionally positively evaluated in retrospect by the individual. To the extent that an individual is biased towards a more positive retrospective evaluation of own well-being, this would be favoured by such a distinction. Thus if an individual subjectively favoured one enjoyment path over another (although both are objectively equal in enjoyments), the subjectively favoured enjoyment path could be given higher normative weight. Since, in this case, the individual is the ultimate judge with regard to well-being, the normative justification for such a distinction could be made with reference to that individual's 'enjoyment sovereignty' (ultimately, the justifying value judgement would be referring to the value of autonomy, thus constituting a qualification of the pure welfarist assessment that ranks all three paths equal). Could one find a justification for ranking paths (2) and (3) not equal? In terms of a strong welfarist measuring rod, I submit this would not be possible. In order to come to an assessment that would rank (2) and (3) differently, one would have to make use of additional information that is beyond the welfarist information used so far. For example, one could argue that path (2) would rank higher because the individual has reached a higher variety of different enjoyment levels in this path. The wider range in which enjoyment levels lie in (2) might thus be interpreted to reflect a wider variety of experiences that could be judged positively if one valued variety or change. Or one could argue that the individual has reached an absolutely higher maximum point of enjoyment in path (2). On the other hand, the individual has also reached an absolutely lower minimum point of enjoyment so that this line of reasoning is not overly convincing. In a purely welfarist perspective, arguments claiming that the deterioration in (2) makes the individual worse off than the constant level of well-being in (3) are not permissible if, per assumption, all relevant enjoyments or sufferings are already reflected in that functional form.[106]

6.4.3 Want–enjoyment dynamics

Let us now examine the interplay between enjoyment and the formation, change or unlearning of wants. In this subsection, we use our positive knowledge of the relation between acquired wants and enjoyments to analyze the implications of want change (relating to enjoyment dynamics) over time. In section 4.4, I have discussed how acquired wants are learned by association with rewarding experiences. This form of operant conditioning (associative learning) leads to the acquisition of a want if behaviour is positively reinforced, i.e. if enjoyment results from an action. For example, if going to the theatre is experienced by an individual as rewarding because it satisfies the innate need for cognitive arousal, a want might be acquired for going to the theatre. Similarly, one could acquire that want because one is rewarded by one's peers when telling them about having gone there. The same acquired want can be linked to different underlying innate needs. Or one can acquire a want for things that are initially not rewarding at all (and may even be aversive). Acquiring a want for spicy food that is seasoned with chilli pepper is an example where the experience is initially aversive (Zajonc and Markus 1982). But if reinforcement is provided (for example from parents who praise the child for eating the dish), a want for chilli pepper can be acquired. We have already seen that wants can also be acquired through the imitation of others who are reinforced (vicarious reinforcement). These cases, where one acquires a want through positive reinforcement (i.e. positive affect), seem to be the most prevalent ones (in particular, this can be conjectured to be the case for many childhood preferences).

But wants can also be acquired by insightful learning, i.e. cognitive judgements precede the positive reinforcement. One thinks about a problem that needs a solution. Based on the reasoning processes, one can acquire a want based on 'more cognitive' reasons, i.e. reinforcement does not play a big role (initially). Over time, there is a difference in how such acquired wants can change or not. Acquired wants that were learned associatively need a certain amount of continued reinforcement or else they become 'extinct'. That is, if an individual has acquired a want for an action and keeps performing it, this must result in reinforcement (enjoyment) at regular intervals or else the acquired want will be unlearned. By contrast, wants that are learned based on cognitive motivations are not unlearned through extinction in the same way. In both cases, the unlearning of a want, however, does not proceed smoothly. First, a want is not unlearned just because enjoyment has not been forthcoming even once. The resistance of a want to unlearning depends strongly on the pattern of reinforcement that was previously exhibited. If the satisfaction of a want has regularly led to enjoyment, the absence of such satisfaction can quickly lead to extinction. Paradoxically, if a want has been satisfied less regularly in the past, extinction occurs less quickly. It has been hypothesized that this effect is caused by the increased difficulty in discriminating whether an action is still reinforced (Mowrer and Jones 1945): it is easier to see that something has changed if previous reinforcement occurred in all instances than if previous reinforcement has occurred only in some, irregular instances. In the case of cognitively acquired wants, unlearning can proceed much more quickly, and preference change is probably more capricious. But wants that were acquired on a purely cognitive basis often become strengthened by affective processes, for example when one gets used to an action or consumption item through 'mere exposure' (Zajonc 2001). Here the mere possession of an item (or the carrying-out of an activity) can lead to increases in enjoyment as one starts liking that item or activity.

Can one normatively distinguish between such various types of enjoyment-want dynamics? I think some tentative distinctions are possible: one could make a normative distinction based on the want-learning dynamics in terms of the stability of acquired wants ('stability distinction'). While the stability of a want may be assessed favourably when that want relates to a non-adaptive enjoyment, one might tend to assess it more negatively when the want relates to an adaptive enjoyment category. Thus the stability of acquired wants would be assessed in relation to (and complementing) our discussion of hedonic adaptation. As decreasing enjoyment through adaptation is not a sufficient condition for the unlearning of a want (the hedonic treadmill is fuelled by the fact the individuals increase the effort to attain enjoyment instead of turning to different enjoyments), the stability distinction is not redundant with the higher normative weight given to non-adaptive enjoyments. Moreover, as has been argued, the stability of acquired wants depends *inter alia* on the reinforcement schedule they follow. But, apart from the relevance for the evaluation of stability of acquired wants, the reinforcement schedule could be taken as the basis for another normative distinction: an acquired want that is more regularly reinforced is normatively more desirable because it is comparatively more closely related to the enjoyment its satisfaction brings ('reinforcement distinction'). Moreover, such a want is more likely to closely mirror external changes in enjoyment, i.e. if the action is no longer rewarding, such a want is unlearned faster. By contrast, wants based on irregular reinforcement tend to be unlearned less easily and thus lead to discrepancies between want satisfaction and well-being. The normative justification for this distinction thus rests on the basic value judgement of the desirability of enjoyments.

Another way to distinguish wants is the reversibility of the want formation process ('reversibility distinction'). This distinction can be made on the basis of a value judgement favouring opportunity: depending on the concrete learning mechanism involved, it can be difficult to lose or 'unlearn' a want. Hence there exists an asymmetry between the ease of learning of a preference and the ease with which it is abandoned. This asymmetry is relevant for cases of adaptive enjoyments because here it would be more desirable to be able to 'unlearn' the want if one recognized the decreasing enjoyments. A similar rationale would apply to 'harmful wants', which were probably acquired on the basis of mistaken beliefs, where, in hindsight, the individual would rather not have acquired that want. On the basis of an evaluation solely in terms of welfare, this distinction would need to be evaluated somewhat differently: while one might *prima facie* think that wants that can be easily reversed because they potentially offer the freedom of either having or not having that want should be normatively prioritized (and thus constitute a larger opportunity set), this intuition needs qualification. It has been shown that the reversibility of decisions has a negative influence on the well-being that results from these decisions (Gilbert and Ebert 2002). There seem to be processes of coping at work facilitating the acceptance of things that cannot be changed (adaptive processes and 'immune neglect', see section 6.3.1). Having fleeting preferences that are easily reversed might impact negatively on actual well-being as opposed to remaining committed to more stable, non-reversible preferences, with which one is 'stuck', but to which one can adapt.

Moreover, there is the possibility of 'crowding out' enjoyments. Acquired wants can lead to enjoyments in several dimensions. In the above example of going to the theatre, such an activity brings pleasure by satisfying the need for cognitive arousal or could bring reinforcement from peers (for example satisfying a status need). Now it is conceivable that an action is reinforced with a low amount of enjoyment for a while. Let us assume that going to the theatre is perceived by a given individual as mildly enjoyable for entertainment reasons. Subsequently, the individual learns to associate these visits with praise from colleagues which is much more rewarding. If that praise continues for a while but is then withdrawn, the reversal to the mild pleasure of the entertainment may no longer be sufficient for the individual to maintain the acquired want: a crowding out of enjoyment will take place. Here again, a normative evaluation (based on a hedonistic value judgement) could be conceived, depending on whether the substituted enjoyment is adaptive or not. If such want–enjoyment dynamics were taking place in relation to an adaptive enjoyment, we would have a case of welfare-degenerating want learning (although the want stays the same, the sources of enjoyment associated with it change for the worse).

A last feature to be normatively evaluated is the possibility that wants are acquired based on stimulus generalization. A want for something can be formed because of the similarity of the underlying stimulus. An individual has a want for X, and as X is very similar to Y, that individual acquires a want for Y (e.g. similar kinds of food or wines). The more closely two activities resemble each other, or the more similar two consumption goods are, the more easily a new want is created for the second, if it exists already for the first of the two. If such generalization occurs with regard to adaptive enjoyments, this could also be evaluated as a negative development. It can be stipulated that such stimulus generalization can lead to large sets of similar acquired wants, which are difficult to satisfy for their sheer number. Such a large set of similar acquired wants could also give rise to what one could term an 'insatiability of wants' because time constraints will make it impossible to satisfy all of these wants. With this, I turn to the subject of the evaluation of want change and take up the discussion on the insatiability of wants in more detail.

6.5 Welfare dynamics relating to wants

Being interested in welfare understood as enjoyment does not deny the importance of individual wants (or the preferences these give rise to) as sources of well-being. For this reason, my aim is a possible normative evaluation of some preference and want dynamics (the third facet of my theory), adding to the previous distinctions and applying insights from other behavioural sciences to a normative analysis (concerning differential satiation patterns of different classes of wants). I will therefore evaluate different want and preference dynamics in light of the positive knowledge we have about these dynamics, their relation to enjoyment as well as other important information. This knowledge allows to make empirically richer distinctions than a purely formal approach, being inspired by Sen's idea of using more information in order to be able to better evaluate interesting cases of preference change (see section 3.4). The naturalistic methodology subscribed to in this monograph can help here to better understand when a preference is formed autonomously (see subsection 6.5.2) or what types of preferences can be satiated, and under what conditions this happens (next subsection).

6.5.1 Want dynamics: satiation

Characteristics of satiation

In this subsection, I discuss the idea of differential satiation patterns with respect to different categories of wants. Before suggesting a normative distinction of different wants according to these satiation patterns, it is necessary to understand more clearly what is meant by 'satiation'. The discussion of this phenomenon is complicated by the fact that the term satiation is used in parts of the economic literature (but also in consumer research) as synonymous with habituation or adaptation:

> Good thing satiate . . . These three words describe a common barrier to happiness, namely, that pleasure often declines with greater consumption. . . . Life has even been compared to an unending 'hedonic treadmill', where we must keep finding better experiences just to maintain our current happiness level.
>
> (Redden 2008: 624)

For Redden, satiation describes the phenomenon that we have already discussed in the section on hedonic adaptation. My argument here is that such an identification of satiation with adaptation is too simplistic with respect to the two. A view that equates adaptation/habituation and satiation is misleading on several counts. Satiation should be carefully distinguished from adaptation (this is done without argument by Baucells and Sarin 2007). In my discussion of the phenomenon, I draw on biology and psychology and their use of the term. While hedonic adaptation certainly plays a role in satiation, I contend that this is only one aspect in satiation, and not the one that is usually relevant in the economic context. Nevertheless, both together can be conjectured to be some of the most important drivers of preference change (Read et al. 1999: 183).

A definition of satiation can be derived by examining its use in the case of the consumption of food. This is a well researched area (see Blundell 1999: 183, for basic terminology): satiation is here understood 'as the complex of processes which brings eating to a halt (cause meal termination)'. Satiety denotes the events that happen after the ingestion of a meal, which suppress hunger and inhibit eating for a certain period of time. It is worth noting that the literature on satiation and satiety with respect to food is very special in terms of the processes involved (e.g. the physiological processes as well as the signals produced by the organism). For the present purpose, I suggest a broader definition of satiation as comprising the processes that terminate the consumption of an item or the carrying-out of a rewarding activity. In the following, I elaborate on its characteristics to show how it can be delineated from adaptation and to what extent both processes may (but do not have to) work in parallel. Satiation does only make sense with reference to a certain time interval. While satiation is reflected in the assumption of a decreasing marginal utility of consumption in the static economic calculus, this neglects the somewhat cyclical character of satiation patterns when related to processes of homeostasis. A first insight refers to the set of innate needs which need to be satisfied at regular intervals to guarantee continued functioning and well-being (see Chapters 4 and 5). Per time interval, the organism needs a certain amount of resources to continue functioning. Upon reaching a certain threshold in the consumption of these resources, satiation sets in until the store of resources in the organism is used up and more are needed. This cyclical character is found in specific deprivation patterns for needs such as those for air, nutrition, fluid intake or sleep.

By comparison, adaptation processes are less cyclical than satiation processes. Exposure to hedonic stimuli leads to decreases in hedonic worth that seem to be monotonic over time. Even when consumption is decreased or the time interval between episodes of consumption is increased, there is no marked reversal in the hedonic quality of the episode. We are getting used to the enjoyment from certain activities, and this adaptation is more stable (via the shift in the adaptation level or desensitization) than the change in affect associated with satiation. Consider, for instance, the so-called 'sensory-specific satiety' with regard to food taste or smell (e.g. Rolls et al. 1981; Rolls and Rolls 1997): during a meal, the pleasantness of the food decreases with consumption. Some researchers argue that at the point of satiation, the food consumed has even become aversive. Nevertheless, after satiety wanes and deprivation sets in again, this decline in hedonic worth is as quickly reversed as it came about in the first place. Such a decline does not seem to be general but sensory-specific, i.e. while the same kind of food is rated less pleasant, other foods are not affected by sensory-specific satiety. The greater variety of a three-course meal is a pleasant experience of which one is not satiated as fast as by a meal consisting of identical dishes (Rolls et al. 1984). The sensory-specific nature of the satiety of food can lead to overeating and obesity given the large varieties of food available. However, it is not fully understood whether sensory-specific satiety would generalize to other non-food stimuli. On the contrary, hedonic adaptation leads to an overall decrease of the pleasure attainable from similar meals over a time horizon that would encompass several satiation-deprivation cycles.

I submit that the main difference between adaptation and satiation is characterized by the two processes we have already distinguished, namely 'wanting' and 'liking' (or motivation and reward). While the key feature of hedonic adaptation lies in its decrease of liking, satiation's main aspect is the decrease of wanting. If one has adapted to an activity, one likes it less, if one is satiated with an activity, the wish to repeat it becomes less intense. By this distinction, we can make sense of some of the features that have been observed with regard to these phenomena: the reasons given for ceasing to eat a meal were not the decline in pleasure resulting from the food but the 'feeling of fullness' (Mook and Votaw 1992: 74), not wanting to continue eating. Thus what we commonly associate with satiation is probably best described as a motivational phenomenon. Based on previous consumption, further consumption of the same good loses its attractiveness in motivational terms. Satiation and adaptation, of course, can and often do work hand in hand. Moreover, the above distinction is not to suggest that adaptation plays no role in satiation (Mook and Votaw 1992). There is a large body of literature on the decrease in pleasantness of food, which is not discounted here (Cabanac 1979). What seems to be misplaced, however, is to argue that satiation is solely a process that decreases liking (with respect to food: palatability) and thereby changes motivation. These distinct processes of a decline in wanting and liking do not have similar magnitudes: the motivation to continue eating successive pieces of chocolate, for instance, declines faster than the hedonic evaluation, i.e. the pleasure gained from the consumption of a single piece of chocolate (Small et al. 2001: 1724). I therefore suggest reserving the term satiation for the more cyclical motivational phenomenon related to the satisfaction of needs and wants that largely depends on, and varies with, the level of deprivation, while adaptation relates to the long-term decline in pleasure that results from such repeated cycles.

In the end, hedonic adaptation can, of course, also have a motivational relevance for an individual, but this is different: a satiated individual will refrain from consuming more of the same good. Satiation is thus important because it may lead to a decrease in demand for a good, but also because the individual may be motivated to search for other non-satiated stimuli. This can be a search for completely different stimuli and be an explanation for variety seeking (McAlister 1982); but sufficiently altered changes in the sensory features of a similar stimulus could also mitigate satiation (e.g. a change in the taste of a yoghurt, cf. Rolls et al. 1984). Even structural features of how an individual perceives a good can play a role in reducing satiation, for example, when fine-grained categorization levels are used to delay satiation (Redden 2008).[107] On the other hand, an individual who adapts to the hedonic qualities of a stimulus will either refrain from consuming more and seek a more rewarding stimulus, or *increase* the consumption of the same stimulus in order to reach higher levels of pleasure. This is an important difference between satiation and hedonic adaptation because it is per definition excluded that satiation leads to an increase in consumption of the good under consideration. The latter case is especially relevant because this is what is usually assumed to happen in the case of habitual preferences, as modelled in economics. Therefore Baucells and Sarin (2007) are justified in modelling satiation and adaptation as two distinct processes. In their contribution, they have not only modelled both processes separately but also shed light on the interplay between satiation and adaptation. An interesting finding is that adaptation mitigates satiation: getting adapted to a stimulus leads to a higher tolerance before satiation sets in. Someone adapted to a certain good can consume more before reaching satiation than someone who is unfamiliar with a stimulus and can become satiated very easily on small amounts.

As the nature of satiation has put upper bounds on the consumption of many goods, it is a rational reaction for producers to look for ways of delaying satiation or pushing back satiation levels, for instance by differentiating categorization levels or by increasing the variety of the goods produced. From the perspective of consumer welfare, a reduction in satiation levels is only beneficial if evading satiation is also associated with increases in enjoyment. As will be shown, this is by no means automatically the case when turning to an evaluation of satiation from a normative perspective.

Normative evaluation

The normative evaluation of differential satiation patterns is conducted within the hedonistic welfare framework, i.e. in terms of a potential contribution towards increasing an individual's enjoyment. Let us briefly return to the learning theory of consumption (Witt 2001). This theory offers insights into the different classes of innate needs. If these are satisfied via direct inputs, satiation is possible with respect to using up these inputs in the consumption process. That is, physical satiation sets in after the consumption of some of these inputs, and the individual is no longer motivated (in that time interval) to continue to acquire the respective direct input (Witt 2001: 26–7). On the other hand, if these needs are satisfied via the service provided by tools, we have to conclude that satiation with respect to these tools is probably inexistent. Although needs that are satisfied via the services of tools are subject to satiation, this does not extend (as in the case of direct inputs) to the number of tools that an individual could purchase. As Witt argues, the consumption of these tools may not necessarily be determined by the underlying deprivation levels of the corresponding needs (Witt 2001: 27).

Moreover, acquired wants have the property that they are conditioned on these innate needs such that one acquired want is conditioned on one innate need, but also that one acquired want is associated with several innate needs. And while deprivation with regard to needs is specific, the deprivation of acquired wants is not, which means that the deprivation of the acquired want depends on the deprivation levels of all needs on which it is conditioned (Witt 2001: 29). Witt thus conjectures that one will seldom feel satiation of acquired wants when many innate needs are involved. We have here a property which serves to normatively distinguish wants in terms of the difficulty to satisfy innate needs (per time interval). If we always experience deprivation relative to wants, this deprivation decreases enjoyment (or brings suffering if deprivation is severe enough). In that sense, if wants are not satiable because their satiation is unspecific and depends on a large number of innate needs, they will tend to decrease our net well-being. The more needs and wants an acquired want is associated with, the less likely it is to exhibit the potential to be satiated.

Besides the unspecific deprivation when an acquired want is conditioned on multiple needs, other strategies for avoiding satiation have been identified. It is possible to put satiation for a want back to a later point in time. i.e. design a good so that satiation is delayed or mitigated. The shift from sugar-sweetened to sugar-free products can be understood as a step to delay satiation and allow for higher levels of consumption (Ruprecht 2001, 2005). In the case of sugar-free products, physiological processes are manipulated in order to delay a biological marker that prompts satiation: when the body absorbs larger quantities of sugar, it seems that bodily processes lead to satiation more quickly than if similar food with artificial sweeteners is consumed. In the case of other needs and wants, similar results could be attained in delaying satiation by varying some features of the stimulus or differentiating the categorization level, as detailed above (Redden 2008).

A normative evaluation of such delays in satiation is not easy. One possibility is that the delay of satiation caused in this way leads to an increase in consumption of the respective product per time interval. Increased exposure to a stimulus over time can trigger adaptive processes that will cause an internality for the consumer (i.e. the individual does not take into account the effects of present consumption on future utility). Consider the following example: by drinking a glass of sugared coke per day, an individual derives a certain amount of enjoyment. Let us assume that the sugar has satiated the individual so that more is not drunk per day. By switching to artificially sweetened diet coke, a larger amount of the product can be consumed per day before satiation sets in. In consequence, the higher amount per day leads to a faster rate of adaptation to the repeated consumption as compared to drinking sugared coke. The consumption pattern described here would then lead to a decrease in welfare of the consumer when satiation is delayed in this fashion (this is the reverse effect to that shown by Baucells and Sarin 2007). Such dynamics could also be conjectured to lie at the heart of the obesity problem, if one considers that similar advances in pushing back satiation have been made with low-fat or fat-free products, which work in a similar fashion. However, delaying satiation could also result in a higher amount of net enjoyment if the increased consumption frequency is not offset by the above-mentioned internality (regarding adaptation). As this is dependent on the domain specifity of adaptation, no unambiguous normative evaluation is possible.

Being in a constant state of deprivation entails a state of unpleasant experiences and is thus welfare decreasing. So avoiding learning a want that is nearly impossible to satisfy might be desirable from this point of view. (A similar reasoning can be applied to these wants where adaptation sets in quickly.) The analysis so far prompts the contention that it could be worthwhile to shift consumption to activities which relate to wants that are easier to satisfy than wants where satiation is rare or nonexistent (of course: regarding similar activities). At least, information on such satiation effects can be used to inform an individual's consumption decisions. In terms of satisfaction patterns of acquired wants, this means that if individuals acquire large and diversified hierarchies of wants, it is easy to see that not all of them can be satisfied in a given time interval and within a given budget: the larger the set of acquired wants, the higher the degree of deprivation an individual experiences with respect to them. In that sense, it is possible to say that more is not always better, because the larger set of acquired wants does not seem so desirable anymore. However, the change of an individual's want set is governed by the acquisition of new wants and the extinction of old wants, which have probably not been satisfied for quite a while. Therefore the above reasoning has to be qualified: the acquisition of new wants is only welfare decreasing in so far as more new wants are learned than old ones are becoming extinct (assuming equal rewards from satisfaction and equal time needed to satisfy the wants). To the extent that the satisfaction of wants takes time, normative priority could also be given to time-efficient wants (regarding comparable activities), i.e. those wants whose level of reward per time unit is higher than that of others.

But a normative evaluation of different satiation patterns can focus on still other aspects. Probably the least controversial suggestion pertains to the case of satiation with regard to positional goods. If the need for status can only be satisfied by positional goods, thus enabling only a fraction of individuals to satisfy such a need simultaneously, the attempt to satisfy it will lead to inefficient and wasteful status races. The 'positional treadmill' literature shows the futility of aiming at the satisfaction of this need. Moreover, the status need is mostly satisfied not by using up direct inputs in the 'consumption process' of satisfying this need but by the service that tools provide. The expensive wrist watch or the rare fountain pen are examples, where one can easily see that large collections of varied goods can be accumulated and the demand for such 'tools' is not limited by the physical properties of the satiation process (Witt 2001). If the status need is satiable per time unit (which is doubtful), at least the demand for status goods might not be affected by the satiation process. Moreover, these positional goods do not necessarily have to be assumed to be available in fixed quantity (as assumed by Hirsch 1995). Rising incomes tend to spur innovative activities towards developing ever new varieties of these positional goods (Frank 1999). As Cooper et al. (2001) have shown, it is possible that such status races lead to an increase in positional good innovations and a concurrent decrease in individual well-being, resulting from an over-proportionate shift in innovative activity towards the production of positional goods. If we accept this analysis, we have found a class of innovations that cannot be seen as beneficial, going by the result of our hedonistic normative analysis.[108] If a status good is used up in the process of consumption, e.g. caviar or expensive wines, there might actually exist a satiation level due to the combination character of the good.[109] When deliberating on policies, an approach based on naturalistic insights might exploit this differentiation between status goods that are subject to satiation because of their association with satiable wants and those that are not subject to satiation.

A different avenue of normative evaluation relates to different dynamics of combination goods. One can argue that there are efficiency gains to be realized in so far as combination goods are able to satisfy multiple needs or wants at the same time. If one good instead of multiple goods can satisfy multiple wants, such an innovation can be beneficial because fewer resources are used up to achieve the same result (assuming that the production of combination goods would be less expensive in terms of resources than the simple goods that would satisfy the multiple wants). On the other hand, this has to be qualified because combination goods might lead to inefficiency if they are more expensive in production than the respective 'single-want goods'. A normative distinction could be made regarding these combination goods that promise to satisfy wants or needs which are characterized as comparatively insatiable. If (unaware) consumers tend to associate such insatiable wants with such a good, they might end up in an 'insatiability treadmill' when trying to satisfy their wants with that good. Two different cases are possible: a good can be set up in two ways to satisfy, besides want A, also a second want, B. If want B has a comparatively higher satiation level, this will lead to increases in consumption of the good going beyond satiation in terms of want A. If, on the other hand, the satiation level is lower, consumption of the combination good will lead to decreased consumption, depending on which of the two wants' satiation levels are relevant in constraining consumption (per time interval). In the caviar example, consumption for status reasons might be limited by virtue of the physical satiation that sets in because of the satisfaction of the need for nutrition. Here the latter satiation level seems more relevant. But it is also conceivable that this dynamic works the other way around, when other needs or wants are catered to by a combination good (these characteristics of goods as being amenable to different satiation patterns for different wants is something which has been by and large ignored in the literature).

Finally, a normative implication of the insatiability of some wants, and the learning of satisfying these wants in ever new ways, could be labelled 'refinement treadmill'. This is probably also fraught with normatively undesirable features, which could account for decreasing enjoyment over time related to its inherent dynamics. If, to escape satiation, ever new and varied combination goods are developed that a consumer can learn to associate with the satisfaction of a certain number of wants, this can lead to what has been labelled the 'refinement effect' of consumption (Witt 2001). To the extent that our wants shape our attention processes and thus influence the consumption possibilities we become aware of, learning tends to be biased towards an increasingly specialized consumption of certain goods with probably decreasing returns to specialization of enjoyment.[110] Although the refinement can push back satiation, the combination of hedonic adaptation regarding the consumption of these goods and the focus on refining this special consumption category could lead to a crowding out of other, more rewarding activities in favour of the refined consumption activity. As the deprivation involved in this activity shapes attention, it can be conjectured that an (unaware) individual could become trapped in a 'refinement treadmill' (which is probably closely related to the hedonic treadmill) due to focusing attention on the refinement category. The driving force here may be the circular focus of deprivation-triggered attention on refinement rather than on hedonic adaptation. Such learning paths of want refinement would probably be as inefficient as the striving for adaptive enjoyments discussed before. It has to be pointed out that a hypothesis of decreasing enjoyment 'returns to specialization' would require further empirical examination as to its existence and effect size.

The considerations in this section allow us to further refine the normative distinction presented in the previous chapter. As I have argued there, a distinction in normative priority between innate needs and acquired wants is quite coarse (see section 5.5). To the extent that we can find differing satiation patterns in these innate needs, we can further distinguish them in a normative classification scheme. As has been highlighted in this section, the status need is difficult (if not impossible) to satisfy because of the inherent characteristics of positional goods. Resulting from this difficulty, a case could be made to decrease the normative weight given to the satisfaction of this status need. Apart from the general concerns about the insatiability of the status need, this is particularly problematic in the context of a normative prioritization of basic needs because it is generally impossible to satisfy this need in an egalitarian fashion (obviously, one cannot entitle everyone to status goods because then these would lose their positional goods character and no longer satisfy the need).[111] Similarly, it can be conjectured that, in principle, the need for cognitive arousal is also very difficult to satisfy and should accordingly be given less normative weight in a basic need prioritization. However, other than the general impossibility of providing the positional goods needed to satisfy the status need, the insatiability discussed here can be conjectured to lie in the vagueness of the families of goods that could satisfy this need (see also Brandt 1979: 33). As large groups of similar stimuli could be provided to satisfy such a need, a comparatively huge class of acquired wants could lead here to an insatiability similar to that involved in the status need. Such line of reasoning would have to be developed further in future research: while differential satiation patterns are – to a small extent – already a matter of empirical research, further empirical results will be needed to develop more fully the rather coarse normative distinctions suggested here.

6.5.2 Want dynamics: autonomy of want formation

In the previous subsection, I have discussed some peculiarities related to satiation dynamics of wants and presented possible normative distinctions. In the present subsection, another application of empirically rich normative distinctions is provided in order to inform a suitable notion of 'autonomy' of want formation and discuss how these insights relate to the problem of adaptive preference formation (a problem already introduced in sections 3.1.1 and 3.1.3). Adaptive preferences are usually understood to be problematic for subjective theories of welfare because of their endogeneity: the preferences used to assess individual welfare are shaped through different processes of coping with objective misery (in terms of an objective list account of welfare, see section 2.2.1). In consequence, subjectively perceived satisfaction of preference (or evaluation of enjoyment) does not reflect the individual's more objective situation and cannot be used as a measuring rod for welfare:

> The hopeless beggar, the precarious landless labourer, the dominated housewife, the hardened unemployed or the over-exhausted coolie may all take pleasures in small mercies, and manage to suppress intense suffering for the necessity of continuing survival, but it would be ethically deeply mistaken to attach a correspondingly small value to the loss of their well-being
>
> (Sen 1987: 45–6)

The circularity involved in the preferences concerned prompts a dynamic analysis, i.e. of the formation and change of these preferences. While there are different ideas in the literature of what 'adaptive preferences' are, authors usually agree that these preferences are normatively special as they are formed as a reaction to a decreased opportunity set. Adaptive preferences are thus a result of a lack of freedom of forming other preferences. This decreased opportunity set can often be related to 'insidious social conditioning', encompassing the manipulative interference with an individual's preferences, be it by another individual, society or the state. Understanding autonomy (in a first approximation) to be 'the capacity of a person critically to reflect upon, and then attempt to accept or change, his or her preferences, desires, values, and ideals' (Dworkin 1988: 48), it can thus be argued that adaptive preferences lack a certain degree of autonomy and should be accounted for differently in the assessment of an individual's welfare. Before discussing the different notions of adaptive preference formation and their normative relevance, note that 'adaptive preference formation' differs from effects of 'hedonic adaptation' in the case where an individual's enjoyment of the same pleasure is dampened by continuous exposition to the same stimuli: adaptation in the context of preference formation can be diametrically opposed to the way the notion of adaptation is used in the context of 'hedonic adaptation' (see section 6.4). While adaptive preference formation results from a decreased feasible set (thus reflecting the limits to one's autonomy), hedonic adaptation can also be the effect of an increase of one's feasible set and the continuous consumption that may be associated with the increase (see also Qizilbash 2008: 58).

The case of adaptive preference formation has been taken as one of the striking counter-examples, where standard views of preference satisfaction go wrong: the 'subdued housewife' or the 'hopeless beggar', who are objectively deprived hold a limited preference set, containing preferences that they can satisfy even under adverse conditions. According to the standard reading of the preference satisfaction view, these preferences are satisfied, and housewife and beggar are not so badly off after all in terms of preference satisfaction. Of course, this is similar in hedonism, where housewife and beggar derive pleasure from small mercies (Crocker 1992: 601). Such being the case, the problem of adaptive preference formation is also relevant for my theory of enjoyment or any subjective theory of welfare in general, because it might lead to a distorted measure of well-being for the extremely poor or otherwise handicapped or deprived. Adaptive preference formation thus shows that a theory of welfare that is solely concerned with welfare information on preferences or enjoyment can seriously fail when such important cases of extreme 'objective' misery are involved. Additional welfare-relevant information, for example on opportunity sets or individuals' autonomy involved in forming their preferences, is therefore necessary to supplement the welfare calculus. Adaptive preference formation is understood differently by different authors: similar differences exist in terms of whether this is understood as a problem of autonomy or opportunity (freedom), depending on the concrete notion of autonomy used in the literature. I therefore begin by distinguishing some relevant though different notions of adaptive preference formation. Following that, I discuss and evaluate various solution concepts for the problem of adaptive preference formation before presenting and defending my own proposal how to deal with these preferences.

Sen's adaptive preferences

Sen's idea of adaptive preferences encompasses the cases discussed above, where subdued housewife, hopeless beggar, exhausted coolie or precarious landless labourer adapt their preferences to situations of misery and deprivation (Sen 1984: 309). This can be the result of different processes as e.g. the habituation to given circumstances or the lowering of aspiration levels. A shift in preferences may happen without conscious reflection of the individual or, on the contrary, as a deliberate 'survival strategy' (Sen 1987: 45–6). The latter notion (already) points to the biological function served by adaptive preference formation, viz. enabling the individual to survive in objectively bad conditions. For Sen, adaptive preference formation is centred on cases of (severe) poverty and deprivation, which are reflected in the severely limited opportunity set of an individual. Resulting from this diagnosis, Sen's argument states that only the potential freedom to be what one wants to be, or to do what one wants to do (the 'capabilities to function', see section 3.2) can be an undistorted measure of an individual's well-being. If a wealthy ascetic chooses a life of deprivation, this case differs from the cases above because the ascetic has a larger capability set and more options to choose from. According to Sen, one can get used to being involuntarily deprived of food, being hungry and nevertheless subjectively quite happy. But this is fundamentally different from someone who deliberately chooses to stay hungry (Sen 1987: 29). Sen's idea of individual autonomy seems to be closely related to the (positive) freedom to do or not to do certain things. What is absent in Sen's treatment of adaptive preferences is a time dimension. Sen's concept is static, and he does not concern himself with the question of how the adaptive preference came to pass, for example whether as a result of social conditioning or a reaction to bad luck or some other influence. On the other hand, in his usage of adaptive preference formation he includes cases where a person is manipulated into having adaptive preferences (e.g. the subdued housewife by her husband). In cases of manipulation, adaptive preferences are induced to the benefit of someone else, e.g. the dominating husband. This is, for example, excluded in Elster's account of adaptive preferences to which I now turn.

Elster's adaptive preferences

Elster's notion of adaptive preferences is in certain ways broader than Sen's, albeit narrower in other respects (Qizilbash 2008). Most of Elster's discussion of adaptive preferences is based on the phenomenon of sour grapes (see section 3.1.1 and Elster 1983), meaning that an individual's preferences are not independent of the feasible set and that one forms a preference based on available options. But while Sen is (unsystematically) interested in the underdogs of a society, Elster takes a much broader view of the phenomenon of adaptive preferences. If the wealthy merchant does not manage to obtain the seat on the city council, he will proclaim, 'I didn't want it anyway!', similar to the fox in Aesop's fable. In his exposition, Elster uses an even more encompassing example of the Industrial Revolution that highlights this fact (Elster 1983: 133): one could conceive of the Industrial Revolution as a process that has increased our opportunity sets and released the individuals of a society from a state of adaptive preferences in t_0 (preferences are adapted to a Pre-Industrial state x), but has led to a cardinally decreased well-being in t_1 (the Post-Industrial state y) because our opportunity sets are so much larger, our wants so ambitious, our aspirations so high that we are frustrated but more autonomous (Elster 1983: 135).

It is worth looking at this example in more detail: imagine that the Industrial Revolution has led to a rise in aspiration levels that is higher than the increased satisfaction of wants it has brought. Were this the case, the utilitarian, without taking into account the effects that adaptive preference formation has had (namely the release from adaptive preferences), might well be led to conclude that society enjoyed higher levels of welfare (in terms of aggregated individual well-being) before compared to after the Industrial Revolution. But for Elster, there must be room for the autonomy of wants to overrule the satisfaction of wants: we might be worse off in terms of well-being but better off in terms of autonomy, and that should be reflected in an assessment of the situation. For a standard (ordinal) preference satisfaction calculus, society would prefer the Pre-Industrial Revolution state ($x > y$) with preferences of Pre-Industrial Revolution (t_0), and the Industrial Revolution state ($y > x$) with preferences adapted to the Industrial Revolution (t_1). Nevertheless, with an ordinal standard, one cannot compare this instance of preference change (compare section 6.1). If one conceives of this situation in terms of a cardinal utility measure, the instance of adaptive preference formation leads the utilitarian to conclude that the Pre-Industrial Revolution state had a higher well-being associated with it, if $u_0(x) > u_0(y)$ and $u_1(y) > u_1(x)$ but also $u_0(x) > u_1(y)$ due to adaptive preferences. As Elster summarizes, 'We were happier before we got these fancy new things, but now we would be miserable without them.' (Elster 1983: 135) For Elster, adaptive preferences constitute a much broader field, and they do not pertain to a less well-off subgroup of individuals: adaptive preferences are an instance of lack of autonomy of preferences. Releasing individuals from their adaptive preferences leads to an increase in their autonomy but can bring a decrease in welfare. There is a trade-off involved. As Elster notes with respect to the economic dynamics that started in the Industrial Revolution, there may be a point where a release from adaptive preferences can even lead to the 'enslavement to addictive preferences' (e.g. the treadmill of striving for ever more material comforts, Elster 1983: 136).

Moreover, while Elster makes the criticism that the process of adaptive preference formation would not matter in a utilitarian welfare calculus (obviously not in an ordinal one, but not even in the cardinal calculus, as the example has shown), he does not use the argument to criticize utilitarianism for its systematic neglect of the poor. I have already mentioned that he carefully distinguishes adaptive preference formation from the preference formation by learning, precommitment, manipulation, character planning or wishful thinking and counteradaptive preference formation (see section 3.1.1). Contrary to Sen (and narrowing down his own concept), Elster excludes manipulation from his analysis. But similar to Sen, Elster considers adaptive preferences as an instance of resignation or habituation to a given situation (largely to reduce cognitive dissonance, cf. Festinger 1957). For Elster, it is relevant to examine the genesis of adaptive preference formation (thereby taking a dynamic perspective) and to ascertain whether there might be a test to detect adaptive preference formation. In this spirit, he has formulated a test whether a preference was formed adaptively, which can be stated as follows (Elster 1983: 131): let S be the global choice set containing all states of the world, and let S_1 and S_2 be two feasible sets for an individual, where S_1 and S_2 induce preference structures $\geqslant_1$ and $\geqslant_2$. Then for no x and y in the global set S there should be $x >_1 y$ and $y >_2 x$. More casually stated, Elster's test for detecting non-adaptive preferences would require that no preference reversal should occur when the set of opportunities is increased.

Von Weizsaecker's adaptive preferences

In sections 3.1.1 and 3.1.3, it has been shown that while von Weizsaecker ostensibly borrows his notion from Elster, he has actually modelled habitual preferences that adapt to a certain situation in terms of a complete consumption vector. For von Weizsaecker, adaptive preferences constitute a convenient way to formalize a somewhat narrow view of endogenous preferences. The main mechanism here is habituation to a given situation, which, however, is assumed for any (!) consumption vector without any reference to problems of poverty or autonomy. In his model, all consumers form adaptive preferences in the sense that, in each time period, they get used to what they have, and other bundles become devalued relative to the status quo. This would still be problematic when an individual is born into a situation of objective misery (in terms of an objective list view of welfare). Moreover, von Weizsaecker has excluded the possibility that preference change leads to decreased welfare but increases autonomy. A more fitting description, as I have argued, would be to call these dynamics a 'mere exposure' effect by which we start liking what we are continuously exposed to, viz. our consumption bundle (Zajonc 2001). Since von Weizsaecker's approach is concerned neither with the aspect of deprivation and misery nor with the autonomy of the preference formation process, I neglect this kind of adaptive preference formation in the following discussion.

Evaluation of adaptive preferences

Any theory of welfare that is not fully objective has to deal with the problem of adaptive preferences and should suggest how to deal with it.[112] For a proponent of the preference satisfaction view, the apparently easiest way out of this predicament is certainly to postulate that adaptive preference formation cannot occur if an individual's *informed* preferences are taken as the welfare measuring rod. Similarly, one could postulate such an information requirement for hedonism and specify that only informed enjoyment, i.e. resulting from the satisfaction of wants that meet an informational requirement, would count for an individual's well-being. Having postulated this, one could assume that an informed preference (or informed enjoyment) does not happen to be adaptive *per definitionem* (of the informational requirement). This has been put forward by Griffin:

> Our desires are shaped by our expectations, which are shaped by our circumstances. Any injustice in the last infects the first. There is no denying that some accounts of well-being will, therefore, distort moral thought in this way. Actual-desire accounts will. A moral theory should not use as its base persons' actual expectations. It has to get behind them to what are in some sense legitimate expectations . . . It does not matter that some persons have modest expectations; their informed desires include what they would want if they raised their sights
>
> (Griffin 1986: 47)

This is certainly a solution to the problem, but it is only a formal one, because the informational requirement is defined in a way that excludes the possibility of adaptive preference formation *ex cathedra*. What would be needed is a material argument that full information does indeed not lead to adaptive preferences, i.e. one needs to spell out how exactly the information leads to non-adaptive preferences. Informed preference or enjoyment accounts, depending on the definition of 'informed', do not have to meet the autonomy requirement automatically. For example, in the account of Brandt (1979), informed preferences are those that would survive 'cognitive psychotherapy' (i.e. a preference that is abandoned by an individual after the laying out of all relevant information in a vivid way and at an appropriate time, see section 6.2). But if an individual has a deep-seated obsessive preference, or has consciously adopted a preference as survival strategy in adverse circumstances, these preferences would survive this full information criterion and could be adaptive (in one sense or the other). Elster's proposal that an informed preference should be grounded in experience, i.e. giving more weight to someone's preference of $x > y$ if that individual has experienced x as well as y, has to be understood similarly (Elster 1983: 113–14). The hopeless beggar or subdued housewife might have experienced both situations but lack one of the options and thus have adaptive preferences. The problem does not stop here. Similarly, in Griffin's account of informed preference (where a preference is fully informed if it advances one's plan of life and further information would not change it, cf. Griffin 1986: 13), adaptive preference formation could also prevail despite the information requirement. In a given situation, one could have informed preferences, while it is still conceivable that they are adaptive in the sense of Sen:

> [S]omeone in unfortunate circumstances forms quite limited and unam-bitious desires that are reasonable given the bleak conditions she faces. Being blind, I don't form ambitions that require eyesight; being impover-ished, I don't form ambitions that require wealth to have a reasonable prospect of success; being unintelligent, I don't form ambitions that would strain my limited brain power; and lacking social connections, I don't form ambitions that can be achieved only with the help of powerful allies. Judged against the baseline of my original grim life circumstances, I am reasonably lucky and most of important desires are fulfilled over the course of my life. These desires are not ill-chosen; they would be endorsed and affirmed by the fully informed and rational ideal advisor
>
> (Arneson 1999: 133)

For such reasons, the structure of preferences evaluated via an informational requirement does not seem sufficient to deal with adaptive preferences. Moreover, full information requirements have been criticized for the 'Herculean' view they impose on human rationality (see section 6.2). Is full information really something that can be realistically attained and, if not, of what use is it (Sobel 1994; Rosati 1995)? Qizilbash argues that such require-ments are too far removed from human cognitive capacities and 'the idealised desires are hardly *human desires* at all' (Qizilbash 2006: 86, emphasis in ori-ginal). Thus they are difficult to make sense of in any case. While this may be too harsh a criticism, I would argue that it is important to materially specify what 'full information' is and relate it to human cognitive capacities. If one formulates 'full information' in less demanding ways, one may end up having to admit that adaptive preferences can still be part and parcel of one's theory.

This refers us back to Elster's idea of what distinguishes adaptive prefer-ence formation from other preferences, namely a lack of autonomy regarding how they were formed (their genesis; see also Christman 1991). Any evalu-ation of a preference in terms of autonomy crucially hinges on what we understand by 'autonomy'. In the present context, I cannot give a fully fledged account of this notion (but see Dworkin 1988). However, what seems to be at the core of the concept is that autonomy has to do with self-determination, freedom, self-information, responsibility, the absence of mani-pulation or of coercion. If we understand autonomy in Sen's and Elster's sense, it is primarily defined in terms of freedom and opportunity, i.e. form-ing a preference without being constrained by one's feasible set. But other concepts of autonomy are conceivable. As stated above, Dworkin has defined autonomy as 'the capacity of a person critically to reflect upon, and then attempt to accept or change, his or her preferences' (Dworkin 1988: 48). On this view, the underdog, who consciously accepts his lot as a survival strategy, would form his preferences autonomously despite his misery: according to

Dworkin's definition of autonomy, some of Sen's cases are not instances of adaptive preference formation. A similar criterion of autonomy has also been used by Sumner in his theory of 'authentic happiness': preferences are only autonomous if they have been formed in a way that did not erode individuals' capacities for their critical assessment (Sumner 1996: 170).[113] Similar to Dworkin's view, Sumner's criterion excludes preferences that came into existence through indoctrination. But it is obvious that he would have to accept that a consciously adopted survival strategy of the underdog can be regarded as based on autonomous preferences: not all adaptive preferences do result from manipulation or social conditioning. Individuals might find themselves in objectively extremely adverse situations and, consequently, their adaptive preferences would be the result of a conscious and critically deliberated strategy of coping.

Lastly, consider Sugden's idea of a responsible individual (section 3.3): Sugden treats each individual as being completely autonomous such that each preference set at each point in time is the outcome of a responsible agent's actions. Individuals having a certain endowment can form whatever preferences they wish in the next stages of the model, and these are considered to be revealing their responsible choices. With such a notion of responsibility, of course, consumer sovereignty is preserved even without coherent preferences. But it also means there is no place in Sugden's model for adaptive preferences at all. If autonomy is understood in the sense that individuals are responsible for whatever preferences they have, the problem of adaptive preference formation does not arise by assumption. The discussion shows clearly that we need to find a test of the autonomy of preference formation that can be used to preserve the intuition of the Elster and Sen examples and to ascertain whether some preferences (and wants) were formed autonomously or not. This is not to deny that other tests could be used in parallel, but any test should be useful in at least some cases. Below I discuss how our naturalistic positive knowledge could help us to specify a criterion for defining whether wants are formed autonomously and then apply it to the different test cases mentioned above.

An alternative proposal

What can be concluded from the discussion so far is that the problem of adaptive preference formation cannot be convincingly solved by recourse to a criterion of full information: it is unclear why exactly a fully informed preference should not nevertheless be adaptive. Also, if one increases the epistemological requirements of full information, one quickly reaches a dimension where this criterion would be vastly beyond human cognitive capabilities and limitations. Within a naturalistic methodology, such a criterion would seem dubious anyway. Moreover, adaptive preference formation is a pervasive problem also for the enjoyment view. Nevertheless, possible solution schemata and tests for adaptive preference formation can be adapted from the discussion of the preference satisfaction view. The question to be asked is to what extent can positive insights of the naturalistic approach be used in providing a different test for adaptive preferences or wants? First, we cannot discuss the autonomy of inborn innate needs *per se*. While one can evaluate the state of consumption knowledge of an individual regarding the satisfaction of these needs, the needs themselves obviously cannot be subjected to a critique of autonomy, as we cannot freely choose to acquire them, nor can we completely refrain from satisfying them. Acquired wants (which are rooted in these inborn needs), on the other hand, can be given a different normative weight. I therefore begin with a proposal on how to assess the autonomy involved in acquiring these wants.

One possibility of testing the autonomy of want formation is provided by the different learning mechanisms that govern the acquisition of wants and their change and by the learning of new consumption knowledge. This idea has been first introduced in a short passage by Chai and Schubert (2007), who argue that if a want is formed through 'insightful learning', one can assume that the agent has sufficiently reflected on the formation of this new want and can thus be considered to have autonomously formed the resulting want. This is not the case (or at least comparatively less so) for 'associative learning', which takes place in a less conscious way. New wants are thus often formed without conscious deliberation. It should be pointed out that this test should be considered to be in addition to assessing the structure of wants with respect to the dimension of differential satiation patterns (section 6.5.1). Making a distinction in wants regarding the way in which they have been formed addresses the *genesis* of a want. To come to different normative assessments of the welfare-theoretic status of preferences as regards the history of how they were formed is not new (see Christman 1991). What is new is a distinction in terms of more or less autonomy, depending on the cognitive involvement in the learning process.

Following Chai and Schubert (2007), let us distinguish two main classes of learning, calling one 'associative learning' and the other 'insightful learning' (see Hergenhahn and Olson 1997). 'Associative learning' refers to learning mechanisms such as Pavlovian and operant conditioning, which play a major role for the learning of acquired wants. Via associative learning, these wants are conditioned on existing innate wants (I have discussed these in detail in section 4.4). A main characteristic of the mechanisms of associative learning is that they operate on a relatively low level of cognitive involvement. On the one hand, this leads to the individual often not being aware of learning wants in this way. On the other hand, such a mechanism produces much more stable results than the more cognitively mediated learning mechanisms (since cognitive interference tends to be low, Zajonc and Markus 1982). Learning via mechanisms of insightful learning is, on the contrary, strongly cognitively mediated. It refers *inter alia* to mechanisms of imitational learning but also to the acquisition of consumption knowledge and the application of such knowledge to problems. In such cases, individuals who are aware of a problem direct cognitive efforts to its solution. While the individuals' perceptions may be affected by all kinds of social dynamics and attention processes at the same time, for example agenda-setting effects and the like, they have the opportunity of reflecting on their wants and the acquisition thereof.

In terms of an individual's autonomy, one can thus argue that the formation of an acquired want is more autonomous if that individual is aware of its formation or has *ex ante* cognitively reflected on it. By contrast, a want that is formed associatively without an individual's awareness lacks a certain degree of autonomy. While insightful learning can be classified as leading to more autonomous wants or more autonomously gained consumption knowledge, this classification is not exclusively bipartite in reality. Associative learning can at times also occur with the awareness or (some) cognitive participation of the individual. On the other hand, even insightful learning can still be subject to some of the well-known anomalies or framing effects known from behavioural economics. What is suggested here is to accord higher normative weight to these wants, i.e. the wants that were learned in a more autonomous way. There is a *general tendency* that this usually includes insightful learning in the process. In terms of Elster's categorization, the distinction suggested here would cut across such categories as learning by experience, deliberate character planning or precommitment, i.e. categories of want formation he has labelled as generally being autonomous (Elster 1983: 111–19). But in light of our positive knowledge of how individuals learn, it is not clear why a preference learned via experience, e.g. via associative learning, should automatically be autonomous, even if the learning has taken place without any deliberate reflection on the part of the individual. In this respect, the test suggested here differs from Elster's characterization.

With this distinction, we can materially explore why some preferences have been formed in a less autonomous way because the individual did not seem to critically reflect on their adoption when learning them in an associative way. This differentiation between insightful and associative learning should be understood in terms of an autonomy as the capacity to reflect critically upon wants, not primarily as an example of better informed want formation (although this may be an instance where this is mutually dependent). To a certain extent, one could also argue that insightful learning is a way of learning that better informs individuals of their wants because knowledge is processed in a more vivid and conscious way. That this is obviously an issue that has to do with an individual's autonomy becomes clear when that individual is manipulated into acquiring a want through associative learning and without awareness. Had the learning of the want occurred on the level of insightful learning, the individual would at least have stood a chance of reflecting on the manipulative character of the learning opportunity and might have refrained from acquiring the want. Especially in the case of reinforcement learning, it might often not be clear for individuals that they are in the process of acquiring a want. Lucid examples can be found in our childhood preferences that are acquired by parental reinforcement, often with very low awareness. Zajonc and Markus (1982) have described a case where Mexican children were (by parental reinforcement) brought to acquire a want for very hot chilli, even though they had a strong initial (innate) aversion at the beginning. Reinforcement through parental praise or the sense of belonging to a community (social pressure and reinforcement) led to the subsequent acquisition of such a want in a large society. Similar processes also operate in adults when wants are acquired by similar reinforcement (in terms of one's status, belonging to a group, etc.). The important point to keep in mind is that such acquired wants (where processes largely work on the level of affect, not cognition) are comparatively more difficult to get rid of than cognitively acquired wants.

Let me point out that defining adaptive preferences as Elster does (by their being reversed when the opportunity set is increased) seems to neglect an important fact about how wants are usually learned by individuals. If the learning of such an adaptive preference has occurred via associative learning, it is not clear whether it would really disappear with the subsequent enlargement of the feasible set, because associative learning is often quite stable, and behaviour that is reinforced over a period of time is maintained as long as it is being reinforced. Many wants that were acquired without much conscious deliberation are still being satisfied (if they are not deliberated on), even if the feasible set is increased. The hopeless beggar who is not aware that his behaviour is based on adaptive preferences might not change it (in some instances), even if his feasible set increases. This is because he is neither aware of the wants he has acquired in the past nor of their adaptive character. Or consider the generation of individuals who grew up during World War II. Despite vastly increased feasible sets after the war, many individuals continued to live a frugal lifestyle (e.g. hoarding food, not being able to throw out leftovers after meals), having acquired adaptive wants during the war and not finding it easy to unlearn them afterwards. Such a situation will largely depend on the strength of reinforcement that is associated with adaptive wants. Here again, only when released from the grip of adaptive preferences does the autonomous individual (in terms of a cognitively deliberating individual) stand a chance of revising and changing existing wants. But often, even more than just cognitive reflection is necessary to get rid of an adaptive want in favour of a non-adaptive one.

As a consequence, the idea of autonomy, linked to the conscious deliberation of want learning, can in fact be compatible with Elster's idea of adaptive preference formation to the extent that some forms of learning lead to autonomous preferences. But according to the scheme suggested here and contrary to Elster and his idea of grounding preferences in experience, some experienced preferences would be counted as having been formed less autonomously. As Elster sees it, if one lives in the countryside and therefore acquires a preference for it and then goes to live in a city and acquires a preference for living there, the preference acquisition is autonomous because it is a result of learning. According to the want-learning test, I would argue that this is not necessarily the case if the preference was acquired without the relevant awareness, i.e. if it was learned in a non-insightful way. Similarly, if, for status-seeking purposes, one imitates a role model because one sees how that role model is (apparently) reinforced for status-seeking behaviour, this can be an instance of non-autonomous preference formation, if it is done without reflection and awareness. Note also that the experience (of imitating the role model) here is vicarious since one can acquire a want via imitational learning even without being directly reinforced oneself. A possible consequence of the peculiar fact of imitational learning is that one is indeed mistaken about the reinforcement the role model receives for the behaviour. In the case of the role model that is reinforced for status-seeking behaviour, the individual imitating the role model may be unaware that the latter has to seek ever increasing amounts of reinforcement due to adaptation effects or insatiability. The apparent reinforcement may have not been reinforcement at all, but the imitator might – without giving it much thought – acquire a similar want nevertheless.

The role of experience, while certainly interesting as an information criterion (see section 6.2), loses some importance regarding autonomy. While such a criterion helps to cope with problems of illusional or delusional enjoyments and preferences, it may not even be a necessary requirement for the autonomy of preference formation. I may have experienced an action, acquired a preference for it, but still may have not critically ('insightfully') reflected on it. Under these circumstances, should one really say that this preference was formed autonomously just because it was learned by experience? That this is not so is especially obvious when we consider that most of our preferences are learned this way, and many of them at a young age and at a time when we generally lack the necessary autonomy (as in the example of the Mexican children). Continuous reinforcement may then keep these preferences alive for the rest of our lives. According to the criterion of autonomy of want formation suggested here, some adaptive preferences of the Sen variety would have to be called autonomous. This is similar to the case of Dworkin's notion of autonomy (Dworkin 1988). When the hopeless beggar consciously reflects on his situation and adopts a modest preference set as his survival strategy, according to the test of autonomous want learning, his preference set has been formed in an autonomous way. Thus being in an adverse situation (even one of extreme misery) and consciously reflecting on and coping with it, for example by accepting deliberately stunted preferences, is counted as an autonomous action. Can our positive knowledge help us in devising a broader-based test that would reveal this type of adaptive preference formation?

A stronger, additional test criterion addressing this issue, and going beyond what has been sketched in Chai and Schubert (2007), could be derived from the discussion of innate needs in general and the necessity to satisfy these. As we all share a set of basic needs which, in one way or another, we need to satisfy in order to guarantee the continued functioning of our organism, one could assess especially Sen's test cases in terms of classes of needs which are not fulfilled. If we assume that adaptive preference formation is a pervasive phenomenon in the face of complete misery and deprivation, we can use the external test to see whether the different classes of innate needs are sufficiently (per time interval) satisfied by a person.[114] So if it turns out that in the case of the hopeless beggar many of these classes of wants are not satisfied, we are justified in inferring that his preferences regarding these wants are adaptive. Accepting the criterion that preferences tend to be formed non-autonomously if large classes of wants are not satisfied at all, can be understood as a different way of saying (as Sen has done) that an individual has or has not had sufficient options for satisfying these classes of wants. Thus a person whose set of satisfied wants only includes {*shelter, nutrition*} and who still reports high levels of well-being could arguably have adaptive wants regarding other needs such as {*status, cognitive arousal, . . .*}.

As with all other tests in the literature, this test is not completely bullet-proof because asceticism is an obvious counter-example. But to mistakenly count an ascetic as being badly off and deprived might be seen as a lesser defect compared to counting a hopeless beggar well off (in a certain sense, erring on the side of potentially privileging the less well off). Moreover, in the case of someone deliberately choosing to leave many classes of innate needs (relatively) unsatisfied (as the ascetic does), we can argue that this is a deliberate decision (in terms of the want-learning test above) and is thus autonomous and non-adaptive. A further complication arises from the fact that adaptive want formation could also affect the means of satisfying innate needs. The hopeless beggar might just seek very modest forms of satisfying his wants, for example watching the crowds passing by in the street instead of watching television or playing a tennis match (to satisfy the need for cognitive arousal). If, in that sense, a deprived person finds modest means of want satisfaction, we need a broader-based criticism of the classes of wants and the means of their satisfaction to detect adaptive want formation. One possibility would be to assess the relation of acquired to innate wants because in those cases where one looks for small mercies, one can expect the individual concerned to have a comparatively small set of acquired wants conditioned on the deprived classes of innate wants. So even if the hopeless beggar can satisfy his need for cognitive arousal, his set of acquired wants, which are conditioned on his need for cognitive arousal, will tend to have considerably fewer elements (e.g. {*watching streets*}) than those of a person who has non-adaptive preferences (e.g. {*watching streets, watching television, playing tennis, . . .*}).

It can, moreover, be conjectured that in a hedonistic framework the 'small mercies' argument is tempered by the characteristics associated with the deprivation of innate needs. Since these are inborn and their non-satisfaction entails severe harm and suffering, many cases of strong deprivation can be hypothesized to be recognized as such by those affected. No one experiencing continued and strong deprivation of (e.g.) food and health would report high levels of well-being (at least if one focuses on well-being related to these classes of needs). Against the background of what has been found for hedonic adaptation regarding innate needs, we can likewise argue that adaptive preference formation does not operate as strongly as in cases of acquired wants:

> Desires for food, for mobility, for security, for health, and for the use of reason – these seem to be relatively permanent features of our make-up as humans, which culture can blunt, but cannot altogether remove.
>
> (Nussbaum 2000: 155)

Adaptive preference formation can thus only work to a certain degree here because it is not possible to completely subdue these innate needs. Their deprivation cannot persist long even for mechanisms of the most insidious cultural conditioning. If one is deprived of the satisfaction of these innate needs, one suffers, and this suffering would figure in an assessment of one's well-being (practical problems of measurement such as false or biased reporting left aside). While it is thus possible that someone deprived when asked about his well-being would state: 'I might be hungry, but overall I have quite a nice life'; it would be less plausible if the person were to hold: 'As far as the need for food is concerned, my well-being is high'. In such cases, it is likely that one could detect adaptive preference formation by assessing more specifically the well-being of an individual with respect to these classes of innate needs.

So even when seeking small mercies, the hopeless beggar is aware that enjoyments (in general and in relation to his needs) are prudentially valuable, otherwise he would not be seeking them. Enjoyment and suffering are recognized for their prudential worth (see also Qizilbash 2006). To what degree awareness is stunted by misery and extreme poverty is debatable, but even in the worst of circumstances, at least the value of avoiding suffering should be acknowledged. I would argue that in terms of *sensory well-being*, even the worst off will experience a lowered balance of net enjoyment (or suffering). Adaptive preference formation, then, finds its expression in reported high levels of *evaluative well-being*, where aspirations are lowered and the 'conscious' evaluation of the situation will be made according to a lowered standard; or else attention is shifted to small mercies. Overall, it seems a comprehensive analysis of the genesis of want formation and the structure of the set of wants and their degrees of deprivation is needed to assess the degree to which a person may suffer from adaptive want formation. The concepts discussed in this section can contribute to that analysis; and while no single one of these concepts (or of those put forward in the literature) can distinguish all possible cases, their combined use can be expected to be valuable in deciding on some of the more problematic cases.

What is the significance of the discussion of these test criteria of want formation for the test case, where an individual acquires all kinds of wants but does not have the resources to satisfy them? In what way can these deliberations provide an answer for an unlucky individual who states, 'Had I not acquired the preferences for all these fancy things, would I not be unhappy not to be able to satisfy them all'? In terms of welfare, a loss might indeed be involved in this situation for the individual concerned. What can be said is that if these wants have been formed autonomously (according to the given definition), then that individual has traded off welfare against an increase in autonomy. For the non-autonomous acquisition of such a set of wants, we can only console the individual for having been tricked into following such a path of preference evolution. Since the increased set of wants is experienced as welfare decreasing by the individual, the normative evaluation is unproblematic: in terms of the individual's welfare, there was a decrease (correctly assessed as such by the individual, so there is no need for correcting the welfare calculus). But in the case of the individual, since the learning was an unreflected process, there was not even an increase in autonomy.[115]

A last approach would be to evaluate the autonomy of innate need satisfaction in terms of the means of satisfaction. This may amount to a critique of an individual's consumption knowledge. Learning also plays a role here for innate needs, namely for acquiring new consumption knowledge, i.e. knowledge about means-ends relationships that specify how to satisfy an existing innate need in a new way. Such knowledge can be learned via mechanisms of insightful learning (e.g. acquisition of knowledge from reading a book), through social learning (e.g. the imitation of role models) or associative learning (knowledge about the satisfaction of a want is gained via experimentation, e.g. trial and error learning). However, with respect to the acquisition of consumption knowledge, no normative distinction immediately suggests itself since, in this case, learning results in a larger knowledge stock of the individual. The indirect welfare effects of a changed stock of consumption knowledge do not allow for a similar and comparatively simple normative distinction of learning mechanisms. Rather, it is the kind of knowledge that is acquired which could be analyzed as to its welfare effects (e.g. one could examine the welfare effects of increased specialization of consumption knowledge), an aspect that is beyond the scope of this book, however. With these qualifications I finish the discussion of the third facet of my evolutionary theory of welfare.

7 Concluding remarks

7.1 Summary

Behavioural economics has brought the conventional revealed-preference approach under attack by finding inconsistencies and context dependencies of the preference formation process (Conlisk 1996). From this emerges a vexing problem for normative economics: when preferences are no longer consistent, one has to consider whether a different measuring rod for individual welfare can and should be found (Sugden 2006a). While Sugden (2004) has promoted a notion of welfare based on opportunities and on a concept of an individual's 'responsibility' as an autonomous agent, a different train of thought has been suggested by authors such as Kahneman et al. (1997) and Ng (2003). They propose to go back, in a Benthamite spirit, to the hedonistic foundations of utility and thus take a step 'beyond' the level of preference to the 'deeper' level of experienced utility (Kahneman) or happiness (Ng) as the actual factor motivating behaviour and the ultimate measuring rod for welfare.

This monograph has added to the hedonistic strain of literature by exploring the normative implications of basing welfare on experienced utility. The argument has been developed in the following way: from an evolutionary viewpoint, preferential change has been identified as a main welfare-theoretic challenge. But the relevance of addressing this phenomenon is broader and extends to welfare economics in general. As discussed in the second chapter, the standard welfare economic approach can be criticized from various angles because of methodological difficulties regarding the assumptions about human behaviour and rationality. Some of the deficiencies pointed out by critics are related to the 'hollowness of utility' (Samuelson 1947: 91) and preference. Ignoring the possibility of enriching both notions with content from psychology and other behavioural sciences has had important implications for economics in general (Lewin 1996; Bruni and Sugden 2007) and for any kind of welfare analysis: it has confined welfare economics to a very 'small box' (Sen 1987: 34). I have argued that welfare economics has been limited in its theoretical and practical relevance due to methodological shortcomings affecting the realism of its assumptions which, in turn, have resulted from behaviourally sparse information. It has further undergone a deliberate confinement to ethically minimal value judgements. This has led, *inter alia*, to the Arrovian impossibility result and practically rendered irrelevant some of the more prominent welfare criteria. I have argued that enriching the welfare-theoretic foundations with a naturalistic perspective would be a promising route to follow. In particular, this concerns the content and formation of preferences as well as the neurological and psychological substrates of well-being and utility.

The reflexions on such criticisms have, not surprisingly, spawned several proposals on how to relax some of these problematic assumptions. I have presented three alternative approaches in more detail. One of them is the model of von Weizsaecker, where preferences are allowed to vary according to the narrow mechanism of habituation to the status quo. A second, less orthodox view involves the capability approach, in which the subjectivistic utility concept has been replaced by two concepts: a functionings vector encompasses aspects of what a person is and does, while the capability set consists of all these functionings vectors an individual can reach and thus captures that individual's opportunities, or freedom, to choose between functionings vectors. The question left open in this purportedly objective account is whether individuals would really be better off in terms of their own evaluation of their situation. The third approach concerns the most radical departure from standard welfare economics, which, as I have argued, consists in the formulation of a purely opportunity-centred concept of welfare by Sugden, where any market allocation is understood as resulting from individuals' behaviour as responsible, autonomous agents, no matter how irrational their preferences are. The main conclusions of the third chapter are that an intertemporal dimension of welfare assessments prompts the need to specify laws governing how these preferences change and to find a more suitable measuring rod to normatively assess that change. In such a welfare-theoretic assessment, the genesis of preferences might matter as regards the autonomy with which a preference comes about, punctuating the importance of understanding how preferences are systematically formed. An identification of these laws, then, expressly introduces an evolutionary perspective into the analysis. History matters in the development of preferences.

After examining to what extent these alternative approaches fare better or worse than orthodox welfare economics, I have discussed the 'learning theory of consumption' (LTC), developed by Witt (2000, 2001, 2005). It has three defining elements: First, utility is conceived as consisting of the net total of pleasure over pain. In that respect, the learning theory of consumption can be understood to be a return to the sensory underpinnings of utility as was present in the early utilitarians. Second, utility is derived from the satisfaction of genetically fixed needs and learned wants. These wants also mark a departure from (axiomatic) preference theory. Third, the learning of wants follows regularities that are also genetically fixed. These elements are all based on material conjectures about the psychological and biological bases of human behaviour (as demanded by a naturalistic methodology, cf. Witt 1987). The dynamics of want acquisition and change are based on learning mechanisms, which function as transition laws governing the change in wants. To understand how wants (or, for that matter, the preferences they are giving rise to) *systematically* change has been identified as an important requirement of a theory of welfare that aims to deal with such dynamic (or rather, evolutionary) features. The discussion of the learning theory of consumption has resulted in a suggestion of a different model of human (economic) behaviour, viz. melioration learning and the matching law (Herrnstein 1997), which does not stipulate exceedingly high requirements on individual rationality. On account of the dynamics of this theory of the learning consumer, a much less pronounced role is attributed to an individual's rationality than in orthodox theory. *Homo discens* is perhaps a more plausible version of man than *homo oeconomicus*.

The core of this monograph are Chapters 5 and 6, the beginning of my contribution towards an evolutionary welfare economics. Here I have developed some important elements of such a theory. My interpretation of the learning theory of consumption as a variety of hedonism has included the two notions of sensory and evaluative well-being. I have also discussed the issue whether we can or should understand utility to be multidimensional. I have clarified some of the aspects of this question with recourse to findings from the neurosciences. My argument has been that a neuro-economic perspective favours a utility notion that is one-dimensional. I have also related the hedonistic notions of well-being to Witt's concept of 'wants' and highlighted (normative) features: innate needs, giving rise to materially specified preferences, constitute an important, more urgent class of wants. Having elaborated on the idea of a naturalistic notion of welfare, it has been necessary to justify the attractiveness of hedonism as the value basis of my theory of welfare and refute some common objections that could be levelled against it. Although hedonism is often considered an unattractive position, I have made a case that such a contention would be premature by showing that it is possible to defend welfare hedonism against common objections from various angles. Moreover, in my framework, the question of how the moral filter of a theory of welfare changes can be addressed separately, with the result that changes in the moral filter no longer prompt scepticism because the concept of sensory well-being is much more stable and can therefore be a sound basis for welfare assessments. Nevertheless, the moral filter is kept open for revisions in light of new 'moral knowledge', a feature that might even be attractive for an evolutionary theory of welfare. It has to be kept in mind that our social norms and values do not change completely capriciously, and by and large, there is still a connection between the Aristotelian notion of a good life and our contemporary notion of a good life (e.g. Sen 1987; Nussbaum 2000; Putnam 2002).

The concept of welfare in this theory has been specified materially as opposed to the usual formal specification of the preference satisfaction perspective used in standard (welfare) economics. Opening up the black box of welfare, utility and preference are important requirements for a naturalistic approach towards welfare economics. While the satisfaction of wants is an important source of welfare the mistake that has been criticized with regard to theories of preference satisfaction is avoided, namely mistaking the sources of welfare for the nature of welfare. This also applies to the difference between this account and the basic needs account, or the capabilities and functionings account: both these accounts merely stipulate lists of needs or functionings whose fulfilment purportedly increases welfare, but no systematic relationship is established between these sources of welfare and the nature of welfare. My account also has some advantages over standard utilitarian accounts since it states the nature of welfare more precisely, without recourse to folk intuitions on that matter. An additional advantage worth stressing lies in the explicit relationship to findings from other sciences not contradicted by the evolutionary theory of welfare.

In Chapter 6, I have discussed the dynamics of well-being resulting from welfare hedonism as envisaged by me. The stronger empirical foundations provided by the naturalistic insights of the previous chapters have been used to normatively discriminate between different sources of well-being and their respective dynamics. I have shown why a hedonistic theory of welfare better fits a dynamic setting than a preference satisfaction view. One does not have to go as far as Brandt (1979) who characterized the preference satisfaction view as 'unintelligible' under a regime of changing preferences; but the difficulties associated with it seem to favour hedonism – especially when considering that the most plausible version of the preference satisfaction view, when allowing for changing preferences, collapses into a hedonistic version of well-being. I have argued that this shift in emphasis from preferences to enjoyment should not be used to belittle the importance of preference satisfaction as perhaps the most important source of enjoyment. In consequence, it does not render obsolete the examination of preference structures or dynamics.

Moreover, I have discussed to what extent we need a kind of 'normative standard of rationality' in order to be able to normatively distinguish between different wants (respective preferences) or enjoyments. Having argued for a measuring rod of enjoyment (as opposed to preference), I have made a case that we can posit the ideal of increasing an individual's lifetime enjoyment as normatively desirable. This does not imply that individuals should actively seek to *maximize* their enjoyments because of the costs associated with such a strategy (Schwartz et al. 2002). Less strict requirements, such as a rule or the tendency to strive for *higher* enjoyments, should suffice (e.g. satisficing). The normative ideal, especially with respect to public policy, could lie in a 'principle of increased enjoyment'. With such a standard at hand, possible normative distinctions of wants (and preferences) and enjoyments can now be discussed. These can be differentiated in terms of the underlying informational structure. This differentiation is called 'informational requirement'.

I have argued that very strict, 'Herculean' requirements on the underlying beliefs have to be rejected on the grounds that they are inoperable and will never be fulfilled by an individual: they violate the naturalistic methodology used in the present monograph. For this reason, they have been rejected in favour of an informational requirement that considers the state of an individual's deprivation. Other types of special preferences, normatively speaking, that have been discussed are adaptive, habitual, addictive as well as insatiable preferences. Most of these distinctions apply also to enjoyments: a special case of uninformed enjoyments is the inability to correctly forecast future affect. Related to this are also enjoyments based on adaptive preferences. The usual way to cope, at least with enjoyments resulting from adaptive preferences, is an 'autonomy requirement'. Having thus paved the way for a general discussion on how to normatively distinguish different wants and enjoyments, I have undertaken a closer analysis of three dynamic facets of my theory of welfare.

The first facet is the 'process view of enjoyment', where I have shown how this view alters the focus when making welfare judgements. While it is conceptually straightforward to conceive of enjoyment as a measuring rod even under a regime of changing preferences, positive evidence has been presented that individuals are relatively poor judges of their future enjoyment. Based on a systematic inability to correctly forecast future enjoyment, I have argued for a shift from predicted enjoyments as a basis for welfare judgements to actual enjoyments. This provides support for an *ex post* understanding of welfare, enabling the welfare analyst to take into account that individuals' future affects will systematically differ from the affects predicted by those individuals. In assessing the effects of a policy on an individual's well-being, such information on the distorted nature of the predictions regarding future affect could be taken into account and inform deliberative policy processes.

The foundations laid out in the previous chapters have been used for an understanding of some dynamics of hedonism, going directly to the layer of enjoyment and suffering. In this second facet of my framework, I have focused on welfare dynamics that relate directly to changes in well-being such as – most prominently – hedonic adaptation effects. While the empirical findings on adaptation are still quite weak, some tentative normative evaluations can nevertheless be proposed: the domain specificity calls for a differentiated evaluation, discriminating between adaptation to enjoyment and adaptation to suffering, and discriminating even further between different sources of enjoyment and suffering. I have suggested taking into account the nature of adaptive enjoyment and suffering in a welfare calculus, which would be relevant should such welfare assessments serve as a basis for judgements of distributive justice. On the grounds of an efficiency argument, I have argued for the normative priority of enjoyments one does not easily adapt to. I have also argued that objections postulating hedonic treadmills can be relativized with respect to our positive knowledge about reduced adaptation dynamics regarding innate needs. While adaptation is a problem to be dealt with by any not fully objective, dynamically oriented theory of welfare, it would be premature to label as self-defeating the striving for the satisfaction of preferences or for enjoyments on these grounds.

Another dynamic aspect is the link between enjoyment and want formation. I have drawn on the aforementioned learning mechanisms and their peculiarities to distinguish the different ways in which wants can be acquired and unlearned over time. This has been captured by a 'stability distinction' and is related to the stability of acquired wants based on their hedonic adaptation properties. Moreover, it is possible to (normatively) discriminate between wants in terms of the reinforcement schedule underlying them because, depending on this schedule, some wants track well-being more closely than others ('reinforcement distinction'). Another distinction has been made in terms of the reversibility of want learning ('reversibility distinction') because, depending on the concrete learning mechanism involved, it can in some cases be difficult to unlearn that want. However, it seems there are some positive effects associated with non-reversibility that complicate the picture. A last distinction has been made regarding the 'crowding out' of sources of reinforcement through other sources of reinforcement, which can lead to undesirable consequences.

Having built a bridge from enjoyment to wants, I have dealt in detail with questions concerning welfare dynamics, relating predominantly to changing wants (and the corresponding preferences). Different types of want change have been discussed, and different normative distinctions have been suggested accordingly. I have discussed two important phenomena. The first is a normative evaluation based on different satiation patterns that can be found in innate needs and acquired wants. This has complemented and extended the discussion of the normative priority of innate needs. Second, I have also suggested differentiating between adaptation and satiation, something that is largely ignored in the literature. I have proposed that adaptation should be understood primarily in terms of 'liking', while satiation is a phenomenon related to 'wanting'. Satiation might be normatively problematic when it comes to differential satiation patterns and insatiable wants are coupled with other wants. This can lead to what I have called a 'refinement treadmill', which can be normatively undesirable under certain conditions.

The third dynamic facet of my framework deals with a distinction that has been made on the basis of different forms of learning mechanisms and regards the way in which wants are formed by the latter. It allows a differentiated understanding of the conditions under which a want is formed 'autonomously'. Such an autonomy requirement plays a role when taking into account possible distortions caused by adaptive preference formation. It has been shown here how differently authors conceive of adaptive preferences and what test criteria were used. Based on a distinction first put forward by Chai and Schubert (2007), I have elaborated on a new test where insightful learning can serve as a first discriminating criterion of whether a want was acquired autonomously. A second criterion can then be applied to determine whether the deprivation that results in adaptive preference formation is also reflected in many classes of innate needs not being satisfied. It has also been shown that experience-based tests serving to discriminate between autonomously and non-autonomously formed wants are only weakly helpful because associative learning occurs via experience, but does not need to be consciously reflected (and may thus lack a certain degree of autonomy).

To summarize, I have presented an overarching framework of an evolutionary theory of welfare, placing the focus on enjoyment and suffering. Based on insights from various behavioural sciences, two hedonistic notions of well-being and their interrelation have been presented and evaluated as to their plausibility. Although the framework does not have the simple charm of the standard (but materially under-specified) notion of welfare, we can now understand the reason why the different theories of well-being contain a grain of truth: hedonism captures the idea that humans experience actions as either pleasant or unpleasant and strive to experience more pleasant situations (the neurosciences are providing increasingly detailed information about what happens in these situations). The preference-based accounts envisage that a common source of pleasant experiences is the satisfaction of preferences. In the (less subjective) needs accounts, it is rightly argued that there are shared elements shaping our preferences (and although there is some variance, a fair basis remains that is common to all humans). By incorporating these insights into the present integrative framework, I hope that, in using a naturalistic methodology, I have been able to make the connection between the essential elements of the theories of welfare under review.

The advantages of such an empirically founded hedonistic approach are threefold. First, a solid ground is established for the resulting welfare implications by basing the positive parts of this work on empirically well-founded assumptions about the behavioural foundations. Second, the informational basis of such a welfare concept is considerably broadened by using the hedonistic, 'experienced utility' framework. A purely formal, subjectivistic stance is avoided. Third, the approach is decidedly dynamic, shedding new light on the normative implications of different learning dynamics with reference to wants. This framework coherently integrates the dynamics of changes in wants and enjoyment, thus connecting strands of literature that have been discussed largely separately so far. A naturalistic methodology can serve to establish the plausibility of some existing normative distinction schemes or normative requirements as well as provide new evaluation schemes and tests (e.g. regarding adaptive preference formation or differential satiation patterns of wants). All in all, the theory suggested here provides a more realistic account of human behaviour, albeit this comes at the cost of the charm of simplicity (the theory is 'messy', as Nelson and Winter (1982: 356) have put it).

7.2 Outlook

In the present monograph, important questions had to be laid aside in order to concentrate on the problems that were addressed in the beginning. What was not addressed extensively were considerations on the interpersonal comparability of the presented concepts of well-being (though I have hinted at psychological findings supporting this possibility), the practical measurability of well-being, the role of opportunities and questions of distributive justice, to name but the most important ones. While any ordinal concept of well-being (or utility) might be sufficient in consumer theory, it has been pointed out that this informational basis is too sparse for social choice and welfare economics (see also Ng 2000). Similarly, interpersonal comparisons of well-being are a necessary component in order to flesh out a theory of distributive justice. While the principle of increased enjoyment counts each person's enjoyment equally (subject to the qualifications made in the preceding chapter), different principles of distributive justice are possible and ultimately need to be taken into consideration.

In order to complete the project of an evolutionary welfare economics, the questions brought up here will have to be addressed in future work, and it can be conjectured that the naturalistic stance taken here can be fruitfully applied in the process. Nevertheless, some tentative implications can already be hinted at: the potential practical relevance for economic policies may encompass several fields. One might think of innovations that fuel individuals' status needs and lead to wasteful status races (a case where an innovation might turn out to be not solely beneficial and which could be a topic to be addressed by innovation policies) or questions of consumer protection. Practical relevance for economic policies could also extend to issues of sustainability, for example via policies promoting or encouraging non-adaptive enjoyments over enjoyments that are highly adaptive to ensure a more efficient use of resources. Probably the most obvious implication stems directly from the possibility of preferential change: in a framework where preferences are allowed to be variable, one has to take into account that economic policies can exert an influence on these preferences and shape their development, something which is neglected in a static framework. These influences can either be deliberate, for example when a policy is instituted with the explicit goal of shaping (i.e. creating or altering) preferences, or they can be an unintentional consequence of a policy measure. In this respect, the framework presented here is a double-edged sword. Going back to the hedonistic foundations of utility and thus take a step beyond the level of preference to the deeper level of enjoyments implies that preferences can be understood as a means that could be legitimately shaped by a policy maker. On the one hand, this would enlarge the policy toolbox for a given problem. On the other hand, for all policies, the possible effect on the malleable preferences has to be considered as well, thus imposing an additional requirement on the information an 'adaptive policy maker' (Metcalfe 1994) needs to have.

I should add that the exposition of different welfare dynamics and the respective normative distinctions do not in themselves constitute an argument for policy intervention. Stating that different dynamics of welfare should be evaluated differently, or given different normative weight, is a theoretical argument. Certainly, such findings could be used as a *basis* to call for policies taking distortions or satiation and adaptation effects into account. However, this would require other careful considerations on a more applied level, including answers to such questions as how to practically measure the phenomena discussed above, or who should implement these policies and how. Associated with these practical policy-related questions are also well-known caveats concerning the imperfect knowledge of a (learning) policy maker or the policy maker's own agenda. Ultimately, this also raises some general questions about the autonomy of the individual and to what degree (paternalistic) policies should be implemented to coerce or 'educate' individuals as regards their own good. None of these questions has been addressed in the present work, but it should be noted that, from the existence of non-ideal preferences, it does not automatically follow that these should be 'laundered' by a benevolent policy maker. For these reasons, one could be sceptical as to whether the theoretical considerations would support the conclusion that something like national happiness or national enjoyment should be actively maximized by a benevolent policy maker (Frey and Stutzer 2007). However, knowledge of the different enjoyment and want dynamics can provide valuable input into the policy process and is certainly a type of knowledge that fosters what Freytag and Renaud (2007) have called 'active learning' in the policy (reform) process.

To conclude, I hope that these elements of an evolutionary theory of welfare constitute some worthwhile initial steps towards solving the 'central welfare economic problem' (Nelson and Winter 1982: 369–70) of assessing welfare when preferences change.

Notes

1　These laws are necessary to avoid the *ad hoc* stipulation of a change in preferences as solution to every economic puzzle unsolved (Yaari 1977: 157).
2　The idea of perfect foresight is at odds with the very idea of innovativeness (Metcalfe 2001: 577–8).
3　I submit that this is compatible with critical rationalist thought, where it is argued that, while there is no strict deductive relationship between factual and evaluative statements ('Hume's Law', cf. Hume 1740: 469), value judgements are nevertheless not completely arbitrary expressions of taste (Popper 1966; Albert 1978, 1991).
4　Similarly, one can test normative assumptions against 'common intuitions'. But as I argue later on, one should not overestimate this criterion (see also Griffin 1998: Ch. 1).
5　Following Witt, we could also call this a criterion of 'Schumpeterian Progress'. This would invite, however, all the problems that are associated with the long tradition of the notion of 'progress' (see e.g. Nisbet 1994). Since a notion of 'economic progress' would imply betterment towards a certain goal, misunderstandings could arise: the notion of 'evolutionary change', as used in this monograph and in biology after Darwin, can no longer be understood as a teleological process leading to (continuous) improvement towards a specified goal. Not all evolutionary change is automatically for the better.
6　This has been shown empirically in the happiness literature (Oswald 1997; Easterlin 2002; Frey and Stutzer 2002b), where it has been found that rising incomes over the last decades did not significantly increase happiness (but see critically Stevenson and Wolfers 2008).
7　To assume that individuals always have the same preferences would limit potential innovations to increasing the efficiency of already known products.
8　This account draws on Warke (2000b) and Witt (2005), but see also Stigler (1950a,b).
9　Hobbes (1651: Ch. VI) has already articulated a similar idea to analyze individual behaviour in terms of desire and aversion, terms he used to define the notions of good and evil in his 'Leviathan' (see Abu Turab Rizvi 1998).
10　The Benthamite idea of a utility notion centred around sensory experiences of pleasure and pain is explored in more detail later together with the issue of its potential multidimensionality (see Chs 4 and 5).
11　Sometimes the third condition of reflexivity ($\forall\, x \in X : x \succcurlyeq x$) is also added, but since reflexivity is implied by the completeness assumption, it is redundant (Mas-Colell et al. 1995: 6).
12　Such a utility function is usually assumed to be twice differentiable, and preferences should also obey local non-satiation. Often a convexity assumption is added, resulting in convex indifference curves (and implying a decreasing marginal rate of

substitution between two goods: the more of good 1 an individual possesses, the less that individual is willing to trade of good 2 in order to obtain more of good 1).

13 This dimension has been suggested by Scanlon (1975) and Sumner (1996), but see critically also Sobel (1997).

14 Proponents of welfarism are e.g. Harsanyi (1976), Hare (1981), Ng (1981), or Mirrlees (1982), Sumner (1996) and Blackorby et al. (2002).

15 This is even admitted by Sen, who states that if utility information is scarce, the welfarist can also use non-utility information as 'surrogates' (Sen 1979c: 471).

16 I abstain from taking up the fundamental question of the existence thesis and instead boldly assume that something such as individual well-being exists. With the same boldness I assume that well-being is also a significant normative maximand. One can indeed agree with Shaver that the 'appeal' of utilitarianism comes from the fact that '[a]ll agree that welfare is valuable' *per se* (Shaver 2004: 238). In order to make a case against the significance thesis, one would have to find a very strong objection against the concept of welfare. This has not been put forward so far (Moore and Crisp 1996: 603). Therefore I agree with Shaver (2004) that the significance of well-being is not contested (even Sen, being *the* critic of welfarism, includes well-being *inter alia* in his account of what constitutes a good life).

17 The author shares the reluctance of Suzumura to part with welfarist consequentialism and leaves Pandora's box unopened in this respect (Suzumura 2002: 24).

18 A similar categorization has been suggested by Parfit (1984: 493–503), who divides theories of welfare into hedonistic theories, desire-fulfilment theories and objective list theories.

19 Such an approach has been put forward by Braybrooke (1987).

20 This distinction has to be taken with caution as desires are also states of mind. However, in desire theories, welfare *additionally* depends on states of the world (Sumner 1996: 82).

21 One could also call this a distinction between formal theories of welfare and those that are substantive (Hausman and McPherson 2006: 119).

22 Ruprecht (2005) has argued, e.g., that this applies to the preference for sugar.

23 It has to be pointed out that welfare and autonomy are two different things and a trade-off may be involved at times between maximizing welfare and individual freedom (autonomy). Therefore sticking to the principle of preference autonomy might be appealing on account of the high degree of autonomy it grants to the individual; it has, however, no direct bearing on whether the resulting notion of welfare is descriptively and normatively adequate.

24 Sen has put that criticism similarly, noting that desiring something does not necessarily equal valuing it (Sen 1987: 45–6).

25 One could assume these normative statements to be hypothetical in nature and then discuss the implications of these hypothetical assumptions (see Ng 1972).

26 This is not intended to imply that this kind of positive economics needs no fundamental value judgements as well. But it is useful to make a distinction between the value judgements in (1) as 'methodological' (Blaug 1992: 144) or 'characterizing' (Nagel 1961: 492–3), pertaining to methodology and other conventional issues, while the value judgements in (2) are those which could be called 'appraising' or 'normative' as they deal with questions of what should be called 'good' in a eudaemonic sense (the border between (1) and (2) is fuzzy since value judgements in (2) might very well impose limits on methodology in (1) and vice versa).

27 Conceptually, there are no problems with this approach, but see Slesnick (1998) for a comprehensive survey on the issues associated with the empirical measurement exercise, which is based on recovering the necessary utility function from the demand function by estimating the latter with econometrical methods. Doing so often implies making strong assumptions on individual preferences.

28 I follow Dutta (1994) in notation.

29 One prominent example is 'single-peaked preferences' introduced by Black (1948).

30 Cf. also the more extensive Becker (1996).

31 Sen (1977b: 325) notes correctly that it leads to a 'remarkably mute theory' if behaviour is interpreted in terms of preferences which are, in turn, defined only by behaviour.

32 In the fairy tale of 'Lucky Hans' by the Brothers Grimm, Hans starts with a nugget of gold, which he subsequently replaces in a series of deals until he is left with nothing but is much happier than before.

33 Following Harsanyi's terminology, it is an 'extended preference' as it compares different histories of preference changes (Harsanyi 1955).

34 I follow Kuklys (2005: 10–11) in notation.

35 Teschl and Comim (2005: 245) note that the capability space would probably have a dynamic, temporal dimension as well. However, they offer no further elaboration on that insight.

36 For the following discussion on the objectivity of Sen's account, cf. also Sumner (1996: 61–8).

37 Jevons was not alone in this project, however: Menger aside, all the protagonists of the 'Marginalist Revolution' were heavily influenced by the mechanics of contemporary physics (see Walras 1926: 71 and Edgeworth 1881: 9–12).

38 Originally, Witt (2001) used the term 'wants' also for the latter subclass.

39 Parts of this section are a revised version of Binder and Niederle (2008).

40 Cf. Everitt et al. (1999) for an overview of the neurological basis of these learning mechanisms.

41 This has been tentatively explored in Brenner and Witt (2003).

42 A different promising option would be Simon's 'satisficing behaviour' (Simon 1956). I have explored this possibility in a different context, cf. Broekel and Binder (2007).

43 Whether one accords a high value to simplicity in theorizing is a methodological question. Mathematical tractability is another methodological value judgement, but so is empirical accuracy. Subscribing to the naturalistic view of evolutionary economics, as outlined in the introduction (see section 1.2), I prefer empirical confirmation over these two other methodological value judgements.

44 There is a distinction between affects and emotions (which are otherwise quite similar): affects are always related to external or internal sensory inputs. Emotions, on the other hand, are triggered by more complex production rules (Johnston 1999: 61–5).

45 There are some (immoral) studies involving human brain stimulation by Heath (1964), which confirm the results, however.

46 Moreover, my use of these notions differs from that of Sumner (1996) in his account of 'authentic happiness'. In his theory, Sumner uses 'enjoyment' and 'suffering' to denote attitudes one has towards one's experiences.

47 A second implication of the evidence discussed here is that apparently humans are better fitted (biologically) to assess the change in a stimulus rather than the (absolute) level of it (Camerer et al. 2005: 28). This may explain why changes in income rather than its level are more important for self-reported happiness (Oswald 1997; Binder and Coad 2008).

48 This, as well as other empirical evidence, is in accordance with the literature on the 'judgement by prototype heuristic' in other fields (Kahneman 1999; Robinson and Clore 2002).

49 When decision utility differs from experienced utility, this can also have normative implications (this will be discussed in Ch. 6).

50 A similar case is made by Ng (2003) and Camerer et al. (2005).

51 Edgeworth (1881) has already expressed the idea that utility is directly measurable and has conjectured that it will be possible to build a 'hedonimeter', an item that

could practically do so (for a discussion, see Colander 2007). Doubts about this have been voiced recently by Zizzo (2002).

52 Similar ideas have also been expressed in Broome (1991b) and Parducci (1995).

53 The axioms are 'concatenation of neutral utility profiles' (total utility of an episode is not affected by adding a neutral episode), 'monotonicity in instant utility' (increases in instant utility do not decrease total utility of an episode) and 'monotonicity in total utility' (if adding two episodes, replacing one of them with another episode with higher total utility increases the total utility of the concatenation, cf. Kahneman et al. 1997: 390).

54 A third distinction, which has not found much resonance, is made by Veenhoven, who differentiates between affective and cognitive concepts of well-being, calling them 'happiness' and 'contentment', respectively (Veenhoven 1991).

55 Schwarz and Strack (1991: 28), e.g., report a low test–retest reliability of such measures even if tests are conducted within consecutive hours.

56 Cf. Michalos' theory of 'multiple discrepancies', which views well-being as being influenced by the difference between standard and achievement in all these dimensions (Michalos 1985).

57 One could also give a normative justification that utility should be conceived as multidimensional. I discuss this possibility in a later section (see section 5.7.1 and Binder 2009).

58 Cf. Rolls (2007) for a more detailed discussion of these brain areas. Descriptions of the location and functions of the OFC can be found in Rolls (2000) and, of the amygdala and the ventral striatum circuits, in Everitt et al. (1999) and Delgado (2007). The OFC is found approximately in Brodmann areas 45, 47, while the amygdala is found in areas 28, 34 and the NAcc/ventral striatum in area 34.

59 The amygdala is well known for its association with fear and negative reward. While there is some evidence that positive and negative stimuli are processed in separate regions of that brain complex (O'Doherty et al. 2001b), it can certainly be stated that negative stimuli have a higher salience for the organism because they have a stronger behavioural relevance. This fact is well documented in behavioural economics through the kink in the value function of prospect theory (Kahneman and Tversky 1979): the loss of 10 euros is higher in (absolute) intensity than a gain of 10 euros. The higher behavioural relevance of negative reward and its neural processing are the basis of the well-known endowment effect.

60 Or for that matter, direct stimulation of brain areas in humans as in the experiments of Heath (1964), whose subjects reported pleasure when stimulated in that way (cited from Berns 2005).

61 The account presented here is compatible with the matching law approach in the tradition of Herrnstein (1997). Shizgal (1999) explicitly builds the matching law, a behavioural model, into his account of behaviour. As such, my account of utility and its representation in the brain are compatible with the theory described in the previous chapter.

62 Evaluative well-being is a derived concept but important nonetheless.

63 It might well be possible to defend a monist framework, where enjoyment is the only intrinsic value and all other values are derived.

64 It is an entirely different matter whether such a pluralist conception could – under the restrictive assumptions employed in social choice theory – be aggregated *consistently* into a social evaluation functional. Blackorby et al. (2005) have shown that under conditions of Pareto indifference, unlimited domain and binary independence of irrelevant alternatives, such a 'pluralist' social evaluation functional would essentially have to be welfarist and *disregard* all non-welfarist information. However, a full discussion of this kind of consideration is beyond the scope of this monograph.

65 One could further distinguish sensory hedonism from attitudinal hedonism by

pointing out that the former links pleasure to sensory experiences while the latter links it to pro-attitudes without reference to any sensory experiences. However, removing pleasure as an attitude from any experiential content would make the account vulnerable to the objection that one could take pleasure in being sad or feeling pain (see Moore 2004).

66 Cf. Davis (1981: 312) and Rachels (2000).

67 This depends also on the rate with which future enjoyments are discounted.

68 Let me add that – the previous argument notwithstanding – for some purposes, it might be better to treat other values besides welfare *as if* they were intrinsic values.

69 But see section 5.2 for some remarks on how enjoyment can be measured via 'experience sampling' or 'day reconstruction' methodologies (Kahneman and Sugden 2005).

70 Cf. also Haslett (1990: 91–2) for a similarly critical attitude towards intuitions concerning far-fetched thought experiments.

71 Interestingly, some philosophers – in a different context – make a point of arguing that we would not be able anyway to really disprove that we are all brains in a vat, experiencing a sort of virtual reality that only exists in our minds (e.g. Putnam 1992).

72 Rawls (1971) has popularized the idea that the defining characteristic of consequentialism is that it describes the right in terms of the good.

73 One could even go so far as to argue that the good should be defined by the right. This is the case when holding that welfare is constituted by virtue (a view held by Aristotle, for example). This would be a normative approach towards well-being because it neglects the empirical fact that many individuals enjoy high levels of well-being without being particularly virtuous.

74 The naturalistic method can be helpful here in giving guidance as to what constitutes a source of enjoyment. Linking pleasures to the satisfaction of primary and secondary reinforcers and a material specification of basic needs (primary reinforcers) can help us to make sense of some of these counter-examples. How realistic or how far-fetched are these counter-examples? One could argue that Porky and the likes of him could be considered exceptions to a rule defined by nature with the usual genetic variance. A modest position like the one developed here holds that the motivational hypothesis of hedonism tends to describe a behavioural *regularity*, not a universal law that holds in every case.

75 Here I neglect the difficulties involved in determining which case applies.

76 But to a certain extent, this problem can also be found in some allegedly objective theories of welfare. Sen has made a virtue of this in his capabilities and functionings approach, making the selection of 'objective' functionings an open matter for social deliberation (see section 3.2).

77 Ultimately, the moral filter might also concern our sensory well-being, for example, if moral norms hold that some pleasures are deemed ethically questionable. This would not deprive these pleasures of their pleasurable character for an individual. But if we enjoy something that is not morally permissible, we feel guilty. The naturalist could argue that emotions such as guilt or shame are genetically hard-wired and triggered when we do harm to others (Tangney and Dearing 2002). This, in turn, might serve to enforce cooperation or non-defective behaviour.

78 Meta-preferences are sometimes also called second-order or higher-order preferences, if more than two layers exist. I use these terms interchangeably. I understand Harsanyi's notion of 'extended preferences', which are preferences for preferences and state pairs, also to be a kind of meta-preference (Harsanyi 1955).

79 It might be possible to construct an argument that innate needs are naturalistically conceived meta-preferences with a high stability across time and similarity between individuals. There are, however, some differences between second-order preferences, as they are usually conceived of, and innate needs. For one thing,

second-order preferences are satisfied by having a certain preference ('$\{X > Y\} > \{Y > X\}$'). They are not located directly on the layer of first-order preferences (if they were, one could arguably drop the idea of meta-preferences in favour of conceiving of the situation in terms of conflicts between 'ordinary' preferences). Innate needs can be directly satisfied and would thus be on the same layer (as acquired wants). Needs are also motivational in a sense that second-order preferences are not, because the former are directly effective in action (Frankfurt 1971). Another difference lies in their being inescapable and given, something directly opposed to the main feature (at least in Frankfurt's conception) of meta-preferences, which are the result of careful deliberation and can be roughly characterized as the defining feature of man's free will: so while one cannot escape one's first-order preferences, one has the freedom of will to have different second-order preferences. In the case of innate needs, one would probably not be free to escape both. Nevertheless, the idea to conceive of innate needs as meta-preferences, though outside the scope of the present work, warrants further investigation. But one could hold that such a view would still be mistaking an important source (needs) for the nature of welfare.

80 Cf. the two selves, at first having a preference ranking $X > Y$ and later $Y > X$, with an individual having a first-order preference ranking $X > Y$ and a second-order preference ranking $\{Y > X\} > \{X > Y\}$.

81 A criticism has been made that these analogies are metaphorically misguided and therefore of limited use for an inter-temporal intrapersonal perspective (Loewenstein 1996: 288–9). There is, e.g., a temporal asymmetry involved between the selves where it is not possible to punish or reward past selves. This asymmetry is not present in the interpersonal context, where one can reward or punish oneself in order to hurt or reward others.

82 Of course one could argue for abandoning this kind of subjective welfare view altogether in favour of objective list or opportunity views. In the previous chapters, I have given reasons why these are less convincing than a hedonistic account (see sections 2.2.1, 3.2.2 and 3.3.2). Nevertheless, the view developed in this monograph is one that is less subjective than a pure preference satisfaction or happiness view as it is anchored in relatively objective features of our human biological make-up.

83 We can understand autonomy with respect to an individual's capacity for critical deliberation, e.g. to be 'the capacity of a person critically to reflect upon, and then attempt to accept or change, his or her preferences, desires, values, and ideals.' (Dworkin 1988: 48). It could also be understood in terms of opportunities, e.g. when a preference is formed without being constrained by one's feasible set (Elster 1982). I will discuss this in detail in section 6.5.2.

84 Similarly, it could be warranted to act contrary to what constitutes the good (welfare), based on ethical considerations of what is right (i.e. one could accept welfare hedonism, but define what is right in terms of something else, but not welfare). I leave these complications aside since my interest is in a theory of *welfare*. Therefore, in cases of self-interested behaviour, it is 'rational' to seek the increase of the net balance of enjoyment over suffering (because of this narrow focus, 'rational' is best to be understood in quotes from now on).

85 These are assessments from a conceptual perspective. Only in a later step and given more practical considerations, could this assessment be used to inform concrete welfare policies. *Per se*, these normative distinctions do not imply that preferences should be corrected by a 'benevolent policy maker', but knowledge of them can, of course, inform the members of a society and thus be useful in a policy dialogue on these issues. These practical considerations are left aside here.

86 A trade-off between welfare and autonomy does not exist in all cases; in some, autonomy can also positively influence well-being.

87 Later I also argue that using an informational requirement does not mean one is

to adequately discern whether preferences were formed in a non-autonomous, adaptive way: see section 6.5.2. In this respect, better information may be only one factor that could help close the gap between preferences and welfare.

88 A sensitization to hedonic stimuli is the opposite of hedonic adaptation, where a desensitization takes place. See also section 6.4.

89 A similar line of argument has been proposed in an economic context by Bernheim and Rangel (2004), who argue that addiction is not rationally pursued but based on decision-making mistakes that basically result from the inability to correctly forecast future enjoyment resulting from drug consumption. In the case of drugs, this is even more problematic than in the case of normal preferences because of the addictive properties of drugs and a potentially higher degree of irreversibility in the formation of addictive preferences (see also section 6.3).

90 This 'incentive-sensitization' of the wanting system happens without affecting the liking system, i.e. it has no effect on the other, dissociated, system that mediates reward (Robinson and Berridge 2001).

91 Moreover, this leaves out all aspects of decreases of autonomy resulting from a decreased possibility of a self-determined life (to the extent that the addict wishes to withdraw from drug use but is not able to).

92 Dolan and White (2006) have suggested a different process model of so-called 'dynamic well-being', which consists of six stages, differentiating between the anticipation stage (an individual predicts the utility of a future episode), the planning stage (the prediction is combined with subjective probabilities of the episode occurring), the behaviour stage (behaviour is executed), the outcome stage (changes in resources occur resulting from behaviour), the experience stage (hedonic reactions to changes in outcomes) and the evaluation stage (evaluation of an episode). While such a model is more complex in terms of its numerous stages, I think it is debatable whether these processes actually work in this order. Especially the behaviour stage seems to be mistakenly conceived to precede the continuous experience of utility associated with an action that is performed. For example, the consumption of a good and the associated enjoyment occur simultaneously, not sequentially.

93 In a framework where preference change is allowed for, one should also, in the *ex post* view, take into account the preference an individual will have *ex post*. In the example of the chemical plant, the policy maker would be well advised to anticipate not only an individual's *ex post* beliefs but also the *ex post* preferences (which will probably have changed by then).

94 In the case where the satisfaction of a preference always results in an increase in welfare (i.e. when preferences cannot be mistaken, beliefs are correct and probabilities related to uncertain outcomes are objective and shared by all), the ex ante view and the ex post view coincide. This would imply that subjectively held probabilities for uncertain outcomes have to be identical across individuals (the ex ante probabilities for a state s can be different for any individual, creating a further problem for the preference satisfaction view under uncertainty, cf. Broome 1991b: Ch. 7). Under these circumstances, individuals' actual preference satisfaction would be identical with their enjoyment.

95 The proponent of preference satisfaction could also use 'undistorted' preference satisfaction, which is different from an individual's stated preference. However, in the face of the problems of changing preferences discussed so far, this seems even more difficult to attain than a corrected estimate of enjoyment.

96 In the present context, I use the terms 'adaptation' and 'hedonic adaptation' interchangeably.

97 The dynamics of enjoyment are mostly researched in terms of how enjoyment changes after external events in different life domains. Also of considerable interest, but less well researched, is how changes in enjoyment influence other life domains (but see e.g. Lyubomirsky et al. 2005; Binder and Coad 2008).

98 Adaptation to pain is rare and mostly incomplete, as shown by evidence discussed below.

99 It is possible that an opposite effect takes place for some stimuli, which would alter the shape of the curve in the opposite direction. Such 'anti-adaptation' will not be discussed here.

100 Of course, there might be other reasons for which an adaptive activity is chosen. I abstract from these arguments here.

101 There could be a small positive element even in the adaptation to enjoyments, because it could prompt an individual to seek other enjoyments, offering more stimulating experiences. Adaptation to known experiences could thus stimulate a certain degree of innovativeness.

102 An internality is an intra-individual intertemporal externality, i.e. the individual neglects effects of present consumption on future utility.

103 Besides such allegations, one can also argue that, on a social level, excessive pleasure seeking might have negative consequences for a society's moral foundations, or that such hedonistic striving tends to be detrimental to the environment by depleting natural resources and overusing and abusing our environment. Whether the latter claims are to be levelled solely at a hedonistic theory of welfare is debatable and would certainly require a much wider discussion than space permits here (see e.g. Frank 1999).

104 The reason for the divergence of findings is that the original findings did not account for breaks in the data, where the wording of the life satisfaction and happiness questions had been changed and thus led to different results. This reinforces the point about the difficulty of empirically capturing subjective well-being through global questions on life satisfaction, see section 5.2.

105 These labels are attributed to Brentano in a philosophical debate on the 'shape of a life' (Feldman 2004: Ch. 6). In this debate, some philosophers have argued that paths (1) and (2) should be evaluated differently, and they have taken this as an objection to hedonism. In the argument presented here, we can find support for differently valuing (1) and (2) without rejecting hedonism.

106 In *purely* welfarist terms, the priority given to (1) would, however, not be permissible either.

107 In experiments, satiation could be delayed by classifying candy more specifically, e.g. 'cherry jelly bean' instead of just 'jelly bean'.

108 As status races tend to be a self-reinforcing collective action problem, the taxing of status good innovations might be a necessary step to curb such dynamics based on the insatiability of the status need.

109 This property might also be due to the direct input character of the good.

110 This would be different for goods where increased specialization can be likened to the dynamics of a 'beneficial addiction'.

111 However, negative effects might be mitigated by increasing the number of status categories in which consumers can compete.

112 In a hedonistic theory, one could also speak of 'small mercies' (Crocker 1992: 601), but, of course, in hedonism, too, a preference formed in order to derive small mercies (pleasures) from its satisfaction would be labelled 'adaptive preference'. Therefore I stick to this terminology.

113 Since Sumner is not interested in the dynamic aspects of his theory of happiness, he does not further elaborate.

114 This could be extended to the classes of acquired wants which are conditioned on innate needs via associative learning processes.

115 There was an increase in the individual's opportunity set. If we assess opportunities in terms of the resulting welfare, in the case of the individual, this was clearly a welfare-decreasing enlargement of the opportunity set.

Bibliography

Abbott, L. (1953). *Quality and Competition*. Columbia University Press, New York.

Abu Turab Rizvi, S. (1998). Utility. In Davis, J., Hands, W., and Maeki, U., editors, *The Handbook of Economic Methodology*, pages 516–525. Edward Elgar, Cheltenham/UK.

Adler, M. D. and Posner. E. A. (2006). *New Foundations of Cost–Benefit Analysis*. Harvard University Press, Cambridge/Mass.

—— (2008). Happiness research and cost–benefit analysis. *Journal of Legal Studies*, 37(S2):S253–S292.

Aharon, I., Etcoff, N., Ariely. D., Chabris, C. F., O'Connor, E., and Breiter, H. C. (2001). Beautiful faces have variable reward value: fMRI and behavioral evidence. *Neuron*, 32:537–551.

Albert, H. (1978). *Traktat ueber Rationale Praxis*. J.C.B. Mohr (Paul Siebeck), Tuebingen.

—— (1991). *Traktat ueber Kritische Vernunft*. J.C.B. Mohr (Paul Siebeck), Tuebingen, 5th rev. edition.

Algom. D. and Lubel, S. (1994). Psychophysics in the field: Perception and memory for labor pain. *Perception and Psychophysics*, 55(2):133–141.

Alkire, S. (2005). Why the capability approach? *Journal of Human Development*, 6(1):115–133.

Altman, M. (1999). The methodology of economics and the survival principle revisited and revised: Some welfare and public policy implications of modeling the economic agent. *Review of Social Economy*, 57(4):427–449.

Anand, P. and Hees, M. v. (2006). Capabilities and achievements: An empirical study. *Journal of Socio-Economics*, 35:268–284.

Anand, P., Hunter, G., and Smith, R. (2005). Capabilities and well-being: Evidence based on the Sen–Nussbaum approach to welfare. *Social Indicators Research*, 74:9–55.

Anderson, A. K., Christoff, K., Stappen, I., Panitz, D., Ghahremani, D. G., Glover, G., Gabrieli, J. D. E. and Sobel, N. (2003). Dissociated neural representations of intensity and valence in human olfaction. *Nature Neuroscience*, 6(2):196–202.

Anderson, E. (1993). *Value in Ethics and Economics*. Harvard University Press, Cambridge/Mass.

Anderson, J. R. (1990a). *Cognitive Psychology and its Implications*. Freeman, New York, 3rd edition.

—— (1990b). Arousal and the inverted-u hypothesis: A critique of Neiss's 'reconceptualizing arousal'. *Psychological Bulletin*, 107(1):96–100.

—— (1995). *Learning and Memory: An Integrated Approach*. John Wiley & Sons, New York.

Andersson, L., Bask, M. and Melkersson, M. (2006). Economic man and the consumption of addictive goods: The case of two goods. *Substance Use & Misuse*, 41(4):453–466.

Arneson, R. J. (1999). Human flourishing versus desire satisfaction. *Social Philosophy & Policy*, 16(1):113–142.

—— (2006). Desire formation and human good. In Olsaretti. S., editor, *Preferences and Well-Being*, pages 9–32. Cambridge University Press, Cambridge/UK.

Arnow, B. A., Desmond, J. E., Banner, L. L., Glover, G. H., Solomon, A., Polan, M. L., Lue, T. F. and Atlas, S. W. (2002). Brain activation and sexual arousal in healthy, heterosexual males. *Brain*, 125:1014–1023.

Arrow, K. J. (1963). *Social Choice and Individual Values*. Yale University Press, New Haven and London, 2nd edition.

Atkinson, A. B. (2001). The strange disappearance of welfare economics. *Kyklos*, 54(Fasc. 2/3):193–206.

Bandura, A. (1965). Influence of models' reinforcement contingencies on the acquisition of imitative responses. *Journal of Personality and Social Psychology*, 1:589–595.

—— (1977). *Social Learning Theory*. Prentice-Hall, Englewood Cliffs/New Jersey.

—— (1986). *Social Foundations of Thought and Action – A Social Cognitive Theory*. Prentice Hall, Upper Saddle River/New Jersey.

Baucells, M. and Sarin, R. K. (2007). Satiation in discounted utility. *Operations Research*, 55(1):170–181.

Baum, W. M. (1974). On two types of deviation from the matching law: Bias and undermatching. *Journal of the Experimental Analysis of Behavior*, 22(1):231–242.

Becker, G. S. (1996). *Accounting for Tastes*. Harvard University Press, Cambridge/Mass.

Becker, G. S. and Murphy, K. M. (1988). A theory of rational addiction. *Journal of Political Economy*, 96(4):675–700.

Bentham, J. (1948[1789]). *An Introduction to The Principles of Morals and Legislation*. Hafner, New York.

Berg, N. (2003). Normative behavioral economics. *Journal of Socio-Economics*, 32:411–427.

Bergson, A. (1938). A reformulation of certain aspects of welfare economics. *The Quarterly Journal of Economics*, 52(2):310–334.

Bernheim, B. D. and Rangel, A. (2004). Addiction and cue-triggered decision processes. *The American Economic Review*. 94(5):1,558–1,590.

Berns, G. S. (2005). *Satisfaction – The Science of Finding True Fulfillment*. Henry Holt and Company, New York.

Berns, G. S., McClure, S. M., Pagnoni, G. and Montague, P. R. (2001). Predictability modulates human brain response to reward. *The Journal of Neuroscience*, 21(8):2,793–2,798.

Berridge, K. C. (1996). Food reward: Brain substrates of wanting and liking. *Neuroscience and Biobehavioral Reviews*, 20(1):1–25.

—— (1999). Pleasure, pain, desire, and dread: Hidden core processes of emotion. In Kahneman et al. (1999), pages 525–557.

Binder, M. (2009). Some considerations regarding the problem of multidimensional utility. SSRN Working Paper No. 1416187.

Binder, M. and Broekel, T. (2008). Applying a robust non-parametric efficiency analysis to measure conversion efficiency in Great Britain. SSRN Working Paper No. 1104430.

Binder, M. and Coad, A. (2008). An examination of the dynamics of happiness using vector autoregressions. SSRN Working Paper No. 1301564.

Binder, M. and Niederle, U.-M. (2008). Institutions as determinants of preference change – a one way relation? In Elsner, W. and Hanappi. H., editors, *Advances in Evolutionary Institutional Economics: Evolutionary Mechanisms, Non-Knowledge and Strategy*, pages 97–120. Edward Elgar, Cheltenham/UK.

Binmore, K. (1998). *Game Theory and the Social Contract II – Just Playing*. MIT Press, Cambridge/Mass.

—— (2005). *Natural Justice*. Oxford University Press, New York.

—— (2006). The origins of fair play. Papers on Economics & Evolution #0614, Max Planck Institute of Economics, Jena.

Binswanger, M. (2006). Why does income growth fail to make us happier? Searching for the treadmills behind the paradox of happiness. *Journal of Socio-Economics*, 35:366–381.

Black, D. (1948). On the rationale of group decision-making. *Journal of Political Economy*, 56(1):23–34.

Black, J. (2002). *Oxford Dictionary of Economics*. Oxford University Press, Oxford/New York, 2nd edition.

Blackorby, C., Bossert. W., and Donaldson, D. (2002). In defense of welfarism. Departement de sciences économiques: Cahiers de recherche, No.2002–02, Université de Montreal.

—— (2005). Multi-profile welfarism: A generalization. *Social Choice and Welfare*, 24:253–267.

—— (1985). Consumers' surpluses and consistent cost–benefit tests. *Social Choice and Welfare*, 1:251–262.

—— (1988). Money metric utility: A harmless normalization? *Journal of Economic Theory*, 46:120–129.

Blaug, M. (1992). *The Methodology of Economics*. Cambridge University Press, Cambridge, 2nd edition.

Blundell, J. E. (1999). The control of appetite: Basic concepts and practical implications. *Swiss Medical Weekly*, 129(5):182–188.

Boadway. R. W. (1974). The welfare foundations of cost–benefit analysis. *The Economic Journal*, 84(336):926–939.

Boadway. R. W. and Bruce, N. (1984). *Welfare Economics*. Blackwell, Oxford/UK.

Bossert, W. and Weymark, J. A. (2006). Social choice: Recent developments. CIREQ Working Paper, University of Montreal, No.01–2006.

Boulding, K. E. (1958). *Principles of Economic Policy*. Prentice-Hall, Englewood Cliffs/New Jersey.

Brandt, R. B. (1966). The concept of welfare. In Krupp, S. R., editor, *The Structure of Economic Science – Essays on Methodology*, chapter 16, pages 257–276. Prentice-Hall, Englewood Cliffs/New Jersey.

—— (1979). *A Theory of the Good and the Right*. Clarendon Press, Oxford/UK.

—— (1992). Two concepts of utility. In *Morality, Utilitarianism, and Rights*, chapter 9, pages 158–175. Cambridge University Press, Cambridge/UK.

Braybrooke, D. (1987). *Meeting Needs*. Princeton University Press, Princeton/New Jersey.

Brendl, C. M., Markman, A. B., and Messner, C. (2003). The devaluation effect: Activating a need devalues unrelated choice options. *Journal of Consumer Research*, 29:463–473.

Brenner, T. (2006). Agent learning representation – advice in modelling economic learning. In Tesfatsion, L. and Judd, K. L., editors, *Handbook of Computational Economics*, volume 2, chapter 18, pages 895–947. Elsevier, Amsterdam.

Brenner, T. and Witt, U. (2003). Melioration learning in games with constant and frequency-dependent pay-offs. *Journal of Economic Behavior and Organization*, 50:429–448.

Brentano, F. (1969). *The Origin of Our Knowledge of Right and Wrong*. Routledge & Kegan Paul, London.

Brickman, P. E. and Campbell, D. T. (1971). Hedonic relativism and planning the good society. In Appley, M., editor, *Adaptation Level Theory*, pages 287–302. Academic Press, New York.

Brickman, P. E., Coates, D. and Janoff-Bulman, R. (1978). Lottery winners and accident victims: Is happiness relative? *Journal of Personality and Social Psychology*, 36(8):917–927.

Broekel, T. and Binder, M. (2007). The regional dimension of knowledge transfers – a behavioral approach. *Industry and Innovation*, 14(2):151—175.

Broome, J. (1991a). A reply to Sen. *Economics and Philosophy*, 7:285–287.

—— (1991b). 'Utility'. *Economics and Philosophy*, 7:1–12.

—— (1993). A cause of preference is not an object of preference. *Social Choice and Welfare*, 10(1):57–68.

—— (2008). Can there be a preference-based utilitarianism? In Fleurbaey, M., Salles, M., and Weymark, J., editors, *Justice, Political Liberalism and Utilitarianism: Themes from Harsanyi and Rawls*, pages 221–238. Cambridge University Press.

Bruelde, B. (2007). Happiness theories of the good life. *Journal of Happiness Studies*, 8:15–49.

Bruni, L. and Sugden, R. (2007). The road not taken: How psychology was removed from economics, and how it might be brought back. *Economic Journal*, 117:146–173.

Buchanan, J. M. (1954). Social choice, democracy, and free markets. *Journal of Political Economy*, 62(2):114–123.

—— (1959). Positive economics, welfare economics, and political economy. *Journal of Law and Economics*, 2:124–138.

—— (1977). *The Relevance of Pareto Optimality*, chapter 15, pages 215–234. Texas A&M University Press, College Station and London.

—— (1994). *Ethics And Economic Progress*. University of Oklahoma, Norman/ Oklahoma and London.

Buck, R. (1999). The biological affects: A typology. *Psychological Review*, 106(2):301–336.

Buenstorf, G. and Cordes, C. (2008). Can sustainable consumption be learned? A model of cultural evolution. *Ecological Economics*, 67(4):646–657.

Cabanac, M. (1979). Sensory pleasure. *Quarterly Review of Biology*, 54(1):1–29.

—— (1992). Pleasure: The common currency. *Journal of Theoretical Biology*, 155:173–200.

Calabresi, G. (1991). The pointlessness of Pareto: Carrying Coase further. *Yale Law Journal Centennial Issue*, 100(5):1211—1237.

Camerer, C., Loewenstein, G. F. and Prelec, D. (2005). Neuroeconomics: How neuroscience can inform economics. *Journal of Economic Literature*, 43:9–64.

Carnelley, K. B., Wortman, C. B., Bolger, N. and Burke, C. T. (2006). The time course of grief reactions to spousal loss: Evidence from a national probability sample. *Journal of Personality and Social Psychology*, 91(3):476–492.

Carter, R. (1999). *Mapping the Mind*. University of California Press, Berkeley and Los Angeles.

Chai, A. (2007). *Beyond the Shadows of Utility: Evolutionary Consumer Theory and the Rise of Modern Tourism*. PhD thesis, FSU Jena.

Chai, A. and Schubert, C. (2007). Rethinking consumer sovereignty: A useful tool for the promotion of sustainable consumption? Mimeo.

Chiappero-Martinetti, E. and Salardi, P. (2007). Well-being process and conversion factors: An estimation of the micro-side of the well-being process. Mimeo.

Chichilnisky, G. (1980). Basic needs and global models: Resources, trade and distribution. *Alternatives*, 6:453–472.

Chipman, J. S. and Moore, J. C. (1976). Why an increase in GNP need not imply an improvement in potential welfare. *Kyklos*, 29(3):391–418.

—— (1978). The new welfare economics 1939–1974. *International Economic Review*, 19(3):547–584.

Chomsky, N. (1986). *Knowledge of Language – Its Nature, Origin, and Use*. Praeger, Westport/Conn.

Christman, J. (1991). Autonomy and personal history. *Canadian Journal of Philosophy*, 21(1):1–24.

Clark, A. E. and Oswald, A. J. (1994). Unhappiness and unemployment. *The Economic Journal*, 104(424):648–659.

Colander, D. (2007). Edgeworth's hedonimeter and the quest to measure utility. *Journal of Economic Perspectives*, 21(2):215–225.

Conlisk, J. (1996). Why bounded rationality? *Journal of Economic Literature*, 34(2):669–700.

Conover, K. L. and Shizgal, P. (1994a). Competition and summation between rewarding effects of sucrose and lateral hypothalamic stimulation in the rat. *Behavioral Neuroscience*, 108(3):537–548.

Conover, K. L. and Shizgal, P. (1994b). Differential effects of postingestive feedback on the reward value of sucrose and lateral hypothalamic stimulation in the rat. *Behavioral Neuroscience*, 108(3):559–572.

Cooper, B., García-Penalosa, C. and Funk, P. (2001). Status effects and negative utility growth. *The Economic Journal*, 111:642–665.

Cooter, R. and Rappoport, P. (1984). Were the ordinalists wrong about welfare economics? *Journal of Economic Literature*, 22(2):507–530.

Cordes, C. and Schubert, C. (2007). Toward a naturalistic foundation of the social contract. *Constitutional Political Economy*, 18(1):35–62.

Cowen, T. (1991). Self-constraint versus self-liberation. *Ethics*, 101(2):360–373.

Crisp, R. (2006a). Hedonism reconsidered. *Philosophy and Phenomenological Research*, 73:619–645.

—— (2006b). *Reasons And The Good*. Oxford University Press, Oxford.

Crocker, D. A. (1992). Functioning and capability: The foundations of Sen's and Nussbaum's development ethic. *Political Theory*, 20(4):584–612.

Damasio, A. R. (2003). *Looking for Spinoza*. Heinemann, London.

Davis, W. (1981). Pleasure and happiness. *Philosophical Studies*, 39:305–317.

Davison, M. and McCarthy, D. (1988). *The Matching Law: A Research Review*. Lawrence Erlbaum Associates, Hillsdale/New Jersey.

Delgado, M. R. (2007). Reward-related responses in the human striatum. *Annals of the New York Academy of Sciences*, 1,104:70–88.

Delgado, M. R., Nystrom, L. E., Fissell, C., Noll, D. and Fiez, J. (2000). Tracking the hemodynamic responses to reward and punishment in the striatum. *Journal of Neurophysiology*, 84:3,072–3,077.

Deutsch, J., Ramos, X. and Silber, J. (2003). Poverty and inequality of standard of living and quality of life in Great Britain. In Sirgy, M. J., Rahtz, D., and Samli, A. C., editors, *Advances in Quality-of-Life Theory and Research*, chapter 7, pages 99–128. Kluwer Academic Publishers, Dordrecht.

Diener, E., Emmons, R. A., Larsen, R. J. and Griffin, S. (1985). The satisfaction with life scale. *Journal of Personality Assessment*, 49(1):71–75.

Dolan, P. and White, M. (2006). Dynamic well-being: Connecting indicators of what people anticipate with indicators of what they experience. *Social Indicators Research*, 75:303–333.

Domjan, M. (2005). Pavlovian conditioning: A functional perspective. *Annual Review of Psychology*, 56:179–206.

Dubanoski, R. A. and Parton, D. A. (1971). Imitative aggression in children as a function of observing a human model. *Developmental Psychology*, 4(3):489.

Duesenberry, J. (1949). *Income, Saving, and the Theory of Consumer Behavior*. Harvard University Press, Cambridge/Mass.

Dutta, B. (1994). Introduction. In Dutta, B., editor, *Welfare Economics*. Oxford University Press, Oxford.

Dworkin, G. (1988). *The Theory and Practice of Autonomy*. Cambridge University Press, Cambridge/UK.

Dyregrov, A. (1990). Parental reactions to the loss of an infant child: A review. *Scandinavian Journal of Psychology*, 31:266–280.

Easterlin, R. A. (1974). Does economic growth improve the human lot? Some empirical evidence. In David, P. and Reder, M., editors, *Nations and Households in Economic Growth*, pages 89–125. Academic Press, New York/London.

—— (2002). *Happiness in Economics*. Edward Elgar, Cheltenham/UK.

—— (2003). Explaining happiness. *Proceedings of the National Academy of Sciences*, 100(19):11,176–11,183.

Edgeworth, F. Y. (1932[1881]). *Mathematical Psychics: An Essay on the Application of Mathematics to the Moral Sciences*. Kegan Paul, London.

Elster, J. (1982). Sour grapes – utilitarianism and the genesis of wants. In Sen, A. and Williams, B., editors, *Utilitarianism and Beyond*, pages 219–238. Cambridge University Press, Cambridge.

—— (1983). *Sour Grapes*. Cambridge University Press, Cambridge.

—— (1985). Weakness of will and the free-rider problem. *Economics and Philosophy*, 1:231–265.

Everitt, B. J., Parkinson, J. A., Olmstead, M. C., Arroyo, M., Robledo, P. and Robbins, T. W. (1999). Associative processes in addiction and reward – the role of amygdala-ventral striatal subsystems. *Annals of the New York Academy of Sciences*, 877:412–438.

Feldman, F. (2004). *Pleasure and the Good Life – Concerning the Nature, Varieties, and Plausibility of Hedonism*. Clarendon Press, Oxford.

Festinger, L. (1957). *A Theory of Cognitive Dissonance*. Stanford University Press, Stanford.

Flanagan, T. J. (1980). The pains of long-term imprisonment: A comparison of British and American perspectives. *British Journal of Criminology*, 20:148–156.

Forbes, K. J. (2000). A reassessment of the relationship between inequality and growth. *American Economic Review*, 90(4):869–887.

Frank, R. H. (1985). *Choosing the Right Pond – Human Behavior and the Quest for Status*. Oxford University Press, New York/Oxford.

—— (1988). Beyond self-interest. In *Passions Within Reason: The Strategic Role of the Emotions*. W.W. Norton, New York.

—— (1999). *Luxury Fever: Why Money Fails to Satisfy in an Era of Excess*. Free Press, New York.

Franke, J. and Kuehlmann, T. (1990). *Psychologie fuer Wirtschaftswissenschaftler*. Verlag Moderne Industrie, Landsberg/Lech.

Frankfurt, H. G. (1971). Freedom of the will and the concept of a person. *Journal of Philosophy*, 68(1):5–20.

Frederick, S. and Loewenstein, G. F. (1999). Hedonic adaptation. In Kahneman et al. (1999), pages 302–329.

Frey, B. S., Benz. M. and Stutzer, A. (2004). Introducing procedural utility: Not only what, but also how matters. *Journal of Institutional and Theoretical Economics*, 160:377–401.

Frey, B. S. and Stutzer, A. (2002a). *Happiness and Economics*. Princeton University Press, Princeton/New Jersey.

—— (2002b). What can economists learn from happiness research? *Journal of Economic Literature*, 40(2):402–435.

—— (2004). Economic consequences of mispredicting utility. Institute for Empirical Research in Economics, University of Zuerich, Working Paper No. 218.

—— (2007). Should national happiness be maximized? Institute for Empirical Research in Economics Working Paper No. 306.

Freytag, A. and Renaud, S. (2007). From short-term to long-term orientation – political economy of the policy reform process. *Journal of Evolutionary Economics*, 17:433–449.

Friedman, M. (1967). Value judgments in economics. In Hook, S., editor, *Human Values and Economic Policy – A Symposium*, pages 85–93. New York University Press, New York.

Gaertner, W. (2006). *A Primer in Social Choice Theory*. Oxford University Press, Oxford.

George, D. (1998). Coping rationally with unpreferred preferences. *Eastern Economic Journal*, 24(2):181–194.

—— (2004). *Preference Pollution – How Markets Create the Desires We Dislike*. University of Michigan Press, Ann Arbor.

Georgescu-Roegen, N. (1954a). Choice and revealed preference. *Southern Economic Journal*, 21(2):119–130.

—— (1954b). Choice, expectations and measurability. *Quarterly Journal of Economics*, 68(4):503–534.

Gierer, A. (1998). Networks of gene regulation, neural development and the evolution of general capabilities, such as human empathy. *Zeitschrift fuer Naturforschung*, 53c:716–722.

Gigerenzer, G., Todd, P. M. and the ABC Research Group (1999). *Simple Heuristics That Make Us Smart*. Oxford University Press, New York/Oxford.

Gilbert, D. T. and Ebert, J. E. J. (2002). Decisions and revisions: The affective forecasting of changeable outcomes. *Journal of Personality and Social Psychology*, 82(4):503–514.

Gilbert, D. T., Gill M. J., and Wilson. T. D. (2002). The future is now: Temporal correction in affective forecasting. *Organizational Behavior and Human Decision Processes*, 88(1):430–444.

Gilbert, D. T., Pinel, E. C., Wilson, T. D., Blumberg, S. J. and Wheatley, T. P. (1998). Immune neglect: A source of durability bias in affective forecasting. *Journal of Personality and Social Psychology*, 75(3):617–638.

Gintis, H. (1974). Welfare critersia with endogenous preferences: The economics of education. *International Economic Review*, 15(2):415–430.

Gorman, W. (1953). Community preference fields. *Econometrica*, 21(1):63–80.

—— (1955). The intransitivity of certain criteria used in welfare economics. *Oxford Economic Papers*, 7(1):25–35.

—— (1980). A possible procedure for analysing quality differentials in the egg market. *Review of Economic Studies*, 47(5):843–856.

Gorn, G. J. (1982). The effects of music in advertising on choice behavior: A classical conditioning approach. *Journal of Marketing*, 46(1):94–101.

Gosling, J. C. B. (1969). *Pleasure and Desire – The Case for Hedonism Reviewed.* Clarendon Press, Oxford.

Gottfried, J. A., O'Doherty. J. and Dolan, R. J. (2002). Appetitive and aversive olfactory learning in humans studied using event-related functional magnetic resonance imaging. *The Journal of Neuroscience*, 22(24):10,829–10,837.

Grassian, S. (1983). Psychopathological effects of solitary confinement. *American Journal of Psychiatry*, 140(11):1,450–1,454.

Griffin, J. (1982). Modern utilitarianism. *Revue Internationale de Philosophie*, 36:331–375.

—— (1986). *Well-Being: Its Meaning, Measurement and Moral Importance.* Clarendon Press, Oxford.

—— (1998). *Value Judgement – Improving Our Ethical Beliefs.* Clarendon Press, Oxford.

Gul, F. and Pesendorfer, W. (2007). Harmful addiction. *Review of Economic Studies*, 74:147–172.

Habermas, J. (1987). *Theorie des kommunikativen Handelns.* Suhrkamp, Frankfurt am Main.

Haidt, J. and Graham, J. (2007). When morality opposes justice: Conservatives have moral intuitions that liberals may not recognize. *Social Justice Research*, 20:98–116.

Haidt, J. and Joseph, C. (2004). Intuitive ethics: How innately prepared intuitions generate culturally variable virtues. *Daedalus*, 133(4):55–66.

Hammond, P. (1983). Ex-post optimality as a dynamically consistent objective for collective choice under uncertainty. In Pattanaik, P. K. and Salles, M., editors, *Social Choice and Welfare*, chapter 10, pages 175–205. North-Holland, Amsterdam.

Hamner, W. C. and Hamner, E. P. (1976). Behavior modification on the bottom line. *Organizational Dynamics*, 4(4):3–21.

Hare, R. (1981). *Moral Thinking: Its Levels, Methods and Point.* Clarendon Press, Oxford.

Harris, R. and Olewiler, N. (1979). The welfare economics of ex post optimality. *Economica*, 46(182):137–147.

Harsanyi, J. C. (1955). Cardinal welfare, individualistic ethics, and interpersonal comparisons of utility. *Journal of Political Economy*, 63(4):309–321.

—— (1976). *Essays in Ethics. Social Behaviour and Scientific Explanation*. Reidel, Dordrecht.

—— (1982). Morality and the theory of rational behaviour. In Sen, A. and Williams, editors, *Utilitarianism and Beyond*, pages 39–62. Cambridge University Press, Cambridge.

—— (1997). Utilities, preferences, and substantive goods. *Social Choice and Welfare*, 14:129–145.

Haslett, D. (1990). What is utility? *Economics and Philosophy*, 6:65–94.

Hauser, M. D. (2006). *Moral Minds – How Nature Designed Our Universal Sense of Right and Wrong*. Little, Brown, London.

Hausman, D. M. (2000). Revealed preference, belief, and game theory. *Economics and Philosophy*, 16:99–115.

Hausman, D. M. and McPherson, M. S. (1994). Preference, belief, and welfare. *American Economic Review*, 84(2):396–400.

—— (1997). Beware of economists bearing advice. *Policy Options*, 18(7):16–19.

—— (2006). *Economic Analysis and Moral Philosophy*. Cambridge University Press, Cambridge, 2nd edition.

Haybron, D. M. (2007). Life satisfaction, ethical reflection, and the science of happiness. *Journal of Happiness Studies*, 8:99–138.

Hayek, F. A. (1945). The use of knowledge in society. *American Economic Review*, 35(4):519–530.

—— (1960). *The Constitution of Liberty*. University of Chicago Press, Chicago.

Heath, R. G. (1996[1964]). *Exploring the Mind–Brain Relationship*. Moran Printing, Baton Rouge.

Henrich, J., Boyd, R., Bowles, S., Camerer, C., Fehr. E., Gintis, H. and McElreath, R. (2001). In search of homo economicus: Behavioral experiments in 15 small-scale societies. *The American Economic Review (Papers and Proceedings)*, 91(2):73–78.

Hergenhahn, B. R. and Olson, M. H. (1997). *An Introduction to Theories of Learning*. Prentice Hall, Upper Saddle River/New Jersey, 5th edition.

Herrnstein, R. J. (1970). On the law of effect. *Journal of the Experimental Analysis of Behavior*, 13(2):243–266.

—— (1990a). Behavior, reinforcement and utility. *Psychological Science*, 1(4):217–224.

—— (1990b). Rational choice theory – necessary but not sufficient. *American Psychologist*, 45(3):356–367.

—— (1997). *The Matching Law*. Russell Sage Foundation, New York.

Herrnstein, R. J., Loewenstein, G. F., Prelec, D. and Vaughan Jr., W. (1993). Utility maximization and melioration: Internalities in individual choice. *Journal of Behavioral Decision Making*, 6(6):149–185.

Herrnstein, R. J. and Prelec, D. (1991). Melioration: A theory of distributed choice. *Journal of Economic Perspectives*, 5(3):137–156.

Hicks, J. (1939). The foundations of welfare economics. *Economic Journal*, 49(196):696–712.

Hilgard, E. R. and Bower, G. H. (1966). *Theories of Learning*. Appleton-Century-Crofts, New York, 3rd edition.

Hirsch, F. (1995). *Social Limits to Growth*. Routledge, London.

Hobbes. T. (1991[1651]). *Leviathan*. Cambridge University Press, Cambridge.

Hull, C. L. (1943). *Principles of Behavior – An Introduction to Behavior Theory.* Appleton-Century-Crofts, New York.

Hume, D. (1978[1740]). *A Treatise of Human Nature.* Oxford University Press, Oxford, 2nd edition.

Jackson, T. and Marks, N. (1999). Consumption, sustainable welfare and human needs – with reference to UK expenditure patterns between 1954 and 1994. *Ecological Economics*, 28:421–441.

Jevons, W. S. (1924[1871]). *The Theory of Political Economy.* Macmillan, London, 4th edition.

Johnston, V. S. (1999). *Why We Feel – The Science of Human Emotions.* Perseus Publishing, Cambridge/Mass.

Jones, E. (1994). The tyranny of 'a priorism' in economic thought. *History of Economics Review*, 22:25–69.

Kagan. S. (1998). *Normative Ethics.* Westview Press, Boulder/Colorado.

Kahneman, D. (1999). Objective happiness. In Kahneman et al. (1999), pages 3–27.

—— (2000). Experienced utility and objective happiness: A moment-based approach. In Kahneman, D. and Tversky, A., editors. *Choices, Values and Frames*, chapter 37, pages 673–692. Cambridge University Press, New York.

—— (2003). Maps of bounded rationality: Psychology for behavioral economics. *The American Economic Review*, 93(5):1,449–1,475.

Kahneman, D., Diener. E. and Schwarz, N., editors (1999). *Well-Being: The Foundations of Hedonic Psychology.* Russell Sage Foundation, New York.

Kahneman, D. and Krueger, A. B. (2006). Developments in the measurement of subjective well-being. *Journal of Economic Perspectives*, 20(1):3–24.

Kahneman, D., Krueger, A. B., Schkade, D., Schwarz, N. and Stone, A. (2004). Toward national well-being accounts. *The American Economic Review*, 94(2):429–434.

Kahneman, D., Slovic, P. and Tversky, A., editors (1982). *Judgment Under Uncertainty: Heuristics and Biases.* Cambridge University Press, Cambridge.

Kahneman, D. and Snell, J. (1992). Predicting a changing taste: Do people know what they will like? *Journal of Behavioral Decision Making*, 5(3):187–200.

Kahneman, D. and Sugden, R. (2005). Experienced utility as a standard of policy evaluation. *Environmental & Resource Economics*, 32:161–181.

Kahneman, D. and Thaler, R. H. (2006). Anomalies – utility maximization and experienced utility. *Journal of Economic Perspectives*, 20(1):221–234.

Kahneman, D. and Tversky, A. (1979). Prospect theory: An analysis of decision under risk. *Econometrica*, 47(2):263–291.

Kahneman, D., Wakker, P. P. and Sarin, R. K. (1997). Back to Bentham? Explorations of experienced utility. *Quarterly Journal of Economics*, 112(2):375–405.

Kaldor, N. (1939). Welfare propositions of economics and interpersonal comparisons of utility. *Economic Journal*, 49(195):549–552.

Kenning, P. and Plassmann, H. (2005). Neuroeconomics: An overview from an economic perspective. *Brain Research Bulletin 67*, 67:343–354.

Keynes, J. N. (1955). *The Scope and Method of Political Economy.* Kelley & Millman. New York, 4th edition.

Knetsch, J. L. (1992). Preferences and nonreversibility of indifference curves. *Journal of Economic Behavior & Organization*, 17:131–139.

—— (1995). Assumptions, behavioral findings, and policy analysis. *Journal of Policy Analysis and Management*, 4(1):68–78.

Knutson, B. and Peterson, R. (2005). Neurally reconstructing expected utility. *Games and Economic Behavior*, 52:305–315.

Komisaruk, B. R., Whipple, B., Crawford, A., Grimes, S., Liu, W.-C., Kalnin, A. and Mosier, K. (2004). Brain activation during vaginocervical self-stimulation and orgasm in women with complete spinal cord injury: fMRI evidence of mediation by the vagus nerves. *Brain Research*, 1,024:77–88.

Koo, A. Y. (1963). An empirical test of revealed preference theory. *Econometrica*, 31(4):646–664.

Koo, A. Y. and Hasenkamp, G. (1972). Structure of revealed preference: Some preliminary evidence. *Journal of Political Economy*, 80(4):724–744.

Koopmans, T. C. (1957). *Three Essays on the State of Economic Science*. McGraw-Hill, New York.

Koukounas, E. and Over, R. (1993). Habituation and dishabituation of male sexual arousal. *Behaviour Research and Therapy*, 31(6):575–585.

Kroeber-Riel, W. (1992). *Konsumentenverhalten*. Verlag Franz Vahlen, Muenchen, 5th rev. edition.

Kuklys, W. (2005). *Amartya Sen's Capability Approach – Theoretical Insights and Empirical Applications*. Springer, Berlin et al.

Laan, E. and Everaerd, W. (1995). Habituation of female sexual arousal to slides and film. *Archives of Sexual Behavior*, 24(5):517–541.

Laibson, D. (1997). Golden eggs and hyperbolic discounting. *Quarterly Journal of Economics*, 112(2):443–477.

Lancaster, K. (1966). A new approach to consumer theory. *Journal of Political Economy*, 74(2):132–157.

Landers, R. M., Rebitzer, J. B. and Taylor, L. J. (1996). Rat race redux: Adverse selection in the determination of work hours in law firms. *The American Economic Review*, 86(3):329–348.

Lawson, T. (1997). *Economics and Reality*. Routledge, London/New York.

Layard, R. (2005). *Happiness – Lessons From a New Science*. Allen Lane, London.

Lebergott, S. (1993). *Pursuing Happiness*. Princeton University Press, Princeton/New Jersey.

LeDoux, J. E. (1996). *The Emotional Brain – The Mysterious Underpinnings of Emotional Life*. Simon&Schuster, New York.

Lelkes, O. (2006). Knowing what is good for you – empirical analysis of personal preferences and the 'objective good'. *Journal of Socio-Economics*, 35:285–307.

Lewin, S. B. (1996). Economics and psychology: Lessons for our own day from the early twentieth century. *Journal of Economic Literature*, 34(3):1293–1323.

List, C. (2004). Multidimensional welfare aggregation. *Public Choice*, 119:119–142.

Loewenstein, G. F. (1996). Out of control: Visceral influences on behavior. *Organizational Behavior and Human Decision Processes*, 65(3):272–292.

—— (1999). Is more choice always better? *Social Security Brief*, 7:1–8.

Loewenstein, G. F. and Schkade, D. (1999). Wouldn't it be nice? Predicting future feelings. In Kahneman et al. (1999), chapter 5, pages 85–105.

Loewenstein, G. F. and Sicherman, N. (1991). Do workers prefer increasing wage profiles? *Journal of Labor Economics*, 9(1):67–84.

Loomes, G., Starmer, C. and Sugden, R. (2003). Do anomalies disappear in repeated markets? *The Economic Journal*, 113:C153–C166.

Loomes, G. and Taylor, C. (1992). Non-transitive preferences over gains and losses. *The Economic Journal*, 102(411):357–365.

Lucas, R. E. and Clark, A. E. (2006). Do people really adapt to marriage? *Journal of Happiness Studies*, 7:405–426.

Lucas, R. E., Clark, A. E., Georgellis, Y. and Diener, E. (2004). Unemployment alters the set point for life satisfaction. *Psychological Science*, 15(1):8–13.

Lumsden, C. and Wilson, E. (1981). *Genes, Mind and Culture: The Coevolutionary Process*. Harvard University Press, Cambridge/Mass.

Lykken, D. and Tellegen, A. (1996). Happiness is a stochastic phenomenon. *Psychological Science*, 7(3):186–189.

Lyubomirsky, S., King, L. and Diener, E. (2005). The benefits of frequent positive affect: Does happiness lead to success? *Psychological Bulletin*, 131(6):803–855.

MacCrimmon, K. and Toda, M. (1969). Experimental determination of indifference curves. *Review of Economic Studies*, 36(4):433–451.

Madsen, C. J. (1968). Nurturance and modeling in preschoolers. *Child Development*, 39(1):221–236.

Martin, M. W. (2008). Paradoxes of happiness. *Journal of Happiness Studies*, 9(2):171–184.

Mas-Colell, A., Whinston. M. D. and Green, J. R. (1995). *Microeconomic Theory*. Oxford University Press, New York/Oxford.

Maslow, A. H. (1987[1954]). *Motivation and Personality*. HarperCollins, New York, 3rd edition.

McAlister, L. (1982). A dynamic attribute satiation model of variety-seeking behavior. *Journal of Consumer Research*, 9(2):141–150.

McClure, S. M., York, M. K. and Montague, P. R. (2004). The neural substrates of reward processing in humans: The modern role of fMRI. *Neuro scientist*, 10(3):260–268.

McDowell, J. J. (2005). On the classic and modern theories of matching. *Journal of the Experimental Analysis of Behavior*, 84(1):111–127.

McFarland, D. J. and Sibly, R. M. (1975). The behavioural final common path. *Philosophical Transactions of the Royal Society of London. Series B, Biological Sciences*, 270(907):265–293.

Meltzoff, A. N. (1990). Foundations for developing a concept of self: The role of imitation in relating self to other and the value of social mirroring, social modeling; and self practice in infancy. In Cicchetti. D. and Beeghly, M., editors. *The Self in Transition: Infancy to Childhood*, chapter 7, pages 139–164. University of Chicago Press, Chicago.

Menger, C. (1950[1871]). *Principles of Economics*. The Free Press, Glenco/Illinois.

Metcalfe, J. S. (1994). Evolutionary economics and technology policy. *Economic Journal*, 104(425):931–944.

——(2001). Institutions and progress. *Industrial and Corporate Change*, 10(3):561–586.

Meuwissen, I. and Over, R. (1990). Habituation and dishabituation of female sexual arousal. *Behaviour Research and Therapy*, 28(3):217–226.

Michael, R. T. and Becker, G. S. (1973). On the new theory of consumer behavior. *Swedish Journal of Economics*, 75(4):378–396.

Michalos, A. C. (1985). Multiple discrepancies theory (MDT). *Social indicators Research*, 16:347–413.

Mill, J. S. (1998[1863]). *Utilitarianism*. Oxford University Press, Oxford/New York.

Millenson, J. (1967). *Principles of Behavioral Analysis*. Macmillan, New York.

Mirowski, P. (1988). *Against Mechanism – Protecting Economics From Science*. Rowman & Littlefield, Totowa/New Jersey.

—— (1991). The when, the how and the why of mathematical expression in the history of economics analysis. *Journal of Economic Perspectives*, 5(1):145–157.

Mirrlees, J. (1982). The economic uses of utilitarianism. In Sen, A. and Williams, B., editors. *Utilitarianism and Beyond*, pages 63–84. Cambridge University Press, Cambridge.

Mitchell, T. R., Thompson, L., Peterson, E. and Cronk, R. (1997). Temporal adjustments in the evaluation of events: The 'rosy view'. *Journal of Experimental Social Psychology*, 33:421–448.

Montague, P. R. and Berns, G. S. (2002). Neural economics and the biological substrates of valuation. *Neuron*, 36:265–284.

Mook, D. G. and Votaw, M. C. (1992). How important is hedonism? Reasons given by college students for ending a meal. *Appetite*, 18:69–75.

Moore, A. (2004). Hedonism. Entry: Stanford Encyclopedia of Philosophy, http://plato.Stanford.edu/entries/hedonism/.

Moore, A. and Crisp, R. (1996). Welfarism in moral theory. *Australasian Journal of Philosophy*, 74(4):598–613.

Moore, G. E. (1903). *Principa Ethica*. Prometheus Books, Amherst/New York.

Mowrer, O. H. and Jones, H. (1945). Habit strength as a function of the pattern of reinforcement. *Journal of Experimental Psychology* , 35(4):293–311.

Myers, D. G. (1999). Close relationships and quality of life. In Kahneman et al. (1999), pages 374–391.

Nagel, E. (1961). *The Structure of Science – Problems in the Logic of Scientific Explanation*. Harcourt, Brace & World, New York.

Nagel, T. (1979). *Mortal Questions*. Cambridge University Press, Cambridge.

Naik, N. Y. and Moore, M. J. (1996). Habit formation and intertemporal substitution in individual food consumption. *Review of Economics and Statistics*, 78(2):321–328.

Nelson, R. R. and Winter, S. G. (1982). *An Evolutionary Theory of Economic Change*. The Belknap Press, Cambridge/Mass.

Ng, Y.-K. (1972). Value judgments and economists' role in policy recommendation. *Economic Journal*, 82(327):1,014–1,018.

—— (1981). Welfarism: A defence against Sen's attack. *The Economic Journal*, 91(362):527–530.

—— (1990). Welfarism and utilitarianism. *Utilitas*, 2(2):171–193.

—— (1992[1979]). *Welfare Economics – Introduction and Development of Basic Concepts*. Macmillan, London.

—— (2000). *Efficiency. Equality and Public Policy: With a Case for Higher Public Spending*. Palgrave Macmillan, Hampshire.

—— (2003). From preference to happiness: Towards a more complete welfare economics. *Social Choice and Welfare*, 20:307–350.

Nisbet, R. (1994). *History of the Idea of Progress*. Transaction Publishers, New Brunswick.

North, D. C. (1999). Hayek's contribution to understanding the process of economic change. In Vanberg, V. J., editor. *Freiheit, Wettbewerb und Wirtschaftsordnung*, 79–96. Haufe, Freiburg.

Nozick, R. (1974). *Anarchy, State and Utopia*. Basic Books, New York.

Nussbaum, M. C. (2000). *Women And Human Development*. Cambridge University Press, Cambridge.

Nussbaum, M. C. (2003). Capabilities as fundamental entitlements: Sen and social justice. *Feminist Economics*, 9(2–3):33–59.

O'Doherty, J., Kringelbach, M. L., Rolls, E. T., Hornak, J. and Andrews, C. (2001a). Abstract reward and punishment representations in the human orbitofrontal cortex. *Nature Neuroscience*, 4:95–102.

O'Doherty, J., Rolls, E. T., Francis, S., Bowtell. R. and McGlone, F. (2001b). Representation of pleasant and aversive taste in the human brain. *Journal of Neurophysiology*, 85:1315–1321.

O'Doherty, J. P., Deichmann, R., Critchley, H. D. and Dolan, R. J. (2002). Neural responses during anticipation of a primary taste reward. *Neuron*, 33:815–826.

O'Donoghue, T. and Rabin, M. (2000). The economics of immediate gratification. *Journal of Behavioral Decision Making*, 13:233–250.

O'Neill, J. (2006). Citizenship, well-being and sustainability: Epicurus or Aristotle? *Analyse & Kritik*, 28:158–172.

Oswald, A. J. (1997). Happiness and economic performance. *Economic Journal*, 107(445):1,815–1,831.

Oswald, A. J. and Powdthavee. N. (2008). Does happiness adapt? A longitudinal study of disability with implications for economists and judges. *Journal of Public Economics*, 92:1,061–1,077.

Pagnoni, G., Zink, F., Montague, P. R. and Berns, G. S. (2002). Activity in human ventral striatum locked to errors of reward prediction. *Nature neuroscience*, 5:97–98.

Parducci; A. (1995). *Happiness, Pleasure, and Judgment*. Lawrence Erlbaum Associates, Mahwah/New Jersey.

Parfit, D. (1984). *Reasons and Persons*. Oxford University Press, Oxford.

Paulus, P. B. and Seta, J. J. (1975). The vicarious partial reinforcement effect: An empirical and theoretical analysis. *Journal of Personality and Social Psychology*, 31:930–936.

Peach, J. T. (1987). Distribution and economic progress. *Journal of Economic Issues*, 21(4):1,495–1,529.

Pollak. R. A. (1970). Habit formation and dynamic demand functions. *Journal of Political Economy*, 78(4):745–763.

—— (1976). Interdependent preferences. *American Economic Review*, 66(3):309–320.

Popper, K. R. (1966). *The Open Society and Its Enemies*, volume 2. Princeton University Press, Princeton/New Jersey, 5th rev. edition.

Pulliam, H. and Dunford, C. (1980). *Programmed to Learn: An Essay on the Evolution of Culture*. Columbia University Press, New York.

Putnam, H. (1990). *Realism With A Human Face*. Harvard University Press, Cambridge/Mass.

—— (1992). Replies. *Philosophical Topics*, 20(1):347–408.

—— (2002). *The Collapse of the Fact/Value Dichotomy and Other Essays*. Harvard University Press, Cambridge/Mass.

Qizilbash, M. (1998). The concept of well-being. *Economics and Philosophy*, 14:51–73.

—— (2002). Development, common foes and shared values. *Review of Political Economy*, 14(4):463–480.

—— (2006). Well-being, adaptation and human limitations. In Olsaretti, S., editor.

Preferences and Well-Being, pages 83–110. Cambridge University Press, Cambridge/UK.

—— (2008). The adaptation problem, evolution and normative economics. In Basu, K. and Kanbur, R., editors, *Arguments for a Better World: Essays in Honor of Amartya Sen*, volume 1, chapter 4, pages 50–67. Oxford University Press, Oxford.

Rachels, S. (2000). Is unpleasantness intrinsic to unpleasant experiences? *Philosophical Studies*, 99:187–210.

Rawls, J. (1971). *A Theory of Justice*. Harvard University Press, Cambridge/Mass.

Read, D. and Leeuwen, B. v. (1998). Predicting hunger: The effects of appetite and delay on choice. *Organizational Behavior and Human Decision Processes*, 76(2):189–205.

Read, D. and Loewenstein, G. F. (1995). Diversification bias: Explaining the discrepancy in variety seeking between combined and separated choices. *Journal of Experimental Psychology: Applied*, 1(1):34–49.

Read, D., Loewenstein, G. F. and Rabin, M. (1999). Choice bracketing. *Journal of Risk and Uncertainty*, 19(1–3):171–197.

Redden, J. P. (2008). Reducing satiation: The role of categorization level. *Journal of Consumer Research*, 34:624–634.

Redelmeier, D. A. and Kahneman, D. (1996). Patients' memories of painful medical treatments: Real-time and retrospective evaluations of two minimally invasive procedures. *Pain*, 66:3–8.

Reiss, S. (2000). *Who Am I? The 16 Basic Desires That Motivate Our Actions and Define Our Personalities*. Berkeley Books, New York.

Rilling, J. K., Gutman, D. A., Zeh, T. R., Pagnoni, G., Berns, G. S. and Kilts, C. D. (2002). A neural basis for social cooperation. *Neuron*, 35:395–405.

Robbins, L. (1935). *An Essay on the Nature and Significance of Economic Science*. Macmillan, London, 2nd rev. edition.

—— (1938). Interpersonal comparisons of utility: A comment. *The Economic Journal*, 48(192):635–641.

Robeyns, I. (2005a). The capability approach: A theoretical survey. *Journal of Human Development*. 6(1):93–114.

—— (2005b). Selecting capabilities for quality of life measurement. *Social Indicators Research*, 74:191–215.

Robinson, M. D. and Clore, G. L. (2002). Belief and feeling: Evidence for an accessibility model of emotional self-report. *Psychological Bulletin*, 128(6):934–960.

Robinson, T. E. and Berridge, K. C. (1993). The neural basis of drug craving: An incentive-sensitization theory of addiction. *Brain Research Reviews*, 18(3):247–291.

—— (2001). Incentive-sensitization and addiction. *Addiction*, 96:103–114.

Rolls, B. J., Duijvenvoorde. P. M. v. and Rolls, E. T. (1984). Pleasantness changes and food intake in a varied four-course meal. *Appetite*, 5(4):337–348.

Rolls, B. J., Rowe, E. A., Rolls, E. T., Kingston, B., Megson, A. and Gunary, R. (1981). Variety in a meal enhances food intake in man. *Physiology & Behavior*, 26:215–221.

Rolls, E. T. (2000). The orbitofrontal cortex and reward. *Cerebral Cortex*, 10(3):284–294.

—— (2007). *Emotion Explained*. Oxford University Press, Oxford.

Rolls, E. T., O'Doherty, J., Kringelbach, M. L., Francis, S., Bowtell. R. and Mc-Glone,

F. (2003). Representations of pleasant and painful touch in the human orbitofrontal and cingulate cortices. *Cerebral Cortex*, 13:308–317.

Rolls, E. T. and Rolls, J. H. (1997). Olfactory sensory-specific satiety in humans. *Physiology & Behavior*, 61(3):461–473.

Rosati, C. S. (1995). Persons, perspectives, and full information accounts of the good. *Ethics*, 105(2):296–325.

Rosenberg, A. (1979). Can economic theory explain everything? *Philosophy of the Social Sciences*, 9(4):509–529.

—— (1985). Prospects for the elimination of tastes from economics and ethics. *Social Philosophy & Policy*, 2(2):48–68.

—— (1992). *Economics – Mathematical Politics or Science of Diminishing Returns?* University of Chicago Press, Chicago.

Rozin, P. and Schiller. D. (1980). The nature and acquisition of a preference for chili pepper by humans. *Emotion and Motivation*, 4(1):77–101.

Ruprecht, W. (2001). *Towards an Evolutionary Theory of Consumption – Conceptual Considerations and Empirical Evidence*. PhD thesis, FSU Jena.

—— (2005). The historical development of the consumption of sweeteners – a learning approach. *Journal of Evolutionary Economics*, 15:247–272.

Ryberg, J. (2002). Higher and lower pleasures – doubts on justification. *Ethical Theory and Moral Practice*, 5:415–429.

Samuelson, P. (1938). A note on the pure theory of consumer's behaviour. *Economica*, 5(17):61–71.

—— (1948). Consumption theory in terms of revealed preference. *Economica*, 15(60):243–253.

—— (1950). Evaluation of real national income. *Oxford Economic Papers*, 2(1):1–29.

—— (1961[1947]). *Foundations of Economic Analysis*. Harvard University Press, Cambridge/Mass.

—— (1967). Arrow's mathematical politics. In Hook, S., editor, *Human Values and Economic Policy – A Symposium*, pages 41–51. New York University Press, New York.

Sapolsky, R. M. (1999). The physiology and pathophysiology of unhappiness. In Kahneman et al. (1999), chapter 23, pages 453–469.

Sartorius, C. (2003). *An Evolutionary Approach to Social Welfare*. Routledge, London.

Scanlon, T. M. (1975). Preference and urgency. *Journal of Philosophy*, 72(19):655–669.

—— (1993). Value, desire, and quality of life. In Nussbaum, M. and Sen, A., editors, *The Quality of Life*, pages 30–53. Clarendon Press, Oxford.

Schelling, T. C. (1984). Self-command in practice, in policy, and in a theory of rational choice. *American Economic Review*, 74:1–11.

Schneider, W. and Shiffrin, R. M. (1977). Controlled and automatic human information processing: I. Detection, search, and attention. *Psychological Review*, 84(1):1-66.

Schreiber, C. A. and Kahneman, D. (2000). Determinants of the remembered utility of aversive sounds. *Journal of Experimental Psychology: General*, 129(1):27–42.

Schubert, C. (2005). A note on the principle of 'normative individualism'. Papers on Economics & Evolution #0517, Max Planck Institute of Economics, Jena.

—— (2006a). A contractarian view on institutional evolution. In Schubert, C. and Wangenheim, G. v., editors, *Evolution and Design of Institutions*, pages 149–179. Routledge, London.

—— (2006b). *Die rechtliche Steuerung urbanen Wandels – Eine konstitutionenoekonomische Untersuchung.* Mohr Siebeck, Tuebingen.

Schultz, W., Tremblay, L. and Hollerman, J. R. (2000). Reward processing in primate orbitofrontal cortex and basal ganglia. *Cerebral Cortex*, 10(3):272–283.

Schumpeter, J. A. (1942). *Capitalism, Socialism, and Democracy.* Harper, New York.

Schwartz, B. (2000). Self-determination – the tyranny of freedom. *American Psychologist*, 55(1):79–88.

—— (2005). *The Paradox of Choice – Why More is Less.* Harper Perennial, New York.

Schwartz, B., Ward, A., Monterosso, J., Lyubomirsky, S., White, K. and Lehman, D. R. (2002). Maximizing versus satisficing: Happiness is a matter of choice. *Journal of Personality and Social Psychology*, 83(5):1,178–1,197.

Schwarz, N. and Strack, F. (1991). Evaluating one's life: A judgment model of subjective well-being. In Strack, F., Argyle, M., and Schwarz, N., editors, *Subjective Well-Being – An Interdisciplinary Perspective*, pages 27–48. Pergamon Press Inc., London/New York.

—— (1999). Reports of subjective well-being: Judgmental processes and their methodological implications. In Kahneman et al. (1999), chapter 4, pages 61–84.

Scitovsky, T. (1941). A note on welfare propositions in economics. *Review of Economic Studies*, 9(1):77–88.

—— (1976). *The Joyless Economy.* Oxford University Press, New York.

—— (1981). The desire for excitement in modern society. *Kyklos*, 34:3–13.

Scully, G. W. (2002). Economic freedom, government policy and the trade-off between equity and economic growth. *Public Choice*, 113:77–96.

Sen, A. K. (1967). The nature and classes of prescriptive judgements. *Philosophical Quarterly*, 17(66):46–62.

—— (1973). Behaviour and the concept of preference. *Economica*, 40(159): 241–259.

—— (1974). Informational bases of alternative welfare approaches: Aggregation and income distribution. *Journal of Public Economics*, 3(4):387–403.

—— (1977a). On weights and measures: Informational constraints in social welfare analysis. *Econometrica*, 45(7):1539–1572.

—— (1977b). Rational fools: A critique of the behavioral foundations of economic theory. *Philosophy and Public Affairs*, 6(4):317–344.

—— (1979a). *Collective Choice and Social Welfare.* Elsevier, Amsterdam.

—— (1979b). Personal utilities and public judgements: Or what's wrong with welfare economics. *The Economic Journal*, 89(355):537–558.

—— (1979c). Utilitarianism and welfarism. *Journal of Philosophy*, 76(9): 463–489.

—— (1981). Plural utility. *Proceedings of the Aristotelian Society*, 81:193–215.

—— (1982). *Choice, Welfare and Measurement.* Harvard University Press, Cambridge/Mass.

—— (1984). Rights and capabilities. In *Resources, Values and Development*, pages 307–324. Harvard University Press, Cambridge/Mass.

—— (1985a). *Commodities and Capabilities.* North-Holland, Amsterdam.

—— (1985b). Well-being, agency and freedom: The Dewey lectures 1984. *Journal of Philosophy*, 82(4):169–221.

—— (1987). *On Ethics and Economics.* Basil Blackwell, Oxford.

—— (1991a). Utility – ideas and terminology. *Economics and Philosophy*, 7:277–283.

—— (1991b). Welfare, preference and freedom. *Journal of Econometrics*, 50:15–29.

—— (1992). *Inequality Reexamined.* Clarendon Press, Oxford.

—— (1993a). Capability and well-being. In Nussbaum, M. C. and Sen, A. K., editors, *The Quality of Life*, pages 30–53. Clarendon Press, Oxford.

—— (1993b). Internal consistency of choice. *Econometrica: Journal of the Econometric Society*, 61(3):495–521.

—— (1999). *Development as Freedom*. Alfred A. Knopf, New York.

Shaver, R. (2004). The appeal of utilitarianism. *Utilitas*, 16(3):235–250.

Shimp, T. A., Stuart, E. W. and Engle, R. W. (1991). A program of classical conditioning experiments testing variations in the conditioned stimulus and context. *Journal of Consumer Research*, 18(1):1–12.

Shizgal, P. (1999). On the neural computation of utility: Implications from studies of brain stimulation reward. In Kahneman et al. (1999), 500–524.

Sidgwick, H. (1907[1874]). *The Methods of Ethics*. Macmillan, London.

Simon, H. A. (1955). A behavioral model of rational choice. *Quarterly Journal of Economics*, 69(1):99–118.

—— (1956). Rational choice and the structure of the environment. *Psychological Review*, 63(2):129–138.

—— (1979). *Models of Thought*. Yale University Press, New Haven.

Skinner, B. F. (1953). *Science and Human Behavior*. Macmillan, New York.

Slesnick, D. T. (1998). Empirical approaches to the measurement of welfare. *Journal of Economic Literature*, 36(4):2,108–2,165.

—— (2001). *Consumption and Social Welfare – Living Standards and their Distribution in the United States*. Cambridge University Press, Cambridge/UK.

Small, D. M., Zatorre, R. J., Dagher, A., Evans, A. C. and Jones-Gotman, M. (2001). Changes in brain activity related to eating chocolate: From pleasure to aversion. *Brain*, 124:1,720–1,733.

Smith, C. A. and Wallston, K. A. (1992). Adaptation in patients with chronic rheumatoid arthritis: Application of a general model. *Health Psychology*, 11(3):151–162.

Smith, D. and Over, R. (1987). Does fantasy-induced sexual arousal habituate? *Behaviour Research and Therapy*, 25(6):477–485.

Smith, V. L. (2003). Constructivist and ecological rationality in economics. *The American Economic Review*, 93(3):465–508.

Sobel, D. (1994). Full information accounts of well-being. *Ethics*, 104(4):784–810.

—— (1997). On the subjectivity of welfare. *Ethics*, 107(3):501–508.

Spash, C. and Hanley, N. (1995). Preferences, information and biodiversity preservation. *Ecological Economics*, 12:191–208.

Spjut, R. J. (1979). Torture under the European convention on human rights. *American Journal of International Law*, 73(2):267–272.

Staddon, J. E. R. and Cerutti, D. T. (2003). Operant conditioning. *Annual Review of Psychology*, 54:115–144.

Steedman, I. (2001). *Consumption Takes Time – Implications for Economic Theory*. Routledge, London/New York.

Stevenson, B. and Wolfers, J. (2008). Economic growth and subjective well-being: Reassessing the Easterlin paradox. *Brookings Papers on Economic Activity*, Spring 2008.

Stigler, G. J. (1950a). The development of utility theory. I. *Journal of Political Economy*, 58(4):307–327.

—— (1950b). The development of utility theory. II. *Journal of Political Economy*, 58(5):373–396.

Stigler, G. J. and Becker, G. S. (1977). De gustibus non est disputandum. *The American Economic Review*, 67(2):76–90.

Streeten, P. (1984). Basic needs: Some unsettled questions. *World Development*, 12(9):973–978.

Streeten, P. and Burki, S. (1978). Basic needs: Some issues. *World Development*, 6(3):411–421.

Stuart, E. W., Shimp, T. A. and Engle, R. W. (1987). Classical conditioning of consumer attitudes: Four experiments in an advertising context. *Journal of Consumer Research*, 14(3):334–349.

Stutzer, A. and Frey, B. S. (2006). Does marriage make people happy, or do happy people get married? *Journal of Socio-Economics*, 35:326–347.

Suedfeld, P., Ramirez, C. Deaton, J. and Baker-Brown, G. (1982). Reactions and attributes of prisoners in solitary confinement. *Criminal Justice and Behavior*, 9:303–340.

Sugden, R. (1993). Welfare, resources, and capabilities: A review of Inequality Reexamined by Amartya Sen. *Journal of Economic Literature*, 31(4):1,947–1,962.

—— (2001). Ken Binmore's evolutionary social theory. *Economic Journal*, 111:F213–F243.

—— (2004). The opportunity criterion: Consumer sovereignty without the assumption of coherent preferences. *American Economic Review*, 94(4):1,014–1,033.

—— (2006a). Taking unconsidered preferences seriously. In Olsaretti, S., editor, *Preferences and Well-Being*, pages 209–232. Cambridge University Press, Cambridge/UK.

—— (2006b). What we desire, what we have reason to desire, whatever we might desire: Mill and Sen on the value of opportunity. *Utilitas*, 18(1):33–51.

Sumner, L. W. (1993). The evolution of utility: A philosophical journey. In Hooker, B., editor, *Rationality, Rules and Utility*, pages 97–114. Westview, Boulder/Colorado.

—— (1996). *Welfare, Happiness, and Ethics*. Oxford University Press, Oxford.

—— (2006). Utility and capability. *Utilitas*, 18(1):1–19.

Suzumura, K. (1999). Paretian welfare judgements and Bergsonian social choice. *Economic Journal*, 109(455):204–220.

—— (2002). Introduction. In Arrow. K. J., Sen, A. K., and Suzumura, K., editors, *Handbook of Social Choice and Welfare*, volume 1, pages 1–32. North-Holland, Amsterdam.

Tangney, J. P. and Dearing. R. L. (2002). *Shame and Guilt*. Guilford, New York.

Temkin, L. S. (1993). *Inequality*. Oxford University Press, New York/Oxford.

Teschl, M. and Comim, F. (2005). Adaptive preferences and capabilities: Some preliminary conceptual explorations. *Review of Social Economy*, 63(2):229–247.

Thaler, R. and Sunstein, C. R. (2003). Libertarian paternalism. *The American Economic Review*, 93(2):175–179.

Thaler, R. H. (1991). *Quasi rational economics*. Russell Sage Foundation, New York.

Thomson, G. (1987). *Needs*. Routledge & Kegan Paul, London.

Tomasello, M. (1999a). *The Cultural Origins of Human Cognition*. Harvard University Press, Cambridge/Mass.

—— (1999b). The human adaptation for culture. *Annual Review of Anthropology*, 28:509–529.

Tversky, A. (1969). Intransitivity of preferences. *Psychological Review*, 76(1):31–48.

Tversky, A. and Kahneman, D. (1986). Rational choice and the framing of decisions. *Journal of Business*, 59(4S):S251–S278.

Vanberg, V. J. (2004). The rationality postulate in economics: Its ambiguity, its deficiency and its evolutionary alternative. *Journal of Economic Methodology*, 11(1):1–29.

—— (2006). Human intentionality and design in cultural evolution. In Schubert, C. and Wangenheim, G. v., editors, *Evolution and Design of Institutions*, pages 197–212. Routledge. Oxford.

Vaughan Jr., W. and Herrnstein, R. J. (1987). *Stability. Melioration, and Natural Selection*, volume 1. pages 185–215. Ablex, Norwood/New Jersey.

Veenhoven, R. (1991). Is happiness relative? *Social Indicators Research*, 24:1–34.

—— (2003). Hedonism and happiness. *Journal of Happiness Studies*, 4:437–457.

Wahba, M. A. and Bridwell, L. G. (2002). Maslow reconsidered: A review of research on the need hierarchy theory. In Cooper, C. L., editor, *Fundamentals of Organizational Behavior*, volume 1, pages 42–67. Sage Publications, London.

Walras, L. (1954[1926]). *Elements of Pure Economics*. George Allen and Unwin, London.

Warke, T. (2000a). Classical utilitarianism and the methodology of determinate choice, in economics and in ethics. *Journal of Economic Methodology*, 7(3):373–394.

—— (2000b). Mathematical fitness in the evolution of the utility concept from Bentham to Jevons to Marshall. *Journal of the History of Economic Thought*, 22(1):5–27.

—— (2000c). Multi-dimensional utility and the index number problem: Jeremy Bentham. J. S. Mill, and qualitative hedonism. *Utilitas*, 12(2):176–203.

—— (2000d). A reconstruction of classical utilitarianism. *Journal of Bentham Studies*, 3.

Wasserman, E. A., Young, M. E. and Cook, R. G. (2004). Variability discrimination in humans and animals. *American Psychologist*, 59(9):879–890.

Wegner, G. (1991). *Wohlfahrtsaspekte evolutorischen Marktgeschehens – Neoklassisches Fortschrittsverstaendnis und Innovationspolitik aus ordnungstheoretischer Sicht*, J.C.B. Mohr (Paul Siebeck), Tuebingen.

—— (1997). Economic policy from an evolutionary perspective: A new approach. *Journal of Institutional and Theoretical Economics*, 153(3):485–509.

Weinstein, N. D. (1982). Community noise problems: Evidence against adaptation. *Journal of Environmental Psychology*. 2(2):87–97.

Weiss, R. S. (1988). Loss and recovery. *Journal of Social Issues*, 44(3):37–52.

Weizsaecker, C. C. v. (1971). Notes on endogenous change of tastes. *Journal of Economic Theory*, 3(4):345–372.

—— (2001). Welfare economics bei endogenen Praeferenzen: Thuenen Vorlesung 2001. *Perspektiven der Wirtschaftspolitik*. 3(4):425–446.

—— (2005a). Is the notion of progress compatible with an evolutionary view of the economy. In Dopfer. K., editor, *Economics, Evolution and the State – The Governance of Complexity*, chapter 2, pages 43–57. Edward Elgar. Cheltenham/UK.

—— (2005b). The welfare economics of adaptive preferences. Discussion Paper, Max Planck Institute for Research into Collective Goods, Bonn.

Wengle, H.-P. (1986). The psychology of cosmetic surgery: A critical overview of the literature 1960–1982. *Annals of Plastic Surgery*, 16(5):435–443.

Williams, B. A. (1988). *Reinforcement, Choice, and Response Strength*, volume 2, pages 167–244. Wiley, New York.

Wilson, T. D. and Gilbert, D. T. (2003). Affective forecasting. In Zanna, M., editor, *Advances in Experimental Social Psychology*, volume 35, pages 345–411. Elsevier. New York.

—— (2005). Affective forecasting – knowing what to want. *Current Directions in Psychological Science*. 14(3):131–134.

Wilson, T. D., Wheatley, T., Meyers, J. M., Gilbert, D. T. and Axsom, D. (2000). Focalism: A source of durability bias in affective forecasting. *Journal of Personality and Social Psychology*, 78(5):821–836.

Witt, U. (1987). *Individualistische Grundlagen der evolutorischen Oekonomik*. J.C.B. Mohr (Paul Siebeck), Tuebingen.

—— (1991). Economics, sociobiology, and behavioral psychology on preferences. *Journal of Economic Psychology*, 12:557–573.

—— (1996a). A 'Darwinian revolution' in economics? *Journal of Institutional and Theoretical Economics*, 152:707–715.

—— (1996b). Innovations, externalities and the problem of economic progress. *Public Choice*, 89:113–130.

—— (2000). Genes, culture, and utility. Papers on Economics & Evolution #0009, Max Planck Institute of Economics, Jena.

—— (2001). Learning to consume – a theory of wants and the growth of demand. *Journal of Evolutionary Economics*, 11:23–36.

—— (2003a). Economic policy making in evolutionary perspective. *Journal of Evolutionary Economics*, 13:77–94.

—— (2003b). Evolutionary economics and the extension of evolution to the economy. In Witt, U., editor, *The Evolving Economy – Essays on the Evolutionary Approach to Economics*, chapter 1, pages 3–34. Edward Elgar, Cheltenham/UK.

—— (2005). From sensory to positivist utilitarianism and back – the rehabilitation of naturalistic conjectures in the theory of demand. Papers on Economics & Evolution #0507, Max Planck Institute of Economics, Jena.

—— (2006). Genes, culture, utility and the resurfacing of the moral dimension. Paper Prepared for the Workshop 'Naturalistic Perspectives on Economic Behavior – Are There Any Normative Correlates', Max Planck Institute of Economics, Jena.

Wong, D. B. (1995). Pluralistic relativism. *Midwest Studies in Philosophy*, 20:378–399.

Wong, S. (1978). *The Foundations of Paul Samuelson's Revealed Preference Theory – A Study by the Method of Rational Reconstruction*. Routledge & Kegan Paul, London, Henley and Boston.

Yaari, M. E. (1977). Endogenous changes in tastes: A philosophical discussion. *Erkenntnis*, 11:157–196.

Yaari, M. E. and Bar-Hillel, M. (1984). On dividing justly. *Social Choice and Welfare*, 1:1–24.

Young, V. L., Nemecek, J. R. and Nemecek, D. A. (1994). The efficacy of breast augmentation: Breast size increase, patient satisfaction, and psychological effects. *Plastic and Reconstructive Surgery*, 94(7):958–969.

Zajonc, R. B. (1980). Feeling and thinking: Preferences need no inferences. *American Psychologist*, 35(2):151–175.

—— (1984). On the primacy of affect. *American Psychologist*, 39(2):117–123.

—— (2001). Mere exposure: A gateway to the subliminal. *Current Directions in Psychological Science*, 10(6):224–228.

Zajonc, R. B. and Markus, H. (1982). Affective and cognitive factors in preferences. *Journal of Consumer Research*, 9(2):123–131.

Zimbardo, P. G. and Gerrig, R. J. (1996). *Psychology and Life*. HarperCollins, New York, 14th edition.

Zizzo. D. J. (2002). Neurobiological measurements of cardinal utility: Hedonimeters or learning algorithms? *Social Choice and Welfare*, 19:477–488.

Index

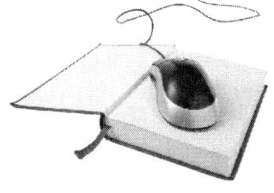